D0918124

ENNIS PUB[redacted]RARY
501 W[redacted]NNIS AVE.
[redacted]NIS, TX 75119-3803

God's Amazing Grace: RECONCILING FOUR CENTURIES OF AFRICAN AMERICAN MARRIAGES AND FAMILIES

TERRY M. TURNER

WESTBOW
PRESS®
A DIVISION OF THOMAS NELSON
& ZONDERVAN

ENNIS PUBLIC LIBRARY
501 W. ENNIS AVE.
ENNIS, TX 75119-3803

Copyright © 2017 Terry M. Turner

Terry M. Turner, Mesquite Friendship B.C, Pastor, Married more than 35 years to the love of his life Nancy. He is the father of four wonderful children and eleven fantastic grandchildren who he enjoys spending time with.

All rights reserved. No part of this book may be used or reproduced by any means, graphic, electronic, or mechanical, including photocopying, recording, taping or by any information storage retrieval system without the written permission of the author except in the case of brief quotations embodied in critical articles and reviews.

WestBow Press books may be ordered through booksellers or by contacting:

WestBow Press
A Division of Thomas Nelson & Zondervan
1663 Liberty Drive
Bloomington, IN 47403
www.westbowpress.com
1 (866) 928-1240

Because of the dynamic nature of the Internet, any web addresses or links contained in this book may have changed since publication and may no longer be valid. The views expressed in this work are solely those of the author and do not necessarily reflect the views of the publisher, and the publisher hereby disclaims any responsibility for them.

Any people depicted in stock imagery provided by Thinkstock are models, and such images are being used for illustrative purposes only.
Certain stock imagery © Thinkstock.

Scripture taken from the New King James Version®. Copyright © 1982 by Thomas Nelson. Used by permission. All rights reserved.

Scripture quotations are from the ESV® Bible (The Holy Bible, English Standard Version®), copyright © 2001 by Crossway, a publishing ministry of Good News Publishers. Used by permission. All rights reserved.

ISBN: 978-1-9736-1083-0 (sc)
ISBN: 978-1-9736-1084-7 (hc)
ISBN: 978-1-9736-1082-3 (e)

Library of Congress Control Number: 2017919050

Print information available on the last page.

WestBow Press rev. date: 10/02/2018

Dedication

I dedicate this book to my wife, Nancy, all the healthy marriages and families today, and our ancestors who endured the trials of life and stayed together.

Epigraph

"Let the wife make the husband glad to come home,
and let him make her sorry to see him leave."

Dr. Martin Luther King Jr.

"No one is born hating another person because of the color of his skin, or his background or his religion. People learn to hate, and if they can learn to hate, they can be taught to love, for love comes more naturally to the human heart, than its opposite."

Nelson Mandela

"Those who deny freedom to others deserve it not for themselves; and, under a just God, cannot long retain it."

Abraham Lincoln

"No matter what, we have the power to choose hope over despair, engagement over apathy, kindness over indifference, love over hate."

Cory Booker

Christian love is the greatest,
Family love is the best,
Let us love and forgive one another
And Jesus will do the rest.

Terry M. Turner

"Dr. Turner has written a book that frames the current demographics of the African-American family in a historical and multigenerational context. He describes how the enslavement of African-Americans affected the bonds of family life through the disruptions of slave unions and parent-child relationships that still have an impact on families today. His effort to trace the relationship patterns across time and generations is an important context that is often missed in discussing African-American families in the present. This is a must read for those who wish to understand the evolution of the African-American family in today's world."

Dr. Anne McKnight
Director of the Bowen Center for Family Studies

"Dr. Turner's book, *God's Amazing Grace: Reconciling Four Centuries of African-American Marriages And Families,* is truly one that I can say is ground-breaking and, at times, disturbing. As a white man, I continue to try to learn from other cultures' perspectives and experiences. This book truly helped me in that regard and will help you. It will also challenge you, as it did me, about misperceptions and prejudices. Biblical, practical, yet scholarly, Dr. Turner's book reveals ugly truths about our culture and our current racial divide. I commend this book from my friend Terry Turner."

Dr. Frank S. Page
President and Chief Executive Officer SBC Executive Committee

"Dr. Terry Turner has given us a sociological study, spiritual journey and academic treasure all in one. God's Amazing Grace: Reconciling Four Centuries of African-American marriages and families is scholarly yet emotionally compelling. African-Americans can gain insight by reading it. Non-African-Americans can begin to understand the heartache experienced through the centuries by our African-American friends. Reading this book will not only change your mind, it will change your heart."

Dr. Jim Richards
Executive Director, Southern Baptists of Texas Convention

"Dr. Turner has provided a very helpful work. Too many dismiss the significance of family dysfunction as one considers the many ills of American society. This book traces the family patterns of African-Americans in the U.S., especially noting the inextricable link between slavery's effects on families and the long-term consequences - and, most importantly, its present manifestations. On a personal note, I am thankful for a work that demonstrates a belief in the sufficiency of scripture, and a belief in the real consequences of sin. Yet, Turner is hopeful, not bitter. Praise God!"

Kevin Smith
Executive Director of the Baptist Convention of Maryland/Delaware

"African-American marriages and families are in crisis in America today. My friend Terry Turner helps us understand why with his historical survey demonstrating the lingering impact of slavery on contemporary Black social structures. More than considering the causes, however, he also proposes solutions found in God's Word and God's grace for resolving this crisis. This book is a means of reconciliation and renewal for all people who consider and are committed to eradicating the slavery-curse from our culture."

Dr. Jeff Iorg
President Gateway Seminary

"I'm happy, excited and elated to recommend "God's Amazing Grace: Reconciling Four Centuries of African-American Marriages and Families." My friend Dr. Terry Turner has written a book to remind us that the eyes of God were always upon us in our historical struggles. This vital work can improve Black and White relationships by increasing our knowledge of the Black family in American history from an African-American Christian perspective. I am so proud he has chosen to write this crucial and critical book evaluating the causes for the social risk factors within marriages and families in the African-American Community."

Dr. Fred Luter
Pastor, Franklin Avenue Baptist Church
Former President Southern Baptist Convention

"Dr. Turner's treatment of slavery's legacy in the African-American family demands a reading because of the synthesis and perspective he brings to the subject matter. By joining history to family systems theory, this book pushes the painful historical legacy of slavery to this day into the reader's understanding. He wades boldly into claims, which will undoubtedly bring a pushback from opposite ends of the cultural spectrum. But to that truth he always adds his ultimately grace-based perspective. For those willing to face rather than ignore some of the most irremediable realities in America's historical and present culture, this straightforward work is an important read."

Dr. Barry Creamer
President Criswell College

"Through *God's Amazing Grace* Dr. Terry Turner helps us better understand the plight and fight for the family in the history and contemporary context of the African-American family. May God use this to help us all equip and encourage faithfulness in partners and parents so needed in a fractured culture."

Dr. Mark L. Bailey
President, Dallas Theological Seminary

"Dr. Terry Turner's book is a much needed word of truth and a breath of fresh air in this season! IT IS A MUST READ FOR ALL, that will educate, enlighten, encourage and enrich! With historical and biblical exegetical insight, life experience and wisdom, he examines the African-American Family dilemma, deliberate destruction and blessed deliverance!! With great courage and strength, he pens our painful inhumane history with integrity, discussing the devastating effects of slavery and the intricacies of slave marriages, and it's effects on the African-American Family then and today! I appreciated the research in the book, especially on America's views of Slavery and the Church's unbiblical justification of this hideous ungodly institution!! Certainly it is by God's amazing grace as a people we have persevered and prospered through a dark and dreary past of oppression and injustice that we are still battling. This book will help the healing and reconciliation for sinner and saint alike! Thank you, my brother, for this excellent work!! It's destined to be a best seller!!"

K. Marshall Williams Sr., Senior Pastor, Nazarene Baptist Church, Past President, National African-American Fellowship, SBC

"Dr. Turner has been a friend and colleague since 1989. It is a privilege to write an endorsement to his new book. Pastors and teachers who are interested in building strong families in their congregations will want to peruse this book. I am highly recommending this book to those from other cultures beside African-Americans who want to understand the role that family has played in healthy spiritual development. As a friend and colleague, I am pleased to endorse Dr. Turner's book."

Dr. Rodney Orr, Department Chair, and Associate Professor of World Missions and Intercultural Studies, Dallas Theological Seminary

"Turner's book, part history, part sociology, part theology, and part autobiography is a significant contribution to those engaged in understanding the family in America and in helping the church strengthen, reclaim, educate, and demonstrate love to families everywhere. His holistic view of the impact of slavery upon all Americans is a singular message not often heard in discussions on the subject. The greatest contribution Turner makes is his unfailing confidence in the grace of God and his unerring ability to see that grace in the darkest that life offers. This book is a must read for anyone serious about the family, American culture, the church's mission, and most importantly, God's Amazing Grace."

Dr. Waylan Owens, Dean of the Jack D. Terry, Jr. School of Church and Family Ministries, Acting Associate Dean of the Research Doctoral Program, Southwestern Baptist Theological Seminary.

"Not only does Dr. Terry Turner offer a sobering history of American slavery and its toll on the African-American family, but he highlights the power of God's grace in the gospel to foster hope, healing and empowerment for racial reconciliation today and into the future. If you want to deepen your understanding of one of the most resilient people groups throughout the ages, this book is for you."

D. Scott Barfoot, Th.M., PhD
Director, Doctor of Ministry Studies, Dallas Theological Seminary

"This book is amazing in the research and in the reason it was written. I see it benefitting the health of the whole family: past, present and the yet unborn. With God's Grace, I see the lessons learned are for the healing and benefit of the whole family not just the African-American family. 'The healing of African-American families and marriages from racial oppression can only be accomplished when slavery is viewed through the word of God and institutionalized racism is acknowledged and ended.' Although I was familiar with Post-Traumatic Stress Syndrome, I had never heard of or thought to apply the effect of years of slavery on the current black family behavior as Post-Traumatic Slave Syndrome. Thank you. My grandmother used to say, 'When you know better. You do better.' My prayer is that we all come to know God's Amazing Grace and do better for the 'healing of the nations.'"

Freda M. Bush, MD, FACOG

Figures List

Contents

Foreword

Terry Turner's monograph *God's Amazing Grace: Reconciling Four Centuries of African-American Marriages and Families* is the rare book that desperately needed to be written, and for the book to be effective, the author needed to be a black pastor. But not just any black pastor was adequate. Of necessity, the author of this book needed to be an African-American who has felt deeply the agonies into which the debilitating horrors of slavery plunged the black community—yet, he needed to be objective enough to be aware of the strengths garnered by the "community of slaves."

Candidly, this book made me ashamed. I never owned slaves and pray that I would not have condoned such a disgusting practice had I lived in the era of American slavery. Thankfully, I grew up in a home in which I was taught that every human of whatever ethnicity was the product of the incredible artistry of God. I was in the fifth grade before I began to reflect on white attitudes and the fact that there was not a single black child in my school. But while I grew up in a home void of racial prejudice, I fell into the morass of the White-American, unable to identify with the experience of the descendants of slaves in America.

A series of events awakened me to my lack of empathy with my brothers of African-American ethnicity. The first was a journey of a lifetime with my parents, circumventing the globe in two months. Against all of my desires to the contrary, I was forced to visit a leprosorium in Korea. Though technically not slaves, I quickly discerned that these precious people were not free. I also experienced the inability of many Koreans to love the Japanese and of the refusal of the Japanese to embrace the Koreans. I asked my father about this. After a short explanation, he added this ice-cold water to my face: "Now, my son, you can understand the difficulties of the Negroes in our country." No, I could not and neither could he. But his comment at least awakened me to how little I did comprehend.

A stint as interim pastor in an African-American church in Beaumont, playing pre-season scrimmages with Black high schools – Charlton-Pollard and Hebert, and incurring the wrath of the Ku Klux Klan in Mississippi for putting an arm around the shoulders of Willie Lee, a station attendant with whom I prayed – all continued to open my eyes.

Then I read Terry Turner's book, and my whole soul blushed afresh with crimson shame at the deeds of Americans in the "land of the free." However, Turner not only assisted me with understanding the impact of slavery generations after the abolition, but he also breathed fresh hope into my heart. I was reassured that God is at work in the darkest night. Turner spoke of the incredible virtues that arose for the Black man amidst the chaffing sorrows of slavery. And he reminded me of the heroism of the few Whites who knew that slavery was stench in the nostrils of a holy God and labored to abolish the ungodly reign of terror at risk of their own lives.

But Turner is a wise, discerning, and biblical pastor. He knows that while one cannot afford the luxury of ignorance of the past, neither can one stake out the past as his residence. To do so is to create bitterness and perpetuate the problems of the past, producing in this case hatred and even reverse racism. As this gifted pastor looks at the dilemma of our day, he senses that what slavery did to the home and family in the Black community has perpetuated itself into our postmodern era, and just may be the cruelest sorrow of all. And he knows only too well that God's healing is the only tonic that will rescue the sacredness of the family. Turner makes clear that this is a malady not only of the Black community, but also one that slavery visited upon the White community.

Throughout the book, the strains of John Newton's "Amazing Grace" are heard repeatedly. That old slave ship devil – saved, forgiven, and changed points to redemption not only for individuals but also for the families. Turner hides nothing, but openly elucidates all the problems visited on Blacks by fatherless families. He knows well the future of young black males forced to development without a disciplining, loving father in the home. In the process, Turner introduces Anglo Americans to many of the heroes of the faith from the days of slavery.

The book assesses the impact of arranged marriages, temporary marriages, and "breeding marriages." He talks frankly about White supremacists who immorally took advantage of Black slave women and fathered children by them. Turner loves the church but also is aware that churches consist of sinners. He discusses, without fear, the frequent contribution of the churches to the virtual demise of God's plan for marriage among many Blacks.

Finally, Turner grasps the solution to the problem. Whatever the contributions of government, social organizations, and psychology – all ultimately crawl defeated from the stage of human life. Using Newton as his paradigm, this godly pastor presents conversion and the awakening of love as the sole means to change the hearts of men. Like Paul admonishing Philemon concerning his runaway slave who has found the Lord, Turner calls on us to "receive him no longer as a slave but as a brother in Christ."

Post-conversion humans must return to the Bible for counsel. Turner begins with the rediscovery of the full humanity of all men. He proceeds to find the outline of marriage as provided in Genesis 1– 3 and amplified throughout the Bible as the hope for communities, whether Black or Anglo. In this solution, Turner rests his case knowing from both study and experience that this alone can resolve the tensions that after all these years affect both oppressed and oppressors in slavery.

God's Amazing Grace is beautifully illustrated. The bibliography provided in this volume is extraordinary, and the reader is engulfed in a sea of books, which will unite in this present time to enlighten the eyes of the reader. For his labor of love in the labor of research, chiefly accomplished in the Southwestern library, all will be forever grateful.

Now, my reader friend, if you are a man or woman of genuine courage, if your thirsty soul seeks enlightenment, and if you wish to be a part of God's solution for the systemic racism that has tarnished the American scene, get a hot cup of tea, sit down by the fire, open *God's Amazing Grace*, and read through your tears a book that will change your life. And as you read, keep humming the tune to "Amazing Grace." After all, this was Newton's story. It is Turner's story. And it must be your story also.

Paige Patterson, President
Southwestern Baptist Theological Seminary
Fort Worth, Texas

Acknowledgements

The writing of this book has been a labor of love by many who, without reservation, gave me their support. I would like to thank Janice Anderson, Robin Foster, Mary Randall, and Nancy Turner for being the first to read the contents of the book and make suggestions. Thanks to Dr. Sarah Springs for her editing support and for recommending revisions to the content and Lori Janke who provided the final proof edit to the manuscript. Drs. Paige and Dorothy Patterson have my gratitude for taking a personal interest in this work and for encouraging me in numerous ways throughout this project. I'd like to thank the staff and members of Mesquite Friendship Baptist Church for permitting me writing time away from the church. I'm grateful to both Kenneth Spresley, who did the cover design, and to my life-long friends, Pastor Larry Joseph Sanders and Willie Bohanan my lifelong friends who daily listened as I read lengthy passages of the book with them over the phone, and in turn, talked through the content with me. To Dr. Willie Peterson, a mentor, friend, co-laborer both in ministry and on this project, thank you for your guidance, support and timely recommendations. Finally, but not least, special thanks to my children, Angela, Caleb, and Levi, my greatest fans and encouragers who believe their daddy can do anything with the Lord's help.

Introduction

> Make the Lord Jesus Christ your refuge and exemplar. His is the only standard around which you can successfully rally. If ever there was a people who needed the consolations of religion to sustain them in their grievous afflictions, you are that people. You had better trust in the Lord than to put confidence in man. Happy is that people whose God is the Lord.[1]
>
> William Wells Brown, 1853

William Wells Brown, a self-taught fugitive slave, penned the first novel by an African-American on the subject of marriage and slavery in the year 1853. In this groundbreaking, non-fiction rendition of *Clotel: or, The President's Daughter*, Brown provided the most profound description of his ideal for marriage and family life: The marriage relationship is the oldest and most sacred institution given to humanity by the Creator. It should be held in the highest esteem by everyone and kept as a holy covenant as initiated from its beginning. Marriage is the first and most important institution of human existence—the foundation of all civilization and culture and the root of church and state. It is the most intimate bond among humankind, and for many individuals, the only relationship in which they feel the true sentiments of humanity. It gives place for every virtue of mankind where love and confidence can develop to the highest degree.

In other words, marriage joins all the cherished feelings, commitments and passions that enrich life. Children within families find themselves secure in the affectionate bond of love between parents who are sympathetically and lovingly concerned for them. This attitude of loving affection that exists between husbands and wives in their role as parents acts with creative influence upon the minds of their young, and promotes every seed of virtuousness within the family. This inestimable inspiration of parental life provides more for children than all means of educational achievements. If this were an accurate depiction of the massive influence for goodness within the institution of marriage, what would be the moral deprivation of people to whom marriage is denied?[2]

This description by Brown enlightens us as to why some sociologists believe the most devastating effects of slavery are the denied roles of family relationships. This issue deserves careful inspection to discover if characteristics within the slave system are responsible for the failures within present-day African-American marriages. This book will explore many tenets of slavery that created this deficiency in the African-American family.

One significant feature of American slavery was its focus on racial differences that kept Black and White-Americans separated by race and economic class. Starting with the colonial period, observations of most people groups disclose events that isolate and divide the people of this country. America claims to be "one nation under God," a nation where the Creator desires every people group to be one in a relationship as the Father, Son, and Holy Spirit are one. In reality, many divisive governmental laws have hindered this oneness, through race-related legislation that created the breakdown of relationships among families, friends, and racial groups. These regulations affected households with a philosophical understanding that the race of a person should determine the treatment of a person. This study will highlight how the histories of two sets of laws in this country have contributed to the breakdown of African-American families.

The turmoil in the streets of America today is a reflection of her past. Systemic racism, in both past and present America, is the cause for many risk factors that exist in the lives of all races and families in the twenty-first century, although some are more disturbing than others. Today, Americans are experiencing the cause and effect of an American history where parents exhibited biased and racial views that caused race relationships to suffer. As a result, centuries of ethnic disharmony has created much of the distress found in African-American families today. When we see the breakdown of unity among people groups like America is experiencing in 2017, it is the outcome of a problem with the history of skin color. Jesus said, "You judge according to the flesh; I judge no one" (John 8:15 ESV). Historically, a person's skin color has been the motivating influence that sustained the failure in relationships between Black and White-Americans. The pigmentation within African-Americans' skin has resulted in a people group becoming the victims of slavery and inherent racial discrimination.

For generations, African-Americans have been on the wrong side of the race problem. They need to heal the pains that link them to the racially charged events of their slave ancestry. Most don't have any knowledge of the source of their frustration beyond a generation or two, and those who have some knowledge of history realize it is deficient and incomplete. For most Black and White-Americans, reliving American history that involves enslavement is agonizingly painful; therefore, most of the intricacies of slavery have been lost for this generation. People of this present generation are left to interpret current events without knowledge of how slavery has had an impact on them, whether negative or positive. It is intrinsic in this book to bridge the knowledge gap about the effects of slavery on present-day Americans, in the hope that we are able to develop a compassionate solution for healing our racially charged country.

We will explore research by social scientists that has determined that present-day African-Americans are still influenced, both in harmful and beneficial ways, by the system of slavery. For example, several investigating reports from family specialists exploring the 2010 Census determined African-American marriages and family structures are suffering from an impending social crisis. This kind of crisis causes family risk factors. African-Americans exhibited the highest risk factors in out-of-wedlock childbirths, single-parent households, and the lowest marriage rates among marrying age adults. Consequently, these troubling conclusions inspired the author to examine the reasons why race makes a difference in family stability, structure, and happiness in the United States.

Why is living in America a social problem for residents in the African-American community? Perhaps a question that better addresses the problem would be, why is there so much social distress from a lack of racial reconciliation between the Black and White races in America? Many people say there is a racial bias embedded the hearts and minds of a majority of the individuals in this country that cultivates division among people groups. An etymological understanding of racial prejudice instructs that it is not a personality flaw that humans are born with, but rather a learned condition that traditionally finds its base in family teachings. In Scripture, the Apostle James provides an example of how prejudice starts. "Have you not then made distinctions among yourselves and become judges with evil thoughts?" (James 2:4 ESV). In life, it is natural to develop an affinity for those who are like oneself, which in turn can create animosity or indifference toward those who are different.

The history of America is the story of two family groups, Black and White. Therefore, the history of African-American marriages and families is incomplete without including the participation of European-Americans, just as American history is incomplete without adding the involvement of African-Americans. With few exceptions, today's understanding of American history is written from the perspective of one race: the White race. This one-sided accounting of the mutual history of Americans has left most uninformed and misguided concerning the dysfunctional social issues in the African-American community.

With this in mind, all Americans are confronted with the task of developing a shared sympathetic knowledge that will result in finding a workable solution for the causes of these social problems for both Black and White-Americans. Although the two races have lived together in this country for four hundred years, there is a deep racial divide that makes racial reconciliation painful. Perhaps the longevity of these racial attitudes has overwhelmed twenty-first century Americans, and because there has been no compassionate resolution, even more tensions have been generated. When dealing with race issues, American history has a way of repeating itself. The notable exception is when kind and regenerate hearts visit the subject and move forward with the intention of improving the racial gap. Throughout this manuscript, we will observe the works of several abolitionists who committed themselves to improving race relationships and freeing African-Americans from slavery.

As African slaves were transported to America in the early seventeenth century, their arrival triggered the beginning of discord of among people groups. Laws were developed to keep them enslaved for life, and to prohibit interracial marriages of Africans and European-Americans. Attached to this legislation was an amendment that also revoked African rights to have marriages and families. In Chapters three throughout five, the rules governing the unions of slaves are examined as first developed throughout the seventeenth and eighteenth centuries. Chapter four deliberates hundreds of years' worth of American legislation that prohibited African-Americans from becoming Christians, because of the misconception that the law forbade Christians to be enslaved. This period of American history reveals a Christianity controlled by the immoralities of slavery. However, any amount of Christian influence in historical America was better than no involvement. The question of whether Christianity and slavery still have an impact today on African-American marriages and families is analyzed. We will examine the following assumption within a spiritual context. The enslavement of African-Americans from 1620-1865 was so ingrained into the American way of life that only God's Amazing Grace could give sufficient comfort to the cruel mistreatment suffered by these families. Within these struggles, you will find a careful spiritual examination of Black history that reveals the hand of God at work in their hearts and minds, keeping them from destruction. You will be challenged with miracles to celebrate when observing the details of survival through the horrors of slavery.

This research must start with the beginning of slavery to get a clear understanding of its history and the impact captivity had on African-American marriages and families. Throughout this book, you will discover the many ways that living the lifestyle of an enslaved person placed them in crisis. Each chapter will consider how the current risk factors of poor education, inferiority complex, low expectations, poverty, poor health, and low marriage rates suffered by the descendants of slaves began in captivity. Because of the intricate details of the American slave system and what has become known as multi-generational impact, history will reveal how centuries of family separation and annihilation affects African-American families today. In spite of these hardships, the African-American past is full of amazing, eye-opening stories of marriage and family survival in the midst of struggles.

Overall, this journey is not a total history of African-Americans, but rather a historical analysis of causes for the high-risk factors that are evident in African-American families today. In recent years, theologians, sociologists and family therapists have begun to "explore how the social history of chattel slavery and the system of Jim Crow segregation shaped the contemporary African-American family."[3] This book will contemplate three questions: 1. What caused African-Americans to rank higher than other racial groups in social risk factors that led to the decline of marriages and families? 2. Are the social issues found in present-day African-Americans the same as those seen during their two hundred and fifty years of bondage? 3. How did Christian slavery remain a positive influence on African-Americans and their descendants despite the atrocities they experienced within the slave system?

Since the impact that slavery had on the family structures of slaves establishes the foundation for this book, narratives of slaves are used to reveal what family life and community structure looked like within the slave lodgings. I use the testimonies of slave marriages and family situations as case studies to assess them by using several social sciences theories and the

Scripture. For Example, in chapter 2, the Pathology and Resilient research methods used by sociologists are contrasting views on the instability and stability of family structures among slaves. On the one hand, the Resilient or adaptable camps teach that slavery was a well-established lifestyle among the slave quarters. In their dwellings, slaves were generally on their own, at least from sunset to sunrise. Husbands and wives, in most instances, experienced the intimacy of a quasi-marital relationship. Fathers and mothers were only able to parent and train their children in the ways of slavery. This being the most favorable view suggests that the influence of slavery did not negatively affect the African-American family, but rather that it became a stronger institution during the slavery period. The Resilient theory also suggests that the African-American family rebounded from slavery and regressed into the present state of risk factors and social issues.

On the other hand, sociologists that are in the Pathological camp considered slavery a destructive force in every area of the lives of slaves. They suggest slavery and its family risk factors are the reasons why twenty-first century African-American marriages and families are an endangered institution. It is not the intention of this research to prove or disprove any of the sociological views, but instead to embrace each as they reflect on the long-lasting effects of slavery. At the same time, while welcoming each philosophy, this study will theologically reveal how God amazingly preserved the African-American family, in spite of the historical and current social factors that plague them.

Finally, in light of slavery representing the start of America's systemic racism, charts have been included throughout the book to help us understand how racism legislated and approved the course of American History. We will travel through centuries of American history to connect the genetic link between slave families and twenty-first century African-American marriages and families. Using the most compelling evidence, we will compare the testimonies of slaves regarding their marriages and families to the risk factors suffered by twenty-first century African-Americans families. When observing the life of slaves, we will see how racial prejudice was intentionally created to have a negative influence on the lives of African-Americans forever. With this in mind, it is the goal of this book to expose the risk factors associated with slavery and racial oppression on African-American families and marriages. Using the word of God and the untold story of American history, it is the goal of this book to facilitate racial healing and bring institutionalized racism to an end.

Chapter 1

What's Wrong with My People?

Trust in the Lord with all your heart, and do
not lean on your own understanding.
In all your ways acknowledge him, and he will make
straight your paths (Prov. 3:5-6 ESV).

Amazing Grace, how sweet the sound,
That saved a wretch like me…

What in the world is wrong with my people? This question is the reason that I needed to write this book, and why I think it's a must-read for America today. What I am actually asking is, what's wrong with me? When analyzing my formative years, trauma in life started for me at age 10 when my father died of a heart attack and my mother became an amputee. Twenty years before that event, he had to have his vocal cords removed so as a child I never heard his natural voice. Having grown up in a single parent household with a sick mother has been a source of motivation and problems in all areas of my life, but especially my home life.

The pain of growing up without a dad in the home was stressful and, at times, very challenging. I watched my handicap mother take care of four of her eight children alone on the income of a monthly social security check. She was employed as a maid for a white family when she had to have her leg amputated. For many years, they continued to help support my family. It was their love for me and my family during this very traumatic time of life that has given me a heart for racial reconciliation.

Although my father died and did not desert us, as is the case with many single-parent households, his absence still left a void in my life that only he could have filled. I am sure this void is also the case for most men and women who grew up in a single-parent household. As a child, I suffered through the fact that daddy was missing, and I often felt consumed with not having his guidance on the things that men must know. While dad's absence left me without a model for marriage as I developed into manhood, I still retained his words of love to my mother that I heard as a child. I gained a sincere appreciation for marriage and family as I watched him love my mom in their sickness. His words and actions hold an essential place in my life today.

My dad was a junk man by day and a small club owner at night. Two nights after my mother came home from the hospital from her amputation, dad came home from the club, went to bed with her and said to her, "Momma, I love you." It was at that moment he turned over and suffered a heart attack and died. His last words have helped shape my thinking about marriage and family. I believe his heart attack was caused by the physical exertion of daily traveling over sixty miles round trip, for weeks, taking care of my mother in the hospital, and then returning home to care for his children. He had all of this added stress while still trying to work. On top of that, he was dealing with a physical disability that affected his breathing. All the years of my youth, as I heard my mother tell this story about the night my daddy died, she never failed to recall his final words.

My parents were uneducated people who had a marriage that lasted thirty-nine years through many hardships. They taught us to love and care for each other through the words dad left in the heart of my mother. As a young man, years after dad's death, I heard rumors of women in town who were supposed to have been his intimate lady friends. For all I will ever know, these were just rumors; however, it would not surprise me if there was some truth to the gossip, as the area of infidelity in marriage has been a problem for most men in my family. My brothers, calling themselves players wrecked their marriages like far too many African American men. I believe that I would have done the same if not for the personal relationship I had with Jesus as a teenager. My youth was spent trying to find myself, making several mistakes along the way. Sundays allowed me to seek prayer, repent in sorrow and confess my failures before the Lord and his church. I don't know what I would have done had it not been for the church and Christianity in my life. I am grateful I had my mother who made her children go to church every Sunday, as long as they lived in her home.

I believe the reason for my zeal to improve the social conditions of marriages and families is because, as a teenager, I, too, became an absentee father. I was responsible for creating the same fatherless void in the life of a child that I suffered through. I am writing with the knowledge of what it is like to have fatherhood risk factors as both a child and a parent.

My experience as an absentee father and as a fatherless child created many sleepless nights and agonizing days. As a teen with a baby, my excuse for not being responsible was, "How could I take care of a child when I needed someone to provide for me? How could I be a father when I didn't have a man to show me what a father does?" My grief was strong, because I had grown up in church and knew God was displeased with my fornication. I knew that it was wrong to have children without being married. For years, I repented to God so often that it seemed like I went to the altar every Sunday asking for forgiveness. It was during this time that my Christianity became real and God began calling me into ministry. I had no doubt that God had forgiven me of my failures, but in my heart, I could not resolve the pain or forgive myself for the heartache I caused others. So, I got caught up in the blame game. But where does the blame rest when our families are missing husbands and fathers because they bailout, instead of remaining leaders of their families?

Friends, we are aware of many reasons that fatherless homes exist, but simply knowing those reasons is not enough. We must begin to make things better for the next generation. When we look at the troubles confronting fatherless families, two other risk factors cause my heart to grieve. First, there are too many men locked up in jail who should be providing for their homes. Secondly, African-American men are being killed by violent crimes, leaving their families without justification for their deaths. No matter the cause, fatherless homes are a severe problem in the Black community. In my opinion, it is at the top of the list for what causes anguish in home life. I am grateful my sons who became single parents broke the fatherless home risk factor and married their children's mother. The social conditions of our families will not become satisfactory until men take their proper place in the house.

Overcoming what has become known as the battle of the sexes is at the core of the breakup in marriages and families. When couples are in competition for control of the household, nobody wins. Sisters, allow me to publicly say something that brothers talk about among themselves but only a few would ever admit openly. Marriage requires a massive dose of humility to stay married, because when spouses stay home and commit to their marriages and families, they are often treated poorly. Couples say that their husbands and wives often talk too much and treat them like children instead of as adults. Disrespectful communication is a negative factor in most African-American marriages and creates a great deal of animosity for both genders. How many of you men have children by your spouses and baby mamas that have left them to care for themselves? I have heard men say many times, "I felt belittled by her in the relationship." How many women have said, "I can do that badly all by myself. I don't need him." Let me assure you that God has given you everything you need to endure the emotional side of your marriages, if you stay strong. It's easy to say problems in marriage are the result of cultural conditioning or discrimination. While it is true that society has failed, mistreated or kept some of us down, in this book, you will find that the hardships we endure today are very small compared to our ancestors. They made their marriages and families work in spite of life's difficulties.

Mothers, wives, sons and daughters, the struggles you are going through are as difficult for real men to watch as they are for you to endure. A good man wants to protect the women in his life, because when they hurt, so does he. Although men handle their frustrations in life differently from women, too often he will leave when he feels incapable of resolving your problems. His desertion is never entirely leaving because he is required daily to live with the knowledge he has failed in his responsibility as a man. Experience has taught me that life is never right for any member of the family once the father is gone from the home, and he can never justify his absence in their daily life. I now realize there is no acceptable apology from absentee fathers that will take away the pain of our absence in the lives of children.

I have been married for over 35 years to my wife, and I helped her raise a wonderful daughter that has become mine in every way. All the women in my life have stolen my heart, and I honor and hold them in the highest esteem. In spite of my family background, I find it overwhelming as I watch with confusion the rates keep going higher and higher for babies born outside of marriage by African-American women and men. I watched three of my five sisters have children before marriage. Three of my sisters also had failed marriages that ended in a divorce. Typically, the risk factor of out-of-wedlock births is placed only at the feet of women. However, how can a woman have a child without a man? Therefore, I give this social issue to both male and female. Although mothers, wives, daughters, and women, in general, are held in the highest regards, the moral standards they have established is lower than any other people group. Their inability to say no to shacking and living with a man, or to not have sex outside of marriage by not demanding to have healthy intimacy within the commitment of marriage, is at the heart of our African-American women's troubles.

Ladies, before you turn me off, please know that I realize that the brothers bring all kinds of pressures to the relationship that influence your decisions. But I have to ask our women the question: What will it take before you learn that unless he is married to you, he will get what he wants and move on to the next woman who will have him? How many of you have given yourself to a man, and he left you with a child or children, only to leave and go to the next? Now you are forced to hope another man will accept you and your children. Ladies, I know the pain of having to watch my sisters, wife and other women in my family struggle with raising children they had before marriage. For decades, I have asked myself the question: what is wrong with African-American women that they are not getting married, and what makes them keep increasing their rates of out-of-wedlock births? While writing this book about the social risk factors present today among African-Americans, and examining the lives of slave families, I have seen you and myself in them time and time again. As you read this book, I encourage you to look for the risk factors in your own life and family, while using the stories of slaves to strengthen your families and marriages.

This book became a driving need on the quest for me to find out if the living conditions of my slave ancestors could reveal the source of present family problems. My need to investigate why African-Americans were overwhelmed by risk factors led me to sociologists that determined the dysfunctions started in slavery. It was at this time that I realized how little I knew about African-American history. My lack of knowledge made me see that, until I discovered why the marriages and families of African-Americans were in trouble, compared to other races, I could not move forward with other projects. This inspired me to start a Sankofa, "(san = to return) + (ko = to go) + (fa = to look, to seek and take"),"[1] into African-American history and learn from my ancestors so that I could move forward.

Let me encourage each of you to go back into history and make your family search personal, as it has been for me. Develop a genogram or a diagram of past family relationshps, as far back as you can, to uncover the past. That will help repair the present risk factors. It's crucial to know centuries of family history and dynamics. The goal is to acquire personal knowledge of one's ancestors, which can then lead to spiritual and emotional healing in broken lives.

However, it's complicated to trace African-American family members back beyond 1870. With this in mind, I have outlined the history of African-American marriages and families, as a people group, with the hope of helping couples who are suffering from marital problems to find strength and stability in historical stories. I encourage you to find in their stories emotional and spiritual ancestral connections, and to develop your own link to the present and past generations of family crisis and satisfactions. The saying is true: when you know better, you can do better. In tracing my family genealogy, I found that this present generation has fallen victim to the same family failures as those of our forefathers and mothers. I believe that knowing their family dynamics should make life better today. I have been able to open my family story back into slavery through a few years of digging into the past. For most of us, slavery seems like a long time ago. In reality, it was not that long ago, and not much has changed in our family issues.

When researching my family genealogy, I realized that the story of my ancestors is also the story of all twenty-first century African-American descendants of slaves and slaveholders. Many African-Americans living today are only three to five generations away from slavery. Allow me to share with you my example of the first discovery of slaves in my family. My paternal great-grandparents were Warren Turner, born in 1847, and Elvira Davis Turner, born in 1851. Their lives will reveal to us some risk factors evolving from the issues of slavery and its complications to families. Both were teenagers at the time of the signing of the Emancipation Proclamation in 1863, and ancestry records informed me that all of their formative years as children were in slavery.

Warren and Elvira spent the majority of their youth in Waxahachie, Texas, where they also married and lived a short time after their wedding. They later lived in Burnham, Ellis County, Texas after the Civil War. They were legally married one month after the Dormancy Marriage Laws were in place for the state of Texas. Dormancy Marriage Laws were the rules established by those states that did not accept the rights of slaves to marry as was provided within the legislation of the Emancipation Proclamation. Their 1869 marriage license displayed the acronyms for the race of Warren Turner as (YMC) Young Man Colored and Elvira Davis as (YWC) Young Woman Colored. The license below on the right is a transposed copy of the original on the left. They were among the first African-Americans to receive a legal marriage license in the state of Texas.

Figure.1 Texas Marriage License Warren Turner and Elvira Davis 1869.[2]

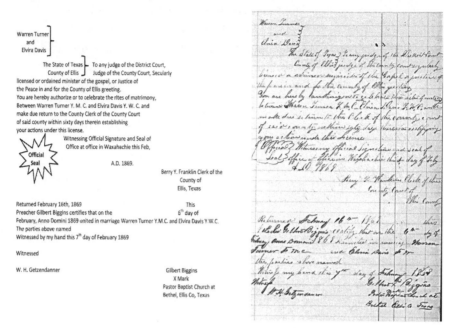

Warren Turner
and
Elvira Davis

The State of Texas
County of Ellis

To any judge of the District Court,
Judge of the County Court, Secularly
licensed or ordained minister of the gospel, or Justice of
the Peace in and for the County of Ellis greeting.
You are hereby authorize or to celebrate the rites of matrimony,
Between Warren Turner Y. M. C. and Elvira Davis Y. W. C. and
make due return to the County Clerk of the County Court
of said county within sixty days therein establishing
your actions under this license.

Official
Seal

Witnessing Official Signature and Seal of
Office at office in Waxahachie this Feb,

A.D. 1869.

Berry Y. Franklin Clerk of the
County of
Ellis, Texas

Returned February 16th, 1869
Preacher Gilbert Biggins certifies that on the This 6th day of
February, Anno Domini 1869 united in marriage Warren Turner Y.M.C. and Elvira Davis Y.W.C.
The parties above named
Witnessed by my hand this 7th day of February 1869

Witnessed

W. H. Getzendanner

Gilbert Biggins
X Mark
Pastor Baptist Church at
Bethel, Ellis Co, Texas

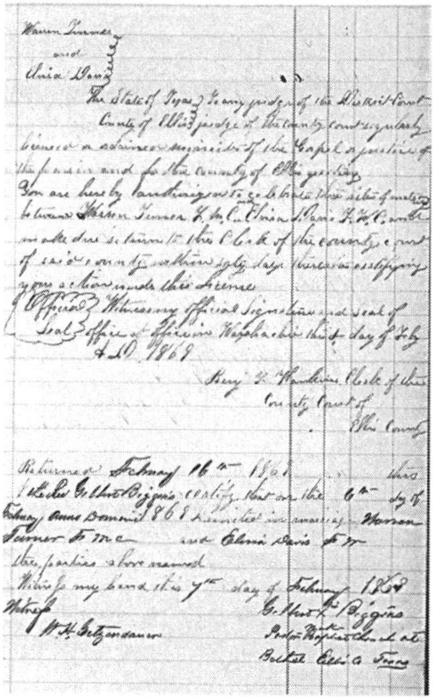

Through ancestery.com their license was discovered, and that has allowed me to piece together several things about my family heritage previously unknown to any of our living family members. Unfortunately, the Turner family records during slavery are unavailable before the 1870 Census for Warren and Elvira—this problem is known as the 1870 brick wall. Genealogists who researched the 1870 brick wall have found collecting information beyond this date usually leads to a dead-end for enslaved African-American families. However, examining the Census for each decade in later years provided more knowledge about their unknown family history. For example, the 1870 Census informed us that Warren and Elvira became a couple during slavery. It revealed that they considered themselves a couple three years before former slaves could make marriages legal. It exposed them as a cohabitating couple in 1867, since marriages in Texas were not legal for African-Americans until 1869. Warren (age 21) and Elvira (age 19) endured two years of cohabitation until they could make their marriage legal as new citizens of Texas. Their marriage license, cited February 7, 1869, revealed that, at the ages of 24 and 21, they legally became husband and wife. The 1900 Census recorded that Warren and Elvira had celebrated 32 years, and their marriage lasted until Warren's death in 1909. Their marital relationship began during slavery and was long-lasting. Warren and Elvira celebrated 41 years of marriage as a free couple before death parted them. However, their marriage was not without the complications that slavery imposed on family relationships.

In case you are thinking this book is only for African Americans, let me assure you that Black and White-Americans have a shared history that makes our stories one. The two people groups are like one coin with two sides. The slave portion of the coin is one story and only half of the complete story. If a DNA test were taken by most Americans, they would discover a mixture of ethnic backgrounds within their family history.

The Census records also revealed that, in 1864 while he was a slave, Warren partnered with a young slave woman, named Cornelia Lockhart, and conceived a son, Lee. In 1864, they were still enslaved, because Texas, in defiance, held its slaves after the signing of the Emancipation Proclamation. Lee was born after the Civil War in 1865 as a free baby. He was the first of my Turner ancestors born as a free person. Lee was first found living with his mother, Cornelia, and grandmother, Martha Lockhart, in a single parent household. These women were both listed as mulatto (a biracial person of black and white genes) on the 1870 Census. Beginning with Lee, is the first occurrence of the White side, or the other aspect of the coin, revealed in my family. Lee Lockhart was born into a single parent home with nine other mulatto children. Ten years later, Lee was listed as a youth living with Warren and Elvira—his name was then Lee Turner.

Legal documents, such as birth records and Census reports, revealed that Warren also had a second child by Cornelia: Willie Ann Turner, born in 1883. Families were still in crisis in spite of their new freedom, only now this was not due to the oversight of a master, but to the dysfunctions that began in slavery. For example, Warren and Cornelia conceived another child after slavery, even though Warren and Elvira were a married couple and free. This infidelity would have created a considerable amount of marital and family stress for all the involved family members. Below is the birth record for Willie Ann, which states her parents were Cornelia and Warren, over fourteen years after the marriage of Warren and Elvira. In this manner, there were two children born outside of their marriage with his slave partner.

Willie Ann was not found on a Federal Census as living with either parent as a child. Willie Ann, a 19-year-old adult, was more than likely living on her own by the 1900 Census. Lee and Willie Ann were unknown to our family down through the years. They were our great aunt and uncle who lived only thirty miles from my current home in Mesquite, Texas. I have told you this history, of the children born between Warren and Cornelia, to raise awareness of the risk factors involved, but the story is not finished. During the same time period, Warren also had six children by his legal wife, Elvira. Elvira must have been a special lady to stay with her family through such hardships. Most women today could not endure this infidelity, and even if they stayed with an unfaithful spouse, the marriage intimacy would be ended.

Figure 2. Willie Ann Turner Birth Record[3]

Warren Turner
mentioned in the record of Willie Ann Turner

Name:	Warren Turner
Gender:	Male
Wife:	Cornellia Lockhart
Daughter:	Willie Ann Turner

Other information in the record of Willie Ann Turner
from Texas, Births and Christenings

Name:	Willie Ann Turner
Gender:	Female
Birth Date:	15 Jan 1883
Birthplace:	Ennis, Ellis, Texas
Father's Name:	Warren Turner
Mother's Name:	Cornellia Lockhart

Indexing Project (Batch) Number: **C00016-4**, System Origin: **Texas-ODM**, GS Film number: **1651033 IT 1-4**

Citing this Record

"Texas, Births and Christenings, 1840-1981," index, FamilySearch (https://familysearch.org/pal:/MM9.1.1/VR3M-Y1L : accessed 24 February 2015), Warren Turner in entry for Willie Ann Turner, 15 Jan 1883; citing Ennis, Ellis, Texas, reference ; FHL microfilm 1651033 IT 1-4.

In slavery, Warren, Elvira and Cornelia became introduced to a crisis lifestyle of sexual tolerance which they did not immediately stop in freedom. Census reports can reveal a great deal about our family background, but it cannot tell of the trauma associated with the issues in their relationships. The risk factor of out-of-wedlock births and marital infidelity started with the slave ancestors in the Turner family and has continued throughout the generations. Warren and Elvira were the parents of my grandfather, Levi Turner. He fathered my dad, Roosevelt Turner, Sr.

Warren and Elvira's family risk factors reveal the problems involved when the issues of blended families cause a breakup. By the 1910 Census report, Lee was again living with his mother, Cornelia. Around 1890, his father, Warren, and stepmother, Elvira, moved to Seward, Oklahoma, along with six of his paternal half-siblings, leaving Lee and Willie Ann with their biological mother in Texas.

The chart below will help explain the importance of knowing the problems in family history and dynamics. It provides a visual of the actual family risk factors and effects that Warren and Elvira Turner had on the stability of their descendants.

Figure 3 First Generation Freedman Risk Factors

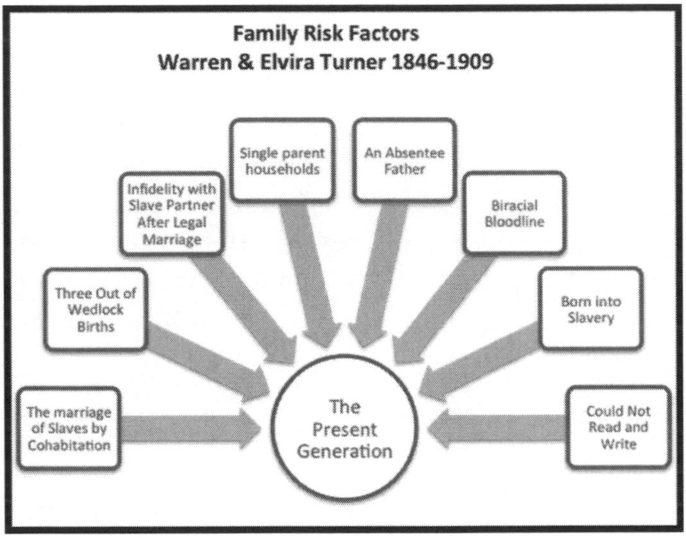

Explanation of Risk Factors Associated with Warren

Perhaps you see the dangers of these risk factors in your marriage and family. They cause those who are related to experience the same problems in life.

A. In cohabiting slave marriages, all children were born outside of a legal wedlock, and slave couples frequently did not stay together after slavery to raise their children into adulthood.

B. Children born out of wedlock and from extramarital relationships create several hardships for both the single custodial parent and the children.

C. Pre-marital sex and extramarital affairs are the source of a tremendous amount of family crisis and can lead to family disruptions.

D. Single Parent homes leave children and single parents without the support of a missing parent and spouse. Family specialists report children are more stable in a dual parent household.
E. Absentee fathers create a void in the life of a child raised without a relationship with the male biological parent. Children with missing dads often experience emotional insecurities in life.
F. Biracial bloodlines have historically been the result of an unacceptable sexual encounter that caused the conception of a child. In America, bi-racial relationships were illegal during slavery and for centuries have remained socially disrespected.
G. Born as a slave was a risk factor, taking from that person the rights of a human. Slavery took a person's citizenship and made their bodies and wages the possession of an owner.
H. The inability to read and write hinders an individual's progress in life. Illiteracy makes a person subject to others to manage their legal contracts, and keeps one from expanding their knowledge beyond what others are willing to teach them. It was illegal for slaves to read and write in America.

This next chart is a compilation of the risk factors for all my discovered slave ancestors and their descendants, for three generations. It is designed to show the magnitude of family problems that are mostly unaccounted for in our past from both a father and mother's family history.

Figure 4 Lineage of Risk Factors for Turner/Laster Family Tree

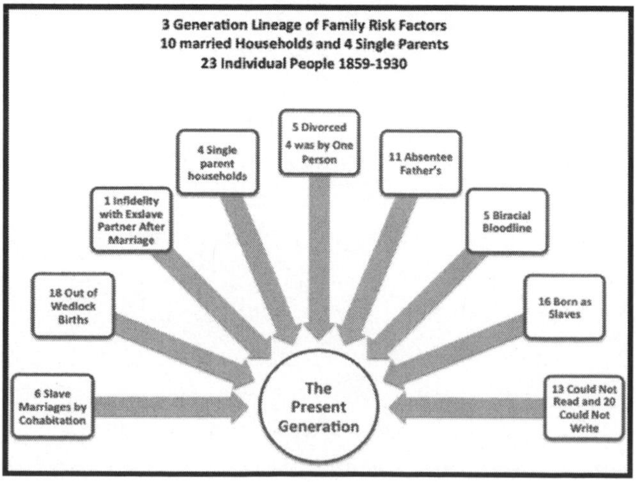

The African American community is filled with social problems that are very troubling to those of us who live through them. In America, it seems that not everyone cares about the issues facing this people group. When I gaze across the landscape of America, I find parallels between my life and what the problem of racism has done to the African-American family experience. We all can talk about the experiences of hate that racial prejudice has created for us in our lives, but few in the African American community can talk about what life is like being fully accepted as an American. How many of you, as my White brothers and sisters, live like Black people are your equal, without any bias? A more significant question may be how many of my Black brothers and sisters are able to live as if Whites consider you as equals in society? There is a more important issue to consider in how many Blacks believe yourselves to be equal with Whites? Statistics would lead African-Americans to believe that we are a troubled, inferior people and that there is something wrong with the entire race. With all the social risk factors in the lives of African-American people, we have begun to think and live as if we are an inferior people. Who cares that single parents are raising more children than married couples? I care that the African-American family is on course to become nonexistent.

Finally, my wife and I both became single parents before our marriage; therefore, we share a blended family of yours, mine and ours. As of June 2017, we celebrated thirty-five years of faithful and committed marriage as a Christian husband and wife. Through the years, our individual differences and failures caused us tremendous emotional pain - but we stayed together. We share some of the failures of past generations, as I have experienced five of the nine areas listed on the chart. Without fully exposing the personal lives of my living siblings, adult children and extended family members, almost every branch of my family has experienced many of the same risk factors as our ancestors. According to family therapists, the discovery of past family dynamics over generations will turn on a light to understanding ourselves and providing stability for our families. Within this book is a historical family resource to reveal past African-American family risk factors. Couples will be encouraged to discover risk factors in their own history so that they can avoid opening the same doors. Having a knowledge of ancestral risk factors will allow for healing in homes and marital relationships, and will provide families the hope of creating a better future. I invite you to travel though this history of African-American marriages and families, to explore their strength to endure problems, and to find healing for your individual family risk factors.

Chapter 2

The Apple Doesn't Fall Far from the Tree

> And I am convinced that nothing can ever separate us from God's love. Neither death nor life, neither angels nor demons, neither our fears for today nor our worries about tomorrow—not even the powers of hell can separate us from God's love (Rom. 8:39 ESV).

I once was lost but now am found,
Was blind, but now, I see.

The Trickle-Down Effect

The Trickle Down of Risk Factors associated with family dysfunctions are referred to as the "apples that fall from the tree." This saying implies that a child is like their parents in some negative or positive connotation. The idiom, "Apples Do Not Fall Far From The Tree" suggests that you are your mother's daughter or your father's son because you are acting as they did at some point in their life. The statement further suggests that a child is a "chip off the old block." Perhaps this saying could find spiritual roots in the Garden of Eden when our first parents ate from the Tree of the Knowledge of Good and Evil, and in doing so, ushered sin into the human race.

This tree, erroneously called an apple tree, actually was the God-determined Tree of Knowledge. Like the tree, humanity can only be what God makes them in life, and who they are is the kind of tree their parents were. No person in life can choose the complexion of their skin, the gender of their sex or who their parents were, and everyone was born with a sin nature. This biblical event provides the account of the entrance of the sin nature into the hearts and lives of the first couple because of their disobedience. Fundamentally, a sin nature became the inheritance of all the descendants of Adam and Eve.

When considering the question "Does the apple fall far from the tree?" a few other questions should also be asked. Why do African-American marriages and families experience the poorest marital and family structure ratings among all racial groups? How did enslaved African-Americans sustain the necessary fortitude to keep their marriages and families as viable institutions? Possibly the answers are in the expression "you are just like your mom and dad."

It helps to clarify a few terms so that we begin with an agreed-upon starting place. The Handbook of Cultural Psychology defines the term "slavery" as "A relationship in which one person or group owns another, with rights to the product of that person's labor and children, and other controls; usually, includes rights to sell the other."[1] The definition of the word "marriage" has changed many times throughout the centuries; however, the following traditional description provides a fundamental understanding:

> Marriage is the uniting of one man and one woman in covenant commitment for a lifetime. It is God's unique gift to reveal the union between Christ and His church and to provide for the man and the woman in marriage the framework for intimate companionship, the channel for sexual expression according to biblical standards, and the means for procreation of the human race.[2]

Based on this definition, the history of marriage for African-Americans was a displaced institution in captivity that did not comply with biblical standards. One of the reasons this book is titled "*God's Amazing Grace: Reconciling Four Centuries of African-American Marriage*" is because it was through the tenets of grace that African-American marriages and families remained an institution, even while surviving two and a half centuries of captivity and racial oppression. Grace was a gift to the descendants of enslaved families and marriages.

Figure 5 A Trickle-Down Pyramid of Institutionalized Racism

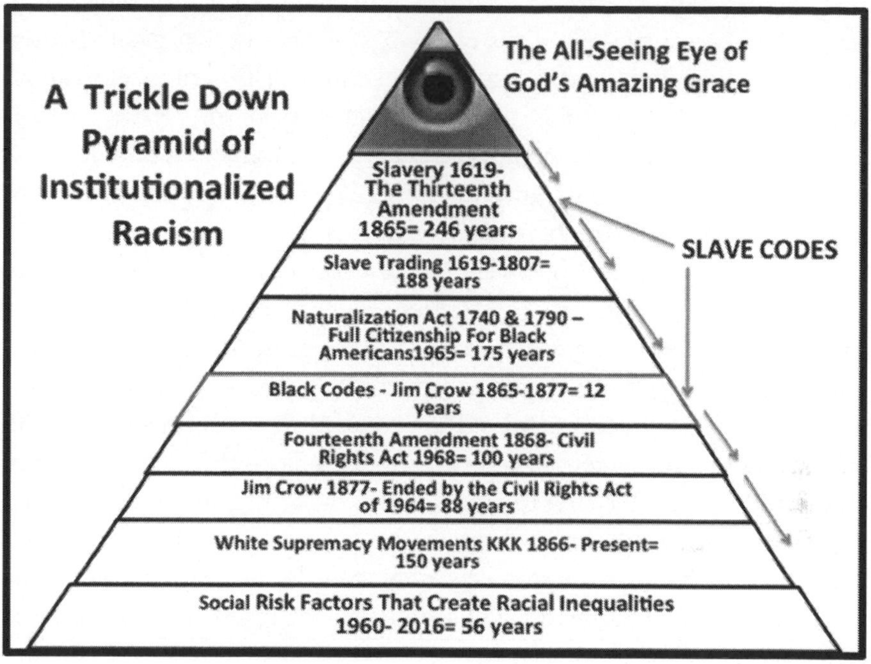

As we begin the twenty-first century, it is important to realize that this country continues to deny its DNA by sidestepping the effects of slavery on its African-American citizens. The DNA, or deoxyribonucleic acid, of the United States is the inherited philosophies and racial ideologies of her citizens. America has advocated being a Christian country that is one nation under God, although there is no reconciling a Christian nation that practices slavery. Scripture speaks profoundly against the practice of racial prejudice in a nation. "So, Peter opened his mouth and said: 'Truly I understand that God shows no partiality, but in every nation, anyone who fears him and does what is right is acceptable to him'" (Acts 10:34-35 ESV).

Historically, there have been two sets of laws in America: one set of rules to govern the lives of White-Americans and another to govern African-Americans. As a result, the initial transfer of emotional trauma to generations of African-Americans started with the hereditary laws for enslavement that defined who would be captive for life. The 1662 Slave Codes, which were written about forty-three years after the first African bondsmen arrived in North America, established that slavery is hereditary and perpetual.[3] Most timelines on the history of slavery list the first enactment of slave codes as early as 1652. According to Darlene Clark Hine, Stanley C. Har, and William C. Hine in *The African-American Odyssey*, slave codes were, "legislation enacted between 1660 and 1710 that further defined American slavery as a system that sought as much to control persons of African descent as to exploit their labor. Slaves could not testify against white people in court, own property, leave their master's estate without a pass, congregate in groups larger than three or four, enter into contracts, or marry. They could not, of course, bear arms."[4]

Slavery, as designed and implemented, was to control family structures for generations. The marriage institution, as developed for slavery, should have destroyed the lives and families of the enslaved. Mental and physical abuse, separation of families, and gender and personal dehumanization were everyday occurrences. All of these mistreatments contributed to the beliefs that African-Americans were mentally inferior to Whites, that they displayed a lack of self-esteem, and that they held no moral integrity. The risk factors associated with these concepts, negative attitudes and social conditions had an impact on almost 4 million enslaved African-Americans. These risk factors are presently widespread in over 45.7 million of their offspring.

The centuries between 1619 and 1865 brought the struggle of bondage to America. These dates represent two hundred and fifty years of multi-generations that endured emotional and psychological anguish. Present-day African-Americans have been left to reverse the scars of their painful history without any socially recognized attempts to heal the inherited traumas of their past. Four centuries of physical abuse, offensive name-calling, and being legally defined as inhuman or second-class citizens has gone virtually unaddressed for those effected psychologically and emotionally.

Freedom did not bring equality, justice, or a legitimate place in the American system of capitalism. And yet the desire for liberty found its place in the hearts of stolen African men, women and children from the Atlantic Middle Passages and lasted throughout the cotton fields of Texas (the last state to free their slaves). Those who opposed the freedom of slaves incurred a different generational consequence as they refused to accept that they no longer had the rights to their slave property. As a result, military forces made Mississippi acquiesce and free their captives in 1865, well before Texas was forced to manumit its bondsmen by the presence of the Union Army. One hundred years after the Civil War, from approximately 1865 to 1965, the United States government produced laws designed to ensure African-Americans would continue to struggle. For example, Mississippi was the last state to legally sanction the 13th amendment in 1995 as a state law. What occurred after slavery, with the United States government refusing to protect its citizens from the onslaughts of racial violence, was in many ways more problematic than the events of slavery.

The Reconstruction Period (1865-1877) provided a new form of oppression through hatred and vengeance against African-American people for the casualties of the Civil War. Nevertheless, this brief period existed to provide equality for the freedman. Reconstruction lasted only 12 years before eventually surrendering to the Jim Crow laws, which undid equalities African-Americans had gained during Reconstruction. The Jim Crow laws (1877- 1965), like those of captivity, relegated the lives of African-Americans to second-class citizens and an inferior legal status in America.

In 1961, during the Civil Rights Movement, the Affirmative Action Programs were signed into law by President John F. Kennedy. These programs served to accomplish a tremendous good, while still providing only a small and inadequate place in the American Dream for African-Americans. The Stanford Encyclopedia of Philosophy said: "Affirmative action means positive steps taken to increase the representation of women and minorities in areas of employment, education, and culture from which they have been historically excluded."[5]

In other words, this effort was not a cure to repair the damage done to African-Americans' identities. After the prohibition of the Jim Crow laws, instead of approving legislation that repaired inequality, legislators consistently approved legislation that covered up America's historical mistreatment of African-Americans. One example is the 1994 Crime Bill that created mass incarceration within the African-American community. Among other facets of the drug policy, the Clinton Administration placed lengthy prison sentences on crack cocaine, a popular drug among addicts in the African American community. At the same time, pure cocaine, a popular drug among addicts in the Anglo community, received light sentences. In 2017, the White community is experiencing an epidemic of Opioid drug use. What we see with this epidemic is a public outcry for help, policies put in place to assist those addicts, and few arrests – a very different response. Over the last forty years, the United States has encountered a flood of arrests placing African-American people in incarceration for what is known as The War on Drugs. The National Association for the

Advancement of Colored People lists the following "Criminal Justice Fact Sheet" for African-Americans:

Drug Sentencing Disparities

1. About 14 million Whites and 2.6 million African-Americans report using an illicit drug.
2. Five times as many Whites are using drugs as African-Americans, yet African-Americans are sent to prison for drug offenses at ten times the rate of Whites.
3. African-Americans represent 12% of the total population of drug users, but 38% of those arrested for drug offenses, and 59% of those in state prison for a drug offense.
4. African-Americans serve virtually as much time in jail for a drug offense (58.7 months) as Whites do for a violent crimes (61.7 months) (Sentencing Project).[6]

Along those same lines, the Welfare Reform Acts created circumstances in which some poor couples had to break up their families to survive. This law caused unemployed mothers, who could not find good paying jobs, to separate from working and unemployed fathers to get welfare support. It was not a rare occurrence in the African-American community that neither husband nor wife could secure a job good enough to sustain the family.

These various kinds of governmental cover-ups in modern America have perpetuated a naiveté among White-Americans and frustration among African-Americans that has resulted in racial tensions. Most Americans, regardless of their ethnicity, avoid the painful subject of racial oppression with those of other races. Therefore, many of the negative perceptions given to African-Americans from the past have remained unaddressed, uncorrected, and unresolved in the minds of too many contemporary Americans. Many of our present mindsets came from slaveholders and other White supremacy members of American society who regarded Black people as inferior, childlike, and untrustworthy.

Post-Traumatic Slavery Syndrome

In 2017, family risk factors within the African-American community continue to shackle lives with many social issues. Consequently, the enduring effects of these misleading stereotypes concerning the African-American identity and their abilities have trickled down in the minds of present-day Black and White-Americans. Robert J. Priest and Alvaro L. Nieves, authors of "*This Side of Heaven: Race, Ethnicity,*" explained how people are judged to have specific characteristics because of race.

> These communications of racialized perceptions of self and others find their stability through stereotypes and prejudices. A stereotype conveys information about an individual based on the individual's group. By assessing an individual as "black," "Asian," or some other race, the observer now supposedly knows something about that individual. Stereotypes provide a shorthand way of identifying a person, or a reason for avoiding a person altogether. Similarly, prejudices are beliefs or feelings, usually negative, held toward an individual or a group. Like stereotypes, prejudices are categorical. People get judged based on their group, not their individuality.[7]

There now exists a trans-generational racial identity linked to the cultural traumas suffered by generations of slaves and slaveholders' descendants. This injury is considered by sociologists and psychologists alike as Post Traumatic Slavery Syndrome (PTSS). "A form of Post Traumatic Stress Disorder (PTSD); a mental illness in which the 'fight or flight' fear reaction is damaged, causing a person to feel as if they're in danger often or always; even though they aren't at risk."[8] This definition provides insight into the effect of American slavery and how it created a trans-generational trauma among the offspring of slaves. Post Traumatic Stress Disorders gave birth to trans-generational trauma, defined as "an anxiety disorder that can develop after a person's exposure to one or more traumatic events, such as significant stress, sexual assault, warfare, or other threats on a person's life."[9] Trans-generational trauma is a transferal of stress associated with traumatic events experienced by ancestors. It describes how generations of surviving descendants have been negatively affected by disorders of extreme stress.

Dr. Joy DeGruy, author of *Post Traumatic Slave Syndrome: America's Legacy of Enduring Injury and Healing,* defined the symptoms as "a condition that exists when a population has experienced multi-generational trauma resulting from centuries of slavery and continues to experience oppression and institutionalized racism."[10] "*PTSS* describes a set of behaviors, beliefs and actions associated with, or related to, multi-generational trauma experienced by African-Americans that may be inclusive of but not limited to undiagnosed and untreated Post Traumatic Stress Disorder (PTSD) in enslaved Africans."[11] The psychological effects of bondage on contemporary African-Americans find their legacy in the physical and mental abuse of slaves. This research on the trauma of captives and their descendants suggests a need for continued historical research into the impact that enslavement and racism has on African-Americans' psychological health today. In my opinion, this analysis should start with exploring the lives of slaves to see how slavery had an impact on them during their lifetime.

For example, Charles Ball, a bondman around 1785, gave this testimony regarding the pain of his family separation: "I was now a slave in South Carolina, and had no hope of ever again seeing my wife and children. I had at times serious thoughts of suicide so great was my anguish. If I could have got a rope, I should have hanged myself at Lancaster. The thought of my wife and children I had been torn from in Maryland, and the dreadful undefined future which was before me, came near driving me mad."[12]

Emotional traumas, like those expressed by Ball, would remain suppressed by captives. A plethora of historical studies teaches that African-Americans were dehumanized and forced to live with unexpressed anger, remorse, revenge, and depression for wrongs to their person, family, or friends. In the presence of slavers, they needed to appear happy and submissive, even when faced with the inhumane treatments associated with extremely oppressive captivity. Having to live with unexpressed grief is an inhumane standard for any people group.

Thomas Fowell Buxton's speech on slavery in the House of Commons on May 15, 1823, expressed first-hand knowledge of traumas associated with the marriages and families of the enslaved. "The slave sees the mother of his children stripped naked and flogged unmercifully; he sees his children sent to market, to be sold at the best price they will fetch; he sees in himself not a man, but a thing - an implement of husbandry, a machine to produce sugar, a beast of burden!"[13] Enslavement was traumatic to every member of the family. Much focus has been given to the pains of enslaved men and women, but the children in captivity were also required to endure great distress.

Post Traumatic Slave Syndrome evolved through generations of suppressed emotional of pain and suffering, and created a mental inheritance, known as Social Pathology, among African-American slave ancestors. Some sociologists prefer the Theory of Resilience or Adaptability when referring to the traumas passed from the enslaved to their African-American descendants, while others prefer the Social Pathology view. The Theory of Resilience sees the negatives of captivity and oppression as a character-builder by reflecting upon the strength of those who endured the afflictions. The Social Pathology Theory examines the negative impact of incarceration and its oppressions as a disease which is revealed within the social factors afflicting African-Americans today. Under these circumstances, African-Americans were forced to find survival by any means necessary, while at the same time enduring the stereotypes associated with their forced enculturation into the American society. "People of African origin have a long history of being labeled pathological because of their efforts to resist racial and economic oppression or their attempts to adapt to such conditions. Also, people of African origin are vulnerable to the same emotional and family problems that affect non-African-descendent populations."[14]

Throughout this manuscript, is the endeavor to uphold both the Pathology and Resilience theories by unfolding how the surviving descendants of slaves exist as a resilient, yet distressed, people. African-Americans are individuals who continue to struggle for a place of acceptance in the present American society through both pathological and resilient methods.

Multi-Generational Transmission

Dr. Murray Bowen of Georgetown University "was the first to realize that the history of our family creates a template which shapes the values, thoughts, and experiences of each generation, as well as how that generation passes down these things to the next generation."[15] Bowen's Family Systems Theory has developed a comprehensive understanding for linking the traumas in families to past generations through eight interlocking concepts that describe the family development and functioning. Dr. Bowen explained the fifth tenet of his theory as Multi-Generational Transmission in the following way:

> This process entails the way family emotional processes are transferred and maintained over the generations.

> This captures how the whole family joins in The Family Projection Process, for example, by reinforcing the beliefs of the family. As the family continues this pattern over generations, they also refer back to previous generations ('He's just like his Uncle Albert - he was always irresponsible too' or 'She's just like your cousin Jenny - she was divorced four times').[16]

A prime example of how the apple does not fall far from the tree is Multigenerational Transmission Process. Families are responsible for the majority of the dysfunctional behavior exemplified by successive generations of family members. The closer a person is to their family, the more likely they are to depict the negative and positive characteristics of their family. Families that experience massive amounts of trauma in their lives will experience emotional issues handed down for several generations. Bowen's Family Systems Theory suggests, "Many whose descendants were affected by the Holocaust, famines or the Great Depression find that until they go back and learn all they can about the impact of that experience on the family, the anxiety continues to manifest itself in the generations. This may be so even though people don't know what the anxiety is about."[17] African-Americans in this country are people in search of an identity, and slavery remains an unresolved issue of which very few have extensive knowledge. If Bowen is correct, African-Americans are on their way to healing by understanding oppression and overcoming the shame associated with their past families.

With this in mind, we find the search for total acceptance has avoided African-Americans since being forcefully transported to America. Nevertheless, the need for full inclusivity remains a desire and concern in the hearts and minds of twenty-first century African-American descendants. This need for inclusivity remains hindered by the historical attitudes of racial prejudice. America has not withheld its innuendos of hateful put-downs to degrade the humanity of African-Americans. These insults created inferior beliefs and perpetuated the burden of a segregated America.

There is misguided speculation that God withheld His protection from African-Americans throughout the centuries of bondage and reconstruction. These thoughts continue to influence social issues in present-day African-American communities. The American society, after inequalities lasting hundreds of years, continues to feed on theories implemented during captivity, one of which is that the African-American race is lesser by nature. This idea has resulted in the belief that many current social factors that are pandemic in African-American marriages and families are the product of an inferior people.

The expressed, or unexpressed, false stereotype that African-Americans are less than other races in moral character and intellectual ability is still ingrained in the minds of mainstream Americans. The media and all spheres of American life persistently misrepresent the disenfranchisement of African-Americans from slavery to the present. Warren Beck and Myles Clowers said, "More Americans have learned the story of the South during the years of the Civil War and Reconstruction from Margaret Mitchell's *Gone With the Wind* than from all of the learned volumes on this period."[18] This statement is made in jest, because this movie glorified bondage and portrayed African-Americans as both inferior and yet happy with their position in life. However, the suggestion does speak to the inadequate amount of teaching on the subject of slavery. Textbooks in the American public-school systems faintly mention the historical contributions of African-Americans to this country. Perhaps this is a subliminal attempt to eliminate the shame of racism associated with slavery, reconstruction and Jim Crow. Carolyn Baker provided some clarity on why textbooks avoid a total history for African-Americans in an online article introducing her book *U.S. History Uncensored: What Your High School Textbook Didn't Tell You*:

> In my opinion, a huge motivator is the desire to purge history of illuminating one's shadowy past. Let's face it, coming to terms with the facts of white European genocide of the Native population on this continent, the trans-Atlantic slave trade, the eclipsing of the U.S. Constitution by corporate capitalism and imperialist expansionism –barbaric and shameful realities in our nation's history is challenging for any American citizen. Conveniently, these are denied, distorted, or eliminated in the fascist history brought to us by mostly fundamentalist Christian conservatives.[19]

After sustaining centuries of negative stereotypes associated with struggles affecting their lives, generations of African-Americans remain afflicted by the racial stereotypes that force them to suffer mentally and emotionally. There are bombardments of social risk factors within African-Americans families, which, consequently, create the impression that African-Americans are inferior. Angela Hattery and Earl Smith, in their book *African-American Families*, compared existing social risk factors to present and past stereotypes. Following is an example of the dilemma of Black America associated with historical stereotypes found within their book:

1. High rates of unemployment, poverty, and welfare dependency are a result of the inherent laziness in African-Americans.
2. High rates of non-marital births and infidelity are the result of an inherent hyper-sexualization of African-American men and the loose social/sexual morals of African-American women.
3. High rates of incarceration of African-American men are a result of a lack of proper socialization and an inherent inclination toward deviance.
4. Low rates of marriage among African-American men and women are a result of a lack of proper socialization (dating back to slavery), loose morals, and a lack of the influence of Christianity.[20]

The unresolved issues involving the history of race relationships have remained too painful for respectful conversation. As a result, the hearts and minds of Americans, both Black and White, remain uninformed regarding the full truth about slavery, reconstruction and Jim Crow. Racial cultures in America continue to perpetuate hundreds of years of racial discriminations intrinsic in the hearts of both White-Americans and African-Americans. Therefore, a considerable amount of the anger and social unrest found in African-American communities can be linked to the traumas of their unexplored history.

The fact that the residuals of racism have filtered down among generations of Americans has prompted emotional questions about our history. The majority of these questions remain unaddressed to public satisfaction. For example, I shared the contents of this book with a retired, White theology professor, who is also a dear friend and mentor. His response was in the form of a question that is at the center of the continuing racial gap in this country. "What is institutionalized racism?" America remains troubled by the phrase, and most White-Americans cannot see where entrenched racism exists in America. This belief is also perpetuated by the majority of African-Americans who find it difficult to explain, but feel they experience it daily. The following chart will help to contextualize traditional racism from a historical perspective. Each of the sections on the pyramid is a past period of racism under the all-seeing eye of God, and considered within the framework of God's Amazing Grace.

Figure 6. A Pyramid of Government Regulated Institutionalized Racism

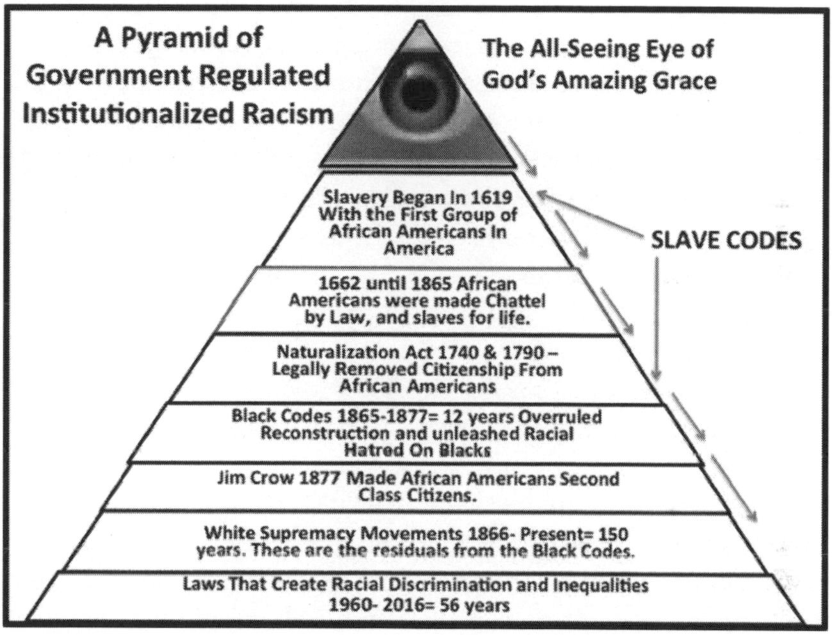

The chart provides a breakdown through the years of legal slavery and discrimination of African-Americans sanctioned by the United States Government. The percentages of slave and free families on the graph are from the US Federal Census from 1790-1865. The family rates, from the years 1865 through 2016, exist in several different research books on the strength of the African-American family. The chart also exposes the impact that the lack of capitalism had on African-American marriages and homes.

There remains an inability to have an active, national conversation on the racial problems that are associated with institutionalized racism within African-American history. This issue has lingered over one hundred and fifty years after slavery. One primary reason that the conversation about race has not resolved is that many Whites fail to see the race problem.

Robert J Priest and Alvaro L. Nieves in *This Side of Heaven: Race, Ethnicity, and Christian Faith* explain the racial divide for White-Americans:

> For people of color, it is often relatively easy to perceive racialization because people of color are reminded daily of how race affects their efforts to survive and thrive in society. Perceiving the presence and dynamics of race is frequently more difficult for white people. First, white privilege often allows white people to engage or ignore racial issues as they please. One of my undergraduate students wrote in an essay, "We [whites] don't have to talk about things because race rarely affects us. We don't even see our own whiteness." Second, whiteness is the American norm—the invisible standard against which difference becomes visible. Another student wrote, "I only learned about other cultures in school, and that was from a white American view … I always thought that I was 'normal.' I was defining myself as the standard, like other Americans do, without even knowing that I was doing it." White people often say they don't see their race, and sometimes say they don't have culture. White food, white music, white child rearing, white dating, and white education just seem "normal," not racialized at all. This invisibility is one of the primary features of whiteness, and so whites must strive to perceive their place in our racialized world.[21]

Because of the inability to confront severe racial injustices that have occurred for centuries in the lives of African-Americans, the historical facts of racism are like a throbbing in the head that remains unresolved. Many suggest that we should not address the issues of our past because of the pain associated with those historical facts. I have often heard it said in personal conversations that slavery was in the past and we must leave slavery and centuries of racial oppression unresolved. Others see this as an attempt to discount the times of agony associated with slavery and its cruelty. Even our public schools have left American students uninformed about African-American history in regards to intricacies of the slave system. These avoidance techniques in US Textbooks fail to mention the overwhelming price paid by slaves, specifically where it pertains to marriages and family roles.

Grace has its most significant effect in the disparaging situations of life. Without the tragedy of sin, God's grace would be useless; however, because all have sinned, grace is capable to solve the problems incurred by sin. Each of the areas on this chart represents a time in which African-Americans suffered under legislation that took qualities of life from them.

African-American Christians find themselves asking many questions about their historical conditions in the midst of their commitment to Christianity. A few of those questions include: Why has God allowed African-Americans to suffer such harsh treatment at the hands of Euro-Americans? Does the fact that African-Americans have the worst ratings in all the social risk factors infer inferiority? Is God punishing African-American people because they are inherently sinful individuals who have displeased Him? Many in the African-American community realize these concepts remain unanswered, and that has left them with a sense of inferiority or animosity. This chart provides a statistical comparison of social risk factors experienced by slaves and their descendants for one hundred fifty years after freedom.

Figure 7 A Historical Pyramid of African-American Social Factors.

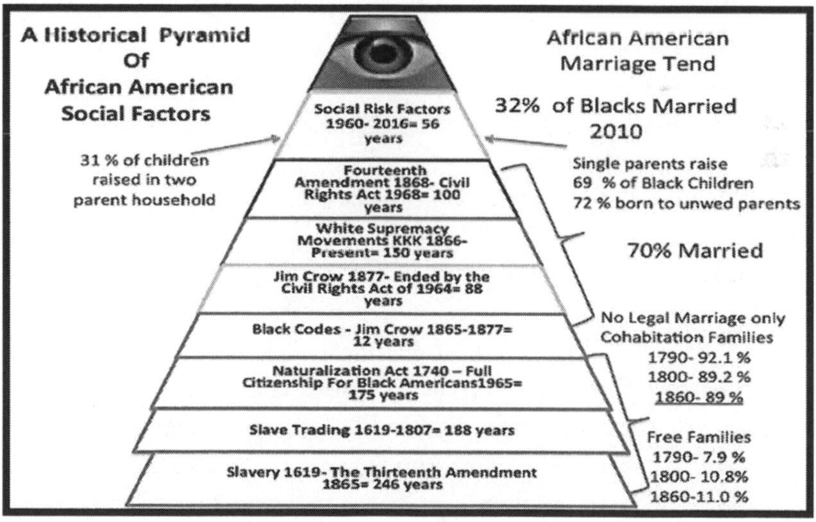

The comparisons in risk factors during slavery and freedom on the above chart are amazingly similar, suggesting that African-American family dynamics have changed very little since living in freedom. The graph shows that the risk factors from multi-generations have rested at our doorstep in this century and discovered God's grace sufficient for our deliverance from sin. Family specialists suggest that knowing the high rates of out-of-wedlock births, and other risk factors among our ancestors, gives us a chance to avoid repeating the same failures. Bowen suggests that family members can prevent these risk factors through differentiation, which is a decision made by an individual to live a different lifestyle from the rest of his or her family. Every person is a collection of their unique life experiences, as well as those of their ancestors. Family specialist, Roberta M. Gilbert, author of *The Eight Concepts of Bowen Theory,* explained how knowing family history can improve life's risk factors by implementing one of the eight concepts, called Differentiation of Self.

> In looking at the generations of our families, we are looking for facts. Emotion-colored stories are interesting but have to be evaluated for factual reliability. It is those facts that will tell a story about differentiation. Important facts include, names, of course, as well as: Longevity of family members, Health, Their locations, including moves, with dates, Their incomes and businesses or professions, including what positions they held, Reproductive history including abortions, stillbirths and miscarriages, Marriages and living-with arrangements, Dates of births, deaths, marriages, and the Highest degree in education, or year in school.[22]

Differentiation of Self places its focus on an individual's ability to overcome the negatives of their family dynamics. The better a person knows the strengths and dysfunctions within their family history, the better they can discern the amount of differentiation needed to develop a process to overcome reoccurring family risk factors.

The theory of Differentiation of Self can be seen in how many African-Americans kept their faith in God through centuries of intentional devastation to their humanity, family structures, and self-esteem. Christianity was their source of strength when many slaves and slaveholders were practicing the ungodly attitudes of slavery. Surely it has been by God's Amazing Grace that the African-American family did not become extinct during these struggles. Of equal importance is the most profound Christian characteristic that aided the African-American family's survival throughout the centuries of slavery and Jim Crow: their ability to forgive their oppressors. One such example of slave forgiveness was Henry Bibb, a runaway fugitive slave in 1844. After Bibb escaped to Canada, he wrote his owner extending forgiveness for the suffering he and his family endured under his ownership.

> Dear Sir: — I am happy to inform you that you are not mistaken in the man whom you sold as property, and received pay for as such. But I thank God that I am not property now, but am regarded as a man like yourself, and although I live far north, I am enjoying a comfortable living by my own industry. If you should ever chance to be traveling this way and will call on me, I will use you better than you did me while you held me as a slave. Think not that I have any malice against you, for the cruel treatment which you inflicted on me while I was in your power. As it was the custom of your country, to treat your fellow man as you did me and my little family, I can freely forgive you. I wish to be remembered in love to my aged mother, and friends; please tell her that if we should never meet again in this life, my prayer shall be to God that we may meet in Heaven, where parting shall be no more. ...I think it is very probable that I should have been a toiling slave on your plantation today if you had treated me differently. To be compelled to stand by and see you whip and slash my wife without mercy, when I could afford her no protection, not even by offering myself to suffer the lash in her place, was more than I felt it be the duty of a slave husband to endure, while the way was open to Canada. My infant child was also frequently flogged by Mrs. Gatewood, for crying, until its skin was bruised literally purple. This kind of treatment was what drove me from home and family, to seek a better home for them. But I am willing to forget the past. I should be pleased to hear from you again, on the reception of this, and should also be very happy to correspond with you often, if it should be agreeable to yourself. I subscribe myself a friend to the oppressed, and Liberty forever.
>
> HENRY BIBB.
> William Gatewood.
> Detroit, March 23d, 1844.[23]

Living in captivity was miserable enough for slaves without having a heart of unforgiveness, so they learned to release the pains and grudges of slavery to stay alive. It did not take much hate for slaves to understand hatred only produced more sorrow. The required demeanor of a slave toward his master, or any white person, was one of humility; therefore, it was essential for them to consistently cleanse their heart of wrongs committed to them or their loved ones. According to Bibb's letter, Christianity was necessary to maintain a forgiving heart while enslaved. These words by Jesus must have had an incredible influence on his life. "You have heard that it was said, 'You shall love your neighbor and hate your enemy.' But I say to you, love your enemies and pray for those who persecute you, so that you may be sons of your Father who is in heaven" (Matt. 5:43-45a ESV). Edward Baptist, the author of *The Half, Has Never Been Told: Slavery and the Making of American Capitalism* said, "Many Christian slaves believed that God had commanded them to put violent vengeance aside, if only for their own souls' sake. But following the command to forgive one's enemies was a difficult task- 'a lifetime job,' said one ex-slave: 'I don't care how long God lets me live, it will still be a hard job.' And forgiveness did not mean that enslaved people believed that the thieving powers of this world would never bow, that the lowest would not one day be the highest, or that their kidnappers would never face judgment."[24] Through forgiveness, slaves discovered the Christian principle of freedom. They grasped the reality that real freedom is in the essence of forgiveness. The Lord's Prayer in Matthew 6:9-14 is often considered the pinnacle of Jesus' teachings, as He encouraged forgiveness among His disciples in verses 12 and 14. "And forgive us our debts, as we forgive our debtors. For if you forgive men their trespasses, your heavenly Father will also forgive you. But if you do not forgive men their trespasses, neither will your Father forgive your trespasses" (Matt. 6:12, 14 ESV). In forgiveness, God's Amazing Grace covers all sin.

When considering the effects of captivity on present-day African-Americans, we are required to seek the findings of sociologists. Like the song "Amazing Grace," sociologists have formulated philosophies that have allowed theologians to discover God's grace in both the positive and adverse events of slave families.

What impact does slavery have on African-American marriages and families today? Did slavery make African-American families weak or healthy? Sociologists E. Franklin Frazier and Herbert G. Gutman, when exploring the history of African-Americans, tried to determine the impact that slavery had on the African-American family. Frazier discovered many abnormalities within the African-American family after slavery, and he labeled it "A Social Pathology."[25] This teaching on Frazier's work suggested a mental disease developed in the African-American family structures through centuries of oppression.

God's Grace in Pathological and Strengthened Families

GOD'S AMAZING GRACE: OVERCOMING AFRICAN AMERICAN FAMILY RISK FACTORS FROM SLAVERY - 2016

SLAVES FAMILIES IN CRISIS 1619-1865	BLACK FAMILY DYSFUNCTION 2010-2016
FATHERHOOD NOT RECONIZED	57.6% ABSENTEE BIOLOGICAL FATHERS
86.3 TO 92 % UNWED MOTHERS	72% UNWED MOTHERS
ONLY COHABITATION HOUSEHOLDS	HIGH RATES OF COHABITATION
MOTHER LEAD FAMILIES	53% OF HOMES HAVE ONLY A MOTHER
AUTHORITY OF PARENTS NOT RECOGNIZED	31% OF HOMES HAVE TWO PARENTS
MARRIAGE NOT RECONIZED FOR 86.3 TO 92% OF ALL PEOPLE IN SLAVERY	70% OF CHILDREN RAISED BY SINGLE PARENTS.
NO LEGAL MARRIAGES	69.1 UNMARRIED IN 2007
NO WAGES/ INEQUITABLE FAMILY STRUCTURES	26.2 OF ALL BLACK FAMILIES LIVE BELOW PROVERTY
FEMALE LEAD HOUSEHOLDS COMPENSATED FOR LARGE NUMBERS OF CHILDREN	40.4% SINGLE FEMALES BELOW POVERTY
FROM CHATTEL	**TO FREEDOM**

Daniel Patrick Moynihan authored "The Negro Family: The Case For National Action" while working as a political appointee for the U.S. Department of Labor. His objective was to help cultivate policy for the War on Poverty during the Johnson presidency. Moynihan coined the term "Tangle of Pathology" while writing under the influence of E. Franklin Frazier's research. He associated this name with the painful conditions the African-American family endured in the poverty-stricken urban ghettos of America. He cited their social risk factors as a result of slavery's oppression, specifically criminality, unemployment, educational failure, and fatherlessness in African-American families. Patricia Dixon evaluated Moynihan's findings in her book *African-American Relationships, Marriages, and Families: An Introduction.*

> The most notable of studies is Patrick Moynihan's (1965) controversial work, The Negro Family in the U.S.: The Case for National Action. In this study Moynihan used Frazier's work to frame his findings but shifted his argument to the "tangle of pathology" where he argued that under the matriarchal family structure, strong women dominate men, causing them to desert their families, subsequently leaving children without fathers. According to Moynihan, this along with the historical factors of slavery, reconstruction, urbanization, the high unemployment rate of African-American males, the wage structure, and the high fertility rate of African-Americans, results in disorganized families and disintegrating communities.[26]

This research "helped to popularize the view in public policy debates that matriarchy characterizes the African-American family."[27] Moynihan further inferred that the development of the "Black community is retarded by a pervasive matriarchy, which, he said, is dysfunctional in a patriarchal society."[28] However, "the real family issue is not the number of unmarried women having many children, but the declining prevalence of marriage as such. Clearly, female marriage rates are closely associated with male marriageability. The decline in marriage rates is in part a consequence of the dramatic increase in the educational achievement of African-Americans."[29]

In contrast, Gutman established the Strength or Resilience Approach that he believed more appropriately represented the impact of slavery on African-Americans. Both theories place the brutal treatment of slaves at the center of their reasoning. Tristan L. Tolman (*The Effects of Slavery and Emancipation on African-American Families and Family History Research)* provided insight regarding the positions of both camps.

> The condition of the black family in America has been an issue of intense debate since the Civil War. At the heart of this discussion is the belief of some scholars that slavery created a propensity for a weak and fatherless family is matrifocal (mother-centered) family, they argue, became typical of African-Americans both during slavery and after emancipation and had been perpetuated generationally to the present time. Other scholars vehemently disagree.

> They counter that black American families cannot classify as either weak or fatherless. These scholars maintain that blacks adapted to their difficult circumstances in creative ways to preserve familial ties.[30]

The adaptable approach suggests that sociological scholars are in disagreement regarding the effect of racial oppression on the African-American family. The two views that have emerged are the pathology and strength approach models to understand African-American families. Sociologist, Patricia Dixon, clarified and defined the strategies that are adhered to by authorities within each school of thought:

> How one understands African-American relationships, marriages, and families depends on the lens or framework through which they are studied. By far the two primary approaches used are the deficit approach and the adaptable approach. Those using a deficit approach compare African-American marriages and families to the nuclear model of the United States and find them to be deviant, and, in some cases "pathological." A precursor to the deficit framework is E. Franklin Frazier's (1966) The Negro Family in the U.S. Although this significant work documented the tremendous negative impact of slavery, emancipation, and urbanization on African-American marriages.[31]

Dixon, a proponent of the resilient or strength approach, or what she titles the *adaptable approach*, defends her theory by pointing out the weakness of E. Franklin Frazier's philosophy and those who adhere to the pathological approach. She continued:

> ...Two major shortcomings of this work were Frazier's argument that slavery had virtually wiped out any memory of an African past and his matriarchal family thesis. Further was his argument that slavery was primarily responsible for shaping African-American marriage and family life. Others (Stampp, 1956; Elkins, 1968) also argued that the African-American family had been shaped mainly by the forces of slavery.[32]

The Pathological view, as discussed by Harvard University Sociologist Orlando Patterson in his book *Rituals of Blood The Consequences of Slavery in Two American Centuries*, is described as "Something that runs deep into the peculiarities of the Afro-Americans' own past. In searching for it, we are inevitably led back to the centuries-long holocaust of slavery and what was its most devastating impact. The ethnocide assault on gender roles, especially those of father and husband leaving deep scars in the relations of Afro-American men and women."[33]

There is a psychological link to the dilemma of slavery, which causes African-Americans to identify with their ancestors in negative ways. This link affects present-day families and marriages in a harmful way. The Resilience view, according to historian Herbert Gutman's book *The Black Family In Slavery & Freedom 1750-1925*, revealed that, "African-Americans, developed a culture shaped by the special ways in which they adapted first to the harshness of initial enslavement, then to the severe dislocations associated with the physical transfer of hundreds of thousands of upper south slaves to the lower South."[34] Gutman, in contrast to Patterson, advocated that African-Americans adapted to the cruelties of slavery with remarkable strength and solidarity. Students of Gutman have expanded on his work providing some convincing theories for how slaves have benefited from slavery.

> Taking an adaptable approach (Blassingame, 1979; Genovese, 1972; Hill, 1972, 1999) argue that African-Americans adapted to their circumstances and their marriages and families have been resilient in the face of tremendous obstacles to their formation and development. They further argue that neither the horrors of the middle passage nor close to 300 years of enslavement were enough to stamp out African cultural patterns in African-American marriage and family practices. Instead, African-Americans have retained some African cultural patterns and, in fact, it is such patterns that have helped them survive.[35]

African-Americans who have a historical knowledge of their past are more appreciative of the contributions made by their ancestors who paved the way for achievements experienced today. This knowledge allows them to understand that life is not without adversities, and the present-day struggles are not close to those of the slaves who sought marriages regardless of their instability. "Although enslaved families were able to function adaptively and feasible given their circumstances, the consequences of slavery were nevertheless devastating on the African-American family (Burgess, 1995). Enslavement had several pervasive, institutional, and long-term effects on the family."[36] The grace of God is effective in every circumstance of life, whether in pathology or resiliency. Perhaps this is the Apostle Paul's understanding of his difficulties in life when he writes these comforting words: "But he said to me, my grace is sufficient for you, for my power is made perfect in weakness. Therefore, I will boast all the more gladly of my weaknesses, so that the power of Christ may rest upon me. For the sake of Christ, then, I am content with weaknesses, insults, hardships, persecutions, and calamities. For when I am weak, then I am strong" (1 Cor.12: 9-10. ESV).

African-American history is linked with the supremacy of God's redeeming grace—which converted the hearts of sinful men to the Christian faith. God's unmerited favor caused many compassionate Christians to rise to the challenge of their generation and fight racial oppression in the face of social opposition. Primarily, God's unconditional love qualified and called His servants to comfort and liberate the oppressed and enslaved through the antislavery movements.

African-Americans have found great strength in loving God as their source for overcoming suffering, and have taught this principle as a method of comfort to successive generations. Moses tells us in Scripture, "The Lord, the Lord, a God merciful and gracious, slow to anger, and abounding in steadfast love and faithfulness, keeping steadfast love for thousands, forgiving iniquity and transgression and sin, but who will by no means clear the guilty, visiting the iniquity of the fathers on the children and the children's children, to the third and the fourth generation" (Exodus 34:6-8 ESV). Because African-American slaves considered their fate similar to the children of Israel in Egyptian slavery, the promises in Scriptures served as a consolation that God would also bless them if they would love Him.

Chapter 3

God's Amazing Grace: A Response to The African-American Family Dilemma

For by grace you have been saved through faith. And this is not your own doing; it is the gift of God (Eph. 2:1-8. ESV).

'Twas Grace that taught...
my heart to fear

The need for more African lives became a valued necessity for the advancement of the industrial revolution beginning in the seventeenth century and ending in the nineteenth century. "By the middle of the seventeenth century, 10,000 slaves per year were being transported across the Atlantic. By the eighteenth century, the slave trade had reached a peak of 60,000 per year. Over the centuries, nearly 10 million African captives found themselves shipped to the Western Hemisphere. About 400,000 came to the American colonies. A rough, conservative estimate would be that a million slaves died en route."[1]

God's grace is amazing! His unmerited favor is entirely unearned or deserved by both slave and slaver. The grace of God came for the sinful to provide restoration, regardless of the depravity existing in the human heart. All races of people on the earth need the grace of God that only Jesus Christ offers. When considering the concept of God's amazing grace in the acts of Jesus, the music and lyrics of the song, "Amazing Grace," are a suitable accompaniment.

The mention of John Newton, who was an abolitionist and who authored the hymn "Amazing Grace," is in no way an attempt to make him the hero of the fight for African-American freedom. It is rather to establish the precedent by which the grace of God used many abolitionists to bring about the end of slavery. Newton and William Wilberforce were among the first advocates in the anti-slavery movements. They serve as a base for establishing an investigation into the impact that American bondage had on African-American families. God was at work in Newton's conversion experience, which provides an example of God's grace working in the life of a changed slave trader to alter the course of history. Likewise, the grace of God used every abolitionist to free the lives of the enslaved in America.

"Amazing Grace" is one of the greatest hymns ever written, and it serves as a witness to God's love in the life of every born-again Christian. The song is a testimony of the way faith leads those who put their trust in God to survive the struggles, failures, and disappointments of life. A deeper analysis into the background of the song is a tribute to God's grace, which inspired the work of the abolitionists' movement through Newton and Wilberforce. The song serves as a tribute to their devotion and tireless work to end the slave trade and enslavement in England and America. Newton, a retired British slave trader in 1754, penned one of the world's best-known spiritual songs as a testimony to his conversion after traveling to the West Coast of Africa in 1748. The song "Amazing Grace has undergone many changes over the 200+ years of its existence."[2] There are those who claim the melody has evolved, assuming many different tunes over the years. Different musical arrangements can occur in any song, depending on the artists; nevertheless, the lyrics of "Amazing Grace" are consoling to Christians.

The song has taken on new meaning for me since first viewing the Bill Moyers' special on YouTube entitled "Amazing Grace." Wintley Phipps suggested the melody originated as a song sung by slaves. Although the origin of the tune is unknown, most American hymnals attribute the sound as early American folk music. Phipps states "John Newton heard the tune he used for Amazing Grace from African captives. He then says that when he gets to heaven, he wants to meet the slave called Unknown."[3] Phipps was not the only one promoting this belief.

Old Calabar

"*The Amazing Grace*" movie directors, Jeta Amata and Nick Moran, also support the theory that John Newton, while capturing slaves in West Africa, heard the melody. This 2006 British-Nigerian historical drama was written to document the slave trading life of John Newton, and has become known as the best movie ever produced in Nigeria. It has won all the film-making awards in that African country. This dramatic commentary tells the conversion experience of John Newton. It also supports the speculation that slaves who were captured in Old Calabar, Nigeria, Africa first sang a song to the melody of *Amazing Grace*. The writings and autobiography of John Newton, however, do not mention Newton traveling to Old Calabar, or to anywhere in Nigeria, on any travels of his slave trading expeditions.

This story exists as a folktale handed down for generations among an African tribe in Calabar. Nevertheless, the opening scene of the movie depicts the Efik tribe during the 1700s in the town of Old Calabar of Creek River, Southeast Nigeria on the West Coast of Africa. They are involved in what appears to be a worship service with a choir director leading a song to the melody of *Amazing Grace*. They sang this tune in their native language, so the lyrics are unknown to anyone who does not speak the language. The narrator of the movie is a young bondwoman who recalls the day slave traders captured her and her people. She explains how they were worshipers of one supreme creator god named Abassi. This Efik tribe, while being taken captive, sang the melody of Amazing Grace both on the shore of Africa and aboard the ship as they endured the atrocities of the middle passage to America.

Historians of Calabar also support theory that "European sailors as far back as the 15th century identified Calabar as an international seaport known around the world from the 16th century. It became recognized as a major slave trade port from the late 17th to 19th century."[4] Newton served on many different ships during his slave trading expeditions. Liverpool, England was his home, and it was a major seaport for transporting captives from the west coast of Africa to the new world. The history of Calabar reports "about thirty percent of the estimated 2.5 million slaves taken from Africa to the new world, passed through the Calabar seaport."[5] Slavery endangered the souls of slave traders who came to Africa from all over the world to steal its inhabitants. "Old Calabar accounted for the export of over 17,000 slaves from 1725 to 1750, and the trade increased dramatically from 1750 to 1775, when the number of persons exported soared to over 62,000. All told, approximately 1.2 million slaves were transported from the Cross and Niger Rivers in the eighteenth century. Merchants in Bristol and Liverpool dominated the trade from Old Calabar, and approximately 85 percent of the slaves exported from the area left Africa on English ships."[6]

John Wesley, a Methodist pastor, abolitionist, and leader of the First

Great Awakening, wrote these words about how the horrors of slave trading had an effect on African families:

> You have seen them torn away, children from their parents, parents from their children: Husbands from their wives, wives from their beloved husbands, brethren, and sisters from each other. You have dragged them who had never done you any wrong, perhaps in chains, from their native shore. You have forced them into your ships like a herd of swine, them who had souls immortal as your own: (Only some of them have leaped into the sea, and resolutely stayed under water, till they could suffer no more from you.) You have stowed them together as close as ever they could lie, without any regard either to decency or convenience. --And when many of them had been poisoned by foul air or had sunk under various hardships, you have seen their remains delivered to the deep, till the sea should give up his dead. You have carried the survivors into the vilest slavery, never to end but with life: Such slavery as is not found among the Turks at Algiers, no, nor among the heathens in America.[7]

Wesley continued by sharing the passivity of the English to change, and he allowed them to see themselves in the shoes of slaves.

> It is surprising that the thoughtful people, where slavery prevails, should so little advert to its dreadful consequent effects to themselves and families, particularly on the necessity they are in of sending away their offspring from under their own paternal care, in very early life, lest their tender minds should be corrupted, and every noble and generous sentiment eradicated by the oppression and cruelty they are daily witnesses of. --That parents should be thus incapacitated and deprived of the opportunity and satisfaction of forming the minds of their offspring to virtue and happiness, but that this most sacred and delightful trust must be left to the care of the hireling and the stranger, must to every tender thinking parent, appear an

evil of so afflictive a nature, and so contrary to the divine order, that no human advantage can compensate for.[8]

Figure 9 John Wesley Slave Abolitionist[9]

Wesley connected with the British Quakers and helped them grow from a small anti-slavery movement into a large group of abolitionists. Although Quakers were small in numbers at their beginning, they became the first Christian group to reject slavery and prohibit its members from owning slaves in America.

John Newton, A Slave Trader Saved by Grace

Figure 10. John Newton Slave Traders/ Abolitionists and Author of Amazing Grace[10]

Newton, abandoning his career of slave trading, became a priest and achieved the credit of being a pioneer of the British abolitionist movement. Newton befriended and mentored William Wilberforce, who fought and won in Parliament to see the British slave trade ended in 1807. "Newton was a spiritual sage, but he also had worldly wisdom. This combination enabled him in his later years to influence William Wilberforce in his campaign to abolish the slave trade. Without William Wilberforce, the abolitionist campaign would not have succeeded, but without John Newton, there would have been no William Wilberforce."[11]

Newton encouraged William Wilberforce to continue a "forty-year fight to abolish slavery in the British Empire. Newton himself appeared before Parliament, giving irrefutable eyewitness testimony to the horror and immorality of the slave trade. Perhaps the surest emblem of his transformation is a town named Newton in his honor in Sierra Leone, Africa where he used to dock his slave ship."[12] Regardless of the accuracy in Wintley Phipps and Jeta Amata's attempts to connect Africans to the origination of the song, Newton's tune told the testimony of God's Amazing Grace at work in his life, in spite of the sinful deeds associated with his many slave-trading expeditions.

When examining the words to the song, Newton used what he called the stages of spiritual growth to pen this testimonial hymn. In the verses of the hymn, we hear the theologies of Justification, Sanctification, and Glorification:

Justification

Amazing Grace, how sweet the sound,
That saved a wretch like me....
I once was lost but now am found,
Was blind, but now, I see.

'Twas Grace that taught...
my heart to fear
And Grace, my fears relieved.
How precious did that Grace appear...
the hour I first believed.

Sanctification

Through many dangers, toils, and snares...
we have already come.
'Twas Grace that brought us safe thus far...
and Grace will lead us home.

The Lord has promised good to me...
His word my hope secures.
He will my shield and portion be...
as long as life endures.

Glorification

Yea, when this flesh and heart shall fail,
And mortal life shall cease,
I shall possess within the veil,
A life of joy and peace.

Harriett Beecher Stowe, in *Uncle Tom's Cabin*, introduced the last stanza of the song as we recognize it today.

When we've been there ten thousand years
Bright shining as the sun
We've no less days to sing God's praise
Than when we first begun.

"This new concluding verse, which had nothing to do with Newton, had never before appeared in any publication of 'Amazing Grace.' However, the four lines beginning 'When we've been there ten thousand years' had been orally around in Afro-American worship for at least half a century"[13] before Stowe wrote her famous novel.

Historically, African-Americans were conditioned to think they had little to claim as their contribution to the making of America. Historical records do not reveal how others have taken credit for many of the contributions made by African-Americans because of their status in bondage. One example of slaves not receiving credit for their inventions is the controversy regarding the actual inventor of the cotton gin in 1794. History gives credit to Eli Whitney, but there may be evidence that the idea came from one of his slaves. "Whitney may have borrowed the idea, which though valuable was still incomplete. He may have used the principle behind the slaves' device and applied it to the broader problem how to clean large quantities of cotton."[14] Perhaps like the cotton gin, the unknown composer of the music to Amazing Grace could have been of African descent. Why would someone remain anonymous with so much to gain? Nevertheless, there are other views concerning the origination of tune to Amazing Grace.

Jonathan Aitken is one of many biographers who researched the life of John Newton in an attempt to dispel the speculation that the song originated with African captives. "The tune now inseparably linked to 'Amazing Grace' was a different hymn until 1835 when it became suddenly popularized by a well-known compiler of spiritual songs, William Walker, a singing instructor from South Carolina."[15] According to Mark Roads' book of hymnology at Bethel University, Aitken wrongly stated his information. Roads believed, "As far as we know the now familiar tune to which we sing 'Amazing Grace' first appeared in two variants (ST. MARY'S and GALLAHER) in the American tune book *Columbian Harmony* published by Shaw & Spilman, 1829.' This tune no doubt existed before for that time in oral tradition and perhaps as a Scottish folk song."[16] It remains that no one knows where the melody got its beginning; however, if there is any truth to the slave speculations, perhaps Newton realized the racial indifference toward slaves would hinder the acceptance of the song if it were attributed to slaves.

James Michael Brodie, the author of *Equal the Lives and Ideas of Black American Innovators,* stated that the answer to the question is within the laws regulating the lives of Black people during this era of American history. He said, "Whether slave or free the Negro could not proceed far in matters requiring the sanction of government except under the tutelage of some White man. Often what the Negro actually developed was exploited by the White man by whom he was employed or through whom he endeavored to find recognition."[17]

Finally, many Christians have experienced a more profound affection and bonding to the music of this beautiful hymn since they have discovered the historical background. That Newton wrote this song while engulfed in the battle to end the English slave trade is a historical fact that is unknown to most Christians. God, in His graciousness, allowed both English and American abolitionists to be a blessing to slaves and their descendants.

Racial Categorizations: A Foundation for Families

African-American marriages and families have a history of slavery that sets them apart from all other races. Never before or since have a people group been enslaved because of race. Priest and Nieves advised that we are all affected by racial attitudes. "Race affects our minds deeply. Though we are born without knowledge of race, we are socialized from birth to perceive the world in racial terms. Each of us is assigned a race and accepts it as part of personal identity. We learn to perceive others as belonging to race categories and learn the stereotypes associated with the categories. In this way, race affects everyone, not just people who experience discrimination."[18] Sociologist Monica McGoldrick, in her book *Ethnicity and Family Therapy,* shed light on when and why racial categorization started.

> During the 18th century, Europeans and Americans were in serious need of a classification of races that would provide justification for Whites to treat people of color as non-human. This was especially important at a time when, with the Enlightenment, there was a focus on the "inalienable" rights of human beings. Having a hierarchy of races helped rationalize slavery. This insidious categorization persists to this day and continues to promote White power because unlike the definition of ethnicity, U.S. official definitions of race have no scientific or historically cultural basis.[19]

The lives of America's founding fathers, George Washington and Thomas Jefferson, substantiate that America initially established separate laws: one for African-Americans and another for Whites. The residuals of these statutes have continued throughout the majority of the twentieth-century in America, regulating differences according to race.

Figure 11 The Five Races of Humanity[20]

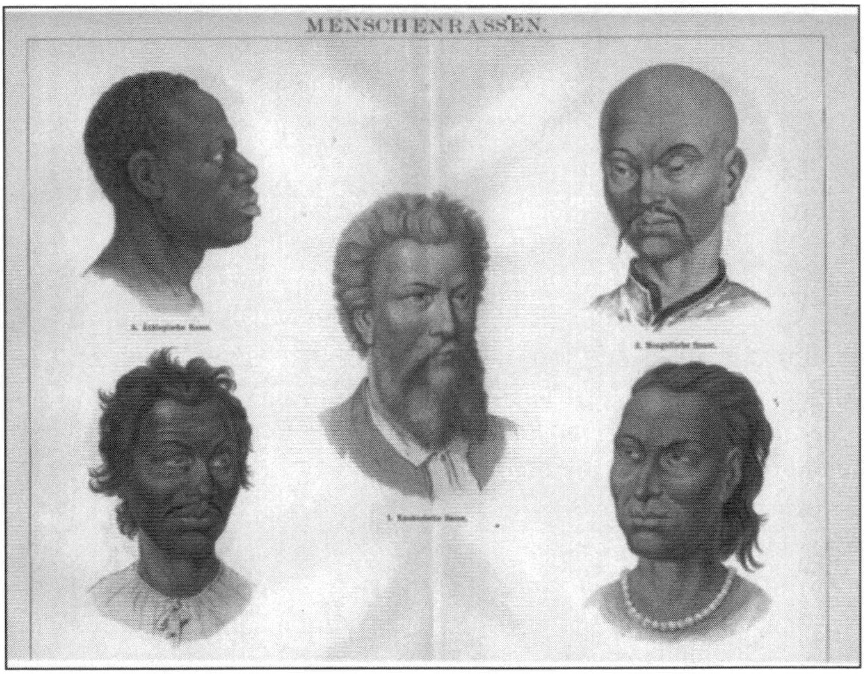

The American culture began categorizing its citizens into different races during the colonial period. During this time, African-Americans were not considered persons or citizens as implied, but undefined in the United States Constitution. "The social construction of race stems from a living history of Whiteness attempting to maintain White power. Categorizing people into different racial categories creates and justifies a racial hierarchy that continues to support White power and privileges throughout the United States. Historically, Whiteness has been set as the standard to which all other races are compared."[21]

George M. Frederickson said in *Racism: A Short History*, "Racial categorization was first articulated in Germany by Johann Blumenbach [*On the Natural Varieties of Mankind* first published 1776[22]]. Johann Blumenbach in his effort to prove the inferiority of Blacks listed them among the people groups that 'he developed into racial categories.'"[23] Blumenbach, who became regarded as the father of anthropology, provides the following geographical breakdown of people groups:

1. The Caucasian variety for the light-skinned people of Europe and the adjacent parts of Asia and Africa.
2. The Mongolian variety for the other inhabitants of Asia, including China and Japan.
3. The Ethiopian variety for the dark-skinned people of Africa.
4. The American variety of most native populations of the "New World."[24]

This work by Blumenbach established the idea that Blacks were not a lower being. However, this research did reinforce many stereotypes that African-Americans deserved captivity during the era of George Washington and Thomas Jefferson. The theory that Blacks were the descendants of Ham and cursed into captivity by God was one of his most widely accepted theologies of the era. "Blumenbach, a German anthropologist, improved on this theory, declaring that while it was true that the White race was the first, yet the other so-called races were in no way inherently inferior and that the difference was due to the environment. He stressed the equality of the Negro with the rest of the human race particularly."[25] Nevertheless, his research emphasized the skull shapes and size of all races, claiming a classification for different races. A combined group of "Anatomists, biologists, and physicians joined in with 'proof' of the superiority of White races over all others. The writing of history became distorted in line with racist notions of African-American inferiority."[26]

America's acceptance of this inferiority will be forever observed in the way American laws deprived African-Americans the rights to claim personhood and having the right to life, liberty and the pursuit of happiness as stated in the Declaration of Independence. This declaration said it was for all people, but was actually only for White men. It silently took from one race what it gave to another - freedom. Some seventy years before the founders framed this great document, "the diminished status of African slaves began in 1705 with the promulgation of the first Slave Codes that defined and governed the lives of African slaves during the antebellum period. As chattel, slaves were considered items of personality with little to distinguish them from horses, cows, or farm equipment."[27] The slave laws would start to decline by the onset of the 1800s when some northern states began departing from slavery because of the incredibly cruel treatment of Southern slaves under these codes.

The founding fathers of this country left out the biblical principle of loving your neighbor, regardless of the color of their skin. Although America was initially established under the values of Christianity, race relationships have been its principal challenge to overcome. No generation since has been able to bridge the racial gaps and create a country that has sufficient love and unity to make us one nation. When will Christians see all people as God's creation enough to stop the madness in our land? Will the church ever stand up and call accountability to those in the body of Christ who are divisive in their statements and actions? We must realize those who love some and not all provide a negative image of the body of Christ. "But if you show partiality, you are committing sin and are convicted by the law as transgressors" (Romans 2:9 ESV). The founding principles of racial difference in American can never be put behind us until the church takes a righteous stand against the evils of racism, thusly fulfilling the requirements of the church to love one another.

The First African Marriage on American Soil/ And the First Slaves in America 1619, Jamestown, Virginia

African-American historians have recorded the name of Anthony Johnson as the first African-American male to marry in America; however, there is a discrepancy with the name of the woman he married. Martha W. McCartney and Lorena S. Walsh in *A Study of the Africans and African-Americans on Jamestown Island and at Green Spring, 1619-1803* refer to his wife as Mary. They said, "Anthony Johnson, Virginia's first demonstrably free African-American, married his wife, Mary, in a Christian ceremony in 1622 and other free African-Americans were united in matrimony."[28]

Jessie Carey Smith, in the article "Black First: 2,000 Years of Extraordinary Achievement," referred to Anthony and Isabella as being among the first Blacks to settle in Jamestown, Virginia in 1619 as indentured servants. The status of their relationship is unknown upon their arrival. It's possible that Anthony Johnson was the same person mentioned by both historians as the first African-American to marry in Virginia because the dates of marriage are the same; however, there remains some question about the different names of his wife, Mary and Isabella. History records they were the parents of "...William Tucker, the first African-American child born, and recorded in the American colonies, he was baptized on January 3, 1624, in Jamestown, Virginia. Anthony and Isabella were also married in 1624."[29] "Anthony and Isabella Johnson named their son, William Tucker in honor of a Virginia Planter."[30] Fortunately, in 1619, the institution of slavery did not yet exist in Virginia.

William Tucker Born 1624, First African Born in America

American Slavery, as we understand it today, evolved gradually, beginning with customs rather than laws. "To further shed light on how this institution evolved officially, from indentured servitude to lifelong slavery, the following laws and/or facts are given as well as other sources on 17th-century servitude among African-Americans in Virginia."[31] The status of indentured servants was different from slavery, because they could serve out their time of service and earn their freedom.

Free Black Marriages in Colonial Dutch New Netherland (New York)/The History of the Dutch Slave Trade 1600-1863

A rare concession for African-Americans living in freedom in early America was in the seventeenth century when seven states, considered the Dutch New Netherland, allowed African-Americans to experience a life of normalcy. "Throughout Dutch rule, African-Americans participated broadly in colonial society. They spoke Dutch, served in the militia, worshipped and baptized their children in the Dutch Reformed Church, and sought legal redress in the Dutch courts."[32] During the brief period of 1609 until 1664, the Dutch New Netherland and New Amsterdam controlled the area known today as New York. "Unlike English Virginia, Dutch New Netherland legally sanctioned slave marriages, and the wedding ceremonies of dozens of slave couples were held in the Dutch Reformed Church soon after slavery was introduced into the colony."[33]

Slavery in its formative years in America brought very few African-American women to the Colonies, creating an imbalance for Black men to find mates. This hardship happened because "The preference for male laborers limited the ability of most African-American slaves in early colonial society from developing relationships with African-American women. Among the Atlantic Creole population in New Amsterdam, however, a more balanced male to female ratio made as many as twenty-six marriages possible."[34] For this reason, the ability to make marriage contracts for slaves gave them a marital credibility that would perish for African-Americans over the next two centuries.

Throughout this time, African-Americans experienced all the niceties of formal weddings and marriages. "These unions took place within the Dutch Reformed Church. The church became an institution through which New Amsterdam African-Americans were able to form independent familial units. In addition to marriage papers, archives of the Dutch Reformed Church contain baptism records that list children according to fathers rather than owners and name Black godparents as witnesses."[35] Unlike the Dutch in the New Netherlands, most Southern states held a very different view of interracial marriages, as we will discover later in this chapter. "When England acquired the colony, most of these privileges were taken away, and the result was a violent rebellion in 1712 that lasted for two weeks and was only suppressed by calling in the militia."[36]

Interracial Marriages Prohibited

In the colonial period before the hereditary laws of 1662, how and when people married depended on whether they were indentured servants, slaves, free laborers, or wealthy people. "On average, free White people in North Carolina married between the age of eighteen and twenty. A free person had to be twenty-one years of age to marry; anyone younger needed the consent of his or her parents."[37] However, because of the term within their contracts, "Indentured servants could not get married until after their term of service, which was usually seven years. Many indentured servants were in their teen years or early twenties when they began their contract, and so they tended to marry later than free people, usually around the age of thirty."[38]

In each of the slave centuries, American laws were passed to stop the marriages between Whites and Blacks. That also affected homogeneous marriages. The heredity law was created to define marriage legislation that prevented the mixing of races, called Amalgamation. This quote by Haram White of Otter Creek Prairie, North Carolina on Jan. 22, 1839 tells us that the prohibition was for everyone but White men. "Amalgamation was common. There was scarce a family of slaves that had females of a mature age where there were not some mulatto children."[39] These children were the offspring of slave masters and overseers who usually refused to acknowledge them as their blood. Only on rare occasions did White fathers raise their mulatto children as their own. More often than not, the mother took the child as her baby to rear without having the rights of naming the father. A White woman having a child by an African-American slave was rare and never reported, because it created a scandal for the family.

Ida Belle Hunter, born in 1844, recalled how the doctor that delivered him later explained the unusual circumstances of his birth. Ida was half White, having a mother who was the White daughter of a slave owner. His father was a slave coachman of his mother's father. He was interviewed at age 93 and recalled the separation he experienced from his mother as an infant:

> My mother was a White woman, and her name was Jane Jenkins. My father was a nigger. He was a coachman on my master's place. I was told this in 1880 by the White doctor, Lyth Smith, which brung me into the world. My master, who was my grandfather, brung me to Texas when I was just seven or eight years old. A few years later, he brung my mother down to Texas, and she had with her three boys, which was her chillen and my brothers. They was White chillen and named Jones. They first names was Tom, Joe, and Lije. They parted from me and I never heerd no more about 'em. I didn't even know my mother when I seen her. All my life I done just knowed my White kinfolks and nothing at all about the other part of my color.[40]

This incident reveals the extreme measures taken by slaveholding families to keep silent the children born to White mothers and slaves. Ida does not mention what happened to his slave father, although based on other occurrences of this nature, his life was likely required by some violent death to appease the crime of having sex with a White woman.

Throughout the seventeenth century, while the institution of marriage was undergoing sweeping changes throughout the world, America was defining marriage along racial lines. Charles Kraft, a noted Christian anthropologist, in his book *Anthropology for Christian Witness,* considered the cause for ethnic distinctions was inbreeding. As Ralph L. Beal's, Harry Hoijer, and Alan R. Beal's' book, *An Introduction to Anthropology* explained:

ENNIS PUBLIC LIBRARY
501 W. ENNIS AVE.
ENNIS, TX 75119-3803

> Racial differences are, like other genetic variations, the result of prolonged inbreeding. Such inbreeding is typically the result of geographical or social isolation. The key factor is reproductive isolation, because "when interbreeding takes place between adjacent breeding populations, the resulting transfer of genetic materials between the two populations will tend to reduce the extent of the biological differences between them."[41]

Interracial marriages in the United States from 1619 to 1660 were by consent of the couple, without any regulations from the church or Parliament. However, things would change when Blacks and Whites began to mate and start family structures in colonial days. "Since almost all the first Africans to arrive in America were males, their only source of companionship was Euro-American female servants and Indian women. Many of these liaisons ended in marriage and produced children. The practice became widespread enough, in a region with a shortage of Euro-American women that laws were passed to prevent it and indentured servitude was ended. Instead, slavery was installed and soon became exclusively associated with the dark-skinned."[42] Sociologist Benjamin Brawley said,

> More than other colonies, Maryland seems to have been troubled about the intermixture of the races; certainly, no other phase of slavery here received so much attention. This was due to the unusual emphasis on White servitude in the colony. In 1663 it was enacted that any free-born woman intermarrying with a slave should serve the master of the slave during the life of her husband and that any children resulting from the union would also to be slaves. This act was evidently intended to frighten the indentured woman from such a marriage. It had a very different effect. Many masters, in order to prolong the indenture of their White female servants, encouraged them to marry Negro slaves.[43]

Because women were scarce in the New World, slaves or indentured servants were not only African-Americans, but also of European descent. Brendan Wolfe's article "Free Blacks in Colonial Virginia" spoke of the foundational law against biracial relationships and oppression. Elizabeth Key, the daughter of Thomas Key (a White man) and his unnamed African-American wife, was enslaved for being African-American. She sued for her freedom and was set free by the General Assembly of Virginia:

Figure 12 Elizabeth Key Won Her Freedom in 1656 as the Child of a White Man[44]

In 1656, Elizabeth Key won her freedom in part by citing to the court her White father and her baptism as a Christian. In December 1662, however, the General Assembly declared that "all children borne in this country shall be held bond or free only according to the condition of the

> mother." In other words, the children of slave women would be slaves. The assembly went further and doubled the fines imposed on any Whites caught having sex with Blacks. Then, in September 1667, the assembly passed "An act declaring that baptism of slaves doth not exempt them from bondage." The paths Key had followed to freedom were now closed.[45]

The victory in court by Elizabeth Key of winning her freedom on the premise that she had a White father and was a baptized Christian, prompted the first laws that determined that the children of any Negro woman would be slaves. Elizabeth Key is also cited in chapter 4 under the section of *slave baptism.* Her freedom established a racial precedent that would last until the end of the Civil War:

> (December, 1662) ACT XII. "Negro women's children to serve according to the condition of the mother. WHEREAS some doubts have arisen whether children got by any Englishman upon a negro woman should be slave or free, Be it therefore enacted and declared by this present grand assembly, that all children borne in this country shall be held bond or free only according to the condition of the mother, And that if any Christian shall commit fornication with a negro man or woman, he or she offending shall pay double the fines imposed by the former act" (Virginia Slave Laws, Virginia General Assembly).[46]

This 1662 marriage law was officially the end to indentured servanthood, and it made the African-American race slaves for life, regardless of their commitment to Christianity. Scripture gives comfort to those who find themselves troubled over the ungodly law to make African-American Slaves for life when it proclaims, "and deliver all those who, through fear of death, were subject to lifelong slavery" (Hebrew 2:15 ESV). The Christian does not need to fear anything in this life, not even death, because we have a savior in Christ that provides freedom from all the issues of life. Based on this biblical mandate, it would only be a matter of time before perpetual slavery would end in death or the rapture for Christians.

The 1662 law also restricted marriage by consent, and Maryland became the first state that placed guidelines on Blacks, Whites, slave, or free who were involved in an interracial relationship where a child was conceived. This was an effort to control interracial marriages. "Prop. XII *Slavery is hereditary and perpetual,*"[47] of the Slave Codes, defined African-American slavery for a lifetime, based on the race of the mother and placed regulations on any male that mated with an African-American woman.

In December of the same year, the Virginia Law Act XII was passed in both upper and lower houses. It defined African-American family formation as, "Negro women's children to serve according to the condition of the mother. WHEREAS some doubts have arisen whether children got by any Englishman upon a negro woman should be slave or free, Be it, therefore, enacted and declared by this present grand assembly, that all children borne in this country shall be held bond or free only according to the condition of the mother."[48]

The Maryland Heredity Laws for enslavement, established in 1664, determined that any child born to an African-American mother would be a slave for life. This law was an addition to the existing law in which the father originally determined the status of a child. "All of the colonies' slave codes had four essential features in common: slavery was defined in terms of life-long service; status descended through the mother; blackness was equated with slavery, and slaves were legally regarded as personal chattels."[49]

George Washington Williams referred to the intermarriages of slaves as the Act of October 1705, also known by the name "An Act Concerning Servants and Slaves." The General Assembly of Virginia's colonial government passed laws by collecting and reviewing old rules from 1619 to 1705 and established new decrees governing indentured servants and slaves. The October Act of 1705, Amendment XX, which placed high fines on ministers who married interracial couples, stated:

> *And be it further enacted,* that no minister of the church of England, or other minister, or person whatsoever, within this colony and dominion, shall hereafter wittingly presume to marry a White man with a Negro or mulatto woman; or to marry a White woman with a Negro or mulatto man, upon pain of forfeiting and paying, for every such marriage the sum of ten thousand pounds of tobacco; one half to our sovereign lady the Queen, her heirs and successors, for and towards the support of the

> government, and the contingent charges thereof; and the other half to the informer; To be recovered, with costs, by action of debt, bill, plaint, or information, in any court of record within this her majesty's colony and dominion, wherein no essoin, protection, or wager of law, shall be allowed.[50]

The Act of 1705 placed strict demands and enormous fines on both the slave and free by forbidding marriages, and children born out-of-wedlock by White people, with anyone of Negro blood. This Act also placed significant penalties on White men and women who intermarried with African Americans:

> And for a further prevention of that abominable mixture and spurious issue, which hereafter may increase in this her majesty's colony and dominion, as well by English, and other White men and women intermarrying with negroes or mulattos, as by their unlawful coition with them, *Be it enacted, by the authority aforesaid, and it is hereby enacted,* That whatsoever English, or other White man or woman, being free, shall intermarry with a negro or man or woman, bond or free, shall, by judgment of the county court, be committed to prison, and there remain, during the space of six months, without bail or main prize; and shall forfeit and pay ten pounds current money of Virginia, to the use of the parish, as aforesaid.[51]

It is important to mention again that, irrespective of ethnicity, God designed marriage to meet the personal needs of couples in a way that only a spouse can satisfy. The cohabitating, quasi-marriages of slaves were human-made, governmental laws. But God does not always function according to man's rules. There is a higher quality of life for married people, compared to an individual who remains single. In principle, marriage and family regulations for the enslaved removed the stability that marriage can provide. Elizabeth Hyde Botume, in *First Days among the Contrabands,* explained the tenet of slavery that proved to be the most destructive to African American family structures. "In old times families of slaves had been broken up by unfortunate circumstances or by the will of the owners.

Husbands and wives thus separated had been advised, and in some instances forced, to form new relations."[52] Consequently, the inconsistency of the American Slave system allowed for occasions where couples would often return to their old partners. Many quasi-marriages of slaves were without one day of love, respect, and consistent companionship, and were instead filled with all the stressors that have been proven to cause marriage dissolution.

> Details differ, but the conclusion that prevails is always the same: after the Emancipation Proclamation, after the Civil War, and after a couple of constitutional amendments, people of African descent still could not love and cherish one another. Black women and black men were at odds. The men, overpowered by the combined assaults of White people on the outside and black women inside their communities, simply could not survive by being loyal and tender. The women, traumatized by regular rape but empowered by greater access to money and work, could not or would not accept masculine authority or protection; thereby not allowing black men to function as real people. Our knowledge of cause and effect informs us that slavery coupled with post-emancipation racial discrimination brought forth the poverty, despair, anger, hurt, shame, and suspicion that characterize too much of African America today.[53]

However, where love was real and committed, the heart stayed married in all circumstances. For example, Elizabeth Hyde Botume records a love story between slaves Kit and his wife Tina, a couple that suffered through the crisis of marital separation, followed by a remarriage situation created by being sold and separated as slaves.

> One day, Uncle Kit came to me greatly troubled. His wife Tina's first husband, who had been sold away from her "in the old secesh (a supporter of the Confederacy) times," had come back and claimed her. "An' I set my eyes by her' said the poor fellow. Tina had been brought up on another plantation to which husband number one had

> now returned. But Kit had belonged to the Smith estate. So the wife went from one place to the other, spending a few weeks alternately with each husband. She had no children, so had nothing to bind her more to one than the other. Kit came to ask me to write a letter to Tina and beg her to come back and stay with him. "Fur (for) him want to come to lib, but him shame," said poor Kit. He was ready to forgive all her waywardness, "fur (for) nobody can tell, ma'am, what I gone through with fur that woman. I married her for love, an' I lub (love) her now more and better than I lub (love) myself." We thought such devotion should be rewarded. I expostulated with Tina over her way of living, and finally threatened to ignore her altogether. She seemed surprised, but replied, "I had Sam first, but poor brother Kit is all alone." Finally, she decided to drop Sam and cling to Kit, "fur he, poor fellow, ain't got nobody but me," she said. They lived happily together for many years. Then Tina died, and Kit refused to allow any person to live in the house with him, telling me he never liked confusion. And folks would talk, and "I don't want Tina to think I would bring shame upon she," he said.[54]

The institution of bondage affected slave marriages and families both physically and emotionally, as seen in the lives of Kit and Tina. Slaveholders, in contrast, widely held the view that slaves would soon be over the trauma imposed on their lives. They contended that marital and family separation was of no effect to enslaved people. This view was so prominent that the United States government attempted to prove validity to the claim in the 1840 Census.

> Epidemiological studies based on the Sixth USA Census of 1840 were used to justify a claim that the Black person was relatively free of madness in a state of slavery, 'but becomes prey to mental disturbance when he is set free'. The underlying supposition was that inherent mental inferiority justified African slavery. However, Benjamin Rush, the father of American psychiatry, refuted such arguments and maintained that the mental capacity of Black people

> could not be evaluated while they were slaves because slavery affected their minds adversely.[55]

One Drop of Black (African) Blood Determines Race

The One Drop Rule finds its base in this 1664 hereditary law at the start of African-American bondage. One drop of African-American blood in a child born to a Black and White couple determines the race of the child as African-American, because it has the blood of an African-American parent. "In essence, the hypodescent concept stemmed from a variety of self-serving motives. Initially, it was an attempt by White European immigrants to maintain racial purity and superiority by passing laws against interracial marriages (anti-miscegenation laws), primarily directed at Blacks and Native Americans."[56] Consequently, the color Black, as in African, became the symbol of enslavement for the African-Americans.

The 1692 Durante Vita Law (slavery for a lifetime) was both a compromise between, and a refinement of, the 1662 and 1681 laws. These new amendments on interracial marriages affected the marriages of homogeneous African-American couples with harsh regulations. These regulations made African-Americans slaves for life and regulated that the children would be slaves in several scenarios. 1) Together these amendments created a situation where, if both mother and father were slaves, their children were also legislated as slaves. 2) These laws also mandated the children of a slave as slaves, even if they had a free Negro mother or father. 3) The passing of these laws took away the responsibilities in the relationship roles of husbands to wives, mothers, and fathers to children, and gave the authority in these relationships to slave-owners. 4) Finally, they defined slaves as chattel and property. The purpose behind these laws was an effort to keep the Black and White races separated.

It all started when the Maryland Assembly broadened and revised their miscegenation provisions. In 1664, Maryland became the first colony to take court action against marriages between White women and Black men. In 1662, judiciary failed to be all-inclusive in its attempt to define the barriers to interracial marriage. According to the 1662 hereditary law, "Apparently, the offspring of unmarried Black men and a White woman, as well as the offspring of any White man and Black woman, were considered to be free."[57] This additional provision in 1664 legislated slave status to include being passed on to descendants by the father of all African-American children. "The third and fourth provisions sought to deal with the 'disgrace' of marriages between African-American male slaves and freeborn English women and to provide a standard for determining the status of the children of mixed marriages." [58] When this law was finally adopted, it had four provisions, which may be summarized as follows:

1. All "Negroes or other slaves," whether already in the Province, or to be imported later, were to serve "Durante Vita."
2. All children born of any Black or other slave were to be "Slaves as their Fathers."
3. To discourage "dives free borne English women" who, "forgetful of their free condition and to the disgrace of our Nation", married slaves, thus inconveniencing courts and masters with legal debates over the status of the offspring, any free woman so marrying after the act's passage was to serve her husband's master during her husband's lifetime.
4. To further discourage such marriages, the children of matches contracted after the act's passage was to be "Slaves as their fathers were." The children of such marriages contracted before the act's passage was to serve their parents' masters until they reached the age of thirty-one.[59]

The final addendum to these early laws would define the penalties for interracial couples and their mixed offspring, when they defied the rules and married outside of their race. The revised provisions may be summarized as follows:

1. Any non-servant freeborn White woman who married a Black man was to become a servant of her church parish for seven years. Her husband, if free, was to become a slave for the parish.
2. If the woman was a servant, she was to serve out her remaining time, with additional time served due to lost time during pregnancies, and then she was to become a servant to the parish for seven years, provided her master did not force the match.
3. Children of mixed marriages were to be servants of the parish for twenty-one years.
4. If the miscegenation couple was not married, the woman was to suffer the seven-year penalty; the child was to serve for twenty-one

years, but, the husband, if free, was only to serve for seven years instead of life.

5. The same penalties are falling a White woman as detailed above were to apply to any White man be getting any Black woman with child.
6. Any master forcing a marriage was to forfeit 10,000 pounds of tobacco.[60]

Virginia led the way with the original 1662 hereditary slave laws, which Maryland took and consistently revised over the next few years. "Although colonists and slaves of African descent had long lived in the colony of Virginia, the legislature did not pass the first law governing interracial marriages until 1753. While free Blacks could marry, Virginia never recognized the legality of slave marriages."[61] By this time, all was in place for the law to penalize everyone involved in bi-racial marriages. Interracial couples were also forbidden to marry, with heavy fines enforced for those who violated the law. This law regulated couples to get a marriage license by placing a bond with sufficient security. For example, if "...there was no existing marriage; the parties were of age; and, if not, were they marrying with permission. Beginning in the 1670s, the General Assembly required colonists marrying by license to obtain the marriage license from the county in which the bride resided."[62]

In spite of all the laws against interracial relationships, the numbers of mixed-race individuals continued to increase by large numbers. For example, earlier in 1755, "...the total number of mulattoes in Maryland amounted to 3,592; and the total number of Negroes, to 42,764. It was reckoned that above 2,000 Negro slaves were annually imported into Maryland."[63] During this time, hundreds of thousands of biracial children were conceived by White men who forced sex on African-American women and girls. If this was not the case, the question must be asked, how a large number of mulatto births occurred, since interracial relationships were against the law?

There were often advantages in being a biracial person. Sociologists suggest that "mulattoes became free much faster than pure Negroes; thus the Census of 1850 showed that 581 of every 1000 free Negroes were mulattoes, but only 83 of every 1000 slaves were biracial. Since the Civil War, moreover, the mulatto element has rapidly increased, advancing from 11.2 percent of the Negro population in 1850 to 20.9 percent in 1910, or from

126 to 264 per 1000."[64] Because African-American women were considered non-human and chattel, the children produced by this union were also non-human, even though they were fathered by White men. Being born mulatto, or half White, did not change their legal status of being a member of the Black race, and therefore, non-human.

Mothers, wives, sisters, and daughters were left to protect themselves daily from the sexual advances of any man who would force himself upon them for sexual pleasure. B. A. Botkin, *Lay My Burden Down: A Folk History of Slavery,* shared how corrupt slave masters were when it came to their sexual desires.

> Aunt Jane Peterson, old friend of mine, come to visit me nearly every year after she got so old. She told me things took place in slavery times. She was in Virginia till after freedom. She had two girls and a boy with a White daddy. She told me all about how that come. She said no chance to run off or ever get off, you had to stay and take what come. She never got to marry till after freedom. Then she had three more Black children by her husband. She said she was the cook. Old Master say, "Jane, go to the lot and get the eggs." She was scared to go and scared not to go. He'd beat her out there, put her head between the slip gap where they let the hogs into the pasture from the lot down back of the barn. She say, " Old Missus whip me. This ain't right." He'd laugh. Said she bore three of his children in a room in the same house his family lived in. She lived in the same house. She had a room so as she could build fires and cook.[65]

The Founding Fathers' Slavery and Marriage

A few years before the American Revolution in 1769, American colonies based its laws on English common law. One tenet of the common law declared "By marriage, the husband and wife are one person in the law. The very being and legal existence of the woman are suspended during the marriage, or at least is incorporated into that of her husband under whose wing and protection she performs everything."[66] This law, however, was null and void for African-American marriages. Because of the shortage of female slaves in America, male slaves found themselves without suitable partners to mate. Around 1730-1750, the number of male and female slaves imported to the North American colonies would finally balance out for the first time.

There were fifty-six signers of the Declaration of Independence in 1776, also known as the Founding Fathers of America. These men would determine the fate of African-American marriages and families for the next eighty-eight years by not including them as American citizens at the time of the Declaration of Independence. This decision had implications that lasted all of the way into the twenty-first century.

When reviewing the present quality of marriage satisfaction rates among couples from different ethnicities, African-American couples rank last. This leads to the question: Why are there different marriage rates when every citizen of the United States has the same unalienable rights concerning the Declaration of Independence, among them life, liberty, and the pursuit of happiness? Consequently, the Declaration of Independence has falsely inspired the citizens of the United States with the idea that all people have the same rights. The framers of the United States Constitution did not recognize African-Americans as residents, nor were they identified as fully human. There were 539,000 slaves in America when the Declaration of Independence was written, and none of them were considered American citizens. The same authors of the Declaration of Independence penned the Three/Fifths (3/5) Compromise determining that slaves counted for only 3 out of five persons in the Electoral Congress.

The compromise was between the Northern and Southern states in regard to how slaves would be counted in the presidential election. Northern states recommended that slaves be counted for taxation. Southern states wanted them counted for electoral representation toward the election. The result was a 3/5 Compromise, determining an incomplete amount of the human status of slaves. They were now 3/5 a person, and yet still chattel (livestock) who could not manage their quasi-marriages and families. The three-fifths person amendment was not a measurement designed to give African-Americans any creditability of human significance; it was an attempt to increase the influence that pro-slavery advocates from the South had in Congress.

William and Ellen Craft, in their autobiography *Running a Thousand Miles for Freedom*, wrote about how they escaped to freedom in 1848 as a married couple. Their story explained how they received motivation from the words of the Declaration of Independence. William and Ellen Craft said:

Having heard while in slavery that "God made of one blood of all nations of men," and also that the American Declaration of Independence says, that "We hold these truths to be self-evident, that all men are created equal; that they are endowed by their Creator with certain inalienable rights; that among these, are life, liberty, and the pursuit of happiness;" we could not understand by what right we were held as "chattels." Therefore, we felt perfectly justified in undertaking the dangerous and exciting task of "running a thousand miles" in order to obtain those rights which are so vividly set forth in the Declaration.[67]

George Washington's Slave Marriages

George Washington, the first President of the United States missed signing the Declaration of Independence while leading troops in the Revolutionary War. Washington was one of the largest slaveholders of his era. Nonetheless, history records him as an advocate for marriages and families among his slaves. In the summer before his death, George Washington's records indicate that roughly two-thirds of the plantation's adult slaves were involved in pseudo-marriages. Both the slave community and Washington acknowledged these marriages within the context of the slave laws. Mary V. Thompson, in "Slavery and Marriage: Mount Vernon Estate and Gardens" explained, "For Mount Vernon's slaves, marriage represented the opportunity to exercise choice in a life that afforded little, if any, personal control over basic life issues such as occupation, housing, clothing, and freedom of movement."[68]

Washington's slaves were better off than most slaves because they were permitted the human dignity of having a family and spouse, even though they possessed no control over their lives and families. His treatment of slaves was also better than most who prohibited marriages among slaves. "However, even this decision had limitations. When one member of a couple lived at a plantation other than Mount Vernon, the pair planning to wed first needed permission from George Washington, as long-distance marriages necessitated a certain amount of traveling back and forth between the two plantations."[69] Long distance marriages for slaves were titled an "abroad marriage." These distance marital relationships and families opened many risky and dangerous doors for both slaves and owners as slaves traveled between plantations. Slave hunters were always on the prowl looking for runaway slaves, and they would often mistake a slave who did not have a pass for a runaway. There were also slave stealers who were in search of an African-American outside of the supervision of a White who could be captured and resold. "Getting the permission of a master would have been in keeping with a 1785 Virginia law that stated that slaves could not travel away from home without a pass or letter of authorization from a master, employer, or overseer."[70]

Washington's slave marriages could enjoy family life with their spouses and children, because the majority of his slaves married slaves on one of his many plantations. Seventy-two slave marriages experienced a quasi-family life among the plantations of the first president of the United States. This could be accomplished because George Washington owned at least 300 slaves who were allowed to travel between his plantations. He also allowed 24 slaves to wed a spouse living on his plantations with other owners. "Distance was a significant stress factor in slave marriages. Of the 96 married slaves working on Washington's five farms in 1799, only 36 lived in the same household as their spouse and children."[71]

Although marriage was the norm for Washington's slaves, there was a majority of 60 married slave households with a single parent. Each of these couples had a spouse living on one of Washington's nearby plantations or a neighboring slave estate with a different owner. Among these 60 separated slave households, "38 had spouses living on one of Washington's other farms, dictated by work assignments. The marriages of the Mount Vernon slaves produced a huge number of children, causing the population to increase dramatically. The population rose from around 50 slaves in 1759 to more than 300 in 1799."[72] Allowing slave marriages proved prosperous for Washington, who increased his number of enslaved people five times the amount over a 40-year period.

"I can only say that there is not a man living who wishes more sincerely than I do to see a plan adopted for the abolition of it [slavery]."
—*George Washington*

Thomas Jefferson Framer of Inequitable Marriages

Thomas Jefferson served as the first Sectary of State, the third president of the United States, and the principal author of the Declaration of Independence.

Nonetheless, he was a slaveholder and fathered many mulatto children by a slave, all the while writing the most important document in American history. He also led in co-authoring the 3/5 Compromise. "In his public life, Jefferson made statements denouncing African-Americans as biologically inferior and claiming that a biracial American society was impossible. Despite these facts, there is much evidence to suggest–if not prove Jefferson had a longstanding relationship with a slave named Sally Hemings, and that the two had at least one and perhaps as many as six children together."[74] There is no evidence that Jefferson ever claimed Sally's mulatto children as his own, as that would have been out of context for this era in America.

Figure 13 Thomas Jefferson[73]

Thomas Jefferson is on record saying, "White-Americans and enslaved African-Americans constituted two 'separate nations' who could not live together peacefully in the same country."[75] Thomas Jefferson also held the belief that Blacks were racially inferior with the status "as incapable as children."[76] Consequently, Jefferson, in a letter to Edward Coles written August 25, 1814, expressed his disdain for African-American people:

> … but of this color we know, brought up from their infancy without necessity for thought or forecast, are by their habits rendered as incapable as children of taking care of themselves, and are extinguished promptly wherever industry is necessary for raising the young. In the mean time, they are pests in society by their idleness, and the depredations to which this leads them. Their amalgamation with the other colour produces a degradation to which no lover of his country, no lover of excellence in the human character can innocently consent."[77]

History records him as an honorable man, although a slaveholder, and only recently has this part of his life become common knowledge. "Thomas was the son of Peter Jefferson, a Virginia landowning slaveholder who died in 1757, leaving the 11-year old with a massive estate. Ten years later, he formally inherited 52 African-American human beings and 5,000 acres of land as well as livestock and other valuables. When he authored the Declaration of Independence in 1776, he held 175 African-American men, women, and children in bondage. By 1822, he had increased that number to 267."[78]

Jefferson was one of the largest slave owners during any time of the American slave system. He, unlike many slaveholders, prospered at the trade, but unlike President George Washington, did not arrange to free all his slaves upon his death. "Thomas Jefferson, on the other hand, freed only 8 slaves, 3 during his lifetime and 5 in his will. Jefferson sold or gave away 161 slaves between 1784 and 1794 and left 130 people to be sold to settle his estate when he died in 1826."[79] After Jefferson's death, his estate sale to relieve his debts created an event that divided off many enslaved marriages and families.

William Wells Brown recorded the indifference Jefferson had to separating families, when three of his house slaves, who happened to be the mother and two of his beautiful mulatto daughters, were sold.

> The slave mother was sold to a trader. Althesa, the youngest, and who was scarcely less beautiful than her sister, was sold to the same trader for one thousand dollars. Clotel was

> the last, and, as was expected, commanded a higher price than any that had been offered for sale. Clotel was sold for fifteen hundred dollars, but her purchaser was Horatio Green. Thus closed a Negro sale, at which two daughters of Thomas Jefferson, the writer of the Declaration of American Independence, and one of the presidents of the great republic, were disposed to the highest bidder.[80]

Thomas Jefferson serves as an example of the attitudes and public opinion about African-Americans during his day. It is incredible that men who believed and fought for their freedom could feel justified by enslaving others. Although, "In his initial draft of the Declaration of Independence, Thomas Jefferson condemned the injustice of the slave trade and, by implication, slavery, but he also blamed the presence of enslaved Africans in North America on avaricious British colonial policies."[81]

The British were responsible for the majority of the influx of people into America and established the first governments that controlled slavery and indentured servants. Bondage existed under British control from 1619 through 1776, before the colonies became states and set their governments. Captivity under the newly formed independent states was more severe than it was under the British. "Jefferson thus acknowledged that slavery violated the natural rights of the enslaved, while at the same time he absolved Americans of any responsibility for owning slaves themselves."[82] Slave ownership became a source of contention and division for the fathers of our nation when the framers of the Declaration of Independence tried to abolish slavery.

When South Carolina and Georgia threatened to succeed from the union if slavery was abolished within the Constitution, the signers of the Declaration of Independence allowed the continuation of captivity as an effort to keep the states united. "The Continental Congress apparently rejected the tortured logic of this passage by deleting it from the final document, but this decision also signaled the Founders' commitment to subordinating the controversial issue of slavery to the larger goal of securing the unity and independence of the United States."[83]

To his credit, Thomas Jefferson did include the following opposition to slavery in the original draft of the Declaration of Independence. Jefferson's statement opposing slavery blamed the British government, controlled by King George III, for the slave system in America, but the explanation was removed as a comprise to keep the states united. Thomas Jefferson wrote:

> He has waged cruel war against human nature itself, violating its most sacred rights of life and liberty in the persons of a distant people who never offended him, captivating & carrying them into slavery in another hemisphere or to incur miserable death in their transportation thither. This piratical warfare, the opprobrium (contempt) of infidel powers, is the warfare of the Christian King of Great Britain. Determined to keep open a market where men should be bought & sold, he has prostituted his negative for suppressing every legislative attempt to prohibit or restrain this execrable commerce. And that this assemblage of horrors might want no fact of distinguished die, he is now exciting those very people to rise in arms among us, and to purchase that liberty of which he has deprived them, by murdering the people on whom he has obtruded (interfered) them: thus paying off former crimes committed again the Liberties of one people, with crimes which he urges them to commit against the lives of another.[84]

The failure of the Continental Congress to abolish slavery would permit the institution to last eighty-nine more years. This inability to do justice to all men is an example of knowing what is right, but not doing what is right. Solomon addressed this when he said, "See, this alone I found, that God made man upright, but they have sought out many schemes"[85] (Ec.7: 29 ESV). The system of slavery in America was a diabolical, man-made plan, an example of what happens to a society that leaves God out by not regulating laws that benefit all people. When man and Satan devised a plan to keep God's people in bondage and suffering, our heavenly Father sent his son as a deliverer to save his children. God's plan of salvation is the antidote for all the sins of humanity. "Humble yourselves, therefore, under the mighty hand of God, so that at the proper time he may exalt you, casting all your anxieties on him, because he cares for you. Be sober-minded; be watchful. Your adversary the devil prowls around like a roaring lion, seeking someone to devour. Resist him, firm in your faith, knowing that the same kinds of suffering are being experienced by your brotherhood throughout the world. And after you have suffered a little while, the God of all grace, who has called you to his eternal glory in Christ, will himself restore, confirm, strengthen, and establish you" (1 Peter 5:6-10 ESV).

Chapter 4

Slave Marriages, Christian Conversions, and the Church

Masters, do the same to them, and stop your threatening, knowing that he who is both their Master and yours is in heaven and that there is no partiality with him (Eph. 6: 9 ESV).

And Grace, my fears relieved.
How precious did that Grace appear...
the hour I first believed.

What I have said respecting and against religion, I mean strictly to apply to the slaveholding religion of this land, and with no possible reference to Christianity proper; for, between the Christianity of this land, and the Christianity of Christ, I recognize the widest possible difference—so wide, that to receive the one as good, pure, and holy, is of necessity to reject the other as bad, corrupt, and wicked. To be the friend of the one, is of necessity to be the enemy of the other. I love the pure, peaceable, and impartial Christianity of Christ: I therefore hate the corrupt, slaveholding, women-whipping, cradle-plundering, partial and hypocritical Christianity of this land. Indeed, I can see no reason, but the most deceitful one, for calling the religion of this land Christianity. I look upon it as the climax of all misnomers, the boldest of all frauds, and the grossest of all libels. Never was there a clearer case of "stealing the livery of the court of heaven to serve the devil in." I am filled with unutterable loathing when I contemplate the religious pomp and show, together with the horrible inconsistencies, which everywhere surround me. We have men-stealers for ministers, women-whippers for missionaries, and cradle-plunderers for church members. The man who wields the blood-clotted cow-skin during the week fills the pulpit on Sunday, and claims to be a minister of the meek and lowly Jesus. The man who robs me of my earnings at the end of each week meets me as a class-leader on Sunday morning, to show me the way of life, and the path of salvation. He who sells my sister, for purposes of prostitution, stands forth as the pious advocate of purity. He who proclaims it a religious duty to read the Bible denies me the right of learning to read the name of the God who made me. He who is the religious advocate of marriage robs whole millions of its sacred influence, and leaves them to the ravages of wholesale pollution. The warm defender of the sacredness of the family relation is the same that scatters whole families,—sundering husbands and wives, parents and children, sisters and brothers,—leaving the hut vacant, and the hearth desolate. We see the thief preaching against theft, and the adulterer against adultery. We have men sold to build churches, women sold to support the gospel, and babes sold to purchase Bibles for the poor heathen! all for the glory of God and the good of souls! The slave auctioneer's bell and the church-going bell chime in with each other, and the bitter cries of the heart-broken slave are drowned in the religious shouts of his pious master. Revivals of religion and revivals in the slave-trade go hand in hand together. The slave prison and the church stand near each other. The clanking of fetters and the rattling of chains in the prison, and the pious psalm and solemn prayer in the church, may be heard at the same time. The dealers in the bodies and souls of men erect their stand in the presence of the pulpit, and they mutually help each other. The dealer gives his

> blood-stained gold to support the pulpit, and the pulpit, in return, covers his infernal business with the garb of Christianity. Here we have religion and robbery the allies of each other—devils dressed in angels' robes, and hell presenting the semblance of paradise.[1]
>
> Fredrick Douglass

In spite of slaveholding Christians, generations of enslaved African-Americans and their offspring benefited from Christianity and lived by Christian principles which enabled them to have hope. Enslaved African-Americans would find relief in the words of the Apostle Paul throughout slavery: "Bondservants, obey your earthly masters with fear and trembling, with a sincere heart, as you would Christ, not by the way of eyeservice, as people-pleasers, but as bondservants of Christ, doing the will of God from the heart, rendering service with a good will as to the Lord and not to man, knowing that whatever good anyone does, this he will receive back from the Lord, whether he is a bondservant or is free" (Eph. 6:7-9 ESV). This text reminded slaves that God would reward them for their faithful service to their masters. Also, they believed this passage divulged the promise that God would judge their owners for their cruel actions during slavery. *Matthew Henry's Commentary* on the book of Ephesians summarized the rationale of both slave and owners. "If masters and slaves would consider their obligations to God, and the explanation they will soon give to the Lord, they would be more thoughtful and sensitive to one another, and then slave families would be more organized and satisfied."[2] Perhaps there were Christian slave owners who took this Scripture to heart and treated their slaves with the dignity of Christian brothers and sisters. "Over the first half of the nineteenth century, as conversion experiences and church-going became the expected thing for proper White citizens, most Christianized enslavers abandoned the claim that African-Americans had no souls to be saved."[3] However, history is silent on the number of slave owners who allowed Christianity to influence how they treated their slaves.

Slave Discipleship Prohibited

Ironically, the institution of African-American slavery finds its roots in Christianity, and would become known among slaves as Christian Slavery. The earliest directive affecting Christianity and American slavery during colonial times is an English law established in 1660 by Charles II, King of England. King Charles ordered the Council of Foreign Plantations to devise strategies for converting slaves and servants to Christianity. The salvation of slaves was an attempt by Great Britain, a Christian country, to follow the Great Commission. English laws determined their mission was to fulfill the Gospel mandate of Matt. 28:20 among all people. Consequently, the afflictions suffered in slavery by early African-American marriages and families were initiated by the motivation to convert them to Christianity.

The following are instructions that were issued by King Charles to the Council of Foreign Plantations: "And you are to consider how much of the Natives or such as are purchased by you from other parts to be servants or slaves may be best invited to the Christian Faith, and be made capable of being baptized thereunto, it being to the honor of our Crown and of the Protestant Religion that all persons in any of our Dominions should be taught the knowledge of God, and be made acquainted with the mysteries of Salvation."[4]

However, the conventional belief among slaveholders in the Americas was that the salvation of any male or female slave granted them their freedom. This was in opposition to the King of England's request to keep the Great Commission and evangelize Africans and Indians. This misunderstanding created a need to protect the institution of slavery.

The colonies rejected the legislation of the council and King Charles. One of the arguments offered in defense of the modern slave trade was the false idea that an African American was an infidel. This belief justified the enslavement of the African-Americans. In the ancient world, all men were considered equally capable of becoming slaves, but with the conversion of the people of Northern Europe to Christianity, the custom of enslaving prisoners of war gradually ceased between Christian nations. Although between Christians and Mohammedans, the practice of enslaving war prisoners continued.[5]

During this era, the concept of African-Americans as chattel became ingrained in the minds of European-Americans, both Christians and non-Christians. As a result, state laws legislated Black people as inferior, which promoted the idea they deserved slavery over Christianity. Additionally, it was believed that to be a Christian, one needed to complete a catechism; therefore, they must be able to read and understand the Bible. As a result, colonial states passed laws that forbade slaves from reading and writing, imposing hefty fines towards violators. South Carolina's Act of 1740 legislated that, because chattel could not be educated, African-Americans could not be educated. This law stated that African-Americans were human, but were to be held in chattel-hood and not receive an education.

> Whereas, the having slaves taught to write, or suffering them to be employed in writing, may be attended with great Inconveniences; Be it enacted, that all and every person and persons whatsoever, who shall hereafter teach or cause any slave or slaves to be taught to write or shall use or employ any slave as a scribe, in any manner of writing whatsoever, hereafter taught to write, every such person or persons shall, for every such offense, forfeit the sum of one hundred pounds, current money.[6]

When it came to educating slaves, Fredrick Douglass explained the penalty for being an educated slave who could read and write:

> This is American slavery; no marriage—no education—the light of the gospel shut out from the dark mind of the bondman—and he's forbidden by law to learn to read. If a mother shall teach her children to read, the law in Louisiana proclaims that she may be hanged by the neck. If the father attempts to give his son knowledge of letters, he may be punished by the whip in one instance, and in another be killed, at the discretion of the court. Three millions of people shut out from the light of knowledge![7]

By 1667, Negro labor had become so profitable that Virginia enacted a law that declared that "the conferring of baptism doth not alter the condition of the person as to his bondage or freedom. Masters, thus freed from the risk of losing their property, could more carefully endeavor the propagation of Christianity."[8] In spite of the early church requirement for reading as a method for catechism, slaves soon found they could have a relationship with Christ regardless of the traditional way of becoming a Christian. Edward Baptist discovered that slaves found Christ through spiritual emotionalism in Christianity that also served as a link to their African religious experiences:

> Enslaved people born in Africa— still in the late 1700s a significant percentage of Chesapeake slaves— came from a part of the world where it was common for gods to throw people on the ground, to breathe in and through them, to ride worshippers' spirits and remake their lives. These new converts demonstrated the same intensity of conversion, and their fervor was catching. White converts modeled their conversions on enslaved people's behavior, learning that shouting and singing were appropriate responses to the breath of the divine.[9]

The real measure of salvation is a spiritually converted heart to the principles of Christianity, regardless of a person's ability to read and write. For African-Americans, "Religion has been used to both oppress and liberate. During slavery, Christian doctrines were used to justify slavery and oppression."[10] This account of an unnamed slave interviewed by the Freeman's Bureau in B.A. Botkins' book *Lay My Burden Down,* set the stage for an approved sermon and attendance for slaves by their slaveholders:

> There wasn't no church on the plantation where I stay. Had preaching in Mr. Ford's yard sometimes, and then another time the slaves went to White people's church at Bear Swamp. Boss tell slaves to go to meeting 'cause he say he pay the preacher. Dean Ears, White man, gave out speech to the slaves one day there to Nichols. Slaves sat in the gallery when they go there. He tell them to obey they master and missus. Then he say, "God got a clean kitchen to put you in. You think you gwine be free, but you ain't gwine be free long as there an ash in Ashpole Swamp." White folks complain 'bout the slaves getting two sermons and they get one. After that, they tell old slaves not to come to church till after the White folks had left. That never happen till after the war was over.[11]

This kind of preaching was the norm for most congregations during this era. "Enslaved people, however, believed otherwise. In 1821, one Georgia slave wrote a letter to a White preacher. 'If I understand the White people,' he wrote, 'they are praying for more religion in the world.' Well then, 'If god sent you to preach to sinners did he direct you to keep your face to the White people constantly or is it because they give you money?'"[12] Slaves knew their enslavement was about free labor and the money earned to provide for their owners. Therefore, when preachers did not preach the truth of the gospel message, they knew that it was about his pay. The above-quoted slave continued his analysis of the watered-down gospel messages that slaves received. He said, "We are carried to market and sold to the highest bidder, and Whites 'never once inquire whither you are sold, to a heathen or a Christian?'"[13] When slaves were allowed to be honest, they could not overlook their substantial contribution of giving two hundred and fifty years of free labor as a financial compensation to the wealth of America. They recognized how the need for money and the laws regulating slave families affected their lives. Economic greed was a primary cause for the ill-treatment of slaves and the longevity of the institution. At the end of slavery, the nearly 4 million slaves were valued around 3.1 billion dollars in an American economy that was 16 billion dollars. The value of slave labor was linked so tightly to the American economy that, to some extent, every industry had the stamp of slavery on it. The foundational years of America depended heavily on free labor to sustain and build it into a great nation. The real master in the hideous institution of slavery was money, and all of the Black Codes regulating captivity were constructed with a greed for capitalism. The southern states of America were devoted to, and survived on, the free labor of the slave system.

Yet, enslaved people continued to flock to churches, "even if ministers turned their backs on them, and hold their own meetings."[14] This serves as evidence of the power of God's word to provide comfort to hurting lives, in spite of the ill will of the messenger. "Enslaved Africans could relate to Christian messages by identifying with the liberation of Jesus Christ who was a persecuted and oppressed figure."[15] Those who became converted Christians found mental escape from the hardships of slavery and sin. Although their inability to read and write left them with little or no theological understanding, they had an excess of spiritual songs that were sung to help them endure their suffering. Slaves also claimed mystical experiences which they related to a conversion experience. Edward Baptist recalled the conversion testimony of a young slave woman who had a near-death experience while worshiping. She dreamed that she had a visit from angels who gave her the message that she had gone through enough pain and suffering to carry the whole world. She stated, "Jesus's helpers, came forward, clothed her with a new robe, and the first voice said: you are born of God. My son delivered your soul from hell, and you must go and help carry the world."[16] "She awoke. She was alive. She believed that the most powerful forces in the universe could name the pains and fears that even she could not. These forces recognized her. From them, she was not stolen. All she had to do in return for this gift was to carry the whole world."[17] For slaves, Christianity provided an inner peace that only God could provide.

> The experience of spiritual death and rebirth reassured converted slaves that they had value and responsibility that went far beyond the number of dollars one could sell for, of pounds one could pick, or of babies one could bear for the fear that their enslavers were, in the end, their final judges. "I heard a voice speak to me," said William Webb. "From that time I lost all fear of men on this earth."[18]

In the 1700s and 1800s, slave owners used Christianity as a means of social control to keep enslaved Africans submissive and docile. Slavery removed the cherished Christian liberties that so many Americans were in pursuit for themselves, while denying millions of slaves their rights to the gospel. Their need for salvation began a trickle-down effect on the lives of African-Americans that lasted until their Emancipation. However, the need for a relationship with Christ was also able to grant freedom to enslaved African-Americans in the midst of slavery. Through many dangers, toils and snares, we have already come.

Certainly Lord: A Catechism of Slaves

Possibly, the old call and response Negro spiritual, "Certainly Lord" served as a catechism for slaves. The author is unknown, and the purpose or meaning leaves the worshiper to his own interpretation; however, Musicologist Horace Clarence Boyer suggested that the song was written during slavery and sung while slaves did their daily work around the plantations. "Certainly Lord" was a song of relief and celebration, steeped in the belief that everyone needed to have a real religion. They believed if they were going to stand before the Lord in glory, it would be essential to answer these fundamental questions correctly. Perhaps it was their way of a self-education in the Christian faith. It seemed to serve as a catechism for the slaves. Each stanza was sung three times before moving to the next. It was a very long song with the leader calling out the verse and the chorus, and the slaves responding with "Certainly Lord." Leaders would, at times, change the order of the verses throughout the song depending on the movement of the Spirit. Because slaves could not develop a relationship with their Lord and Savior Jesus Christ through Bible study and baptism, they established their religion in their songs.

> "Have you got good religion? Certainly Lord. Have you been baptized? Certainly Lord. Is your name on the row? Certainly Lord. Do you really know the Lord? Certainly Lord. Do you love the Lord? Certainly Lord. Do you love everybody? Certainly Lord. I know I have religion. Certainly Lord. I been born again? Certainly Lord. Is your soul set free? Oh, certainly, certainly Lord."[19]

The nature of the American slave system allowed for many mental games that African-Americans had to play for survival. It was required of the enslaved to understand their roles in every area of life. Slaves needed to know and adhere to the unwritten rules of living in bondage. They had to learn how to live in disrespectful situations, keep self-respect while pleasing their masters. This required subliminal messages in their mannerism and conversations with Whites, which aided their ability to cope with life. A closer evaluation of the song "Certainly Lord" shows how songs had concealed messages for both slave and owner. The question "Have you Got Good Religion?" was also an attempt by slaves to have their masters examine the purity of his own Christianity. Each phrase called for the introspection of one's conversion experience by relating the principles of slavery to those of Christianity. Verses associated with baptism, church membership, knowing God, and loving God would remind masters of their relationship with God. The phrase "Do you love everybody" was a reminder to owners and slaves that the Bible commands everyone to express love in their dealings with neighbors, enemies and even slaves. Finally, the call "Is your soul set free" was a reminder of the importance of freedom to the slaves. Although they were in physical bondage, the soul was free in Christ. For slaveholders, it was a reminder that owners could control the body but not the soul. The strength of the song is found in the conviction of the response "Certainly Lord" after each call.

Christianity's Endorsement of Slavery

"The First and Second Great Awakening represented the first times African-Americans embraced Christianity in large numbers."[20] This was a time filled with many glaring messages against both sin in general, and in the evils of slavery, all shared expressively from great preachers of the abolitionist movement. Essentially, God was changing the hearts and minds of Europeans and Americans about the slave trade and slavery. The year 1833 bought a spiritual revival to England among anti-slavery movements. They received motivation and teaching around the idea of freeing Africans from the chains of slavery; however, the inspiration to end slavery in America would take another thirty years of abolitionists struggling to be heard. America needed to be educated as to the evils of slavery. The message of many of the anti-slavery movements of the North was that, before there could be a revival in America, Christians would need to repent for their racial hatred and abuses.

Historically, a significant threat to African-American families and marriages was the prohibition of educating slaves. This, of course, hindered their ability to study God's Word. Keeping slaves uneducated made them seem less in character, perpetuated the idea that they did not have the capacity to learn, and made them look unworthy of the rights and treatments assumed by the free population. This cleared the conscience of slaveholders, and slaves alike, as they violated biblical principles concerning infidelity.

The early American church's endorsement of slavery also supported the abusive methods forced upon African-American marriages and families. Edward Baptist, in his comprehensive book on the history of slavery in America, informed us,

> The vast expansion of slavery in the United States happened in tandem with the emergence of evangelical Protestantism. At the time of the American Revolution, most Americans had not participated actively in organized religion. Though most were nominally Protestant, few outside of New England attended church services on a weekly or even monthly basis. But by the 1850s, half or more of all White Americans had come to participate regularly in some church. The vast majorities were in evangelical denominations, among which the Methodists and Baptists were the most popular choices.[21]

Consequently, information like this quote by Baptist is not included in an overwhelming majority of Christian history books. Therefore, the impact of evangelical Christianity's endorsement on the growth of the America's slave system is unknown by most Americans. This writer's fascination with investigating slavery during the era of the early American church led to the discovery of the abusive lifestyles enforced on African-American marriages and families by church members. Baptist portrayed this in the life of:

> James Smylie, a prominent Presbyterian minister from Mississippi, and (by 1840) the captor of thirty men, women, and children, argued in 1836 that a slaveholder "whose conscience is guided, not by the word of God, but by the doctrines of men"— i.e., by the anxiety that anti-slavery Christians might have a point—" is often suffering the lashes of a guilty conscience. "But he should not suffer. God had created some people unfit for freedom. Slavery was God's will. To worry about slavery was to doubt God. To oppose it was heresy.[22]

My experience as a Christian has made me naive to the cruel attitudes that many Christians are capable of displaying toward their fellow mankind. Growing up in a Christian home and having my parents teach me to love everyone, regardless of their race, was a foundation of my education and a rewarding experience. Having parents who raised their children to practice Christian love remains one of my life's greatest blessings. They taught us this principle of loving all races, in spite of the fact that they, themselves, had been victims of a lifetime of racial prejudice associated with being a minority in America. The commandment of Christ to "love the Lord our God with all our hearts, mind, and soul and our neighbor as ourselves" (Matt. 22:36-40) is a Christian principle for living that I have taken seriously throughout my life.

Their Christian teaching, however, led me to see the world through partly rose-colored glasses. I had never attributed the acts of racism to Christian persons. Christians who assaulted and abused people over skin color were not living the lifestyle of a believer. In my naivety, I believed godly love was a principle taught in all Christian homes in the United States. I have now found my belief to be a false assumption. Although children are born racially unbiased, they soon realize that racial prejudice is a part of living in this country, and it usually is first taught in the home. Racial discrimination is a learned behavior and is a prime example of how Multi-Generational Transmission works within families to hinder race relationships.

A solace for me is the reminder that many of the abolitionists were just as confused as I am about the Christian principles portrayed by their slaveholding Christian brothers and sisters. Christian abolitionist, Judge William Jay, wrote an introductory letter in William Goodell's book *The American Slave Code In Theory And Practice: Its Distinctive Features Shown By Its Statutes, Judicial Decisions, & Illustrative Facts 90.* His words bring us full circle to the reality that not all churches and Christians held to the conventional views of American Slavery. Judge Jay encouraged the work of Goodell when he said, "May God make your book a means of awakening the consciences of our cotton divines to the deep sin of upholding, in the name of the blessed and adorable redeemer, a system so damnable as American Slavery!"[23] It is astonishing how the majority of the church and Christians were able to endorse slavery, even as they could see all the suffering this bondage placed on slave families and marriages.

Slaveholder and leader of the Great Awakening, Jonathan Edwards, is one of America's most respected evangelical messengers of all ages. And yet, he preached the following excerpt from a sermon as his defense of slavery in America. This was preached while advocating the abolition of the slave trade and not enslaving Africans in Africa. This speech was presented to an anti-slavery group, called the *Connecticut Society for the Promotion of Freedom and the Relief of Persons Unlawfully Holden In Bondage,* on September 15, 1791. Edwards used the following arguments to justify keeping his own slaves enslaved: "A man who has been bred up in domineering over negroes, can scarcely avoid contracting such a habit of haughtiness and domination, as will express itself in his general treatment of mankind, whether in his private capacity, or in any office civil or military with which he may be vested."[24] In this statement, Edwards captures the essence of Bowen Theory of Family Systems Multi-Generational Transmission and its impact on the offspring of American slaveholders.

Edwards also exposes the concerns of slaveholders over legislation that would free the massive slave population. He said, "After all, it is not safe to manumit the Negros: they would cut our throats; they would endanger the peace and government of the state. Or at least they would be so idle, that they would not provide themselves with necessaries: of course, they just live by thievery and plundering."[25]

This sermon served to excite the fears of his Christian hearers by describing an angry African-American population that would take vengeance on their masters by viciously killing them in several different ways. It seems this philosophy has trickled down to the twenty-first century by instilling a fear of African-American vengeance. We see scores of innocent African-Americans being killed in this century because someone else feared for their life. This often happens at an innocent event, like being stopped for minor traffic violations. Edwards challenged the congregation of abolitionists to support American slavery with this reminder: "In all countries in which the slaves are a majority of the inhabitants, the masters lie in a great measure at the mercy of the slaves, and may most rationally expect, sooner or later, to be cut off, or driven out by the slaves, or to be reduced to the same level and to be mingled with them into one common mass."[26] When sermons like this are preached by one of the world's greatest evangelists, it will affect the lives of many.

Jonathan Edwards serves as an example that the American church fathers were a mixed bag of theological and biblical views on the subject of slavery. In Edwards, we see the combination of good and evil bound up in the same individual. His statements reveal his fear of the enslaved by keeping them in slavery, while delivering a message with the intent of stopping the slave trade to America. Paul, in his letter to the Romans, effectively speaks to this point:

> For I do not understand my own actions. For I do not do what I want, but I do the very thing I hate. Now if I do what I do not want, I agree with the law, that it is good. So now it is no longer I who do it, but sin that dwells within me. For I know that nothing good dwells in me, that is, in my flesh. For I have the desire to do what is right, but not the ability to carry it out. For I do not do the good I want, but the evil I do not want is what I keep on doing. Now if I do what I do not want, it is no longer I who do it, but sin that dwells within me (Rom. 7:15-20 ESV).

In both Paul and Edwards, we see how God has always used flawed persons to advance the gospel, because all have sinned and come short of God's glory (Rom. 3:23 ESV).

James Roberts, born in 1753, wrote an autobiography about his experiences as a former slave and a soldier in the Revolutionary War. He described his prayers and bewilderment with a system of slavery that could exist within Christianity. He recalled:

> For more than eighty years I have desired that Providence would, in some way, enable me to contribute my mite to the destruction of the iniquitous and soul and body destroying system of Slavery in this country --a system, the cruel effects and soul-sickening tendency of which no human being that God ever made can tell me anything more of than I have seen and experienced in my own mind and person, and in my fellow sufferers.[27]

While we do not have exact records, it is assumed that Roberts while a slave served his master at war and would not have fought on the side of the British, who promised African-Americans their freedom upon victory over the Continental Army. Some 9,000 African-American soldiers were either fugitive slaves or men who gained their independence by other methods. Roberts expressed his disgust with the system of slavery, even while he proclaimed his faith in God, who he saw as a deliverer of the less fortunate. As he reflected upon his own slavery, he linked the brutality of the institution to the Christian faith of slave owners. "But while I look back over the long history of my life, and can see many, many events of the most heart-sickening character connected with the system of Christian slavery, I can now see hopes of a brighter day for those who suffer under that system."[28] Roberts described the emotional impact of what he called "Christian Slavery" in his life.

This title "Christian Slavery" is originated in truth, because history tells us that the American society is established upon Christian principles. Slaves also felt the impact of Christian lifestyles reflected in their owners who were both spiritual and carnal. Edward Baptist reported, in his comprehensive book, how slave auctions were commonly held in churches. Baptist recorded the content of an 1816 newspaper advertisement by William Robertson: "auction, at a New Orleans church, of 20 or 30 Negroes, just arrived from Tennessee, consisting principally of working hands."[29]

Conducting a slave auction at a church is beyond imagination for twenty-first century believers. During this era, Sunday was a day of leisure and recreation that drew large gatherings of people to one location. Slave auctions, for many, were often treated as recreational activities, complete with side events to help draw crowds. "In the old Southeast, White people bought and sold African-American people on exceptional days. It was customary, wrote ex-slave Allen Parker of the early nineteenth century, for those having slaves to let, to take them to some prominent place for community auctions, while Sundays, when gentlemen traded horses and people in the yard outside of the church, were also typical sale days."[30] In spite of mistreatment slaves endured from Christian owners and their church dominations, they continued to receive Christianity by faith.

Fugitive slave Roberts expressed how slaves were blessed by their belief in God despite their captivity. "Their long prayed for day is dawning in the horizon of public sentiment, East, West, North and South, and over the civilized world. It is dawning in the improving condition of my race."[31] He implied that slaves were a people of prayer, and that they could see the effects of their prayers as the anti-slavery sentiments spread across America. Prayer is always a source of comfort for people who are suffering and who need deliverance from the difficulties of life. A committed prayer life provides hope in the most desperate situations. Roberts said, "I can myself, during a period of upwards of one hundred years, see all the improvement that they have made, in habits and manners, in refinement and education, in morals and religion; and in all these respects no one knows the favorable change that has come over them, but one who has been an eye-witness of all that germ, bud and growth of the happy change."[32]

Looking back over one's life is often the best thing to do in a desperate situation. Roberts recalled the changes he observed during his lifetime. He was almost a hundred years old at the time of writing his autobiography, and it is likely he lived over a hundred years. He was born in 1753, but his autobiography wasn't printed until 1858. Roberts continued, "These improvements will go on in public sentiment and in personal elevation, till somewhere in the future, God, in his inscrutable providence, will strike a blow to the system of human bondage in this country, which the combined forces of earth will not be able to resist. This shall be my unceasing prayer while life lasts."[33] Prayer in the life of the suffering has a fantastic ability to strengthen and sustain during extended periods of persecution. Throughout history, in the narratives of former slaves, these attributes are revealed.

Roberts exposed the mindset of a slave who understood that the system of slavery within Christianity was out of God's will. Nevertheless, he maintained a faith that allowed him to commit his sufferings into the hands of God through prayer. In prayer, he further suggested that his ancestors found hope for the future despite the disparaging conditions of their life. The church and Christianity have always been the strength of the African-American community, even in the days of slavery. "And if it is evil in your eyes to serve the LORD, choose this day whom you will serve, whether the gods your fathers served in the region beyond the River or the gods of the Amorites in whose land you dwell. But as for me and my house, we will serve the LORD" (Joshua 2:15 ESV).

Christianity Provides Physical and Spiritual Freedom

"Slave owners along with their clergy taught slaves a partial truth that Christianity would save their souls and provide them with a good afterlife if they were obedient to their masters. This emphasis on afterlife was one difference seen in religious beliefs among Africans before they became enslaved in America."[34] Salvific teachings also provided slaves with a mindset of freedom, as they viewed the afterlife as an escape from the hardships of slavery. Death among slaves became known as a "Home Going Celebration."

The old African belief was that one returned to their native homeland upon death. At the passing of a friend or loved one, the African custom of releasing the dead was demonstrated as they placed an item in the grave that related to their native country. When a slave died in America, it was a time of celebration because they were free from the master's oversight and would experience real freedom for the first time. Although funeral services of slaves could not exist in churches, there was a celebration of dancing around the graveside to represent the hope of liberty for the dead. Of course, this kind of burial service required the master's permission.

The concept of celebrating remains widespread, as Rick Paskin, an authority in African-American funerals, explained: "For many in the African-American community, funeral services and expressions of mourning contain a theme of celebration, rather than the melancholy emotions associated with death in other cultural settings. This attitude grew out of the period of slavery when most slave owners would not allow slaves to gather for funerals."[35] He continued, "During this dark time, death was often seen as freedom and a reason to celebrate amidst the grieving. Africans believed that the deceased's soul returned to their African homeland. From this arose the concept of a home going, which survives today, although it is now seen as the soul entering heaven or joining with ancestors."[36]

There are several similarities between what African slaves believed about death and the afterlife and what Christianity teaches. Both teach that there is another life in a world beyond this world. In the next existence, they believed that we will see our ancestors, friends and present family, and that it will be a place without suffering and without the misery of this world.

One significant difference is that Christians believe you must have a saving faith in Christ to enter that world, or heaven. First generations of slaves thought that you would travel to the homeland of Africa where the spirits of their ancestors lived. However, after conversion to Christianity, they recognized heaven as that place where their ancestors lived. "After slavery was abolished, the newly freed slaves could openly gather to honor their dead, and the opportunity to honor their loved ones became an important time in their community. Extravagant celebrations of the deceased's life became common, including music and dancing, helping fuel the growth of the Jazz Funeral."[37]

Today, African-American Christians continue to view death as a time of celebrating freedom from the suffering of this world, and as a reward for living as a Christian. The celebration of death and dying continues, although Africa is no longer the homeland desired. B. A. Botkins shared this interview of an unnamed slave preacher and his preaching experience during slavery:

> I been preaching the *gospel* and farming since slavery time. I jined the church 'most 83 years ago when I was Major Gaud's slave, and they baptizes me in the spring branch close to where I finds the Lord. When I starts preaching I couldn't read or write and had to preach what Master told me, and he say tell them niggers iffen they obeys the master they goes to Heaven; but I knowed there's something better for them, but daren't tell them 'cept on the sly. That I done lots. I tells 'em iffen they keeps praying, the Lord will set 'em free.[38]

As Christians, what saves sinners is our obedience to the word of God and accepting Jesus as Lord and Savior. Although slaves received a partial and often false gospel message, they could determine when it was not the truth. Their inability to read and write made them vulnerable to what others told them was in the Bible, but their moral compass guided them to the essentials of what it took to get to heaven. They knew the basic difference between right and wrong. They also knew true bible teaching from distorted teaching. They held closely and remember the true teachings, while casting away the corrupt.

Christianity and Slave Marriages

When evangelical church leaders approached Black Slavery in America, they adjusted their hermeneutic to suit the prevailing slave practices. In other words, they held close to a hermeneutic of convenience. William Goodell exposed the mind of Christianity and slavery in his day: He said:

> The legal relation of master and slave, with all the vestal robes of its spotless innocence, and saintly Biblical paternity has never, in this country, been held to be compatible with marriage. So as in colonial times, when parish ministers, all over New-England, owned slaves, it was held by learned civilians, in good old Connecticut, that when a slave master, though inadvertently, gave verbal license to a female slave to marry, the license made her free. Being married, she was not a slave, and the husband bore off his prize in triumph, before her master![39]

The original law prohibiting marriages among African-Americans appears first established in the Commonwealth of Virginia during the days of the New England Colonies. This law defined the slave status of the children born to slave owners and African women slaves. It also penalized White Christians, both male and female, who involved themselves in sexual relationships outside of marriage with a free or enslaved African-American.

> Some masters favored marriage for religious reasons, and it was in the interests of plantation owners for women to have children. Childbearing started around the age of thirteen, and by twenty the women slaves would be expected to have four or five children. To encourage childbearing, some plantation owners promised women slaves their freedom after they had produced fifteen children.[40]

Slave mothers of many children were usually granted a life of favor and ease because of the wealth in bearing children she brought to her master. Encouraging women to have more children to gain financial support is compared to our modern-day welfare system that provides support based on the numbers of dependent children.

Many good Christians lived a life of agony over the institution of slavery and took every opportunity to complain about the outrageous treatment of families. Mr. William Allan, abolitionist and the son of the Rev. Dr. Allan (a slaveholder and pastor of the Presbyterian Church in Huntsville, Alabama) reflected on his life of growing up as a slaveholder, as well as what he saw as the cruel treatment of enslaved families by some Christian slavers in the city. He made the point that marriages between slaves held very little meaning to some preachers and men of God. "Legal marriage is unknown among the slaves, they sometimes have a marriage form--generally, however, none at all. The pastor of the Presbyterian Church in Huntsville had two families of slaves when I left there. One couple were married by a Negro preacher--the man was robbed of his wife a number of months afterwards, by her owner."[41] Slavery as an acceptable institution grew so interwoven into the American church that it removed the spiritual convictions that would have prevented the separating of newlywed couples and families.

Mr. William Allan was not a pastor or a spiritual leader, but he felt the convicting power of God's Spirit over the treatment of slaves in his hometown. "The other couple just 'took up together, without any form of marriage. They are both members of churches--the man a Baptist deacon, sober and correct in his deportment. They have a large family of children--all children of concubinage--living in a minister's family."[42] His account revealed that in many cases, slaves were leaders in their churches, but were unable to live morally because of their inability to marry.

Nevertheless, the forced conditions of immorality within the marriages and families of slaves gave no reason for the majority of Whites to lay down their sinful ways. Numerous laws were made to regulate marriages between the Black and White races. During this era, legislation usually included an addendum for Christians that prohibited actions that would violate the law because of their faith. By 1705, Massachusetts made marriages and sexual relations between Blacks and Whites illegal. The Act of 1705 also forbade any "Christian" from marrying a Negro, and imposed a penalty of fifty pounds upon any clergyman who joined a Negro and a "Christian" in marriage. It stood as the law of the Commonwealth until 1843 when it repealed the "Act relating to Marriage between Individuals of certain races."[43]

Virginia Bell, a former slave, living in Houston, Texas, recalled her days as a slave living on the Thomas Lewis plantation in Opelousas, a city in South Central Louisiana.

> We didn' have no schoolin' or preachin'. Only the White folks had them, but sometimes on Sundays we'd go up to the house and listen to the White folks singin'. Iffen any of the slave hands wanted to get married, Massa Lewis would get them up to the house after supper time, have the man and woman join hands and then read to them outen a book. I guess it was the Scriptures. Then he'd tell 'em they was married but to be ready for work in the mornin'. Massa Lewis married us accordin' to Gospel.[44]

Countless slave owners misrepresented the principles of the Bible, because their scripture knowledge was not any better than that of their uneducated slaves. However, this was not the case with Rev. Thornton Stringfellow, who was born March 6, 1788 and died March 6, 1869. Stringfellow was the well-known author and pastor of Stevensburg Baptist Church of Culpeper County, Virginia. He was best known for his biblical apologetics in defense of African-American slavery. Stringfellow gave testimony to the mental triviality Christian slave masters placed upon the sexual promiscuity of their cohabitating slaves on John Swan's plantation from 1824 to 1835 around Wilmington North Carolina. He recalled, "There were on his plantation about seventy slaves, male and female: some were married, and others lived together as man and wife, without even a mock ceremony. With their owners generally, it is a matter of indifference: the marriage of slaves not being recognized by the slave code. The slaves, however, think much of being married by a clergyman."[45] Stringfellow's remark was an effort to make a pro-slavery statement as an indifference to slave marriages. In this declaration, a highly respected Bible scholar of his day accepted the cohabitating lifestyles of slaves because he believed the sin of adultery to be a matter of irrelevance among the enslaved.

When trying to understand how these biblical principles were dismissed so easily by Christian slavers, Phillip Schaff shed a little light for us. His historical research on the subject of slavery and Christian tolerance led him to express that "No marriage, no education, no liberty, no pure gospel! This, dear reader, is American Slavery, an institution, not of some far-off pagan land, but of Christian, Republican America!"[46]

Slavery and all its accompanying sins were a way of life in America, even for many who loved and embraced their freedom from sin in Christ Jesus. Accepting slavery was the attitude in churches all over America, especially in the South, even as late as the year 1853. "It is estimated that in the United States, members of the Methodist church owned 219,363 slaves; members of the Baptist church owned 226,000 slaves; members of the Episcopalian church own 88,000 slaves; members of the Presbyterian church owned 77,000 slaves; members of all other churches owned 50,000 slaves; in all, 660,563 slaves owned by members of the Christian church in this pious democratic republic."[47]

Carter G. Woodson enlightened us to the internal turmoil within the Presbyterian denomination as it studied the destructive effect slavery had on African-American families. Woodson reported,

> In this straddling position these churches tried to discountenance as far as possible all cruelty of whatever kind in the treatment of slaves, especially the cruelty of separating husband and wife, parents and children, and that which consisted in selling slaves to those who would either themselves deprive these unhappy people of the blessings of the gospel or who would transfer them to places where the gospel was not proclaimed, or where it was forbidden to slaves to attend upon its instruction.[48]

The spiritual and moral issue of slavery forced many within Christendom to question the positions of their pro-slavery churches. They debated among themselves about how the deprivation of their spirituality allowed them to accept the cruelty of separating slave families and prohibiting slaves from learning God's word. Consequently, ten years later, a decision was announced that revealed the resolution made by the Presbyterian Church in regards to slave owners and their acceptance as members of the denomination. "When, as a result of various memorials on slavery, the Assembly, deploring the division of the church on slavery, passed a resolution that the church could not legislate where Christ has not legislated, that as Christ and the Apostles admitted slaveholders as members of the church, they could not be expected to do otherwise."[49] They based their decision on the biblical positions of the Apostle Paul in Scripture when he instructed slaves to obey their masters, and on the fact that Christ was silent on the topic of slavery and did not out-right denounce it. However, after much division over many years, they offered a justification. "Some disclaimed, however, any desire to deny that slavery is an evil, or to countenance the idea that masters may regard their slaves as real property and not as human beings. They merely intended to say that since Christ and his Apostles did not make the holding of slaves a bar to communion, the church organizations as the court of Christ had no authority to do so."[50] One of the most influential pro-slavery arguments was the idea that the New Testament does not condemn slavery. Jesus and the apostles were silent, even though Roman slavery was alive and well during the days of the first church. The Presbyterian Church was not the only denomination to justify their position on slavery. The Baptists also re-established their views on the marital status of slaves, despite the brutalities that enslaved families and marriages endured in the mid-1800s.

On the topic of slave marriages, the Baptists in South Carolina deliberated over the state laws, in most cases disregarding the biblical principles for husbands and wives. William Goodell said, "The Charleston Baptist Association in support of its states legislations resisted the calling of professed disciples to stand with Christ who came to proclaim the jubilee of deliverance to the captives!"[51] Although South Carolina was among the strongest slaveholding states, there appears to be a measure of remorse over their stance on the topic, especially when Christ's statements regarding setting the captives free came in conflict with what was required to be a slaveholding Christian. Goodell presented the case of the Savannah River Baptist Association in an attempt to expose the imbalance between Christians and the issue of slavery. "Now Baptist slaveholders understand the tenure of their assumed rights of property in man, and at what expense they expect those rights to be maintained by their State Legislatures, may be learned from the following: In 1835 the following query, relating to slaves, was presented to the Savannah River Baptist Association of ministers."[52]

The Savannah River Baptist Association also deliberated what their position would be in regard to the issues surrounding slavery. One such topic they investigated was the problem that arose when a second marriage for slaves was required if they were sold away from their families. The question and its conclusion was recorded as follows: "Whether, in case of involuntary separation of such a character as to preclude all future intercourse, the parties may be allowed to marry again? That such separation among persons situated as our slaves are, is civilly a separation by death, and they believe that, in the sight of God, it would be so viewed."[53]

The church leaders' concern for the desperate situation of the enslaved was at the base of their discussions. They realized that when a family was separated from each other, knowing that they would never see each other again, it was emotionally experienced as if the separated family member had died. In a stretch for compassion, they determined that it would be cruel to disallow another marriage and require celibacy for the remainder of their lives. They alleged, "To forbid second marriages in such cases, would be to expose the parties not only to greater hardships and stronger temptations, but to church censure for acting in obedience to their masters, who cannot be expected to acquiesce in a regulation at variance with justice to the slaves, and to the spirit of that command which regulates marriage between Christians."[54]

Goodell pointed out that it was beyond the control of the slave, as it was not their choice to either remain with their spouse or be sold away. He argued the case of the enslaved, "The slaves are not free agents, and a dissolution by death is not more entirely without their consent and beyond their control than by such separation. Incidentally here, the fact leaks out that slave cohabitation is enforced by the authority of the masters, for the increase of their human chattels, and that this is done in utter contempt of the divine institution of marriage."[55] This argument suggests they needed to appear pious before others. These men knew slave marriages were not legal, so their discussion was rendered worthless. Goodell continued his explanation of the false conclusions by the Savannah River Baptist Association of churches. He reprimanded their decision:

> And a body of devout ecclesiastics gravely decide that inasmuch as this process, in connection with the frequent and forced separation from each other of wives and husbands belonging to Baptist churches, is inseparable from the slave system, the divine institution of marriage, as expounded by Christ, must be modified in conformity with the slave code, in order that those whom God hath joined together, may, by man, be put asunder, that Baptist wives

> may have two husbands and Baptist husbands may have two wives, without being subjected to church censure.[56]

The discussions were obviously influenced by the legislation of the day that was controlled by the influences of slavery - their conclusions were not in line with God's biblical laws. It was evident they were more concerned about their good standing within the church than with the souls of the slaves who were being led into adulterous relationships. Goodell concluded his reproach of this Christian body of believers by pointing out the reality that marriage and slavery cannot coexist. "The censoring of such churches, verily, must be of vast benefit in rebuking the sin of adultery! If any testimony were wanted, to establish the fact that slavery is incompatible with marriage, the Savannah River Baptist Association have furnished it to our hands."[57]

The Baptists maintained their long-held view of slavery and continued to teach that slave marital relationships do not require the same morals that White's require for marriage and sexual standards. When addressing the Baptist decision, Frederick Douglass said, "Here we find a deliberate setting aside of the Marriage Institution and the deliberate sanction of a wholesale system of adultery and concubines; and, yet the persons who authorize and enforce such wickedness calling themselves Christians!"[58]

Around the same time, on January 20th, 1788, the First Colored Baptist Church in North America was constituted in Savannah, Georgia. The first African-American missionary Baptist was George Liele, who also became the pastor of the First Colored Baptist church in Savannah. As a part of the old Georgia Baptist Association, leaders remarked about the difficulty and slowness in converting African-Americans into the church. "These humble slave worshippers stately met at their meetinghouse, as it was called; and the good seed sown by the good Lord, through the instrumentality of Brother George Liele, began to spring up and bear fruit."[59] In the initial stages of the ministry, about 20 new converts provided a convincing profession of their faith in Christ and received baptism. "This number, however, is not an indication of the extent of his success, for many who may have been converted could not receive this ordinance, being so bound by the power of slavery that they required the consent of their masters in writing to enable them to obey God and satisfy this earnest religious desire of the soul."[60]

The Black Creek Baptist Church and the Lots Creek Baptist Church were soon started as African-American church plants. All three

African-American slave churches started before a Baptist Association existed in Savannah. As the need arose for a fellowship of churches in Southern Georgia, Black and White, and slave and free churches joined together and started the Savannah River Baptist Association. "They met in convention at Savannah in 1802 and organized the Savannah River Association. Who the officers were, we have no knowledge, as the file of minutes has been lost, it appears; but this we are certain of, that the churches were enrolled according to the date of constitution, and the First Colored Church stood at the head of the roll."[61] By the time the Association began, the First Colored Baptist Church's membership roll had grown. George Liele was no longer the pastor, but his leadership had laid great foundations.

Tensions grew over the details of slavery and the use of African-Americans in ministry positions. Georgia Baptists would test the General Convention's position on slavery when James Reeves, a slaveholder, was nominated to become a missionary to the South. His rejection created a split in the General Convention and caused the Southern Baptist Convention (SBC) to be structured.

> The attempt of the General Convention to maintain an uneasy neutrality over the issue came unstuck in 1844 when the Georgia Baptist Convention sponsored slaveholder James E. Reeve as a missionary to the Cherokees in a test case. When the General Convention's Home Mission Society rejected Reeve's nomination and its Foreign Mission Board affirmed later in the year that it would not appoint a slaveholder, southerners concluded that abolitionists had seized control of the convention. In response, they met in Augusta, Georgia, in May 1845 and organized the SBC.[62]

The SBC supported the South in its defense of slavery, even as America, specifically during 1850s and 1860s, saw some of the more severe divides around the issue. For Southern Baptists, it would take until the 1930s for both the principles of Christianity to affect convention life, and for the majority of its leadership to see the ills of racial oppression. "As far back as 1939, the Southern Baptist Convention adopted a resolution that expressed 'a deep sense of sorrow and shame' over the continued practice of lynchings and recognized that 'inequalities and injustices ... still exist' in matters such as public school funding, unequal and impartial administration of justice, inadequate wages and the lack of opportunity for African-Americans."[63] The convention had come full circle from oppressing slaves to supporting the causes that advanced the stability of African-Americans. "The resolution pledged that Southern Baptists would 'use our influence and give our efforts' to correct those inequalities and secure opportunities for 'full development in [the] education, industrial and religious life' of African-Americans."[64]

In 1995, the Southern Baptist Convention officially apologized for its earlier defense of slavery, in the form of a resolution on the convention floor. The messengers to the 150th annual meeting of the Southern Baptist Convention said that its "relationship to African-Americans has been hindered from the beginning by the role that slavery played in the formation of the Southern Baptist Convention."[65]

The bulk of this book thus far has explained the ways slavery has influenced African-Americans. However, we now see an open admission from a body of White believers as to the impact slavery had on their convention. These men, with a penitent heart for their sins and those of centuries of ancestors, wrote a document revealing their intent for racial reconciliation. "The resolution apologized to African-Americans 'for condoning and/or perpetuating individual and systemic racism in our lifetime' and resolved, 'to eradicate racism in all its forms from Southern Baptist life and ministry.'"[66] In 2016, the SBC passed a resolution that declared that they would stop displaying the Confederate flag. And as recently as 2017, with some prompting from the floor, the SBC voted in support of denouncing the "alt-right." The decision to denounce this ideology that advocates white nationalism, demonstrated their sincere interest in racial reconciliation.

The Southern Baptist Convention has continued to change in its racial and ethnic makeup. In 1995, at the time of the apology, approximately 1,600 predominantly African-American churches were affiliated with the Southern Baptist Convention. By 2005, 3,038 African-American Churches enjoyed membership in the convention. Today in 2017, the number has risen to over 3,500 African-American churches holding membership in this denomination. The Grace of God has incredibly placed both forgiveness in the hearts of African-Americans and a renewed spirit of love for all people of color in the hearts of White Southern Baptist Christians.

We have heard testimonies from many former slaves who shared stories about how the indifference of the church, and specifically Christian slave owners, was responsible for the moral breakdown of their friends and family. It should be noted this was also a time when church members endorsed and protected the slave's involvement in sexual sins. Bill Herd, in his ex-slave interview, recalled the experiences of what Christianity meant to him and his family, in spite of its cultural and racial differences:

> Folks didn't even git married back in dem days lak dey does now, leastwise slaves didn't. If a slave wanted to marry up wid a gal, he knocked on his Marster's door and told him 'bout it. If his Marstar laked de idea he told him to go on and take de gal and to treat her right; dat was all dere was to slaves gittin' married. My Daddy said slaves went to de White folks' church 'til dey got some churches for colored folks. Church days was big days wid folks den 'cause dey didn't have meetin' evvy Sunday. Slave 'omans had percale or calico dresses, brogan shoes, and big home-made bonnets wid slats in de brims for Sunday-go-to-meetin' wear, and if it was cold dey wropt up in shawls. Menfolks wore cotton shirts and pants. Dey had grand preachin' dem days and folks got honest-to-goodness 'ligion. [67]

Some African-American slaves lived their entire lives never having experienced a marriage or wedding ceremony involving two slaves. There is one recording of a slave, named John Jasper, who suffered three marriages. Most slave marriages did not last, for many different reasons, as we have already discussed. As there were no marital statistics on the divorces and separations of slave marriages, perhaps the three matrimonies of Rev. John Jasper were not out of the norm.

> "Mr. Jasper was for the first time married. His marriage was with a woman whose name was Elvy Weaden, a slave, of the city of Williamsburg. Mr. Jasper left Williamsburg on the same night of his marriage for Richmond, leaving his bride behind him, and was not allowed to return to see her again."[68]

A major component for owners who permitted marriages for their slaves was to use family ties to keep them enslaved. No one would have expected a male slave to abandon his wife on the night of the wedding to escape to freedom. Soon, Jasper's wife, Elvy, wrote him a letter requesting a release from their marriage vows. "It must be remembered that marriages between the slaves in the South were not recognized by the law as being anything. The method of getting a divorce was easy for both of the parties, all that was necessary was to notify the other of his or her intention to marry again. Nevertheless, in many cases this was not done although separation was a simple process for slaves."[69]

Figure 14. Rev. John Jasper Escaped Slave: Married Three Times[70]

The marriages of slaves were not binding by any legal legislation; nonetheless, it held great meaning for slaves, and they often approached their marriages with a commitment to becoming one flesh. In Jasper's case, since there was no need to obtain a legal divorce, Jasper was free to marry again at his convenience. "His second marriage was with Candus Jordan in 1844, by whom he had nine children, though there never existed a very pleasant relationship between them; and after long years of trouble and dissatisfaction Mr. Jasper finally obtained a divorce from her upon good and just grounds."[71]

Jasper's second marriage was an unhappy one, but it was fruitful with children. The relationship dissolved because of marital incompatibility. "On the second day of September, in the year 1863, he was married to Mary Anne Cole, the widow of a man whose name was Archer Cole."[72] Rev. John Jasper was a great slave preacher who filled the church weekly because of the incredible command of scripture in his sermons. The fact that he could not keep his marriages together was an issue that plagued him his entire ministry. After Mary Anne died, Jasper remained single the remainder of his life.

Early Slave Laws on Baptism and Freedom

Baptism is an ordinance based on the commandment of Christ for those committing their lives to him. The act of baptism is an open symbol to the world that Jesus is Lord, and it symbolizes that the baptism candidate believes Jesus Christ died, was buried and raised from the grave to a new life. Colonial Christians held their faith in high regard for all people, although African-Americans were forbidden the rites of Christianity. "Morgan Godwin, an English divine who spent several years in Virginia, decried the priorities of the colonists in a sermon published in 1685 with the accusatory title: *Trade preferred before Religion and Christ made to give place to Mammon.*"[73]

Christianity had a significant influence on the creation of laws that determined the treatment of Black people. The problem of Blacks and mulattos claiming freedom after they had been baptized was solved in 1664 by an addendum to a 1662 piece of legislation. From 1619 to 1775, the governmental system in Colonial America was the Upper and Lower House. Virginia was the first colony to establish this method of the legislature. The issue of baptizing African-Americans prompted a request from "the Lower

House of the Assembly to outline the problem for the Upper House: It is desired by the lower house that the upper house would be pleased to draw up an Act obliging negroes to serve Durante Vita they thinking it very necessary for the prevention of the damage [that] Masters of such Slaves may sustain by such Slaves pretending to be Christened and so plead the law of England."[74] The term *pretending* suggests that slaves were unable to receive salvation based on their inability to be catechized. However, in the event of a slave receiving salvation, laws were passed by several states that protected slaveholders. This kept owners from losing slaves who had already acquired baptism, as well as those who would become Christians in the future.

Carter Godwin Woodson, in *The History of The Negro Church,* described a situation that demonstrated that conversion and baptism were important enough to a slave that he ran away when his Christian freedom was lost.

> Having enjoyed for some time the boon of freedom in the church, moreover, the Negroes were loath to give up this liberty. The escape of a young Negro, a slave of Thomas Jones, in Baltimore County in 1793 is a case in evidence. Accounting for his flight his master said: "He was raised in a family of religious persons commonly called Methodists and has lived with some of them for years past on terms of perfect equality; the refusal to continue him on these terms gave him offense and he, therefore, absconded. He had been accustomed to instruct and exhort his fellow creatures of all colors in matters of religious duty."[75]

The 1656 case of Elizabeth Key set the stage for the heredity of slavery to be determined through the mother, as was observed in Chapter 3. Her case also was a consideration when the courts decided to disallow baptism for African-Americans. This court ruling served a hardship in both marriage and baptism for African-Americans.

> In 1656, Elizabeth Key won her freedom in part by citing to the court her White father and her baptism as a Christian. In December 1662, however, the General Assembly declared that "all children borne in this country shall be held bond or free only according to the condition of the

> mother." In other words, the children of slave women would be slaves. The assembly went further and doubled the fines imposed on any Whites caught having sex with Blacks. Then, in September 1667, the assembly passed "An act declaring that baptism of slaves doth not exempt them from bondage." The paths Key had followed to freedom were now closed.[76]

This victory by Key forced the 1667 law, imposed by King Charles II, to convince the colonies that there was no need to fear conversion of their slaves into Christianity. The king implemented the following code in the province of Virginia.

> September 1667 - 19th Charles II, ACT III, 2:260. An act declaring that baptism of slaves doth not exempt them from bondage. WHEREAS some doubts have risen whether children that are slaves by birth, and by the charity and piety of their owners made partakers of the blessed sacrament of baptism, should by virtue (sic) of their baptism be made free; It is enacted and declared by this grand assembly, and the authority thereof, that the conferring of baptism doth not alter the condition of the person as to his bondage or freedom; that diverse masters, freed from this doubt, may more carefully endeavor the propagation of Christianity by permitting children, though slaves, or those of growth if capable to be admitted to that sacrament.[77]

Virginia became the first state to devise laws that prohibited freedom for slaves based upon their baptism into Christianity. The 1667 law stated, "Virginia declares that Christian baptism will not alter a person's status as a slave."[78] The Baptism Laws would be revisited in 1715 by "Maryland, Forasmuch as many people have neglected to baptize their negroes, or suffer them to be baptized, on a vain apprehension that negroes by receiving the sacrament of baptism, are manumitted and set free, Be it enacted that no negro or negroes, by receiving the holy sacrament of baptism, is thereby manumitted or set free, nor hath any right or title to freedom or manumission, more than he or they had before, any law, usage or custom to the contrary notwithstanding. The Act of 1715, chap. 44, 23."[79]

According to this new agreement, Maryland first passed laws that implied becoming a Christian would not enfranchize an African-American. The 1671 law was less confusing, observing that many slaveholders were still hesitant to see their slaves receive a religious education for fear of losing them due to baptism. "This arose from a contrary apprehension growing out of ancient usages in England, and the opinion of some jurists that Christians could not be lawfully enslaved."[80] The colonies thereby legislated an act obliging Negroes to serve Durante vita (slaves for life). The legislation served as an insurance policy to prevent slaves from pretending to be christened.

The law was a detour to any effort by an African-American who would plead to the non-existent law of England. Although colonial Americans originally believed baptism granted liberty to slaves who became Christians, for nearly 250 years, the need of African-Americans to become Christians would cost generations a lifetime of freedom. "By 1706 at least six colonial legislatures had passed acts denying that baptism altered the condition of a slave 'as to his bondage or freedom.'"[81]

Although colonial states passed legislation protecting the rights of slaveholders to keep their slaves, regardless of their religious convictions, most slave owners did not want to risk the baptism of their slaves. "Even after colonial assemblies had declared baptism to be no threat to a planter's legal right to hold slaves in perpetual bondage, the process of religious instruction which had to precede baptism was seen by many slaveholders as an economic detriment."[82]

Besides fearing that baptism might lead their slaves to think they were free, religion also had the potential to distract their slaves from their work. A conversion experience was typically followed up with religious instruction, and those times of instruction would take time away from the slave's daily work. From sunrise to sundown, the work schedules of slaves were very demanding and did not allow time for instruction in Christian catechisms. Slaveholders realized their personal needs would be left unmet and the plantations would be unmanned if the requirements of the church were met to convert slaves to Christians.

Also, there were many stereotypes about slaves that were central to the belief shared by slavers: African-Americans were too uncivil to have the ability to receive salvation and education. One example in history that would disprove this theory is the 1795-1820 time period of religious revivalism known as the "Second Great Awakening." "Slaves converted to Christianity in large numbers for the first time. As African-Americans embraced Christianity beginning in the 18th century, especially after 1770, they gathered in independent church communities and created bigger denominational structures such as the African Methodist Episcopal Church, the African Methodist Episcopal Zion Church, and the National Baptist Convention."[83]

Some Northern and Southern churches developed among African-American congregations. The small number of free Blacks in the South resulted in their churches aligning with White religious institutions. Nevertheless, these churches and denominations became significant areas for spiritual support, educational opportunity, economic development and political activism. Black religious institutions served as environments in which African-Americans made meaning of the experience of enslavement, interpreted their relationship to Africa, and charted a vision for a collective future.[84]

Albert Raboteau articulated the societal beliefs of the era about slaves and baptism and the difficulty in converting first-generation Africans into Christianity. He said, "Masters also objected to slave conversion because they believed that Africans were too 'brutish' to be instructed. In part, this objection was based on the linguistic and cultural barriers between African-born ('Guinea') slaves and English colonials."[85] This statement expresses the difficulty of enculturation for Africans into the American society. Most were defiant to the brutal and inhuman treatment of slave-traders during the Middle passage travel. They were afraid and despaired of their new life that was in every aspect not of their understanding. "Even missionaries despaired of overcoming the linguistic and cultural gap and directed their attention primarily to children and to American-born slaves, who had some facility in English."[86]

From 1619 until 1808, the American Slave Trade brought African-born slaves to America against their wills, producing 189 years of extreme difficulty in evangelizing Africans for those devout believers who made attempts. Africans were made to submit until eventually their wills nearly broke. Nevertheless, "toward the end of the seventeenth century Col. Francis Nicholson, governor of Virginia, was instructed by London to recommend to the Virginia Assembly that it pass laws ensuring the education of Indians and Negroes in the Christian faith."[87]

The growing colonies, now filled with slavers who knew of the difficulty involved in the education of their slaves, were once again commanded to convert Indians and slaves. Virginia responded to London's direct command with the following from the House of Burgers. "The negroes born in this country are generally baptized and brought up in the Christian religion; but for negroes imported hither, the gross bestiality and rudeness of their manners, the variety and strangeness of their languages, and the weakness and shallowness of their minds, render it in a manner impossible to make any progress in their conversion."[88] This response was a partly true statement, because laws were passed that permitted baptism of slaves, although said baptism and Christianity did not make a slave free. Slave owners held plenty of suspicion towards the law; therefore, few slaves were baptized and allowed instruction in the word until the 1800s.

Although most slavers believed that African-Americans would not benefit from the rites of baptism and objected to their indulgence in any form of Christian rituals, some eventually allowed them to participate. However, it was not until slavery ended that African-Americans received the full rites of baptism. George Washington Williams clarified:

> As to the political rights of the Negro, it should be borne in mind, that, as he was excluded from the right of Christian baptism, hence from the Church; and as "only church-members enjoyed the rights of freemen, it is clear that the Negro was not admitted to the exercise of the duties of a freeman. Admitting that there were instances where Negroes received the rite of baptism, it was so well understood as not entitling them to freedom or political rights, that it was never questioned during this entire period. Free Negroes were but little better off than the slaves." While they might be regarded as owning their own labor, political rights and ecclesiastical privileges were withheld from them.[89]

These nationally-held views on slavery and baptism, by both Northern and Southern states, made it difficult for them to work through the religious rites of the African-Americans. Carter Godwin Woodson wrote about early eighteenth century baptisms, conversions and catechisms of Negros in colonial Pennsylvania. These baptisms happened while Pennsylvania was a slave state. It was not until 1787, after the American Revolution, that the state became free for slaves. He also revealed the catechisms of Negros before their baptism, which was the required method to receive salvation during the era. Woodson recorded:

In Pennsylvania, the missionary movement among the Negroes found apparently fewer obstacles. Records are showing the baptism of Negroes as early as 1712. One Mr. Yates, a worker at Chester, was commended by the Rev. G. Ross "for his endeavors to train up the Negroes in the knowledge of religion." Mr. Ross himself had on one occasion at Philadelphia baptized as many as twelve adult Negroes, who were examined before the congregation and answered to the admiration of all who heard them. "The like sight had never been seen before in that church." Giving account of his efforts in Sussex County in 1723, Rev. Mr. Beckett said that many Negroes constantly attended his services, while Rev. Mr. Bartow about the same time baptized a Negro at West Chester. Rev. Richard Locke christened eight Negroes in one family at Lancaster in 1747 and another Negro there the following year.[90]

The religious development of slaves suffered a severe setback by the most famous insurrection in the history of slavery. An African-American preacher, named Nat Turner, claimed to have visions from God revealing to him that slavery would end in bloodshed. These revelations plagued him, and many slaves believed these were prophetic visions. Turner was pastor of a Southampton, Virginia, slave congregation. "Nat, a slave who by the custom of the country had acquired the surname of his first master, was the foreman of a small plantation, a Baptist exhorter capable of reading the Bible, and a pronounced mystic."[91]

Unlike many slaves, his ability to read and write from a young age gave him comfort in religious worship. This enabled him to deal with the hardships of slavery. Turner and 70 members of his local congregation, both slave and free, armed themselves with knives, axes and other tools. They traveled from house to house freeing slaves and killing any White people they encountered.

They killed a total of 60 White men, women, and children, although many could have been innocent of any wrongs against slaves. A White militia armed with guns killed more than 100 African-American people, the majority of whom had not been involved in the insurrection. This slave rebellion caused the states to tighten their laws on the unsupervised worship services of African-Americans. The abolitionist movements of Judge Stroud, Judge Jay and William Goodell all record the quickly passed legislation calling for control of the worship experiences of slaves. "In 1831 planters became so alarmed about the potential for religious messages to cause other revolts that they passed legislation in 1832 requiring that White pastors lead all African-American churches. The planters believed they could ensure control of the message that Whites would deliver. This situation lasted until after the Civil War when African-Americans took back control of their church."[92] Virginia Codes of Assemblies passed a law that assured control of the public worship of all African-American Christians. "In Virginia, it will be remembered, that all meetings of slaves, free negroes and mulattoes, mixing with such slaves at any meeting house, or any other place, in the night, under any pretext whatsoever, are declared to be unlawful assemblies, and the civil power may disperse the same, and inflict corporal punishment on the offenders. Slaves may, however, attend at church on any day of public worship."[93]

The state of Mississippi Rev. Code, 390 in 1831, "adopted the law of Virginia, with a proviso, that the master or overseer of a slave may, in writing, grant him permission to attend a place of religious worship, at which the minister may be White and regularly ordained or licensed, or at least, two discreet and reputable White persons appointed by some regular church or religious society, shall attend."[94]

According to Carter Godwin Woodson, toward the end of slavery, some slave owners were committed to the conversion of their slaves. Owners recognized an appreciative difference that Christianity had upon the lives of slaves. For the first time, slavers were admitting to the intellectual abilities of slaves.

> In 1854 Bishop Polk owned 400 slaves himself but endeavored to bring them up in a religious manner, baptizing all of their children and teaching them the catechism. All without exception says Olmsted, attend the church service, and the chanting is creditably performed by them in the opinion of their owner. Ninety of them are communicants, marriages are celebrated according to the church ritual, and the state of morals is satisfactory.[95]

The country had primarily forgotten the rebellion of Nat Turner by 1854, and African-Americans were allowed to worship and serve God again openly; however, the gospel African-Americans heard was influenced by the dictates of their owners. Former slave, Lina Hunter, described the excitement of a Spirit-filled worship and baptism service. She stated:

> Honey, back in dem good old days us went to church wid our White folks. Slaves sot in de gallery or in de back of de church. I'se been to dat old Cherokee Corners Church more times dan I knows how to count, but de fust baptizin' I ever seed was at de old St. Jean church; dere was jus' three or four baptized dat day, but Lordy, I never did hear such prayin', shoutin', and singin', in all my born days. One old 'oman come up out of dat crick a-shoutin' 'bout she was walkin' through de pearly gates and wearin' golden slippers, but I looked down at her foots and what she had on looked more lak brogans to me. I kin still hear our old songs, but it's jus' now and den dat dey come back to my mind.[96]

Baptism among captives was a joyous occasion. Having been denied the rites for many years, they considered it a blessed privilege. Several essential factors made this a significant occurrence. Along with the fact that they now enjoyed salvation, baptism also represented their new birth into Christ and was an acknowledgment of their humanity. Baptism gave testimony to the fact that they possessed a soul that could be saved, and this established the slave above chattel. The actions of White Christians who accepted the baptism of slaves into Christ also confirmed their belief that slaves were members of humanity and were people with a soul that need salvation. Attached to baptism was the promise of heaven and the commandment to practice Christian principles.

God's Amazing Grace has kept African-Americans in a relationship with Him despite the history of Christianity having been used as an instrument to control slaves. African-Americans, for centuries, have remained committed to their Christian faith, as a recent 2004 study by Robert J. Taylor, Linda M. Chatters and Jeff Levin showed. Their comprehensive study, entitled *Religion in the Lives of African-Americans: Social, Psychological, and Health Perspectives,* found that church involvement of African-Americans in the twenty-first century is as follows:

> Less than 10 percent that has not attended church services. 80 percent considered themselves to be either strongly or moderately religious. 70 percent affirmed they attended church worship services a few times a month, plus two-thirds conveyed that they are church members. 80 percent of African-Americans stated they pray almost every day, 27 percent shared they read religious books and 21 percent tune into religious broadcast stations on both television and radio every day.[97]

Understanding and living by the principles of Christianity in every phase of life will provide deliverance that only God is capable of giving. God's gift of salvation to the African-American during the years of slavery was their most reassuring relief. Studies have shown that "religious and spiritual beliefs are associated with better coping, and better mental and physical health."[98] Salvation is the best thing that can happen in life and eternity. To accept Jesus Christ as one's personal Savior is the highest accomplishment in this life, because it is the only action that can provide a blessing both in this world and in heaven. A relationship with Jesus as our Savior gives believers the ability to cope with the struggles of life, knowing that our troubles will not always exist. Christians recognize that Jesus Christ saves us from sin and provides us the strength to handle danger, harm, and failure. Because Jesus is Savior, He rescues and delivers from the trials and temptations of life.

Chapter 5

Slave Codes: Their Impact on Marriages and Families

> But if the slave plainly says, "I love my master, my wife, and my children; I will not go out free," then his master shall bring him to God, and he shall bring him to the door or the doorpost. And his master shall bore his ear through with an awl, and he shall be his slave forever (Exodus 21:5-6. ESV).

Through many dangers, toils, and snares...
we have already come.

The Bible does not condemn slavery, but does prohibit the mistreatment of the enslaved by their owners. Exodus 21:6 describes God's concept of relationships between the master, a slave, and his family. The text reveals an intimacy where the slave is in love with his owner and struggles with the choice of freedom over slavery if his family remains enslaved. "I love my master, my wife, and my children; I will not go out free." Therefore, the slave decides to stay a slave for life. Jesus, however, revealed his mission was to announce the freedom of slaves, though not going as far as to condemn the institution of slavery.

Jesus said, "The Spirit of the Lord is upon me because he has anointed me to proclaim good news to the poor. He has sent me to proclaim liberty to the captive and recovering of sight to the blind, to set at liberty those who are oppressed, to proclaim the year of the Lord's favor" (Luke 4:18-19 ESV). Within this scripture are two conditions found in the American slave system that are opposed to God's requirements for the slave/master relationship. First the announcement of freedom to the captives, and second the giving liberty to the oppressed. Both were essential to relieve slaves of the way they suffered during American slavery. In light of the stated mission of Christ, we can contemplate the Godhead saw captivity and oppression as sins for which human beings needed a deliverer. In the book *Uncle Tom's Cabin*, Harriett Stowe described Uncle Tom's conversion experience using this Scripture to represent a means of relief for slaves in America.

> Those who have been familiar with the religious histories of the slave population know that relations like what we have narrated are very common among them. We have heard some from their own lips, of a very touching and affecting character. The psychologist tells us of a state, in which the affections and images of the mind become so dominant and overpowering, that they press into their service the outward imagining. Who shall measure what an all-pervading Spirit may do with these capabilities of our mortality, or the ways in which He may encourage the desponding souls of the desolate? If the poor forgotten slave believes that Jesus hath appeared and spoken to him, who shall contradict him? Did He not say that his, mission, in all ages, was to bind up the broken-hearted, and set at liberty them that are bruised?[1]

In this text, Jesus becomes all things to those caught in the spiritual and physical snares of life. In the case of African-American bondage, the captured and oppressed people from Africa needed deliverance from the Constitution of the United States of America. The United States Constitution remained silent on the subject of African-American slavery.

The Constitution yielded its regulations to Slave Codes, enforced by state laws, which were designed to regulate captivity. These codes were not always in harmony with biblical methods for how people became a slave. Biblically, "There are many ways a person can become a slave. One-way is by stealing and not being able to make restitution payment (Exodus 22: 3). Or, if someone is an unbeliever, they can be sold as slaves (Leviticus 25: 44-46). Someone can also sell themselves into slavery due to their terrible poverty (Leviticus 25: 47). Slaves are also captured through warfare (Deuteronomy 20: 14)."[2]

Here we must be clear that the rules mentioned for bondage throughout the Bible are far from what happened in America. Yes, God did approve of slavery in Scripture, but under very specific conditions. He put in place many safeguards for the right treatment of the enslaved. Biblical enslavement, when based on God's commandments, was often loved and appreciated by slaves so much that they chose to remain slaves for life, even after gaining their freedom. It is also important to mention that the race of a person was never a condition to be enslaved in the Bible, and they were never reduced to chattel.

During Biblical bondage, masters were always required to hold in high regard the roles of enslaved husbands, wives and children. The principle of love found in both the Old and New Testaments is the standard for how mankind must treat one another. "Love the Lord your God with all your heart and with all your soul and with all your strength and with all your mind, and love your neighbor as yourself" (Luke 10:27 ESV).

Slave Codes Defined

Men, like abolitionists William Goodell and Judge George M. Stroud, wrote books examining the Slave Codes of each slaveholding state. These books served to influence the manumission of slavery in a way that other literature only hoped to accomplish. The books placed the focus on the scandalous laws within the slave system. George M. Stroud, in his book *A Sketch of the Laws Relating to Slavery In the Several States of The United States*, described the boundaries of slavery. Stroud said, "'The sate (sig. state) of slavery in this country, so far as it can be ascertained from the laws of the several independent sovereignties, which belong to our confederacy, is the subject of the following sheets."[3]

In 1827, at the time Stroud wrote his book, the slave and free states were divided evenly, with twelve states each. Stroud explained, "This (book) comprises a particular examination of the laws of the states of Delaware, Maryland, Virginia, North Carolina, South Carolina, Georgia, Kentucky, Tennessee, Louisiana, Mississippi, Alabama, and Missouri."[4] The District of Columbia was also considered as a slaveholding territory but was not mentioned in Stroud's list.

Stroud said, "With respect to the remaining states, slavery, in some, having been abolished, and in others, never tolerated, a cursory notice of a few of their laws, chiefly important for the evidence which they furnish of the right of these states to the appellation of non-slave-holding, is all which the title or object of this work requires."[5] When the Civil War started, the United States consisted of 34 states: 15 slave states and 19 free states. Eleven slave states seceded from the United States to form the Confederacy. The rules of Maryland, Missouri, Delaware and Kentucky became known as Border States, because they committed to the Union.

Judge Stroud worked the court systems as an abolitionist. He recorded this compilation of the following Slave Codes in his offense against slavery. These Codes were still in place for the slaveholding states at the beginning of the Civil War:

Prop. I. The master may determine the kind, and degree, and time of labor, to which the slave shall be subjected.[6]

*II. The master may supply the slave with such food and clothing only, both as to quantity and quality*as he may think proper or find convenient.*[7]

III. The master may, at his discretion, inflict any punishment upon the person of his slave.[8]

IV. All the power of the master over his slave may be exercised not by himself only in person, but by any one whom he may depute as his agent.[9]

V. Slaves have no legal rights of property in things, real or personal; but whatever they may acquire belongs, in point of law, to their masters.[10]

VI. The slave being a personal chattel is at all times liable to be sold absolutely or mortgaged or leased, at the will of his master.[11]

VII. He may also be sold by process of law for the satisfaction of the debts of a living, or the debts and bequests of a deceased master, at the suit of creditors or legatees.[12]

VIII. A slave cannot be a party before a judicial tribunal, in any species of action, against his master, no matter how atrocious may have been the injury received from him.[13]

IX. Slaves cannot redeem themselves, nor obtain a change of masters, though cruel treatment may have rendered such change necessary for their personal safety.[14]

X. Slaves being objects of property, if injured by third persons, their owners may bring suit, and recover damages, for the injury.[15]

XL. Slaves can make no contract.[16]

XII. Slavery is hereditary and perpetual.[17]

This former American system of oppression is a model of the slave laws found in ancient Rome. The American and British method of captivity, however, unlike Roman enslavement, allowed only people of African descent to be bound and reduced to an inhuman status. While Roman history records having a slave system that prohibited the family institution, a person's race was not the determination for slavery. "Roman slaves were men and women taken prisoners when Rome conquered more and more territory. Their children helped ensure a continuing supply. Citizens at the bottom of the socio-economic ladder who got so far into debt they could not get out lost their freedom and became slaves along with all members of their families. Unwanted children in Rome, especially girls, were abandoned at birth: many were picked up by passers-by and sold as slaves."[18]

Roman slaves could not lawfully wed, but some owners within the Empire, with sizeable numbers of slaves, allowed cohabitation and intercourse. Every child conceived by any slave parent was a slave; this became a standard for increasing the number of slaves owned by a slaveholder. This aspect of slavery was a total denial of God's designed order for the family. When the government outlaws the divinely inherited rights of marriage, it is a desecration of God's first institution.

The legal condition of the slaves established by Roman law was described in Taylor's *Elements on Civil Law p.429*, Cooper's *Justinian*, p. 411 And Stroud's *Sketches*, p. 21, and were as follows:

> .... *pro nullis, pro mortuis, pro quadrupedibus*; nay, were in a much worse state than any cattle whatsoever. They had no head in the state, no name, no title, or register; they were not capable of being injured; nor could they take by purchase or descent; they had no heirs, and therefore could make no will; they were not entitled to the rights and considerations of matrimony, and therefore had no relief in case of adultery; nor were they proper objects of cognation or affinity, but of quasi-cognation only; they could be sold, transferred, or pawned, as goods or personal estate, for goods they were, and as such they were esteemed; they might be tortured for evidence, punished at the discretion of their lord, and even put to death by his authority; together with many other civil incapacities which I have no room to enumerate.[19]

Roman Law served as a pattern for the courts and legislatures of the United States when creating regulations for African-American families and marriages. "In the centuries that followed the fall of the Roman Empire, marriage was a mess. The Roman Catholic Church made a significant contribution to marriage in the Middle Ages, helping to define marriage as a matter of free consent between husband and wife rather than as a contract between families. Basing marriage on consent was an accomplishment for the church in the Middle Ages, but it also led to ambiguities, misunderstandings, and sometimes legal disputes."[20]

Dr. John Taylor's book, *Elements of the Civil Law,* provided the standard quote when interpreting Roman law concerning slave marriages. He said, "It is clear that slaves have no legal capacity to assent to any contract. With the consent of their master they may marry, and their moral power to agree to such a contract or connection- cannot be doubted; hut (shacking or cohabitating) while in a state of slavery it cannot produce any civil effect because slaves are deprived of all civil rights."[21] This form of marriage was the only option to which slaves were allowed to commit as they created their families.

After this time, "Marriage evolved as an alternative to constant warfare between the sexes. But it took centuries of struggle to transform marriage from a political arrangement made by patriarchs to a relationship based on the free choice and mutual consent of the couple."[22] History does record the lawful marriages of free African-Americans in the North and South. As America progressed as a nation, new laws were created to better assist with the management of slaves. The Slave Codes, prohibiting slaves from marrying without the consent of a slaveholder, began in 1724 and lasted in America until 1865. The origination of the Louisiana Law reads, "Article VIII of the Louisiana Black Code forbids marriages between slaves without the consent of the slave master. French Louisiana prohibits slaves from marrying without the permission of their owners."[23]

Slaves tried to legalize and sanction their marriages by having a description of their ceremony written up. Following is a written statement in 1844 for the wedding proof of Benjamin and Sara Mason. This copy of their marriage was found online in the archives of the Freeman Bureau of Records. Notice that it was by the consent of the master, who held no legal standing or authority in the state of the marriage.

Figure 15. The 1844 Documentation of Benjamin and Sara Mason's Slave Wedding[24]

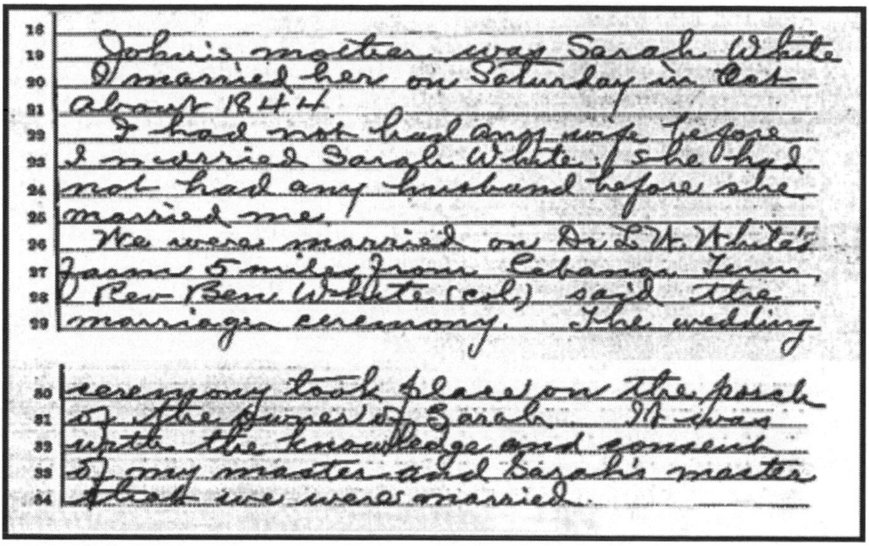
John's mother was Sarah White
I married her on Saturday in Oct
about 1844.
I had not had any wife before
I married Sarah White; she had
not had any husband before she
married me.
We were married on Dr. L.W. White's
farm 5 miles from Lebanon Tenn.
Rev Ben White (col.) said the
marriage ceremony. The wedding
ceremony took place on the porch
of the owner of Sarah. It was
with the knowledge and consent
of my master and Sarah's master
that we were married.

The owners who allowed this letter demonstrated a rarely seen compassion by slave owners who wanted to create better living conditions for their slaves. In most cases, this was an effort to make slaves loyal to the slave system, as the slaves, in turn, would feel a need to reward owners for his/her exceeding kindness. Owners believed that giving slaves a relationship that required commitment would keep them from running away or leaving their families. Slave masters knew this letter held no authority, and owners held the privileges within the Slave Codes to refuse or permit an enslaved couple the right to marry. The most scrupulous owners realized the need for marriage among slaves and gave their permission, while others among the unprincipled owners did not. When slaves wanted to wed, the male slave was both required to ask their own masters first, and then to ask the woman's master for permission to marry his slave. The following is an example from The Narrative of Lunsford Lane:

> I next went to her master, Mr. Boylan, and asked him, according to the custom, if I might "marry this woman." His reply was, "Yes, if you will behave yourself." I told him I would. "And make her behave herself?" To this I also assented; and then proceeded to ask the approbation of my

> master, which was granted. So in May 1828, I was bound as fast in wedlock as a slave can be.[25]

The act of behaving of as slave couple was to remain subservient to their masters in everything as a family. When finding God's grace in all the situations of life, we must look beyond the surface of an event to see the providential work of God. This law was at least an acknowledgment that slaves had the rights of a relationship similar to marriage according to the Slave Codes. These codes gave credence to the humanity of slaves by acknowledging their need for spousal and family companionship, while continuing to define them as chattel.

Men and women of all races are designed for intimacy with people of the opposite sex. Solomon teaches us in Proverbs that the marriage institution has satisfying qualities in the relationships of a husband and wife. "He who finds a wife finds a good thing and obtains favor from the LORD" (Prov.18: 22 ESV). It is a covenant to a partnership that provides a lifelong spouse and a companion which whom you can share all the blessings and hardships of life.

Modern sociologists suggest, "During slavery, African-Americans had no legal means of creating a family, but this did not mean that they weren't families in every other sense of the word. And today, as noted above, many African-American children live in a 'family' that is not composed of either biological or legal ties."[26]

Abolitionist Thomas Morris said, "Moreover, by facilitating the transfer of slaves by deed, auction, mortgage, or will, the law normalized masters' lack of concern for slave families, and readily allowed for the annihilation of slave family structures."[27] Although the slave family in many ways did not exist, the family was as crucial to slaves as it was to their White masters. For financial reasons, male and female slaves were often paired to live together and marry according to the plantation rules established by slaveholders. Planters realized slaves progressed and worked better when allowed to have families, with the promise that good behavior would ensure their family would never be sold or separated. Slaves who were committed to quasi-marriages were happier and usually had large families. This served planters with the same economic benefits of breeding to enlarge their plantations without the stress associated with normal slave reproduction.

Prop. XI: Slaves Can Not Make Marital Contracts

Proposition XI was the most devastating of the Slave Codes on the daily life of men, women and children for whom it was designed to control. The inability to make contracts had far-reaching consequences into their powerlessness to manage any business. Making legal agreements between persons and doing business to care for themselves and their families was, and still is, essential in life. When investigating the ways this law put slaves into a hopeless situation, it is clear that the ability to acquire a marriage contract was beyond their grasp. Prop. XI established the unscrupulous principle that slaves could only live together as man and woman, thereby setting the stage for cohabitation.

The heritage of forced cohabitation during slavery has influenced the past and present rates of African-Americans' marital stability. Some researchers have found that the residuals of culture and oppression are still attached to modern-day African-Americans. The cohabiting family structure is one of the traumas from captivity found among African-American families today. There are risks associated with cohabitating before marriage, and yet the majority of couples today choose this route. The following list is a set of risk factors that are likely to occur because families cohabitate: 1) Husbands and wives have a poor relationship with each other and their children. 2) Children are unable to enjoy family stability when they are not born into a married family. 3) Children are less likely to thrive in complex households. 3) Growing up outside of an intact marriage increases the likelihood that children will divorce or become unwed parents. 4) Cohabitating couples build less wealth than married couples. 5) Children who live with two married parents enjoy better physical health. 6) Cohabitation is associated with higher levels of psychological problems among children. 7) Boys raised in cohabitating families are more likely to engage in delinquent behavior. 8) Cohabitating women are at a higher risk of experiencing domestic violence.[28] Each of the tenets of this risk factor has a chance to be found in the lives of cohabitating families.

Prop. XI made it clear that cohabitation was not the functional equivalent of marriage, but cohabitating was the norm for African-American families under the slave systems. Judge George Stroud interpreted this law and reported, "Besides such of the laws referred to under Proposition V. ... it may be added, that a slave cannot even contract matrimony the association which takes place among slaves and is called marriage, being properly designated by the word contubernial a relation which has no sanctity, and to which no civil rights are attached."[29] Prop. V of the Slave Codes took from slaves all rights to own property, whether it was wildlife, homes, land, or even relationships with other people, such as family members. When we are consumed and worried about material things, scriptures teach us, "The earth is the LORD's and the fullness thereof, the world and those who dwell therein" (Psalms 24:1 ESV). Although African-American slaves were deprived of ownership of material things and family members during their life of slavery, we recognize that the slaveholders were not the real owners, either. God is the owner of all our relationships and material things.

What a beautiful world this would be if every individual lived as if God owned everything. Perhaps this would allow all humans to have everything in common. Having everything in common was the goal of the apostles in the era of the first church. Prop. XI removed the abilities of slaves to negotiate and contract themselves to get ahead in life. This law forced them into a life of poverty and illiteracy without the support of the judicial system for advancement. Their inability to make contracts took away all of their decision-making power.

Figure 16. Rev. William Goodell Abolitionists 1792-1878 [30]

William Goodell's book provides an interpretation of the slave laws listed by Judge George Stroud. In *The American Slave Code In Theory And Practice: Its Distinctive Features Shown By Its Statutes, Judicial Decisions, & Illustrative Facts*, we find the following citations and interpretations of the United States Slave Codes. Prop. XI "Slaves can make no contract."[31] When considering the marriage possibilities of slaves, William Goodell interpreted the No Contract Law as it relates to the conditions of slaves for marriage. He said, "A slave cannot even contract matrimony the association which takes place among slaves, and is called marriage, being properly designated by the word contubernial a relation which has no sanctity, and to which no civil rights are attached."[32]

Contracts are legally binding when entered into by two or more parties; the law promises to enforce all contracts certified by a notary or a witness to the agreement. Over the last four centuries, contracts have taken on many different methods. There have been personal, written, handshakes, verbal and court validated contracts. Contracts are binding to all parties, regardless of error or lack of understanding. Once the agreement has been sealed, by whatever means, the contracting parties agree.

Such was the case in an 1810 decision involving Fletcher vs. Peck. The dispute was over the purchase and sale of 35 million acres of land that were later used for the expansion of slavery. Supreme Court Chief Justice John Marshall ruled, "The contract might have been accomplished by bribery. It may have contravened the will of the majority of White Georgians. But the sale to the investors' land companies was a sale of property all the same, and property rights, by the chief justice's interpretation of the contract clause of the Constitution, were absolute."[33]

This land decision rendered an overarching effect on all property in an era where personal property served as a motivating backdrop for land expansion that was needed to produce more cotton. Contracts were necessary for business transactions, and slaves could have no business. Slavers made deals everywhere for the sale and purchase of slaves that could happen anywhere, from trading blocks to local churches following Sunday morning worship services.

Contubernium (The Marriage of Slaves)

The Slave Codes did more than establish the status of slaves as non-human and as objects of property. Prop. X. stated, "Slaves being objects of property, if injured by third persons, their owners, may bring suit, and recover damages for the injury."[34] The ability to make contracts would give slaves capacity to make binding agreements. A slave with negotiating power could make deals that would not be in the best interest of his master or that could possibly arrange his freedom. Prohibiting slaves from making contracts would affect every area of a slave's life, including his marriage and family.

Allowing couples to live together would remove the disagreement between abolitionists and slave owners regarding the moral state of slave families and marriages. Contubernium answered the question when, "The slave is one who is in the power of a master to whom he belongs. How, then, can the slave marry?"[35] The term contubernial defined the relationship of slave marriages, according to slave laws. It means to live together in a tent or dwelling without the commitment of a legal marriage.

The Free Online Dictionary provides the following definition of marriage by two Roman slaves or with a free person. "Slaves had no civil state, their marriages, although valid according to natural law, when contracted with the consent of their masters, and when there was no legal bar to them, yet were without civil effects; they having none except what arose from natural law; a marriage of this kind was called contubernial."[36]

Adeline Willis, who in 1937 was the oldest living slave in Wilkes County, Georgia, provided an account of her slave wedding to her husband Lewis when she was fourteen years old:

> When we married, my Marster and Mistess said they didn't care, and Lewis's Master and Mistress said they didn't care, so they all met up at my White folks' house and had us come in and told us they didn't mind our marryin'. My Marster said, 'Now you and Lewis wants to marry and there ain't no objections so go on and jump over the broom stick together and you is married'. That was all there was to it and we was married. I lived on with my White folks and he lived on with his and kept comin' to see me jest like he had done when he was a courtin'. He never brought me any presents 'cause he didn't have no money to buy them with, but he was good to me and that was what counted.[37]

Contubernium, or a slave's marriage, placed them in a better situation than couples who just got together, because it was a consented marriage with the approval of the master. Most slave couples were married realizing that natural law dictated a license that superseded the government or the owner's permission. "The term natural law is derived from the Roman term jus naturale."[38] The option to live together as a couple needed the approval by a master. According to natural law, slaves were provided an unwritten body of universal moral principles. Slave believed this inspired the "ethical and legal norms which human conduct is evaluated and governed."[39] Also, natural laws became synced to principles inherent in human nature that exist regardless of whether or not governments recognize or enforce them. Their commitment to the natural laws fulfilled the need for companionship between men and women, and the need for emotional and physical love.

A slave's master held the authority to recognize or refuse contuberium, completely controlling whether or not a slave couple could share a life together. This form of marriage was no more than living together by mutual law or, in other words, to the hut. The "hut" was a term referenced in the Slave Codes that referred to a man or woman who moved into a shelter with someone of the opposite sex with the intent of living without the responsibilities of home life.

Although slaves had no formal education or learning, they had the moral awareness to understand the purpose of having legal marriages. Nevertheless, they possessed no civil rights to sanction their marriages. They only had the right to live together, or cohabitate, which required no civil rights. William Goodell continued this explanation of how Slave Codes defined marriage: "It is clear that slaves have no legal capacity to assent to any contract. With the consent of their master they may marry, and their moral power to agree to such a contract or connection cannot be doubted; but while in a state of slavery it cannot produce any civil effect, because slaves are deprived of all civil rights."[40]

According to post-enslavement civil rights laws in 1865, it became "illegal to discriminate on the basis of race, color, religion, sex, age, handicap, or national origin. The right to marry requires citizenship in the United States."[41] The authors of United States Constitution implemented the Bill of Rights without protecting the rights of African-American slaves. "The first ten amendments to the U.S. Constitution ratified in 1791… guarantee certain fundamental rights and privileges of individuals, including freedom of religion, speech, press, and assembly; guarantee of a speedy jury trial in criminal cases; and protection against excessive bail and Cruel and

Unusual Punishment."[42] The majority of these principles were withheld from African-Americans until the middle of the twentieth century.

God never willed men to enslave other men using the cruelties of the American slave system. Scripture confirmed the slaveholder's status, but without the freedom that comes from Jesus, his dependency on sin made him a slave to the sin associated with slavery. Jesus clarified this statement when he said, "Truly, truly, I say to you, everyone who practices sin is a slave to sin. The slave does not remain in the house forever; the son remains forever. So, if the Son sets you free, you will be free indeed" (John 8:34-36 ESV). Jesus came to provide freedom, but the laws that controlled slavery in America legislated that African slaves would remain physical slaves for life.

A Marriage Without Spousal Rights Decreed

Fundamental to African-American slavery practices in America was the intentional destructive effort to eradicate God's universal design that each person is linked or related to a family. How bewildered is the heart, mind and will of the man who cannot lead his wife, lead his children or provide for his family? Marriage and family specialist, W. Bradford Wilcox, through comprehensive research discovered, "Marriage increases the likelihood that fathers and mothers have healthy relationships with their children."[43] Parenting is a natural expectation for couples that have children, and parents have an inherent need to protect and provide for their needs. Downhearted is the heart of the woman who cannot submit to her own husband, raise her children and nourish her family. "Marriage and a normative commitment to marriage fosters high-quality relationships between adults, as well as between parents and children."[44]

Uncle Shang Harris was 97 years old at the time of his ex-slave interview. He remembered vividly his time as a slave in Franklin County, Georgia and told Vanessa Bell (his interviewer) about the complications he faced as a slave without a marriage and family. He recalled:

> Lots o' folks did sell dey (they) niggers, and sometimes dey'd (they'd) take yo' chile (children) and go to Alabama or Virginia, and you wouldn't never see him no mo'. Dey kept de dark ones together and de bright ones together. Hit (it) didn't make no diffunce (difference) 'bout families. Dey warn't (weren't) no marryin' 'mongst de niggers way

> back in time. De marsters (master) wanted you to increase to give 'em more niggers, but dey didn't had no marryin'. I had three wives and I got my fourth one now. Dey all treated me good.[45]

According to Uncle Shang Harris, his family life was only good for increasing the number of slaves for his master. What is a marriage when a husband and wife cannot perform the divinely designed duties that are essential in the marriage relationship? God created marriage between a man and a woman for the success of the family. Scripture best defines the roles of husbands and wives in Ephesians 5. When providing the woman with instructions for marital happiness and success, the passage says, "Wives, submit to your own husbands, as to the Lord. For the husband is the head of the wife even as Christ is the head of the church, his body, and is himself its Savior. Now as the church submits to Christ, so also wives should submit in everything to their husbands" (Eph. 5: 22-24 ESV). The wife's submission to her husband is God's way of fulfilling both his and her needs. This suggests a wife gives the husband leadership of his home. She builds his ego (self-worth) so that he desires to be the man in her life. He becomes driven to protect, provide and love her as she remains in submission to him. Scripture encourages the husband to lead his wife with love. It states:

> Husbands, love your wives, as Christ loved the church and gave himself up for her, that he might sanctify her, having cleansed her by the washing of water with the word, so that he might present the church to himself in splendor, without spot or wrinkle or any such thing, that she might be holy and without blemish. In the same way, husbands should love their wives as their own bodies. He who loves his wife loves himself. For no one ever hated his own flesh, but nourishes and cherishes it (Eph. 5: 25- 29 ESV).

Husbands are to love their wives with the unconditional agape love of God. When a husband loves his wife in the same way that he would his own body, she will be cherished and nourished by him; she will respond to him in a way that meets his needs to the best of her ability. Taking away the rights to function as husbands and wives would leave slave couples unfulfilled in all their marital commitments.

All slave marriages knew their allegiance belonged first to their owner. Goodell explained that the roles and responsibilities of a slave husband and wife could never be fulfilled toward each other when their ultimate responsibility was to meet the needs of their owner. He said, "The obligations of marriage are evidently inconsistent with the conditions of slavery, and cannot be performed by a slave. The husband promises to protect his wife and provide for her. The wife vows to be the helpmeet of her husband. They mutually promise to live with and cherish each other, till parted by death."[46]

The Slave Codes were designed to interrupt any intimacy between slave couples that would assist them in developing an independence from others and dependence on each other. The law takes from the couple their rights of manhood and womanhood. Any marriage with a husband who cannot protect or provide for his wife is considered a dysfunctional spouse, and the marriage will soon dissolve. In the wedding vows, couples made all the promises of free men and women with every intention to fulfill the commitments. "But what can such promises by slaves mean? The 'legal relation of master and slave' renders them void!"[47] Even though a master could regulate most areas in their slaves' lives, no master or owner could control the hearts of two people in love. A heart of humility and the need for belonging made slave couples happy; it was all they had to give each other. Marriage laws served to establish legal relationships and contracts; but for the slave, there was only a natural moral law that solidified their marital relations.

Proponents for enslavement continued their arguments against the normalization of anything that might endanger slavery. The most favorable inference from this decision was that the joint action of master and slave can legalize a slave's marriage. Each slave state enforced this law while allowing owners to give consent to the marriages of slaves. The only legality for slave marriages was in the permission for marriage given by the master who determined the contents and made up what he wanted for his slave property. In essence, an owner could do as he chose with his property. Goodell continued, "What, then, can the marriage vows of slaves mean? The laws annulling slave marriage are explicit, as has been seen. The corresponding position of the judiciary, as attested by the Maryland Reports, has been adduced. Will anyone inquire whether or not, in this particular, Code is a 'dead letter.'"[48] Goodell contended that no one would pay any attention to this law, so why present it at all. An examination of the meaning of this statute revealed that it is a dead letter or rule, and the people cannot comply with its content because they do not know its content. Simply put, why call the relationship of slaves a marriage when they have no rights as husbands, wives, and parents?

The question now takes on a different issue. Goodell asked, "...whether the institution of marriage among slaves may not have survived the annulling action of the legislatures and the courts? As a recognized legal relation, most assuredly the marriage relation among slaves does not and cannot exist."[49]

The letter of the law prohibited the legal marriage contracts for men and women in slavery; however, the spirit of the law allowed the owner to have complete oversight over his property. Within the institution of slavery, with the consent and authority of slave owners, marriages existed. But outside of slavery, within the laws of society, marriages between slaves was not legal. Slave Codes were confusing and not uniformly adhered to, because the codes left all to the discretion to owners as to how strictly they would enforce the codes. By some concepts, the codes state, "And no master shall unreasonably deny marriage to his Negro with one of the same nation, any law, usage or custom to the contrary notwithstanding."[50]

Another tenet of the Slave Code stated: "The slave is not ranked among sentient beings, but among things, and things are not married."[51] Consequently, because the law did not recognize slave marriages, not many seventeenth to nineteenth-century owners made a diligent effort to keep marriages and families together. However, the slaves took their commitments to marriage extremely seriously, regardless of the method of their marriages. Some slaves were fortunate enough to be married in a church, while others decided to cohabitate with a person of their choice. Some masters allowed their slaves to make formal announcements of marriage, which were often followed by a reception with their friends and family present. However, there were those slaveholders who chose a partner for their slaves and forced them to cohabitate without celebration. Nevertheless, when couples were allowed to celebrate marriage with a wedding ceremony, they knew they were not legally married. "Slaves were not entitled to the conditions of matrimony, and therefore they had no relief in cases of adultery; nor were they the proper objects of cognation or affinity, but of quasi-cognation only."[52]

Although marriages were not permissible, most slave communities tried to keep their moral standards by requiring cohabitating couples to make a commitment to their methods of marriage. In this way, they could consider themselves as husband and wife. Everyone was forced to endorse contuberium as a valid marriage after the order of natural law. For the slave community, the sharing of a tent became the norm. The community of slaves validated the marriages of enslaved African-Americans by treating the couple as though they were married. "Many slave masters encouraged slaves to choose a spouse and tried to keep families together. A slave was less likely to run away if he or she had a spouse and children. However, when there were bills to pay, or when the property was divided up at the time of the slave master's death, families were broken up. Slave owners might also sell a spouse to punish an unruly slave."[53]

Weddings without a celebration for Africans "contrasted sharply with customs in Africa, where marriage was a religious rite often accompanied by weeks of celebration."[54] On plantations where owners sanctioned marriage among slaves, most plantation slaves developed a family structure that owners were unable to control. Ira Berlin, author of *Many Thousands Gone: The First Two Centuries of Slavery in North America* said:

> The recognition of the slave family also provided a modicum of protection for slave women-at least married women-as planters came to understand that violation of the sanctity of the marriage bed wreaked havoc on plantation discipline. Most importantly, the emergence of the slave family created a powerful source of opposition within the plantation, as a cadre of respected elders bearing the titles of mother and father, aunt and uncle took their place at the top of the plantation order.[55]

What would our world be like without any laws to govern the actions of ungodly men? This chapter has been an example of how poorly men legislate when God's principles are left out of their decision-making, specifically as it concerned the marriages and families of slaves. When total power is left in the hands of one man over another man's life, the outcome is usually to the detriment of the person who has no authority. We would do well to leave the power over human beings in the hands of a Holy God who will establish laws in the hearts of men to benefit all men. King David, a man after God's heart, reported this in Scripture. He said, "Then David said to Gad, 'I am in great distress. Let us fall into the hand of the LORD, for his mercy is great; but let me not fall into the hand of man'" (2 Samuel 24: 14

ESV). The authority given to slaveholders found in the Slave Codes to give and take a life should never find its way into the hands of sinful men. The Marriage Covenant, as defined in God's natural law, should have been the guide for African-American family legislations within the slave codes of America.

Chapter 6

Sexual Immorality Legalized for Slaves

'Twas Grace that brought us safe thus far...
and Grace will lead us home."

The Lord is close to the brokenhearted and saves those who are crushed in spirit. Psalm 34:18. ESV.

Couples Defenseless Against Sexual Abuse and Assaults

When studying American history, very little has been written concerning the centuries of institutionalized assaults on African-American families. Henry Bibb, in writing his autobiography entitled *Narrative of the Life and Adventures of Henry Bibb, An American Slave 1849*, addressed his broken heart over the moment that he was sold off and torn apart from his wife. He said, "A poor slave's wife can never be true to her husband contrary to the will of her master. She can neither be pure nor virtuous, contrary to the will of her master. She dares not refuse to be reduced to a state of adultery at the will of her master."[1]

There is no doubt that there were many broken hearts among enslaved men and women over their inability to protect the sexual purity of themselves and their loved ones. Within the following Slave Codes and their amendments is found the legalization of sexual immorality in the lifestyles of a slave.

V. Slaves have no legal rights to property in things, real or personal; but whatever they may acquire belongs, in point of law, to their masters.[2]

VIII. A slave cannot be a party before a judicial tribunal, in any species of action, against his master, no matter how atrocious may have been the injury received from him.[3]

X. Slaves being objects of property, if injured by third persons, their owners may bring suit, and recover damages, for the injury.[4]

XL. Slaves can make no contract.[5]

Daniel Dulany, a slave-owner, judge, Attorney General and member of the legislature of Maryland from 1722 to 1742, recorded his interpretation of the Slave Codes in his book of reports regarding the legal sexual disadvantages of slaves. Dulany explained, "A slave has never maintained an action against the violator of his bed. A slave is not admonished for incontinence, or punished for fornication or adultery; never prosecuted for bigamy, or petty treason for killing a husband being a slave, any more than admitted to an appeal for murder.[6]

The legalization approving sexual immorality and criminal actions among slaves would serve as a bridge to immorality in their families and marriages. This legislative bridge would, for generations, serve as a major block for the enslaved who wanted to establish healthy marriages and families. When laws approve actions that are considered criminal acts, immorality becomes a lifestyle for the people who are forced to obey the rules of ungodly legislation. Under this law, slave couples found it very difficult to lead healthy marriages, because it removed the essentials for a happy marriage. Healthy marriages require faithfulness to each other and the protection of a spouse against sexual intruders, even when the relationship is a quasi-marriage. William Goodell said, "It severs the plighted pair, at the will of their masters, occasionally, or forever! The innocent 'legal relation' of slave-ownership does or permits all this, and without forfeiting clerical favor, or a high seat in the Church, or in the Senate, or Presidential chair."[7] Goodell makes the point that the sins of slavery that were allowed by the American government, the Kingdom of God prohibited. The Bible states "now the works of the flesh are evident: sexual immorality, impurity, sensuality, idolatry, sorcery, enmity, strife, jealousy, fits of anger, rivalries, dissensions, divisions, envy, drunkenness, orgies, and things like these. I warn you, as I warned you before, that those who do such things will not inherit the kingdom of God" (Gal. 5:19-21 ESV).

The above propositions and their interpretations are amongst the most devastating of all the Slave Codes as it pertains to the marriages and family structures of African-American slaves. The proposition is in violation of Scripture, and put slave marriages in a defiled status with God: "Let marriage be held in honor among all, and let the marriage bed be undefiled, for God will judge the sexually immoral and adulterous" (Hebrew 13:4 ESV). There are several tenets of this law, which created a legal forum for sexual infidelity among marriages in the slave community. Its most damaging effect on female slaves was the ability of any man to sexually abuse or rape any African-American woman without fear of legal prosecution. Her inability to defend herself placed her in a constant position to be the victim of sexual assault, at any time.

Ronald Mincy, Professor of Social Policy and Social Work Practice at the Columbia University School of Social Work, made several observations about the consequences of sexual exploitations to slave marriages. He said, "The relationships between African-American men and African-American women began to undergo lots of stress during slavery. After all, men could not protect women from sexual assault during slavery. The meaning and relevance of marriage were ridiculous under slavery. The basic conditions of marriage were undermined during slavery."[8]

According to the American Psychological Association, many mental and emotional traumas develop when a person is the victim of sexual abuse. "Sexual abuse is the unwanted sexual activity with a perpetrator using force, making threats or taking advantage of a victim not able to give consent. Most victims and perpetrators know each other. Immediate reactions to sexual abuse include shock, fear or disbelief. Long-term symptoms include anxiety, fear or post-traumatic stress disorder."[9]

There must have been psychological damage to the psyche of female slaves who were the constant victim of sexual abuse. This caused generations of their descendants to suffer from their traumatic experiences. Likewise, African-American men in the twenty-first century often struggle mentally with the shame of having male ancestors who were forced to tolerate the abuse of their women and daughters. The limited knowledge of how African-American men and women handled these sexual violations has left room for much-undesired speculation.

The residuals of pain between couples over the inabilities of male ancestors to protect their female family members from mental, physical, and sexual abuse are seen in gender relationships today. This topic has created much confusion, tension and conflict in the bonds of present-day African-American men and women, because sexual purity is highly valued, but seldom achieved. Also, sexual infidelity is one of the most challenging problems to overcome in relationships, because sex is the highest level of intimacy reserved for spouses. As a result, marriages that find themselves confronted with adultery, unfaithfulness and disloyalty are never the same, and often end in divorce.

W.E.B. Du Bois, in the *American Negro Family,* compared the social factors of African-Americans in his day (1908) to the social elements of slaves in America. He discovered the following similar traits in both slave and free Negro communities: "1. No legal marriage; 2. No legal family; 3. No legal control over children."[10] His final discovery found: "Sexual immorality is probably the greatest single plague spot among Negro Americans, and its greatest cause is slavery and the present utter disregard of an African-American woman's virtue and self-respect, both in law court and custom in the South."[11] In spite of the sexual abuses incurred by African-American couples, most attempted to maintain a morally pure lifestyle in a climate of sexual philandering.

> The assumption that Black women were by nature sexually promiscuous was widespread among Whites. Such ideas would continue long after slavery, justifying the rape of Black women with impunity in most southern states. In Mississippi in the late nineteenth century, it was not a criminal act to rape a Black girl over the age of ten. In an ideological climate that attributed hypersexuality to Black women, some slave women did not resist their master's advances, because they knew it would be futile to do so. Others sought the master's advances because of the prestige or material advantages that such a relationship might bring. The historical record also discloses cases of genuine affection between a master and his female slave.[12]

Robert Staples, one of the foremost authorities on Black sexuality, is professor emeritus of sociology at the University of California, San Francisco. He explained, "Due to the sexual vulnerability of Black women in the South, the common American stereotype that emerged was that of a sexual seductress. This was in strong contrast to the Southern White woman as sexually pure, a fact that led some behavioral scientists to conclude that Afro-American women tend to draw the un-sublimated sexual feelings of Euro-American males."[13] In contrast, within the slave communities,

African-American couples who desired to find sanity in their marriages held to the principle that husbands and wives established a mental guard against all sexual aggressors. Any man accosting a slave woman did so with the understanding that she was a person practicing sexual integrity. This moral value, which was highly emphasized and practiced within the slave community, was the only safeguard for the enslaved female. Her man learned to trust her, because he knew that she would never, without strong compulsion, give her body to anyone. However, for many, the overwhelming pull of human depravity and sexual desire was too much for them to overcome. Often times this resulted in providing sex for favors.

W.E.B Dubois implied that sexual relationships were not a subject for everyday conversation, but for their value to the Negro, sex either corrupts or makes stronger:

> That while the sexual appetite is the most easily abused of all human desires and most deadly when perverted, that nevertheless, it is a legitimate, beneficent desire when normal, and that no civilization can long survive which stigmatizes it as essentially nasty and only to be discussed in shamefaced whispers. The Negro attitude in these matters is in many respects healthier and more reasonable. Their sexual passions are strong and frank, but they are, despite example and temptation, only to a limited degree perverted or merely commercial.[14]

As previously stated, a healthy sexual relationship in the life of twenty-first century African-Americans has been determined as one of the top reasons for marital satisfaction. The Slave Codes put a strain on both the husband's and the wife's responsibility to fulfill their partner's sexual needs. Scripture speaks to the intimate duties needed by husbands and wives, and what happens when the desire goes unfulfilled.

> The husband should give to his wife her conjugal rights, and likewise the wife to her husband. For the wife does not have authority over her own body, but the husband does. Likewise, the husband does not have authority over his own body, but the wife does. Do not deprive one another, except perhaps by agreement for a limited time, that you

> may devote yourselves to prayer; but then come together again, so that Satan may not tempt you because of your lack of self-control (1 Cor. 7:3 ESV).

In essence, the Slave Codes removed any practice or rights to sexual virtue for the enslaved. How tragic to the race of any people when their women and girls become the prey of anyone who chooses to take advantage of them sexually without suffering adverse consequences. These particular Slave Codes were written for the benefit of White men to do as they pleased with enslaved women. "Slaves were not entitled to the conditions of matrimony, and therefore they had no relief in cases of adultery; nor were they the proper objects of cognation or affinity, but of quasi-cognation only."[15]

Figure 17. Josiah Henson Bought his Freedom and Escaped With his Slave Family[16]

Slave Josiah Henson was born in 1789, and he recalled the physical and psychological effect that an assault on his mother by an overseer created for his family. He said:

> The only incident I can remember, which occurred while my mother continued on N.' s farm, was the appearance of my father one day, with his head bloody and his back lacerated. He was in a state of great excitement, and though it was all a mystery to me at the age of three or four years, it was explained at a later period, and I understood that he had been suffering the cruel penalty of the Maryland law for beating a White man. His right ear had been cut off close to his head, and he assault on my mother, and this was his punishment.[17]

Here is seen the treatment of a man who was trying to protect his wife from being victimized by another man. Only among slave men was it not considered admirable to rescue one's spouse in the event an assailant abused her. According to Josiah Henson, this was a life-changing event for his father, and it forever changed their family structure. He continued:

> Furious at such treatment, my father became a different man, and was so morose, disobedient, and intractable, that Mr. N. determined to sell him. He accordingly parted with him, not long after, to his son, who lived in Alabama; and neither my mother nor I, ever heard of him again. He was naturally, as I understood afterwards from my mother and other persons, a man of amiable temper, and of considerable energy of character; but it is not strange that he should be essentially changed by such cruelty and injustice under the sanction of law.[18]

Henson does not mention whether the assault was of a sexual nature, but many sexual assaults on the wives of slaves by overseers were the cause for extreme acts of violence by slave men. This was dangerously outside of the will of God. Many slave men lost their lives because they opposed their owners forcing their wives into committing marital infidelity.

> The African-American male could do nothing to protect his wife from the sexual advances of any White man. Most Whites, however, realized that a liaison with a slave's wife could be dangerous. Occasionally, enslaved husbands would kill White slaveholders and others for such acts. The women had no choice but to submit to the sexual advances of White men and as a general understanding to divulge the action meant harm to her family."[19]

Women who resisted could be beaten, or even killed, for not complying with the wishes of their owners. The brutalities of the American slave system serve as a reminder of how depraved the human heart can become in its abuse of fellow humans. "Sexual abuse was not confined only to female slaves. The males were treated as studs, shuffled from plantation to plantation to mate with slave women and produce children who would also be legally defined as slaves."[20] When masters sexually suffered from gay and lesbian tendencies, slaves would have been subjected to these behaviors. "For their women exchanged natural relations for those that are contrary to nature; and the men likewise gave up natural relations with women and were consumed with passion for one another, men committing shameless acts with men and receiving in themselves the due penalty for their error. And since they did not see fit to acknowledge God, God gave them up to a debased mind to do what ought not to be done" (Rom. 1: 26-28 ESV).

The Bible says a great deal about sexual immorality, because unhealthy sexual lifestyles consumed the biblical world. Paul encouraged Christians to pursue holiness by controlling their sexual appetites. "For this is the will of God, your sanctification: that you should abstain from sexual immorality; that each of you should know how to possess his own vessel in sanctification and honor, not in passion of lust, like the Gentiles who do not know God; that no one should take advantage of and defraud his brother in this matter, because the Lord *is* the avenger of all such, as we also forewarned you and testified. For God did not call us to uncleanness, but in holiness"[21] (1Thess. 4: 3-7 NKJV).

Having this law, that approved of promiscuous sex, violated the relationships of married slave couples by eliminating the physical consequences of adultery, and encouraging sexual exploitations outside of marriage. It further removed the sanctity of the intimate relationship among married couples, which is designed by God for His glory and the satisfaction of marital unions. Any sexual encounter outside of the marriage relationship is a cause for disparagement among couples, and today, it is the cause of many marital disruptions that often lead to divorces. Paul encouraged the Corinthian church to, "Flee from sexual immorality. Every other sin a person commits is outside the body, but the sexually immoral person sins against his own body. Or do you not know that your body is a temple of the Holy Spirit within you, whom you have from God? You are not your own, for you were bought with a price. So glorify God in your body" (1 Cor. 6:18-20 ESV). Sexual sins are physical acts, which affect both the victim and offender spiritually.

The consequence of any act of sex abuse is devastating to victims and families. Charles Swindoll, in his counseling manual *Insight for Living, Counseling Insights: A Biblical Perspective on Caring for People* said, "Sexual abuse always has an enormous impact. It teaches the victim: that love and affection can only be 'bought' by giving oneself away sexually he or she has value only as a thing or object, and that powerlessness is a way of life that relationships can only bring betrayal."[22] Slave victims and families were defenseless against the perpetrators; therefore, they could not follow the suggestions of today's counseling professionals who advise victims to fight back for healing to take place. A defense involves several methods of fighting, such as through the legal systems or confronting the violator with their wrongs. When sexual abuse occurs in a family, the entire family feels victimized and needs healing.

African-American slave marriages suffered physically and spiritual whenever an owner exercised their legal power and took away the virtue of a couple. No male slave (father, husband, brother, son) had the legal authority to protect his female relative from any man (slave, free, or White) who chose to victimize his female family members. The slave code "forbids the slave to protect even himself. It clothes his master with authority to bid (make a slave whip or kill his own family members) he inflict deadly blows on the woman he has sworn to protect in marriage. It prohibits his possession of any property wherewith to sustain her, his labor and his hands it takes from him."[23]

Slavery and Sexual Bonding

Perhaps modern-day studies in neuroscience research can shed light on what was happening in the lives of enslaved individuals caught in the snare of many forced sexual partners. Neuroscientists Freda McKissic Bush and Joe S. McIlhaney Jr., in their book *Hooked: New Science on How Casual Sex is Affecting Our Children*, discovered new developmental studies in neuroscience revealing how the brain works in happy and unhappy relationships. Humans are designed to live in monogamous relationships, and more than one sexual partner during a lifetime hinders a person's ability to bond with his or her mate. Bush and McIlhaney stated, "From an experiment on hugging, we also know that oxytocin (fluid on the brain that stimulates sexual arousal) is naturally released in the brain after a twenty-second hug from a partner—sealing the bond between the huggers and triggering the brain's trust circuits."[24]

One parallel between the sexual promiscuity of slaves and the decline of marriage rates among African-Americans in 2017 can be found by observing today's African-Americans. It is not uncommon for present-day African-Americans to have numerous sexual partners. In *Race and Ethnicity in Fragile Families,* authors Robert A. Hummer and Erin R. Hamilton's research discovered that "out-of-wedlock births rate highest among African-Americans and least among Asian American women."[25] 2016 statistics reveal that 72% of African-American children are born to unwed mothers, while the statistics among the Hispanic population is 52%, among Asians is it 17%, and 29% among the White population. Could the many sexual traumas perpetrated on slaves have any bearing on these numbers? Perhaps this implies that there is a cultural trauma from slavery still existing among African-Americans. Bush and McIlhaney explained how sexual promiscuity with more than one sex partner causes brain damage. They discovered:

> An individual who becomes sexually involved, and breaks up and is sexually involved again, and who repeats this cycle, again and again, is in danger of negative emotional consequences. People who behave in this manner are acting against, almost fighting against, the way they are made to function. When connectedness and bonding form and then are quickly broken and replaced with another sexual relationship, it often actually causes damage to the brain's natural connecting or bonding mechanism.[26]

The above quote reinforces the concept that slaves suffered from a sexual pathology by having many sex partners, which in turn obstructed couple bonding. Sexual promiscuity has become a significant problem in the American culture, as evidenced in all the out-of-wedlock births experienced in each of the ethnicities. According to Bush and McIlhaney, when the members of a couple have multiple sexual experiences before marriage, there is an inability to connect and bond. Perhaps this helps to explain why the decline of marriage is so high among cohabiting and dating couples who have sex without commitment. Bush and McIlhaney have rejected the American social philosophy that suitors must sexually evaluate all possible marriage partners for compatibility before getting married.

The Sexual Revolution and African-American Marital Satisfaction

Slavery has not caused all of the marriage and family problems that create risk factors in African-Americans. Orlando Patterson, the author of *Rituals of Blood,* provided insight into one of the major tenets of the 1960s Sexual Revolution. "With the sexual revolution, men and women gained greater freedom to have sex outside of marriage. One result was a surge in unwed pregnancies and births."[27] Other researchers have revealed that non-marital births are highest for Africans-Americans and lowest for Asian-Americans. However, because of the huge population difference between African-American and White-American women, there are more White-American women having children out-of-wedlock. The Sexual Revolution receives credit for several of the risk factors for the marriage decline. The freedom for couples to cohabitate removed shame and seduced a society with the benefits of marriage without marital responsibilities:

> In the 1960s effective contraception (especially the birth control pill) made it possible for single individuals to engage in sexual activity without the complications of unwanted pregnancies. As peoples' attitudes toward non-marital sex became more liberal, increasing numbers of men and women chose to live together in sexually bonded relationships outside marriage.[28]

Contraceptives reduced the risks and consequences of sexual activity outside of marriage. This allowed cohabitating couples to reap the benefits of marriage without the responsibility. From the baby boomer generation until the present millennial generation, couples moved away from the values of their parents and became open to the cultural revolutions and movements of society. "Cohabitation has become very common. In fact, by the age of twenty, approximately the same numbers of young people live in cohabiting relationships as are married (20 percent)."[29]

Katherine Anderson, Don Browning and Brian Boyer are authors of the book and documentary "*Marriage-Just a Piece of Paper: Just a Piece of Paper.*" The research was done by the Religion, Culture, and Family Project located at the University of Chicago Their research found, "What we had in the late '60s into the '70s were the sexual revolution and the feminist movement. What happened inside marriage and for people considering marriage was a historically high emphasis on individual happiness and satisfaction out of marriage."[30] Don Browning, the leader of the research, revealed how the revolutions often influenced each other to have an impact on marital satisfaction. The Psychological Revolution (individualism) significantly influenced the movements of the Sexual and Feminist Revolutions. "Throughout history, marriage had always been more about duty, family, property, raising children. What we had in the late '60s into the '70s was a real reversal of that, marriage was about personal happiness and fulfillment more than anything else."[31]

These revolutions brought the glamorizing of free sex, the solicitation of sex or a pimp culture, and a general moral decline within the American culture. By the 1990s, the homosexual revolution began, and gay and lesbian couples started coming out of the closet. "The number of same-sex cohabitating couples recorded in the U.S. Census rose sharply."[32] The sexual revolutions of the 90s had a significant effect on the number of out-of-wedlock births for African-American families.

> For Afro-American young women, a worst-case scenario may have developed since the sixties. Their own sense of shame and of feeling stigmatized in having a child out-of-wedlock may have declined at a much faster rate than did the perception of stigma by the men whom they expected to marry. Indeed, these same men, while continuing to devalue women who had children out-of-wedlock, encouraged these women's "liberated" post-sixties view of out-of-wedlock childbearing.[33]

The 60s, in the midst of a sexual revolution in America, reveal a link between the irrational sex lives of promiscuous slaves and the senseless sex lifestyles of African-Americans in this era. Slavery produced the ideology that African-Americans have illegitimate children as a way of life. Now it has become the same for African-Americans in post-slavery. All slave marriages were lived in cohabitation, even when couples enjoyed a wedding ceremony designed for slaves. Their children were born out-of-wedlock because slave couples could not be legally married. Cohabitation, rather than providing benefits, produces problems. Consider the following facts from Bush and McIlhaney Jr.'s book:

1. Cohabiting relationships are not as permanent as marital relationships. The majorities of cohabiting couples either break up or marry within two years.[34]
2. Couples who live together and then get married face a greater chance of divorcing than couples who never cohabited.[35]
3. Cohabiting couples often get pregnant. Over a quarter of unmarried mothers are cohabiting at the time of their children's birth.[36]
4. Lack of commitment is a standard attitude in cohabiting relationships. Even when cohabiters have been together for extended periods of time, they often do not feel obligated to remain with a partner forever.[37]
5. Cohabiting couples experience violent behavior much more often than married couples. Cohabiting couples are also much more likely than married couples to say that arguments between them have become physical.[38]

Bush and McIlhaney Jr. provided a clear picture of the adverse effects that cohabitating has on families. Therefore, since slave families were all cohabiting family structures, these risk factors would apply to their lives. We need to ask ourselves that if being an enslaved people is the reason for African-American family dysfunctions, why have African-American marriages declined more the farther we are from slavery? Perhaps the answer is found in these revelations that took away respect for family roles and responsibilities from Black and White families alike. However, African-Americans were only two or three generations removed from slavery and had not long begun to adjust to having the legal, moral rights of marriage.

The culture shock of the sexual, psychological, marriage, feminist, drug and consumer revolutions overwhelmed all Americans, but was extremely difficult for African-American families and marriages. After 100 years,

African-Americans were still seeking to gain their part of the American dream and were highly motivated to excel. However, despite their best efforts, they remained disenfranchised. This era also brought the Civil Rights Movements, and most African-Americans felt the need for equality. With this desire in hand, they embraced these revolutions, even with all their negative qualities. While some liberties were gained, the cost was that it sent the family into dysfunction. This happened in part because they never entirely overcame the impact of slavery, and their adjustment into the American social and economic structures had failed to become a reality.

These revolutions allowed African-Americans to rebel against the unfair treatment they suffered at the hands of an unjust American society. The negative influences of the 60s revolutions did not improve the reputation of African-Americans as a people group, which prompted the stereotypes associated with slavery to remain intact. During the 60s and 70s, African-American women were reminded that they were loose like Jezebels, prostitutes, wanton wenches, and oversexed women. African-American men told that they were studs, animalistic brutes, oversexed, lazy, and thieves.

Many would suggest that 100 years is a sufficient amount of time to overcome 250 years of being labeled sexually promiscuous. The problem is, though, that the stereotyping never ceased. We see it on TV in the gang and crime shows, and we hear it on our radios in the lyrics of rap songs. We see it in the way people dress by exposing the intimate parts of their bodies, and we hear it in the names that African-Americans call each other in movies. The minds of many African-Americans are still in chains and shackles to the enslavers who controlled their bodies and their intellect. Lots of research on the Sexual Relationships of African-Americans discovered few positives, because of the way society sexually portrays them.

The negative sexual stereotypes that are attached to African-Americans, from slavery to the present, have falsely educated our American society and have contributed to the risk factors among this ethnicity. "A common stereotype of African-American men is that they are viewed as oversexed beings and dreadfully promiscuous."[39] This stereotype has erroneously educated an overwhelming majority of African-American men to think they are great lovers, capable of pleasing any woman, and that they are expected to be unfaithful in relationships. "Research suggests that marriage can lead to an enhanced sex life, but black males are less likely to believe that marriage will enhance their sex life."[40]

Delores Williams, in her book *Sisters in the Wilderness,* reported on stereotypes associated with African-American women. Williams said, "One of the most prevalent images of black women today has its roots in the antebellum slave-woman/ slave-master sexual liaison. [This era portrayed] Black women as loose, over-sexed, erotic, readily responsive to the sexual advances of men."[41] Bell Hooks, in her book *Ain't I a Woman*, contended, "This kind of white, antebellum image making about black women's sexuality has contributed greatly to the process of devaluing black womanhood that continues to this day."[42] According to Hooks, "The rape of slave women led to the devaluation of black womanhood in the American psyche. And television keeps this notion of black womanhood alive today. American television continues to project images of the black woman as a fallen woman, slut [an offensive term for a woman thought to be sexually promiscuous], [and a] prostitute [a woman paid for sexual intercourse]."[43]

In my opinion, sexual stereotypes are the predominant reason that African-American couples rank last in the decline of marriage. They heavily contribute to the fact that African-Americans experience the majority of risk factors that lead to dysfunctions today. These myths have caused irreparable damage to the sexual psyche of African-Americans throughout history, which presently remains un-reversed in a majority of marriages and families. Lee Butler explored the psychological and physiological effect of sexual stereotypes on the relationships of African-American men and women in his book *A Loving Home: Spirituality, Sexuality, and Healing Black Life.*

> Unfortunately, both the African American husband and wife have been affected by the various historical messages of sex and gender that have had painful consequences for marital relationships. We battle with Eros and spirituality by attracting and repelling one another. These activities make it difficult for us to be at home with anyone. We continue to live with the old inappropriate ideas that our manhood and womanhood are defined by our reproductive organs and procreation. The gift of procreation has been distorted into personal power and authority. Prowess and reproduction have become the defining features of what it means to be African American women and men.[44]

Sexual promiscuity among African-Americans, reported in the most recent research polls, has negatively influenced marriages among

African-Americans. This perception has caused many couples to enter marriage with unhealthy concepts regarding sexual expectations in their relationship. African-Americans who do not have a Christian foundation contribute significantly to the social risk factors. They also continue to be angry over the past, while unknowingly remain in a lifestyle that is designed to destroy their marriages and families.

In contrast, African-American Christian couples, when confronting the negative sexual connotations and stereotypes, were inspired to remain sexually committed. This commitment is an effort to live by biblical standards, while at the same time overcoming the stereotype and cultural bias that African-Americans are sexually indiscriminate by nature. When African-Americans practice Christian principles, they can break the stereotypes. African-American marriages and families find their greatest satisfaction in life when they live by principles that guide them away from sins that are morally unacceptable to each other and to God. Paul instructs the church at Ephesus on the importance of holy living. He said, "But sexual immorality and all impurity or covetousness must not even be named among you, as is proper among saints. Let there be no filthiness nor foolish talk nor crude joking, which are out of place, but instead let there be thanksgiving. For you may be sure of this, that everyone who is sexually immoral or impure, or who is covetous (that is, an idolater), has no inheritance in the kingdom of Christ and God" (Eph. 5:3-5 ESV). The Grace of God, as found in the word of God, will deliver those who are captive to evil ideologies and philosophies in life. Slaves were not given the liberty to choose a good lifestyle, but African-Americans today who live promiscuous lives must learn to change their ways.

Chapter 7

Marriage: For Humans Only

"What therefore God has joined together let no man separate" (Mark 10:9 ESV).

The Lord has promised good to me...
His word my hope secures.

Prop VI. "The slave, being personal chattel, is at all times liable to be sold absolutely, or mortgaged or leased, at the will of his master."[1] Bewildered is the heart, mind and will of the man who cannot keep his wife, be a father to his children and provide for his family. The question "Am I Not a Man?" when spoken by an African-American husband, father or son is directed at America's institutionalized injustices upon his God-designed person. In other words, the lasting corruption and mistreatment of African-American men are entrenched and deeply rooted in the fundamental institutions of American society. "The slave has no rights, of course, he or she cannot have the rights of a husband, a wife. The slave is a chattel, and chattels do not marry. 'The slave is not ranked among sentient beings, but among things;' and things are not married."[2]

The tenets of marital satisfaction, referred to as partner style and habits along with roles and responsibilities, would have been significantly affected by the laws defining chattel slavery. William Goodell's interpretation of this law informed us that "The slave is not ranked among sentient beings, but among things, and things are not married."[3] Goodell said that, because slaves remained legally defined as "property, and incapable of making any contract, they cannot contract a marriage recognized by law."[4] According to the proponents of the abolitionist movement, the redefined manhood of

African-American men was intentional in producing lasting effects upon the relationships of slave families. Goodell contended that defining slaves as chattel was the genius of the American slave system, a concept that will never be forgotten. "Men may forget or disregard the rules of logic in their reasonings about slavery, but the genius that presides over American slavery never forgets or disregards them. From its well-defined principle of human chattel-hood, it never departs, for a single moment."[5]

A Marriage Designed for Breeding

The biblical teachings of Christianity established the principle that marriage comes first in the making of a family. If children come before the marriage, it is considered sinful. One trauma that continues to have an impact on the African-American culture was the breeding of slaves. Manning Marable, the director of African-American studies at Columbia University in New York reported, "Slave breeding in the United States was those practices of slave ownership that aimed to influence the reproduction of slaves in order to increase the wealth of slaveholders."[6]

The sexual immorality that accompanied breeding continues to plague African-American marriages more than any other atrocity of slavery. When comparing the risk factors of divorce to the effects of inbreeding among slaves, sociologist Heather Williams believes, "Slave breeding included coerced sexual relations between male and female slaves [non-marital sex, forced cohabitation], promoting pregnancies of slaves[single parent households, absentee fathers]. The comparison continues, sexual relations between master and slave with the aim of producing slave children [rape, adultery, out-of-wedlock births,], and favoring female slaves who produced a relatively large number of children [children born to unwed mothers for welfare]."[7] In America, a nation considered Christian, the marriages and families of all should have remained protected, as the Scripture requires. "Let marriage be held in honor among all, and let the marriage bed be undefiled, for God will judge the sexually immoral and adulterous" (Heb.13: 4 ESV).

Elite Davison described his slave life and marriage as a promiscuous male breeder in Virginia: "I been marry once before freedom, with home weddin. Massa, he bring some more women to see me. He wouldn't let me have just one woman. I have about fifteen and I don't know how many chillen. Some over a hundred, I'se sure."[8] This is a case of a single male slave with over a hundred children by fifteen different women, but was married to only one wife. At the time of the interview, Elite Davison was 81 years old living in Madisonville, Texas following the Civil War.

There was a method to breeding robust and healthy slaves for labor. George Womble was born in 1843 in Clinton, Georgia as a slave of Robert Ridley. As a small child, both of his parents were taken and sold away. After his master Robert Ridley died, George became the property of Enoch Womble. George was a small-framed man of about 5 feet 6 1/2 inches tall and one hundred and seventy-five pounds, and he recalled some of the intricacies of slave breeding.

> A man who was small in stature was never allowed to marry a large, robust woman. Sometimes when the male slaves on one plantation were large and healthy looking and the women slaves on some nearby plantation looked like they might be good breeders the two owners agreed to allow the men belonging to the one visit the women belonging to the other, in fact, they encouraged this sort of thing in hopes that they would marry and produce big healthy children. In such cases, passes were given freely.[9]

Open visitation for robust male slaves was a method for increasing the workforce by slave owners, which developed into a philosophy of breeding slaves to create healthy workers. What slave couples considered marriage, their slaveholders often viewed as breeding. Former slave, Carrie Davis, from Smith's Station, Alabama recalled, "When any of de slaves got married dey (they) went up to de White folks' house an' jumped over de broom. Dat (that) was de ceremony at de weddin'. And if marster (master) wanted to mix his stock of slaves wid (with) a strong stock on 'nother (another) plantation, dey would do de (the) mens an' women jest lak (like) horses. I 'members dat when two niggers married, dey got a big supper."[10]

An evaluation of "slave breeding describes the practice as a systematic mode of enslavement which was based on the sexual and reproductive exploitation of female slaves made possible by force, coercion, and oppression-all done for the socio-economic uplift of slave owners."[11] Breeding of slaves was not always between male and female slaves. Male masters, their sons, and White overseers often targeted enslaved women for the conception of children. "White women were penalized for forming sexual liaisons with

Black men, and Whites who married someone of African descent had to leave the colony during the early colonial settlements. In contrast, any slaveholder who produced a child with a Black female stood to gain, for the youngster was classified according to his/her mother's race and status."[12] In North Carolina, "Slave mothers are there licensed by their masters to be breeders, not wives, and thus they are retained as slaves. A slave cannot even contract matrimony, the association which takes place among slaves, and is called marriage, being properly designated by the word contubernium, a relation which has no sanctity, and to which no civil rights are attached."[13]

Pamela D. Bridgewater, in her research "Un/Re/Dis Covering Slave Breeding in the Thirteenth Amendment Jurisprudence," made several observations about the traumas suffered by many slave women:

> Aspects of the culture of the slave south justified widespread sexual attacks on female slaves. The first facilitating factor was the socially accepted view of female slaves as deserving of sexual abuse because of their allegedly heightened sexual appetites and lascivious natures. The second factor was the lack of legal protection for female slaves against sexual assault. The third factor was the presence of laws that effectively encouraged the sexual assault of female slaves. These factors combined to validate a slave culture that based its needs for labor on unlimited sexual access to female slaves.[14]

The Slave Codes were able to force enslaved people to face the realities of their plight, as revealed in the abuses that took place at the auction block. "Enslaved females headed for the auction block were raped, fondled, and forced to remove their clothing for inspection by crowds of prospective buyers."[15] A predominate aspect of slave trading was the sale and purchase of slave women for breeding and prostitution. Robert James, a soldier in the Revolutionary War and former slave of Colonel Francis De Shields in Washington's Army, recorded the planned interracial breeding of African-American women to White men to produce mulattos for the slave market on the Smith's Plantation or the Bargrass Farm. He wrote:

> From fifty to sixty head of women were kept constantly for breeding. No man was allowed to go there, save White

> men. From twenty to twenty-five children a year was bred on that plantation. As soon as they are ready for market, they are taken away and sold, as mules or other cattle. Many a man buys his own child. That is the cause of the rapid increase, already alluded to, of the mixed race. The Anglo-Saxon must blame himself for all the consequences that may result, in time or eternity, from such an unnatural state of things. I have seen brother and sister married together, and their children, some of them, as White as any person in the world. These children, marrying among the Whites, their children are White, and these have slaves, in their turn, after having been slaves themselves. On Wade Hamilton's farm the same process went on to a great extent, each planter vying with the other to see who could raise the greatest number of mulattoes a year for market, (as they bring a higher price than the Blacks,) the same as men strive to raise the most stock of any kind, cows, sheep, horses.[16]

The outrageous history breeding of slave women by White slavers, their "Johns" or other male slaves, is so mentally outrageous it can only be resolved in hearts and minds with hope in Jesus as savior. Robert James reminded us that the sexual appetite, apart from Christ, has no limits to its sinful boundaries. Andreas Kostenberger and David Jones in *God, Marriage, and Family* propose, "In the end, therefore, it is only Christians who are liberated to enjoy pure and joyful sex within the context of monogamous marriage, and those who persist in pursuing sexual pleasure apart from the Creator must first come to Christ as sinners in need of salvation, so that he can save them in every way that a person can be saved."[17]

The sexual part of man's sin nature is one of the most challenging aspects to control. Sex in the hands of weak and powerful men is a major struggle, especially for those who have not experienced a conversion to the Christian life. However, the principles of Christianity are designed to give mankind the ability to overcome the temptations of their immoral sex drives.

Although forced breeding of female slaves was a major contributor to the economic success of the institution of slavery, it also serves to expose the depth of a sinful mankind outside of God's will. Consequently, "in his fallen state, man still exhibits traces of the image of God in him or her, but this image is now distorted. Prostitution, pornography, and other sexual sins dehumanize and degrade a person, and sex, rather than being enjoyed as the Creator's good and gracious gift to his glad and grateful creatures, becomes a burden, bondage, a form of slavery."[18]

As a result, enslaved females could be subject to a life of prostitution and breeding, depending on the demands of her master. Slaveholders also forced their slaves to indulge in many forms of illicit and degrading sexual appetites. Breeders and slavers, although not subject to the personal consequences endured by slaves, were also enslaved to the sin of breeding and the sexual supremacy they exerted over both male and female slaves.

Slavery Instigates Sin

In modern society, the sin nature associated with slavery has become an evident link inherited by both Black and White Americans. John Calvin's Theology of Total Depravity informs us that mankind has a sin nature that prohibits his ability to do right, apart from the reconciling grace of God. Sinful men, void of a relationship with God, have no boundaries and are unsympathetic to the treatment he gives to his fellow man. When defining total depravity, sin negatively affects the spiritual lives of mankind in all aspects of life. An analysis of this teaching explains "(1) depraved people cannot or do not perform actions that are good in man's or God's sight … (2) that fallen man has no conscience which judges between good and evil for him. (3) that people indulge in every form of sin or in any sin to the greatest extent possible."[19] Although John Calvin lived before slavery existed in America, his doctrinal treatment of Total Depravity supported the positions of the anti-slavery movement. This doctrine helps us understand the complexities of the mind portrayed in slaveholders, and their ability to reduce fellow humans to chattel.

Enslavers found themselves the victims of their sin natures and an immoral secular American culture that opposed Christian virtues. In response to that, Anti-Slavery Movements found motivation and called for the end of slavery. Most anti-slavery advocates had a firm conviction to help the less fortunate and agonized over the mistreatment of slaves. While they, too, wrestled with their sin natures, they exemplified a Christian regeneration over their depravity and relied on their faith. "Total depravity does not mean that everyone is as thoroughly depraved in his actions as he could possibly be, nor that everyone will indulge in every form of sin, nor that a person cannot do acts of goodness. But it does mean that the corruption of sin extends to all men and there is nothing within the natural man that can give him merit in God's sight."[20]

It was the grace of God that worked through the abolitionists to change the status of African-Americans. While the abolitionists were victims of the sin nature, they acknowledged the humanity of slaves and their need for the grace of God to deliver them from slavery and sin. Similarly, the doctrine of Total Depravity suggests, "All men are conceived in sin, and born the children of wrath, indisposed to all saving good, propensity to evil, dead in sin, and the slaves of sin; and without the regenerating grace of the Holy Spirit, they neither are willing nor able to return to God, to correct their depraved nature, or to dispose themselves to the correction of it."[21] All men, both the slave and free, White and Black, are in the same condition without the salvific grace of God.

Abolitionists William Goodell and George Stroud highlighted the absurdity of reducing the humanity of slaves to chattel and livestock. The following is an enumeration of the integral parts of chattel-hood within the American slave system, provided by William Goodell:

1. The unlimited authority of the slave-master or owner.
2. The nullification of marriage and family relationships among slaves.
3. The power to enforce labor without wages.
4. The incapacity of the slave to acquire or hold property.
5. His incapacity to make contracts or bargains.
6. His incapacity to enjoy civil, domestic or political rights.
7. The liability of the slave to be sold, like other chattels, and separated from relatives. The authorized prosecution of the SLAVE TRADE!
8. The absence of any adequate legal protection for the slave.
9. The power of the master to forbid education and social religious worship, at his own discretion.
10. The power of the legislatures of slave states to prohibit education, even by the masters, and to prohibit or restrict free social worship.
11. The power of the legislatures of slave states to abolish freedom of speech and of the press, in general.[22]

All these parts were lawful and intentional in making an animal or object out of slaves. They also gave sanction to the cruelties imposed by owners. The full effect of each of these tenets of chattel slavery on the lives of enslaved men and women will never be known. Likewise, one will never know of the full effects that chattel slavery had on the lives of slaveholders. Pamela Bridgewater states, "Some slave laws were rooted in Whites' fear that those they enslaved would rebel."[23]

Human nature dictates that an abusive people will fear retaliation from abused people. American society permitted slave owners to perpetuate the lie that slaves loved and enjoyed their treatment as inferior beings. Reducing the humanity of slaves was an avoidance mechanism to relieve slaveholders from acknowledging their own abusive actions. Any admission to the inhumane treatment of slaves in the psyche of most slave owners was convicting evidence of their own lack of civilized humanity.

The physical and mental abuses inflicted on slaves were not considered for any possible psychological trauma for over two and a half centuries. Family specialists have discovered that individuals who suffered from traumatic events also infected their families with generational physical and mental distress. According to Murray Bowen, founder of the Bowen Family Systems Theory, there are eight concepts of family systems. Among them is "Multigenerational Transmission Process" or a concept that links generations of family members to their past family distress. "A key implication of the multigenerational concept is that the roots of the most severe human problems as well as of the highest levels of human adaptation are generations deep."[24]

Multigenerational Transmission Process is also implied in scripture: "For I, the Lord your God, *am* a jealous God, visiting the iniquity of the fathers upon the children to the third and fourth *generations* of those who hate me, but showing mercy to thousands, to those who love Me and keep My commandments."[25] African-Americans have an association with the traumas of slavery and are left to self-cure the impact that hundreds of years of slavery had on them.

The Cruel Effects of Slavery on the Person of Slave Men

African-American males have struggled with the stigma of the cruelties of slavery and racial prejudice that shaped their existence for centuries. These vestiges of oppression serve as a constant reminder that his presence in

American society is unwanted and unappreciated. Some sociologists have claimed the greatest tragedy of slavery was the emasculation of the African-American male and his inability to rebound. Male slaves, coming from a male dominated society, were denied the essential elements of manhood. All qualities of male leadership were stripped from the African-American male. They were either given to the owners - most means of subsistence were supplied by the slaveholdlers, or given to mothers - rations were often in the mother's name. Even the children were under the control of either their mother or their owner.

The Merriam-Webster Dictionary defines the term *emasculation* with four definitions, namely "unnerve, enervate, unman, emasculate mean to deprive of strength or vigor and the capacity for effective action."[26] Each of these terms applies to the lives of enslaved men. The term "unnerve implies a noticeable often temporary loss of courage, self-control, or power to act *unnerved* by the near collision."[27] An unnerved man loses his dignity and integrity, forcing him to live a life of shame and disgrace.

Men of every race are expected to remain brave when facing the dangers of life, especially when it involves the welfare of their family. When the men of any people suffer from a loss of courage, self-control and power, they are labeled as cowards, both in the face of their own people and in the face of opposing forces. Men are expected to give their lives confronting all challenges, even in the presence of death, to protect their country and people. The enforcement of cruel disciplines over hundreds of years took the enslaved African-American male to the lowest point of honor as a man. Enslaved African-American men became what Merriam-Webster defined as a race of enervated men. "Enervate suggests a gradual physical or moral weakening until one is too feeble to make an effort."[28] Although his physical prowess could be compared as equal to men of other races, his inability to control his status in life kept him docile to the systems of slavery.

The psychologies within the systems of slavery were designed to control the minds of the enslaved. The autobiography of Charles Ball, written in 1837, provides an example of the despair suffered by male slaves who were rendered helpless in their ability to protect and secure their families.

> This man came up to me, and, seizing me by the collar, shook me violently, saying I was his property and must go with him to Georgia. At the sound of these words, the thoughts of my wife and children rushed across my

> mind, and my heart died away within me. I saw and knew that my case was hopeless and that resistance was vain, as there were near twenty persons present, all of whom were ready to assist the man by whom I was kidnapped. I felt incapable of weeping or speaking, and in my despair, I laughed loudly. My purchaser ordered me to cross my hands behind; which was quickly bound with a strong cord, and he then told me that we must set out that very day for the south. I asked if I could not be allowed to go to see my wife and children, or if this could not be permitted if they might not have leave to come to see me, but was told that I would be able to get another wife in Georgia.[29]

The enslaved African-American male could only be concerned with the things he could control, which was nothing. Total despair about the situations of life will devolve into a weakening of morals and immorality. In every way, the African-American male was stripped of his ability to fight back by the harsh regulations imposed by slavers to keep him in bondage.

Several aspects of the slave system obstructed the determination of the male slave's spirit for battle against his oppressors. The most significant obstacle was a lack of knowledge concerning strategic battle tactics. It was illegal for a slave to read, write, and bear arms. Therefore, slaves did not have the weapons to protect themselves. Enslaved men could not make money to buy their freedom or the freedom of their family. His days were filled with work, but the earnings from his labor belonged to his owner. His loss of valor was formatted by a lifetime of witnessing the punishments of those who dared to oppose slavery in their fight for freedom. Although there were many failed slave insurrections by enslaved men, they typically revealed the hopelessness of any rebellion. There were as many as 250 slave rebellions, which included The Stono Rebellion. This uprising was a failed revolt in South Carolina in 1739, the biggest slave revolt before the American Revolution. Gabriel Prosser led a failed insurrection in Virginia in 1800, and Denmark Vessey led a failed uprising in South Carolina in 1822. As we already discussed, Nat Turner killed 60 White people in Virginia in 1831 before being caught and hanged.

Each of the above events revealed the hopelessness in the fight for freedom, and each served to emasculate the African-American male in America. "Emasculate stresses a depriving of characteristics with force by removing something essential to any existing safeguards.[30] African-American men in slavery lost the ability to care for their families safely. "If a man was a big strong man, neighboring plantation owners would ask him to come over and see his gals, hoping that he might want to marry one of them, but if a Negro was a small man he was not cared for as a husband, as they valued their slaves as only for what they could do, just like they would horses. When they were married and if they had children they belonged to the man who owned the woman."[31]

During slavery and for almost a century following, African-American men were severally punished for looking into the face of a White person. Looking into another person's eyes suggested equality and dignity, something that no African-American man was allowed. Any African-American man accused of having a sexual relationship with a White woman was tortured and killed. The White woman involved was ruined for life, even if she blamed the Black man of rape.

> While Black men could be killed for expressing any sexual interest in Euro-American women, those who were charged with sexually assaulting them were often innocent of the crime. Because a White women who engaged in intercourse with a male slave would be ruined socially. In situations where they consented to it, they cried rape in order to save themselves. Even those who claimed rape was regarded as "damaged goods" and never received the normal opportunities of marriage offered to "decent White women."[32]

Any involvement in an interracial relationship for an African-American man was signing his death warrant. African-American men were often the victims of mob activity who feared the idea of interracial relationships. "Before the political state took over the duty of avenging the Euro-American woman's honor by executing Afro-American men, it was left to vigilante justice. The number of African-American men lynched by mobs between 1865-1955 was approximately five thousand, about a quarter of them accused of the 'crime' of having touched, approached, or imagined to have looked at a White woman."[33]

One final note on the effects of slavery and African-American men is the attempt to destroy the authority of fathers. "Through a history of slavery, segregation, exploitation, oppression, overwhelming prejudice, emasculation, and well-intentioned but degrading government assistance programs, African-American families have lost their leaders—the fathers."[34] Douglass seems to have favored the pathological view that was later followed by W.E.B Dubois, E. Franklin Frazier, and Orlando Patterson. All have advocated the theory that slavery is responsible for the absence of fatherhood in African-American families. Frederick Douglass explained his reasoning for a time during slavery:

> I say nothing of father, for he is shrouded in a mystery I have never been able to penetrate. Slavery does away with fathers, as it does away with families. Slavery has no use for either fathers or families, and its laws do not recognize their existence in the social arrangements of the plantation. When they do exist, they are not the outgrowths of slavery but are antagonistic to that system.[35]

Since it is a matter of legal documentation that federal, state and local laws failed to recognize the family structure of African-Americans as Douglass' statement suggested, it is evident that Douglass also influenced future scholars who found the purpose behind slavery to be an intentional destruction of African-American fathers and families. Dubois, at the turn of the 20th century, described the effect of slavery on the authority of fathers. He described what slave relationships looked like in homes where husbands and fathers were present:

> The absence of the father along with the lack of authority in the slave father to govern or protect his family. His wife could be made his master's concubine, his daughter could be outraged, his son whipped, or he himself sold away without his being able to protest or lift a preventing finger. Naturally, his authority in his own house was simply such as could rest upon brute force alone, and he easily sank to a position of male guest in the house, without respect or responsibility.[36]

These are all links to the dilemmas of slavery for African-American males. The effects have remained intact well into the twenty-first century, one hundred fifty years after slavery. Orlando Patterson claimed, "Perhaps the most important group specific problem of Afro-Americans is the fact that the roles of father and husband are very weakly institutionalized, possibly the worst heritage of the slave past. Afro Americans had their cultural scripts for the roles of fathers and husbands destroyed, and were never quite able to redefine them."[37] King Solomon, the wisest man to ever live, expressed the importance of fatherhood roles and children keeping a father's guidance: "My son, do not forget my teaching, but let your heart keep my commandments, for length of days and years of life and peace they will add to you. Let not steadfast love and faithfulness forsake you; bind them around your neck; write them on the tablet of your heart. So you will find favor and good success in the sight of God and man" (Proverbs 3:1-4 ESV). According to this Scripture, one benefit of having a father teaching in the home is the path to success for children. Richard Land, former head of the Ethics Religious Liberty Commission, an entity of the Southern Baptist Convention, reported:

Using a comprehensive study from the U.S. Department of Health and Human Services and other sources, Land noted the many benefits provided to children who grow up with a married mother and father who stay married. Compared to other children, Land said, they are seven times less likely to live in poverty, six times less likely to commit suicide, less than half as likely to commit a crime, less than half as likely to become pregnant out of wedlock, more likely to finish high school and college, more likely to get married and stay married, less likely to experience physical or sexual abuse, and are more physically and emotionally healthy.[38]

While this study looks at the benefits children receive for having a father present in their homes, it is also helpful to take this study and read into it the risk factors families face when fathers are missing. Lands statement can serve as an insight into the struggles present in the homes of slaves where the authority of the father was canceled.

The Cruel Effects of Slavery on the Person of Slave Women

The relationship of an enslaved woman in marriage was defined by the following addendum to the Slave Codes. "It bids the woman assist, not her husband, but her owner! Nay! It gives him unlimited control and full possession of her own person, and forbids her, on pain of death, to resist him, if he drags her to his bed!"[39] This was a law in total violation of biblical standards for the wife in her relationship with her husband. "She, being in the image of God as is her husband and thus equal to him, has the God-given responsibility to respect her husband and to serve as his helper in managing the household and nurturing the next generation."[40]

Figure 18. A Captured Runaway Slave Woman[41]

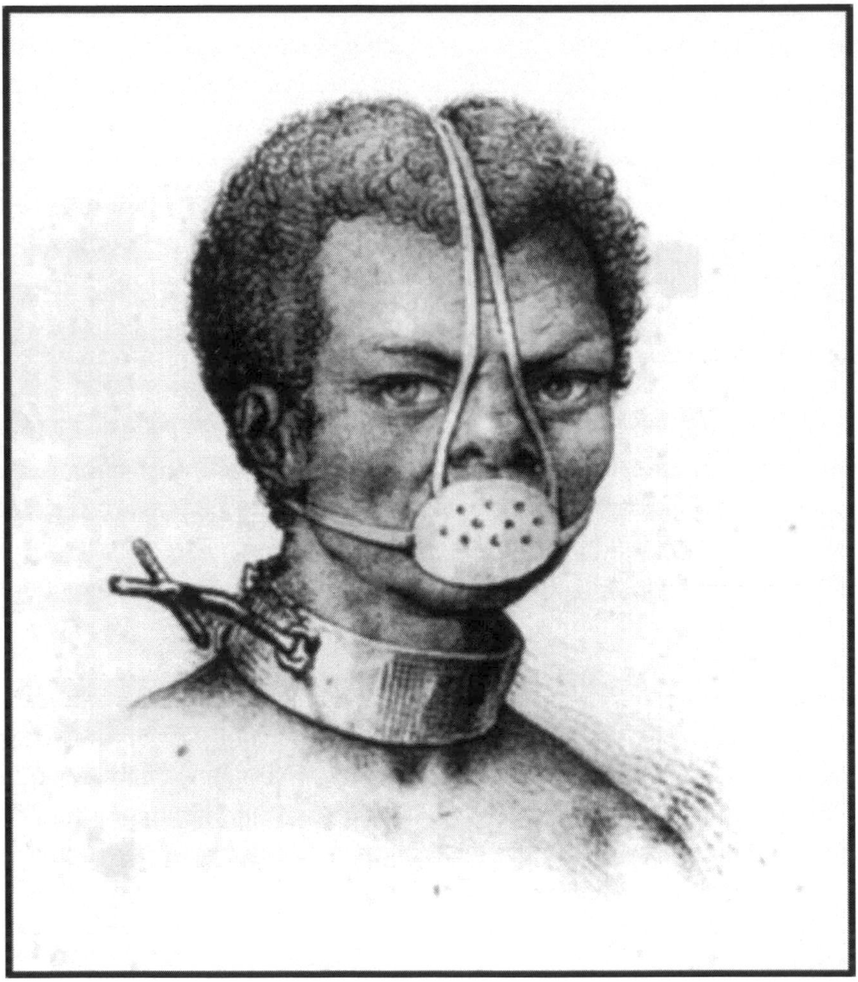

Just as African-American men were emasculated to dehumanize them, African-American women were defeminized during slavery as a process of dehumanization. The American slave system removed the systematic human requirement to protect and care for the weaker female sex. African-American women were left to fend for themselves with neither Black nor White men to aid them. Enslaved women were treated with the same level of harshness as their male slave counterparts. This made them more masculine in the eyes of their abusers. The "defeminization of African-American women and girls is one form of implicit bias that contributes to social approval of violence against them."[42]

The stereotypes associated with Black femininity have created the "perception that Black women are more masculine than White women are an implicit bias that has serious consequences for the treatment of Black female victims in real life."[43] The misconception that African-American women are sexually promiscuous has negatively twisted their image and reduced the public concern for their sexual chastity. Sonya Tonnesen described the present sexual risk factors related to conditions of schoolgirls discovered in studies of young women. "A hypothetical date rape is more acceptable with a Black female victim. Among the many negative images of rape survivors, one is that the victims become less attractive following victimization or deserved to be raped because of their sexually provocative or aggressive appearance, traits associated with masculinity."[44]

The skin complexion of women has been associated with beauty. Lighter skin, because of its closeness to the White skin, is considered better looking and pure. Slavery and its racial concepts produced the idea that the skin of White women was chaste and beautiful in contrast to Black women, who were unattractive and adulterated. It was established in the Slave Codes that both raping and the sexual abuse of African-American women were legally permitted.

The implications of this law still affect the safety of twenty-first century African-American women. For example, "rapes of Black women lead to far fewer convictions than rapes of White women. This finding suggests that society does not take the sexual victimization of Black women and girls seriously, implicating depictions of Black women and girls as unworthy of protection."[45] It should be noted that masters considered this a favor to slave women when they were forced to have sex with their owner. They claimed that sex with them was a favor to her because it kept her from having sex with African-American men, who were considered animalistic and brutal.

Being dehumanized affected African-American women both physically and mentally in the most severe ways. Faye Z. Belgrave and Kevin Allison describe the many consequences of slavery on African-American women. They discovered "Enslavement had several pervasive, institutional, and long-term effects on the family. These included earlier ages of intercourse, childbearing, and establishing a household. In African communities, natural spacing techniques such as breastfeeding and polygamous unions allowed women to space childbearing."[46]

The roles of wives and mothers made a tremendous change for enslaved women as they made the transition from their lifestyles in Africa. Women and girls no longer enjoyed the safeguards that protected their femininity and the natural use of their bodies for motherhood. Robert Mallard, a wealthy slaveholder and author of *Plantation Life Before the Emancipation* recalled his experience with his slaves and nanny.

> They are our constant and inseparable associates; whither we go they go; where we dwell they dwell; where we die and are buried, there they die and are buried; and, more than all, our God is their God. What parts men most closely connected in this life from each other, that can only part us from them, namely, crime, debt, or death. Indeed, they are with us from the cradle to the grave. Many of us are nursed at their generous breasts, and all carried in their arms. They help to make us walk, they help to make us talk, they help to teach us to distinguish the first things we see and the first things we hear.[47]

Slave mothers were often required to take care of their master's children above their own. Nannies nursed, breastfed and raised the master's children like they were their own biological babies. Mallard remembered, "As a babe, I drew a part at least of my nourishment from the generous breasts of a colored foster mother, and she and her infant son always held a peculiar place in my regards. A black nurse taught me, it is probable, my first steps and first words, and was as proud of both performances as the happy mother herself."[48] Married life and motherhood held different expectations for African women while in Africa, but in America, this understanding of matrimony and maternity was challenged. According to family specialist Andrew Cherlin, this caused them to have mixed allegiance.

> Childbearing could occur before the ceremony, in which case the couple was expected to marry. But on the other hand, if the couple produced no children in the early stage, the elders might cancel the marriage. It was the lineage—the larger kinship network—that mattered more than the

marriage itself. In other words, both the slavery system and cultural survivals could have influenced the development of the African-American slave family. Slavery did not allow formal marriage; while African culture allowed it, the married couple was subordinated to the lineage.[49]

Figure 19. A Slave Mother Breastfeeding a Black and White Baby[50]

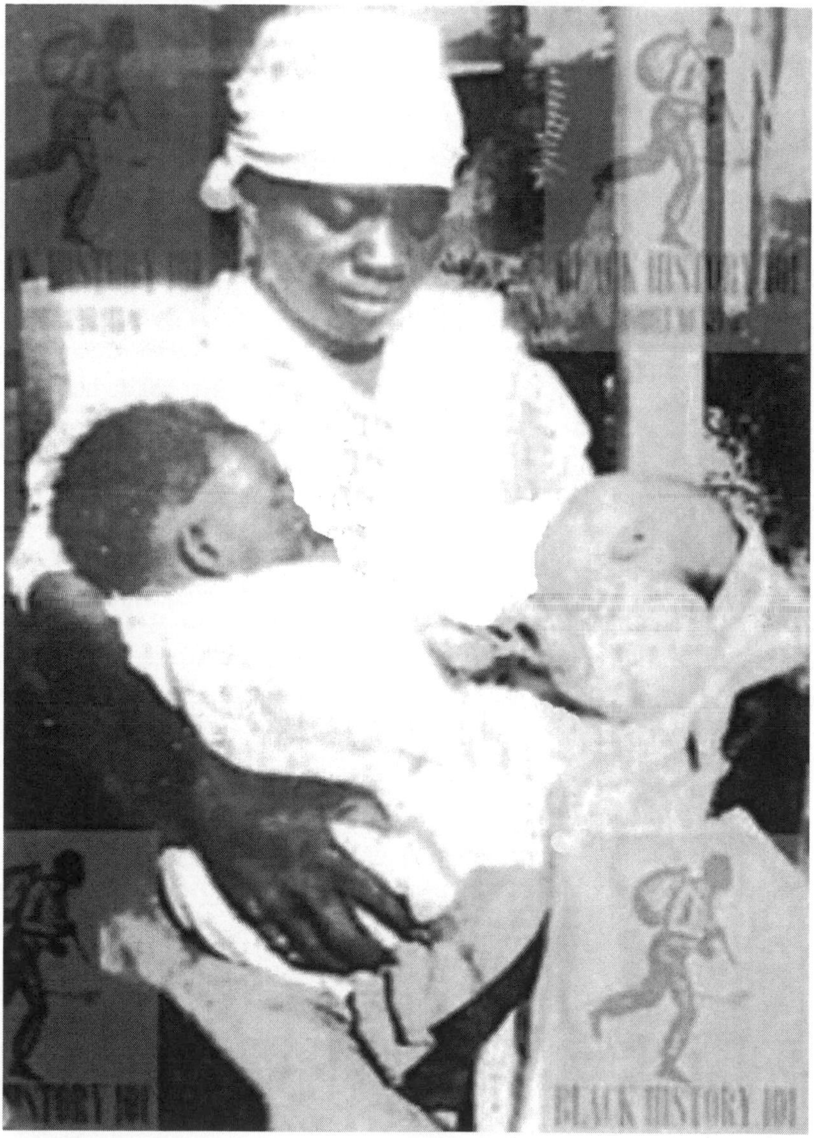

Julia Brown, born a slave in Commerce, Georgia in 1852, described the treatment of slave mothers during their times of delivery and post-delivery recovery on the plantation where she was raised:

> They didn't mind the slaves matin', but they wanted their niggers to marry only amongst them on their place. They didn't allow 'em to mate with other slaves from other places. When the women had babies they was treated kind and they let 'em stay in. We called it "lay-in," just about like they do now. We didn't go to no hospitals as they do now. We just had our babies and a granny to catch 'em. We didn't have all the pain-easin' medicines then. The granny would put a rusty piece of tin or a ax under the mattress and this would ease the pain. The granny put a ax under my mattress once. This was to cut off the after-pains and it sure did, too. We'd set up the fifth day and after the "layin-in" time was up we was allowed to walk outdoors and they told us to walk around the house just once and come in the house. This was to keep us from takin' a 'lapse.[51]

African-American women, into the twenty-first century, kept the tradition of women staying in the home and allowing their bodies to heal for a month after the birth of a child. Whereas this was a post-natal requirement from the motherland, "Within the New World, there was an emphasis on increased economic production and thus human reproduction. Therefore, enslaved African women began parenting at earlier ages and had greater numbers of children than did their foremothers in Africa."[52] Historian John Hope Franklin recorded one of many offenses that occurred to enslaved women having to mature quickly. He says, "David Dickson was forty years old when he fathered a child by his twelve-year-old slave Julia Lewis."[53] Today, this would have been statutory rape of an underage child enforced by a punishment of prison time.

"In 1855 Missouri v. Celia, a Slave, a Black woman is declared to be property without a right to defend herself against a master's act of rape."[54] Female slaves experienced the most deplorable conditions under the Slave Codes, suffering the inability to protect their virginity and chastity. Generations of unprotected African-American women faced the cruelties of the world that removed from them all the natural rights of her personhood.

This created an understanding in Euro-Americans that an African-American woman's sexuality developed out of the conditions of slavery. These circumstances also influenced the African-American female's perception of her sexual morality, by forcing her to accept her situation. "Once she accepted the fact that she had no control over her body, the importance of virginity to her was considerably reduced. The Black woman came to look upon herself as the South viewed and treated her. In fact, she had no other morality by which to shape her womanhood."[55] Although humiliated in life as the victims of an institution that approved the actions of sexual predators, not all African-American women submitted for their entire lifespan. Robert Newsome and his slave girl, Celia, serve as a case study of the legal protection provided by slave owners in respect to their female slaves. Robert Newsome held the mental attitude of his day regarding African-American female sexuality, and Celia suffered the mental and physical abuse of many slave women. Her retaliation is a rare incident, but serves to identify the severity of the trauma imposed on many female slaves. The judicial ruling on the case of Celia Newsome revealed that she and all African-American women were not to be treated as women. The second article in Section 29 of the Missouri statutes of 1845 forbade anyone:

> "... take any woman unlawfully against her will and by force, menace or duress, compel her to be defiled," Judge William Hall refused to instruct the jury that the enslaved Celia fell within the meaning of "any woman"—giving the jury no latitude to consider Celia's murder of her sexually abusive master a justifiable act of self-defense.
>
> In 1850, the recently widowed Robert Newsom purchased the 14-year-old Celia, ostensibly to help his daughters with the housework. En-route from Audrain County, the site of the transaction, to his own home in neighboring Calloway County, Missouri, Newsom raped the young girl. Back at his farm, Newsom ensconced her in a small cabin 150 feet from his home. Between 1850 and 1855, Celia bore two of Newsom's children, both of whom became her master's property. She also began a relationship with a fellow slave named George. When she became pregnant in 1855,

> she was unsure which of the men was the father. At that point, George told Celia "he would have nothing more to do with her if she did not quit the old man."
>
> Celia first asked Newsom's daughters to intercede. She told Mary (19 years old, as was Celia in 1855) and Virginia (36 and returned to her father's home with her own three children) that her pregnancy was making her feel unwell and that she wished Robert Newsom to respect her condition and leave her alone. There is no indication that either Newsom daughter challenged her father.
>
> Celia herself pleaded with Newsom on June 23, but he brushed aside her objections and said: "he was coming to her cabin that night." That afternoon, Celia brought a heavy stick, "about as large as the upper part of a Windsor chair, but not so long," into her cabin. When Newsom arrived and refused to back off, she killed him with two blows to the head. She spent the night burning his corpse in her fireplace. As morning approached, she ground the smaller bones into pieces with a rock; the larger bones, she hid "under the hearth, and under the floor between a sleeper and the fireplace." Later that day, she gave Newsom's unwitting grandson, Virginia's son Coffee Waynescot, "two dozen walnuts [to] carry the ashes out." Coffee disposed of his grandfather's remains on the ground beside "a beat down like" path on the property.[56]

The years of sexual abuse upon Celia by her master Robert Newsome created a mental rage, causing her to murder him ruthlessly. Celia was found guilty and hanged for the murder of Newsome, who sexually molested her throughout her adolescence and adult life. Newsome's power over this young woman deprived her of any hope of a satisfying marriage. By fathering two of her children through his continued sexual assaults, he devastated her mentally and corrupted her family structure. Newsome had bought and owned Celia, therefore, he held the legal right to sexually abuse her and father as many children as he desired. Celia serves an example of the mental effects suffered by many slave girls and women when exposed to long-term sexual abuse.

Louise Oliphant and John N. Booth of the Federal Writers' Project, an entity of the Freemans Bureau, recorded the testimony of an unnamed former slave in Richmond County Augusta, Georgia, who belonged to Bob Lampkins.

> In them times, White men went with colored gals and women bold. Anytime they saw one and wanted her, she had to go with him, and his wife didn't say nothin' 'bout it. Not only the men, but the women went with colored men too. That's why so many women slave owners wouldn't marry, 'cause they was goin' with one of their slaves. These things that's goin' on now ain't new, they been happenin'. That's why I say you just as well leave 'em alone 'cause they gwine to do what they want to anyhow.[57]

One reason God designed sex is for the procreation of the human race. Children are the result of intercourse, regardless of whether each person gave consent, or if rape was perpetrated. The brutality of the slave system forbade the recognition of White blood in the child of an African-American mother. Although the White father, according to the legal system, was considered human, the child was not. It was a most egregious, shocking, appalling and awful act to deny the humanity of one's own child. Children born to biracial parents were counted as African-Americans, a practice that remains today. This reduces the rate of White children born out of wedlock with interracial parents, but increases the African-American percentage. Nonetheless, the intent of the slave system in America was to dehumanize men, women and children with any percent of African-American blood. At the beginning of the nineteenth century, powerful anti-slavery appeals began to prove that the image of God existed in slaves. "In 1841, when former slave Frederick Douglass first told his story in public, people were 'well prepared to see both his sufferings and his survival as evidence of the imago dei.'"[58] There is nothing that "can annul the birth-right charter, which God has bequeathed to every being upon whom he has stamped his own image."[59]

The impact slavery had on African-American women was intensified by the sexual and feminist revolutions. These revolutions promoted a disregard for traditional family values. The question of how much of an impact the forced, promiscuous sexual lifestyle of slave women had on the social risk factors of African-Americans in this generation must be deliberated. In 2016, the Center for Disease Control reported, "The percentage of non-marital births varied widely among population groups, from 16.4% for Asian, Pacific Islanders mothers to 70.9% for non Hispanic black mothers."[60] This report also revealed that White women experienced non-marital births at 29 percent and Hispanic 53 percent. These statistics show a breakdown of African-American family structures that far surpass other ethnicities.

There is something incredibly wrong within the disparity of non-marital births for African-Americans compared the other ethnicities. Marriage, families and children are a gift of God, according to His Amazing Grace, and humans were designed to enjoy the experience of family relationships. The separation of families during the centuries of slavery had its most tragic and demoralizing effect on the lives of mothers, wives and daughters. The African-American female in bondage was left without the protection and guidance of a man to fill the male gender roles in her race. This vacancy of male leadership remains an emotional hardship for generations of women today who find themselves the victims of homes with absentee husbands and fathers. Fatherless homes have caused the African-American female to suffer from rejection and low self-esteem that only fathers and husbands can give to their wives and daughters. This void in their lives has caused many to look for someone to fill the loneliness by getting involved with the wrong person. In my opinion, many of the stereotypes and risk factors associated with the African-American female finds its origin in missing fathers.

Children Born in Slavery

The forceful split-up of children from their parents was one of the most disturbing and demoralizing aspects of captivity upon the marriages of slaves. "Control over black children passed into the slaveholders' hands after the mother had given birth and successfully completed her breeding function."[61] Agreements were often made between slave owners to give a newborn baby as a gift to family or friends or to pay off a debt. Also, children were given away in some cases when new mothers needed to return back to labor and the care of newborn slave children was considered a burden on plantations. "As a Boston observer explained to a correspondent in the late eighteenth century: Negro children were reckoned an encumbrance in a family; and when weaned, were given away like puppies. They have been publicly (sig) advertised in the newspapers to be given away."[62] This article in the Boston observer was evidently posted in a newspaper that was supportive of the abolition of slavery. This newspaper's advertisement was unusual, because the bondage was about economics, and Southern slavers needed and wanted as many children born to slaves as possible: slaves were money to their owners. "When a man strikes his slave, male or female, with a rod and the slave dies under his hand, he shall be avenged. But if the slave survives a day or two, he is not to be avenged, for the slave is his money" (Exodus 20: 20-21 ESV). The objective of the article was to bring awareness to as many people as possible to the cruelties of slavery. However, the reality is "More accurately, slave children were put up for sale, as is evident in the numerous slave advertisements in Massachusetts newspapers."[63] Most slave children suffered from the need to bond with their mother as the primary caregiver. Psychologists report that children taken away from parents in the first three years of life are hindered in the development of their right brain. The right brain is the area that produces their ability for emotive bonding and attachment. Infant children who are separated from their mother can suffer a lifetime of emotional detachment.

The Friends of the Negro, Leeds Antislavery Series no. 68, is an extract from, "Five Hundred Thousand Strokes for Freedom," A Series of Anti-Slavery Tracts. This tract reflected on the mental depression of a slave mother. It reported, "One woman was told by a slave dealer who lived near her, that he had bought her; she said, 'Have you bought my husband?' 'No.' 'Have you bought my children?' 'No.' She said no more, but went into the courtyard, took an axe, and with her right hand chopped off her left. She then returned into the house as if nothing had happened, and told her purchaser she was ready to go; but a one-handed slave being of little value, she was left with her children."[64]

Slave mothers and fathers who lost their infant children would naturally suffer from depression. Today we recognize post-partum depression as a feeling of sadness, hopelessness and being overwhelmed with anxiety. The National Institutes of Health: Medline Plus states mothers and fathers "have a higher chance for postpartum depression if they had a stressful event during the pregnancy or delivery, including personal illness, death or illness of a loved one, a difficult or emergency delivery, premature delivery, or illness or birth defect in the baby."[65] According to this description, slave couples facing the emotional trauma of their infant child being sold away from their care could have resulted in their being diagnosed with post-partum depression.

This must have developed into health issues for many enslaved mothers and fathers, and would have created pain and misery within any slave marriage. Infancy death rates were very high among slaves because of the atrocities of oppression. "But from the planters' perspective, the slave family also had its drawbacks. The domestic relations that slaves pieced together, especially the claims African-American parents made to their own children, challenged their owners' dominion. If plantation patriarchs demanded the loyalty of their 'children,' so did slave parents. In the contest between the metaphoric parents of plantation owners and the parents of birth, the master and mistress fared poorly."[66]

Harriett Jacobs, in the writing of her life story, recalled the struggle of slave parents and their children when determining parental authority. She said, "My brother was a spirited boy; and being brought up under such influences, he daily detested the name of master and mistress. One day, when his father and his mistress both happened to call him at the same time, he hesitated between the two, being perplexed to know which had the strongest claim upon his obedience. He finally concluded to go to his mistress. When my father reproved him for it, he said, 'You both called me, and I didn't know which I ought to go to first.' 'You are my child,' replied our father, 'and when I call you, you should come immediately, if you have to pass through fire and water.'"[67] This young man knew there would be painful consequences in not answering the call of his mistress; his decision saved both him and his father from possible hardships and punishment.

The French controlled states were more accommodating to slave marriages in their Slave Codes than the Spanish or British. Code Noir was the name of their Slave Codes, and they were mostly supportive of slave families and marriages. "According to the Catholic slavery code, the master could not deny his slaves permission to marry."[68] The Code Noir "required that slaves be married by a priest, granting slave marriages the same standing in the eyes of the law and church as white marriages. In Louisiana's Catholic parishes, marriage rites between slaves were often performed by priests."[69] Slaveholders outside of the Catholic Church did not always strictly adhere to the Code Noir to allow their slaves marital rights. "The law also prohibited owners, in the process of selling slaves, to break up a family unit of a husband, wife, and children under the age of fourteen. Nevertheless, by not recognizing slave marriages as legal, owners routinely evaded this section of the code."[70] Slaves could not be sold to pay plantation debts except when the entire estate was seized. A distinctive intent of the

Noir Code was to keep families together between six years old to sixty. The French code did not simply govern slave behavior. Owners also lived under particular guidelines concerning their slaves. "After Louisiana became a territory of the United States, the Protestant slavery code came into effect and the legality of black marriages was abandoned."[71]

Slave Codes in every state decreed slaves not be tortured, mutilated, or killed by owners, although masters who did so were rarely rebuked. Both state and local Slave Codes were designed to be intentionally terroristic on the Negro family to keep them subservient. "Slavery in the United States was governed by an extensive body of laws developed from 1640 to 1860. Every Southern slave state had its own slave code and body of court decisions."[72] For almost two hundred and fifty years, the laws that governed and enforced captivity upon African-American men, women, and children were responsible for the inhumane treatments of entire families. These laws established the quality of life for both African-American slaves and slaveholding Whites. "All Slave Codes made slavery a permanent condition and defined slaves as property, usually in the same terms as those known for real estate. Slaves, being property, could not own property or be a party to a contract. Since marriage is a form of a contract, no slave marriage had any legal standing."[73]

Each of the Slave Codes was designed to take away the slaves' rights to freedom, marriage and family by confiscating their independence and creating a total dependency on their owners. The most devastating effect of these codes was "on the roles of father and mother and husband. There was no room for the role of husband and father, as we normally understand the terms. There was no room for progenitor or male progenitor father."[74]

The role of fatherhood in the black community is still overwhelmingly missing, which is a significant contributor to the cause of risk factors in most African-American homes. Pew Research Center, a Social & Demographics Trend think tank, discovered the following risk factors in African-American families. In 2015, just 38% of African-American children had two parents living in the household. This was compared to 84% in Asian households, 78% for White children, and two-thirds for all Hispanic children. This same article revealed 54% of African-American children live with a single parent.[75] The separation of families, whether through a divorce, out-of-wedlock births or slavery, cause families to experience living complications that lead to risk factors that cannot be denied. In contrast, Brad W. Wilcox in *Why Marriage Matters, Third Edition: Thirty*

Conclusions from the Social Sciences, discovered the importance of both parents being intact for each family member.

1. Marriage increases the likelihood that fathers and mothers have good relationships with their children.
2. Children are most likely to enjoy family stability when they are born into a married family.
3. Children are less likely to thrive in complex households.
4. Cohabitation is not the functional equivalent of marriage.
5. Growing up outside an intact marriage increases the likelihood that children will themselves divorce or become unwed parents.
6. Marriage reduces poverty and material hardship for disadvantaged tagged women and their children.
7. Marriage, and a normative commitment to marriage, foster high-quality quality relationships between adults, as well as between parents and children.
8. Marriage has important biosocial consequences for adults and children.[76]

These findings reveal the many ways that parental commitment to God's divine gift of marriage and family is essential for the physical and emotional well-being of all people. Families that firmly adhere to positive relationship roles and responsibilities make each other stable and complete people.

Chapter 8

Marriage the First Institution: God's Grace Designed for Mankind

> The LORD God said, "It is not good for the man to be alone. I will make a helper suitable for him." So the LORD God caused the man to fall into a deep sleep; and while he was sleeping, he took one of the man's ribs and then closed up the place with flesh. Then the man said, "This, at last, is bone of my bones and flesh of my flesh; she shall be called Woman, because she was taken out of Man." Therefore, a man shall leave his father and his mother and hold fast to his wife, and they shall become one flesh. And the man and his wife were both naked and were not ashamed (Genesis 2:18, 21, 23-25. ESV).

He will my shield and portion be...
as long as life endures.

The Definition of Marriage

Marriage, as God created, is a divine institution; therefore, its benefits apply to all who enter into a marriage covenant. Man has often attempted to define his own rules for marriage, as you have witnessed in earlier chapters. Today, America is seeing this with the changing of societal norms about marriage.

The highest standard for getting married is from the biblical perspective. It is important to know that, from a biblical viewpoint, a license or certificate is not a requirement. It is making a life-long covenant between a man and woman. The Baptist Faith and Message 2000 (a revision of the 1964 doctrinal statement of the Southern Baptist Convention) provides us with a biblically based definition of marriage and family.

The Christian principles in the Baptist Faith and Message 2000, which did not exist during slavery but expresses the biblical standard for Christian families, states it this way. "God has ordained the family as the foundational institution of human society. It is composed of persons related to one another by marriage, blood, or adoption."[1] How could family commitment exist among slaves, when children were often born from breeding parents who did not like or love each other? Sadly, slaves were forced to accept that their existence was to provide a lifetime of free labor. The hope of creating a better life for themselves, including getting an education, was cruelly withheld from them.

On the other hand, when couples married for love, it was impossible to be secure in family loyalty, especially in light of their function to fulfill the owners' command of producing more slaves by having children. No slave wished captivity on anyone, and they hated the fact that his or her children would be enslaved. The Baptist Faith and Message 2000 highlighted the importance of having children for both God and man. "Children, from the moment of conception, are a blessing and heritage from the Lord. Parents are to demonstrate to their children God's pattern for marriage. Parents are to teach their children spiritual and moral values and to lead them, through consistent lifestyle example, and loving discipline, to make choices based on biblical truth. Children are to honor and obey their parents."[2] In light of these instructions, one great hardship for slaves was the usurpation of their rights to teach family values. The parental authority of a slave for his or her child was worthless, and anything they had modeled or taught became nullified when the child heard a different command from a master or any White person.

Sociologists have defined a secular definition of marriage as "a legally and socially recognized relationship between a woman and a man that includes sexual, economic, and social rights and responsibilities for partners."[3] The slave's marriage could not be established on the biblical principles as defined in the Baptist Faith and Message, which says: "Marriage is the uniting of one man and one woman in covenant commitment for a lifetime. It is God's unique gift to reveal the union between Christ and His church, and to provide for the man and the woman in marriage the framework for intimate companionship, the channel for sexual expression according to biblical standards, and the means for procreation of the human race."[4] The historical absences of these principles are the reason for the dysfunction within the family structures of African-Americans in the twenty-first century.

America in 2017 has discovered that when the institution of marriage is defined by any definition other than the Bible, social issues materialize. The biblical standard requires that marriage be a holy relationship between a man and a woman. However, state codes suggest, "Marriages are legal relationships, but just the consent of the adults is not sufficient. Each state has its own laws about who can and cannot marry."[5] In 2003, Massachusetts became the first state to allow gay marriage. By 2016, the Supreme Court ruled that it was unconstitutional in all fifty states to forbid same-sex marriage, which took the marriage laws out of the hands of state governments for the first time in American history. Same-sex marriages are a violation of the biblically designed command for marriages and families. God warns against violations of his divine institution of marriage in scripture: "Let marriage be held in honor among all, and let the marriage bed be undefiled, for God will judge the sexually immoral and adulterous" (Hebrew 13:4 ESV).

A Genesis 2 Marriage

"He who finds a wife finds a good thing and obtains favor from the Lord" (Proverbs 18:22 ESV). God performed a marriage ceremony between Adam and Eve that was without all the luxurious trimmings associated with the wedding ceremonies experienced throughout history. However, the inaugural wedding was held in a garden called Eden, the world's most beautiful oasis to ever exist. Their first intimate dating experience was initiated by a surgical procedure performed by God, and their wedding was the same day they met.

The Father, Son, and Holy Spirit were the only persons who attended and witnessed their marriage vows. When the Trinity prepared them for marriage, it was necessary that Eve was formed from the rib of Adam to represent their compatibility and oneness. This couple stood before the Great High Priest in the most beautiful wedding garments, which was the innocence of their nakedness, and they were not ashamed. In as much as they were the first man and woman, there were no parents to give them the consent to marry.

Adam and Eve never received a marriage license, but their matrimony was consented and sanctioned by their creator. Therefore, there has never been a more compatible couple to marry. They were divinely made for each other, as God intended to make them suitable spouses.

Adam stated their vows when he said, "This, at last, is bone of my bones and flesh of my flesh; she shall be called Woman because she was taken out of Man" (Genesis 2:24 a, ESV). The Godhead declared them husband and wife with the divinely inspired words, "therefore a man shall leave his father and his mother and hold fast to his wife, and they shall become one flesh" (Genesis 2:24 b, ESV). This divine announcement recognized Adam and Eve as husband and wife and has served as the patent for Christian marriages throughout the ages.

The Godhead declared that they made them male and female for the purpose of marriage. Christ makes reference to God's original intention for marriage in Genesis 1:27-28. "So God created man in His *own* image; in the image of God He created him; male and female He created them. Then God blessed them, and God said to them, 'Be fruitful and multiply; fill the earth and subdue it; have dominion over the fish of the sea, over the birds of the air, and over every living thing that moves on the earth.'" Looking at God's divine providence, His image exists in men and women as a blessing of fruitfulness, multiplication and dominion, and all are associated with the institution of marriage. Marriage is rooted in God's creative act of making humanity in his image as both male and female.

When Paul clarified the values of Christian marriages in Ephesians 5, he focused more on how husbands and wives should relate to one another than on what makes a marriage. Perhaps a study of Genesis 2 and the creation ordinance will help certify the importance that God places on marriage to satisfy husbands and wives as they establish domination in his image. The first thing to notice is that marriage is God's idea (2:18); therefore, he created the relationship between a man and woman based on their need for companionship.

After God created the world and the first man, it was evident that man should not be alone. Therefore, God created the animals. Adam named them, but none was suitable as a helper for him (2:19–20). God created humans for marital and family relationships, and without such, man is incomplete. Therefore, God then created Eve from Adam's rib and brought her to him (2:21–22). Eve was designed and handpicked by God for Adam. Whenever I prepare a couple for marriage, I counsel them using premarital evaluation tools to determine if they are a good match for each other. For this original wedding, no premarital counseling or marriage compatibility assessment was required by the God of ages.

In the garden wedding, there was not an assessment or a compatibility test to provide ways to help improve their marriage. Adam and Eve joined together in the first marital covenant, and since God put them together, He was their compatibility assessment. There has never been any grander wedding than that of Adam and Eve. As the first man and woman, they stood before the throne of God who pronounced them husband and wife. In verse 23, Adam's word of acknowledgment that Eve was appropriate to be his helper was the "I Do" to their marriage commitment. When Adam acknowledged her as a woman, the building of their relationship as husband and wife started.

They had no dating period nor time set aside to get to know each other. It was not necessary, because they were perfectly compatable. And on top of that, the first couple could not have found an alternative suitor if they had wanted one, because there was no one else. The passage concludes (v. 24) by setting forth the fundamentals that go into making a marriage as God determined. Verse 24 tells us that, when a man distinguishes that he has the exact woman to be his wife, one who is appropriate to be his companion, he then leaves his parents. "The word for leave (*'āzab*) is a very strong word that means more than simple departure. At times, 'to forsake, leave destitute, or refuse.'"[6]

Marriage also includes a cleaving to one's mate. The word cleave (*dabaq*) is "to cling to, remain close, adhere, glued firmly."[7] The overarching meaning of this verse helps us understand that parents are forsaken, and the man does not return to live under their guidance and supervision. He establishes his home with his wife and pours his affection and attention into her, and she does the same to him. Marital cleaving instructs us that one's mate is to be our primary relationship, leaving all others. Often this is interpreted to mean not taking other suitors, but it also embraces the idea that every relationship is secondary to the marriage. Cleaving must occur in order for couples to remain faithful and to bond with their spouse.

The verse concludes by instructing us that marriages consist of couples that become one flesh, partners who commit to a lifelong merger that is broken only by death. Becoming one flesh does not mean that marriage makes two individuals only one person. Adam and Eve both retained their own body and mind. Likewise, the explanation is not merely alluding to the sexual intercourse between partners. "Surely, the phrase refers to the sex act, but the context demands that it means more. We believe the phrase is a metaphor intended to signify the bonding or uniting of the two as a married couple. The sex act outwardly and physically points to the bond marital intimacy. Some argue that the phrase also signifies the creation of kinship or blood relation (cf. Gen. 29:12–14; 37:27; Judg. 9:2; 2 Sam 19:13)."[8]

Consequently, a married couple is committed for life to one another, which signifies forsaking others and cleaving to each other. "The second is an act of God constituting or uniting them together. Jesus' command in Matthew 19:6 not to put asunder *those whom God has joined* emphasizes the divine element in establishing the bond. Some might think God unites only believers, but Matthew 19 and Genesis 1 and 2 suggest otherwise."[9]

It is equally important to clarify that marriage is always portrayed as an institution for all, not just for Christians. "Unless the marriage involves those who should not marry because of some biblical prohibition (e.g., some unions are forbidden because they would involve incest"[10] (Lev 18:6ff.). It is important to remember God's Amazing Grace defines the institution of marriage by the word of God and not the definitions of men. Marriage has always been a covenant between a man and a woman, establishing oneness based on the principle that God made them and then put them together. Therefore, they are no longer two, but one flesh. What God has joined, let not man separate (Matt.19: 6 ESV). "The husband and wife are of equal worth before God, since both are God's image. The marriage relationship models the way God relates to His people. A husband is to love his wife as Christ loved the church. He has the God-given responsibility to provide for, to protect, and to lead his family."[11] Given all the above-mentioned advantages of following the biblical design for marriage, let each husband and wife love and respect each other, knowing you were designed to satisfy each other.

The Beginning of Marital Conflict

Adam and Eve's fall was the beginning of the marital conflict between a husband and wife. Their disobedience ushered sin into the human race, and ever since, men and women have complained of incompatibility in marriage. For this reason, "Sin is depicted as the result of humanity's rebellion against the Creator at the instigation of Satan, himself a fallen creature, and as becoming so much a part of the human nature that people ever since the fall are by nature rebelling against their Creator and his plan for their lives."[12]

Orlando Patterson, in his book *Slavery and Social Death*, analyzed marriage and family as God's first institution within the social sciences. "Sociologically, marriage and the family are closely related but different institutions; the former regulates the sexual unions of adults, the latter provides the framework which children are born and reared. Usually, marriage legitimizes not just the cohabitation of the parents but the status of their children."[13]

Theologically, the Bible discloses marriage and family as one institution, with the family evolving from marriage. Biblical manhood and womanhood are found in filling the roles of husband and wife and being men and women according to the instructions of scripture. Men, by God's design, are created to lead, and women are by design made to help. Marriage is "the partnership of two spiritually equal human beings, man, and woman, the man bears the primary responsibility to lead the partnership in a God-glorifying direction."[14] Postmodern perceptions of marital relationships have blinded Christians and non-Christians alike into believing that marriage is a broken institution.

Marriage in the twenty-first century no longer holds the moral value or importance it once held for new couples, because they are marrying at an older age.[15] Half of all married couples are getting divorced today, creating the belief that wedlock is unsustainable. That belief makes cohabiting look like a valid choice. A team of family research specialists "reported that 50 percent of marriages end in divorce, the implication is that the remaining half is happy. It obscures the fact that many couples remain married but are unhappy, or one person is happy, and the other is not."[16] The relationships of husbands and wives must find success in developing a co-dependency upon God, who provides the strength to sustain a satisfying marriage.

In the beginning, God's creation of the first man and woman served as an eternal patent for intimacy. "So, God created man in his image, in the image of God he created them; male and female he created them" (Gen. 1:27 ESV). "The Bible is quite clear that men and women are equally God's image bearers and therefore equal before God and in a relationship with one another, and also they are fellow-heirs in the Christian life, equal in their spiritual standing before God."[17]

Fundamentally, marriage relationships have the potential to satisfy the needs of both men and women. Those necessities are as follows: 1. The man was relieved of his loneliness. 2. Their flesh was made of the same substance unlike any of the other of God's living creation. 3. For the first and last time, the body of a man would produce a living human life. From that point forward, the woman was designed to give birth to their children. 4. The relationship of men and women would surpass all other levels of intimate relationships. 5. In their nakedness, they would be comfortable with each other, representing the closeness and oneness of their relationship.

The above needs are necessary across all races of people. These requirements are by God's design for the essence of marriage and human existence. When these principles are absent in any adult man or woman, they are incomplete as a person.

In African tradition, before young couples married, "Adults carefully controlled and monitored courtship and marriage. What matters most is not the happiness of a young married couple but rather the birth of children who could be retained by the lineage. Getting married was more of a process, a series of steps that occurred over a long period of time, then a single event."[18] In contrast to the marriages of African couples in that era, current statistics suggest that 88% of Americans marry for love. Represented in those stats are the importance of physical attraction, personality traits, and intimate time courting; all are essential to a couple's decision to marry. Again, we discover that the conditions of oppression prohibited many African-Americans from choosing their marriage partner based on the intimacies of a dating relationship, like other ethnicities had the opportunity to do.

When slave owners allowed the quasi-marriages of slaves, it was the slaveholders who often made the choice of which partner a slave could marry, mate or cohabitate. Owners ruled over the lives of slaves with the authority of a supreme lord. A majority of Americans held in captivity never experienced the usual intimacy of dating a person by choice. Nor could they profess to have a quasi-marital love that was initiated because they had dated various suitors before making a marriage decision. It is important to note a few African-Americans, who existed among free persons, experienced the benefits of making the marriage selections of their choosing.

Due to the lack of marriages for love, the social risk factors found in quasi-African-American marriages and families grew in insurmountable numbers between 1619 and 1865. As the number of slaves increased, the number of family risk factors associated with slavery also increased. The following statics demonstrate the high risks that slaves faced from the beginning until the end of their captivity was "86.3 to 92% in the social risk factors involving: Cohabitation, out of wedlock birth, fatherless homes because fatherhood was not recognized, and single-parent households."[19]

Today couples marry for love, but often end up pursuing a divorce in the absence of feeling loved. Comparing the timeline for the African race versus those living in countries where slavery did not exist, the marital risk factors for people of African descent were in line with other ethnicities. Starting with the first biblical man and woman until 1600 years after the death of Christ, Africans enjoyed freedom in marriage based on their customs. Is not it possible to contribute this marital success to the fact they were not targeted as slaves, nor were they denied the rights of stable families like in they were in America? For example, the marriage customs forcefully dictate "... in traditional West African societies, when a couple gets married, they [do] not start families, they [join] families. And although marriage is highly valued, most marriages are lifelong unions, and there are strong sanctions against having children outside of marriage."[20]

Authors Robert A. Hummer and Erin R. Hamilton wrote an extensive explanation on fragile families and the reasons for their frailness. The focus of this scholarly 2006 research was on out-of-wedlock births. They found that weak families vary substantially by race and ethnicity. The global ethnic breakdown of out-of-wedlock births among African-Americans and Blacks in other countries is as follows: "Black-Americans 75%; non-American Blacks 40%."[21] The percentage for non-American Blacks, which is at 40%, is more in line with the other ethnicities in America. For example, Hispanic Americans are higher at "53% with Asian-Americans at 31% and White-Americans 27% in out-of-wedlock births."[22] African-Americans are hugely disproportionate in out-of-wedlock births compared to non-American Blacks and other ethnicities. Family specialists say that blended families that result from children born out-of-wedlock who experience marriage disruptions can consider this a reason. "This is important because having more partners is linked both to an increased risk of having a child outside of wedlock and to a high risk of divorce later in life."[23]

Who Needs a License to Marry?

Traditionally, outside of African-American bondage, couples that desired to be married needed to comply with the rules of society. Each period of history created new challenges and requirements for entering into the marriage institution. In ancient cultures, families arranged marriages for their sons and daughters based on the needs of the families. The arranged couple had no say about the selection of their future spouse. In most societies, arranged marriages ended by the Middle Ages; however, the custom is still in place in various countries. The Middle Ages began with the end of the Roman Empire, approximately AD 476, and ended by the fifteenth century AD.

During the Middle Ages, the church adopted marriage by consent and ended arranged marriages. In the beginning, marriage by couple approval was without the oversight of lawful or spiritual authorities and left families and spouses without documented proof that a union took place. "For the first time in five thousand years, marriage came to be seen as a private relationship between two individuals rather than one link in a larger system of political and economic alliances."[24] Before this era, society basically took the word of the couples that a marriage had happened. Throughout this time, many unions existed only by the couple's consent. No witnesses or ceremony was needed. Getting married was as simple as a man and woman going fishing together and deciding we are husband and wife because we want or need each other.

The research team of Katherine Anderson, Don Browning, and Brian Boyer, in their acclaimed documentary *Marriage-Just a Piece of Paper*, provided insight into the problems created by marriages of consent without oversight. They discovered that "Marriage in the eleventh and twelfth centuries, right before the papal revolution inaugurated by Gregory the VII, was a mess. It was a mess in part because there was no authority, there was no law, there was no academic tradition, and there was no consistent theological education."[25]

At the beginning of the 16th century, during the religious Reformation, the church and state redefined marriage and added a blessing. In 1564, the Council of Trent also made several revisions to enhance matrimony by making it a more responsible institution. The council declared that parents must give consent to minors who married. Before this decision, young girls were permitted to marry at age fourteen. The Council of Trent decided that two witnesses must accompany all marriages, and the marriage must be registered by the state and consecrated by the church. These rules made marriage a more viable institution, protecting the welfare of husbands, wives, and children.

Everything was different for slaves. Ex-slave, Lina Hunter, from Athens,

Georgia described slave marriages on the plantation on which she was raised. She stated:

> Slaves didn't even git married lak folks does now. Dere warn't none of dem newfangled licenses to buy. All dey had to do was tell Marster dey wanted to marry up. If it was all right wid him he had 'em jump over a broom and dey was done married. Slaves couldn't git out and do no courtin' on other plantations widout deir marsters knowed it, 'cause dey had to have passes to leave de place whar dey lived. If dey was brash enough to go off widout no pass de paterollers would cotch 'em for sho, and dey would nigh beat 'em to death. Dat didn't stop courtin', 'specially on our place, 'cause dey jus' tuk anybody dey laked; it didn't matter whose man or 'oman (woman) dey had.[26]

This testimony reveals the chaos suffered by slaves when the institution of marriage held no sacred meaning for them or their master.

A key factor during the Enlightenment era was the development of slavery in the United States to support the demands of the Industrial Revolution. The advancements in commerce during this era created an enormous market to keep people of African descent as slaves. Free labor served to build a new country and make wealthy slaveholders. "During the eighteenth century, the spread of the market economy and the advent of Enlightenment (1685-1815) wrought profound changes in record time."[27]

The fact that this era brought changes to African-American marriages has primarily gone unexplored by historians and sociologists. It's my opinion that no other period in American or world history affected the African-American family structure as negatively as the laws instituted to regulate marriage during the Industrial Revolution and the Enlightenment (1760-1840). The principles for marriage were reduced for all Americans, which made the quasi-marriages of slaves seem justifiable for slaveholders. Katherine Anderson explained how marriage was:

> No longer a sacrament, marriage is no longer a covenant marriage, is no longer a social estate in which the broader community participates. Marriage is simply a privately negotiated relationship between two parties. Marriage is

> reduced to that. No other party should participate in its formation. No other party pre-marital its dissolution. It's the parties themselves who are the decision-makers about what the contract entails. It is that contractual notion that the Enlightenment begins to adumbrate in the eighteenth and nineteenth century and that increasingly drives the reformation and revolution of marriage in the twentieth century.

These principles for marriage were developed along racial lines, with one for people of color and slaves, and another for White citizens and European immigrants. "By the end of the 1700s, personal choice of partners had replaced arranged marriage as a social ideal, and individuals were encouraged to marry for love."[28] The idea of marrying for love ushered in the need among early Americans to stop interracial marriages or mixed-race cohabitation. It placed all marriages, both slave and free, under the control of the government. This forced everyone to stay in line with the societal norm to promote racial prejudice, which would stabilize African-American bondage as a money-making institution. "Slaves were not allowed to marry at all. Marriage was used as a weapon to dehumanize them and to say that they were not worthy of the law's respect and that their love and their commitments and their families meant nothing under the law."[29]

Consequently, this lead to creating a new marriage law, called the Act for the Orderly Solemnization of Marriage, which required a marriage license that would regulate, validate, enforce, sanctify and formalize marriage. This Act for the Orderly Solemnization of Marriage was created to help America to establish its marriage laws after America won its independence from England.

Sociologist George Washington Williams suggested that free Negroes and slaves could be married, but not according to this Law. He said, "In 1786, when the 'Act for the Orderly Solemnization of Marriage' passed. … Negro slaves were united in marriage; there is abundant evidence, but not many in this period. It was almost a useless ceremony when 'the customs and usages' of slavery separated them at the convenience of the owner. The master's power over his slaves was almost absolute."[30]

The passing of the Act for Orderly Solemnization of Marriage required a license before a couple could be married, but it also established the precedent for the Church and State to control marriage as a legitimate contract.

Their design was to turn marriage into a legal and religious institution. This agreement would emphasize the authority of the church by making marriage a spiritual and sacramental covenant, and it made marriage a social estate, regulating property and family inheritance. Marriage became a contract by agreement between two consenting parties based on love or their personal needs. Finally, this law recognized the natural association of couples to be married as divinely designed for the human race – with the exception of slaves. Before this law existed, all slaves, indentured servants, free, African-American and Whites were married with or without a license. Does a license or marriage certificate constitute a marriage? What purpose does a marriage license serve?

The Bureau of Vital Statistics provided the following purposes for a marriage license to exist. "Marriage information is most commonly found in the United States in the form of a Marriage License, a requirement for all marriages. The certificate of marriage is the most common family record and is typically available at county offices."[31] County clerks are responsible for selling and keeping the records of all marriages within their jurisdiction. The cost of a license is determined by each state's legislature; therefore, fees range from $10 to $115. "What makes this tricky is that marriage licenses are typically filed in the location of the wedding, not the residence. So if your ancestors married in a remote location, their documents could be hard to find. The good news is that a marriage certificate is typically given to the bride and groom, so be sure to check the family paperwork."[32]

Las Vegas, Nevada has been the nightmare for many couples and ministers who travel to its centers of entertainment with the desire to get married. The Nevada marriage laws require you to apply and receive a license one month before the wedding, although many couples go there to get married, thinking it will happen on the spot. "Note that there are marriage licenses and marriage certificates. A marriage license is issued as permission for a marriage to take place. Once the marriage has taken place, the married couple is provided with a co-dependency certificate. The marriage certificate serves as proof of marriage."[33] One of the greatest joys of a loving couple is to know that they have the papers that validate they belong only to their spouse. "Legally, marriage licenses are required for recording family history and getting permission from the local government,"[34] but a license or certificate does not make a marriage.

When getting married, it is essential that the citizens of the country follow the laws of its society. Paul instructed the Christian citizens of Rome,

"Let every person be subject to the governing authorities. For there is no authority except God, and God has instituted those that exist. Therefore, whoever resists the authorities resist what God has appointed, and those who resist will incur judgment. For rulers are not a terror to good conduct, but to bad"[35] (Romans 13:1-3 ESV).

This scripture provides little consolation for the slaves who were denied marriages by law. Nor does it provide sacredness for the same-sex marriage licenses that are being issued today. The difficulty with this scripture, in the context of slavery, is the depravity of the elected leaders who established the man-made laws and placed their own decrees over God's Laws. When Christians practice civil disobedience in the face of ungodly laws, they experience the penalties for their unlawful actions. By the grace of God, secular laws are made to change, while the moral laws of God are unchanging, as He is unchanging. "I am the same yesterday, today, and forever" (Hebrew 13: 8 ESV).

The natural laws of God insist that men and women were made for companionship, regardless of their race. The Slave Narratives, a Work Projects Administration Project of the United States from 1935-1943, interviewed former slaves about their experiences during enslavement. These interviews were conducted on behalf of the Freemans Bureau to reconnect slaves with lost family members. However, the stories from the Slave Narratives can now serve African-Americans in recovering the customs and lifestyle of their ancestors.

The marriage of Arthur and Gordon Bluford provides insight into the longevity and fruitfulness of some slave marriages. Arthur and Gordon lived in Newberry, South Carolina for the extent of their marriage. Gordon was ninety-two years old at the time of this interview. Nevertheless, when remembering her marriage to Arthur, she said: "I married at 14 years old to Arthur Bluford. We had 10 children. I now have about 8 grandchildren and about 7 or 8 great-grandchildren. I was married in the town of Newberry at the White folk's Methodist church, by a colored preacher named Rev. Geo. De Walt."[36]

This marriage stands out as a lasting, stable and happy marriage among slaves; however, how much of this union was actually during captivity is questionable. The year of the wedding is not stated in her interview, and slaves were not usually correctly informed about dates. As we do our own math, based on the calculation of the eight years (1935 to 1943) the United States Works Projects interviews were performed, Gordon Bluford married at age 14 and was 92 years old at the time of the interview. That would have placed her birth around 1843 to 1850, allowing her marriage to take place between 1857 and 1865. These numbers reveal this couple could have experienced up to eight years of marriage as slaves. Although eight years does not seem like a long time, the first ten years of a couple's marital life are the most important to the health of a marriage. The research of a family specialist discovered that during this period, couples tend to settle into their marriages. Fewer couples get a divorce after ten years.[37] Arthur and his wife, Gordon, survived difficult years of marriage as slaves and remained together until death parted them. Matrimony for the slave or free African-Americans was a difficult task, and it required couples to endure extremely challenging demands to stay married.

Frederick Douglass was born a slave and gained his freedom after escaping to New York in 1838. His first wife was Anna Murray. She was an African-American woman born as a free person in Maryland. Although Maryland was a slave state, her parents received their freedom before her birth. "He and Murray were friendless in the big city and lacked any of the usual embellishments of a traditional marriage ceremony, but they were delighted to find a clergyman available. Douglass noted later that they had no money for a marriage fee, but that Pennington 'seemed well pleased with our thanks.'"[38] Douglass, America's most celebrated African-American abolitionist, observed the marriages and families of slaves living within the plantation systems of America. He explained:

> The marriage institution cannot exist among slaves, and one-sixth of the population of democratic America is denied its privileges by the law of the land. What is to be thought of a nation boasting of its liberty, boasting of its humanity, boasting of its Christianity, boasting of its love of justice and purity, and yet having within its own borders three millions of persons denied by law the right of marriage? —What must be the condition of that people?[39]

Douglass provided an impressive condemnation on the integrity of American Christian principles regarding the conduct of America and its treatment of slaves. In other words, he is saying America talks loud about her beliefs, but fails to live up to them in how she treats African-Americans. Perhaps Douglass was reminded of the apostle Paul's message to the

Corinthian church, "If I speak in the tongues of men and of angels, but have not love, I am a noisy gong or a clanging cymbal" (1 Cor. 13:1. ESV).

Figure 20. Frederick and Anna Douglass married 1838-1882[40]

"The slave does not remain in the house forever; the son remains forever" (John 8:35 ESV). Harriett Ross Tubman, an escaped slave, developed the famous Underground Railroad that led thousands of enslaved men and women to freedom. "About 1844 she married a local free African-American named John Tub-man, shedding her childhood name, Minty, in favor of Harriet, possibly in honor of her mother."[41] Their marriage must have been difficult for John, because as a freeman, he lost all rights to his enslaved wife and family. According to slave laws, the master-slave relationship usurped the marriages of all slaves, which also placed the marriages of free African-Americans under the slave owner's control. "Any union between a slave and a free African-American was not a legal marriage but an informal arrangement. A slave's master could choose to honor or ignore the couple's commitment, rendering such unions inherently unstable. The sale of the slave spouse might throw the entire relationship into limbo."[42] For this reason, instability of slave marriages and families was a major cause of fugitive slaves. Couples living on different plantations would escape trying to find their spouse and family. Any slave women who married a free African-American male feared to have children who would be born slaves.

This gave many fugitive slave women an incentive to escape captivity. "But in Maryland, especially along the Eastern Shore, marriages between free African-Americans and slaves were increasingly common."[43]

By this time in Maryland, the ratio of African-American men to African-American women was reversed. "Women outnumbered men within the free African-American community, and with this kind of gender imbalance, often a free woman of color would attach herself to a slave husband."[44] History records that John and Harriett Tubman's marriage was short-lived because Harriett escaped to freedom five years after they united, and John was left behind to marry again.

Harriett Tubman's sale from her home and family was the turning point in her life. "These sales in 1849 marked a turning point for the transformation of Tubman from a slave to a liberator. The first step for her was to make her hazardous journey of self-liberation. Spurred by rumors of her impending sale to satisfy creditors of Brodess's estate, and against the wishes of her free husband, John, Harriett Tubman took the initiative and set out."[45]

Motherly descent represented a departure from English common law, which determined that descent would be paternal, or both mother and father. "The switch was due to several factors; the prospect of slave mothers raising free children was problematic; the stigma placed upon miscegenation; and the desire for more slaves. The equivalence of Blackness with slavery put the burden of proof to the contrary on free Blacks."[46] There were some occasions in Northern states where slavery was determined by the race of the father:

> In the case of Angola and his wife, Elizabeth. Angola, probably born in the 1630s, arrived in Massachusetts Bay via Bermuda. Angola's master, Robert Keayne, arranged for him to be married to Elizabeth, the African slave of Edward and Abigail Hutchinson. Their marriage in 1654 was the first recorded marriage of two Africans in Boston. After their marriage, Elizabeth continued to reside with her mistress. Upon Keayne's death, his will freed neither his African nor his Scottish servants. Angola was eventually permitted by Keayne's widow to purchase his freedom, after which he and Elizabeth started a family. However, Elizabeth appears to have remained enslaved.

> Interestingly, their children were not born slaves. They did not follow the condition of their mother, although in this case the children's freedom simply resulted from the benefit of timing. After 1670 in Massachusetts Bay slave status became hereditary.[47]

Angola purchased his freedom and provided a free life for his children, but their mother remained a slave. In most cases, the majority of the states adopted the 1662 law legislating the mother-determined enslavement of her children. Negroes who came to Virginia as indentured servants after the year 1682 were not permitted to acquire their freedom. "Nevertheless, the free Negro population continued to increase until the Civil War."[48] John Russell has indicated the five sources through which the free Negro population increased: "(1) children born of free colored persons; (2) mulatto children born of free colored mothers; (3) mulatto children born of White servants or free women; (4) children of free Negro and Indian parentage; and (5) manumitted slaves."[49] We find that in 1752 in Baltimore County, Maryland, 196 of the 312 Mulattoes were free, while all of the 4,035 Negroes, except eight, were slaves.[50] Russell's findings suggest being born with a White parent was attached to most of the ways freedom existed for people of color.

During these years, the US Census was not in existence. Therefore, there was no tabulation of the African-American slave population. We know a considerable amount of the growth among slaves was because of the slave trade. This side of slavery, Census statics from 1865 through 1880 show the population of African-Americans in freedom produced the most significant growth, quadrupling for the same period as those in captivity. These statistics confirm that after slavery, African-Americans were substantially inclined to have children that were free, unlike they were in bondage. Freedom brought a blessing to the family. "For freedom, Christ has set us free; stand firm therefore, and do not submit again to a yoke of slavery" (Galatians. 5:1 ESV).

Chapter 9

The Marriage Covenant of Slaves

> If he comes in single, he shall go out single; if he comes in married, then his wife shall go out with him. If his master gives him a wife and she bears him sons or daughters, the wife and her children shall be her master's, and he shall go out alone (Ex. 21:3-4. ESV).

Yea, when this flesh and heart shall fail,
And mortal life shall cease,

African-American Historian, George Washington Williams, was born in Bedford Springs, Pennsylvania in 1849 as a free African-American. He documented the marriage ceremony of slaves, Bob and Sally. These vows revealed a three-way commitment between the slaves and their owner who gave them the consent to be married. This slave wedding must have taken place in the early eighteenth century, around 1710, since this was the date given for the minister's credentials who performed the ceremony. Bob and Sally's marriage vows said they were committed, not until death, but until they are no longer in this place. They were required to make promises to their master and remain committed and loyal slaves. Their vows suggest they received a marriage license, which was the permission of their owners.

George Washington Williams records the following in his sociological manuscript, *History of the Negro Race in America From 1619 to 1880. Vol. 1 Negroes as Slaves, as Soldiers, and as Citizens*:

> Rev. Samuel Phillips of Andover. His ministry did not commence until 1710; and, therefore, this marriage

occurred after that date. He realized the need of something and acted accordingly.

Slave Husband

You, Bob, do now, in ye Presence of God and these Witnesses, Take Sally Promising, that so far as shall be consistent with ye Relation which you now Sustain as a servant, you will Perform ye Part of an Husband towards her: And in particular, as you shall have ye Opportunity & Ability, you will take proper Care of her in Sickness and Health, in Prosperity & Adversity; And that you will be True & Faithful to her, and will Cleave to her only, so long as God, in his Providence, shall continue your and her abode in Such Place (or Places) as that you can conveniently come together.—Do You thus Promise?

Slave Wife

You, Sally, do now, in ye Presence of God, and these Witnesses, Take Bob to be your Husband; Promising, that so far as your present Relation as a Servant shall admit, you will Perform the Part of a Wife towards him: and in particular, You Promise that you will Love him; And that as you shall have the Opportunity & Ability, you will take a proper Care of him in Sickness and Health; in Prosperity and Adversity: And you will cleave to him only, so long as God, in his Providence, shall continue his & your Abode in such Place (or Places) as that you can come together.—Do you thus Promise?

I then, agreeable to your Request, and with ye Consent of your Masters & Mistresses, do Declare that you have License given you to be conversant and familiar together as Husband and Wife, so long as God shall continue your Places of Abode as aforesaid; And so long as you Shall behave yourselves as it becometh servants to doe:

For you must both of you bear in mind that you remain still, as really and truly as ever, your Master's Property,

> and therefore it will be justly expected, both by God and Man, that you behave and conduct yourselves as Obedient and faithful Servants towards your respective Masters & Mistresses for the Time being:
>
> And finally, I exhort and Charge you to beware lest you give place to the Devil, so as to take occasion from the license now given you, to be lifted up with Pride, and thereby fall under the Displeasure, not of Man only, but of God also; for it is written, that God resisteth the Proud but giveth Grace to the humble. I shall now conclude with Prayer for you, that you may become slave owners Christians, and that you may be enabled to conduct as such; and in particular, that you may have Grace to behave suitably towards each Other, as also dutifully towards your Masters & Mistresses, Not with Eye Service as Men pleasers, ye Servants of Christ doing ye Will of God from ye heart.[1]

This 18th-century wedding ceremony designed for a slave couple has the necessary wording of the traditional marriage vows in the 21st century. Bob and Sally's wedding vows found solidification by the master's consent. This slave couple was required to make a more significant commitment to the owner than the bride and groom secured to each other. In this, we see the wedding of a slave couple according to the laws regulating slavery.

A slave marriage with the splendor of Bob and Sally's was very unusual in the North or South. However, slave marriages in the North were not as threatening to the status of slavery as it was to the Southern states. "The slaves were socially ostracized. The marriage of Whites with slaves was forbidden, as was also the concubinage of Whites and manumitted or freeborn African-Americans with slaves. The consent of the parents of a slave to his marriage was not required. That of the master was sufficient, but a slave could not be forced to marry against his will." [2]

George Washington Williams further explained the law regulating slave marriage from the Ancient Charters and Laws of Mass:

> True, there wasn't [sic] any prohibition against the marriage of one slave to another slave, —for they tried to breed slaves in Massachusetts! —but there never was any

> law encouraging the lawful union of slaves until after the Revolutionary War, in 1786. We rather infer from the following in the Act of October 1705 that the marriage relation among slaves had been left entirely to the caprices of the master.[3]

Historically, systems of oppression took on many different forms on plantations. Although slave marriage was usually allowed, it was not a binding institution. Most slave systems outside America required the selling of the entire family when selling a slave; however, this was not the law in the American slave system.

America's Foundation for Slave Marriages

The basic scriptural principles to keep families intact and healthy were ignored in slavery: "Wives, submit to your husbands, as is fitting in the Lord. Husbands love your wives and do not be harsh with them. Children, obey your parents in everything, for this pleases the Lord. Fathers, do not provoke your children, lest they become discouraged" (Col. 3:18-21 ESV). Olaudah Equiano, when writing his life story, *The Life of Olaudah Equiano the African 1789,* explores the family hardships associated with the cruelties of separating slave marriages and families. "Why are parents to lose their children, brothers their sisters, husbands their wives? Surely, this is a new refinement in cruelty, which, while it has no advantage to atone for it, thus aggravates distress; and adds fresh horrors even to the wretchedness of slavery."[4]

African-American men and women desiring to become husbands, fathers, wives or mothers must recall a painful history that records millions of struggling ancestral marriages and families. Generations of parents and children who never received the commitment of a father or mother now find it challenging to be what they never experienced as a child. The most significant tragedy of any family is the breakup of a marriage causing a family to be separated; likewise, the misfortune of quasi-marriages was being united unlawfully, without legality and void of a binding commitment. Cohabitating couples are usually able to leave the relationship without violating the commitments of a married couple. However, regardless of the legalities and difficulties of married life, God has designed it with an attached intimacy to fulfill a need in both for male and female to unite in holy matrimony. And if they cannot or will not marry, they will find it necessary to cohabitate.

Leo Tolstoy said, "All happy families are alike; each unhappy family is unhappy in its own way." It initially seems that Leo Tolstoy has captured the essence of family happiness and unhappiness. If there were only one pattern that shaped happy families, a solution to repair difficult marriages and families would be evident. Stephanie Coontz, a well-known author and sociologist on the history of marriage and family disagreed with Tolstoy's quote. She said, "the more I study the history of marriage, the more I think the opposite is true."[5] Perhaps a consideration of the opposite meaning of the quote would read, each happy family is happy in their way, all unhappy families are alike. She continued to support her theory by offering evidence that "Most unhappy marriages in history share common patterns, leaving their tear-stained— and sometimes bloodstained— records across the ages. Nevertheless, each happy, successful marriage seems to be happy in its own way. And for most of human history, successful marriages have not been happy in our way."[6]

In 1724, the state of Louisiana initiated the law that set a precedent for slave marriages throughout the history of American slavery: Article VIII of the Louisiana Black Code "prohibits matrimonies among slaves without the permission of the slave master."[7] Slave couples were not allowed to give consent for their own marriages. An owner's permission was the determining factor of whether their unions were for honor or obedience. All the Black Codes were responsible for regulating captivity with a greed for capitalism. In comparison, the happiness of slaves in marriage was no match for money.

Slavery was a system in defiance of God's natural order for the family and marriage. America established laws that prohibited the legal marriages of couples from African descent; however, with permission given by their owners, slaves could choose a partner and develop a relationship that allowed for some of the needs associated with love and intimacy. The following is a letter between slave owners A. R. Wright of Louisville, Georgia, and Howell Cobb at Cherry Hill, whose plantations were in the same county. This letter gives recognition to a slave's fondness in picking their own mate and a validation of his preparation for marriage. "As my boy Reuben has formed an attachment to one of your girls and wants her for a wife this is to let you know that I am perfectly willing that he should, with your consent, marry her. His character is good; he is honest faithful and industrious."[8]

This letter expressed the feelings of a male slave, by the name of Ruben, who wanted a wife. The slave woman he wants to wed is unnamed because it would have been her responsibility to inform her master of her desire to marry, thereby allowing her master to give consent. Their owners' letters of approval would serve as the only permission for a slave marriage to take place. Married life among slaves provided many benefits that brought happiness and satisfaction, even though they did not control their unions. This slave and his wife would not have the experience of living together since they had different masters who lived in a different part of the county. Unless a spouse became the property of another owner, they would have only occasional visits. The selling of a spouse would often end the marriage and family relationship, depending on the new owner's wishes and residence. This lifestyle was not unusual among slave marriages, known as abroad marriages. The bright spot is that they were given the privileges of conjugal visits on some weekends and holidays, depending on the distance of travel.

Martin Richardson, who was born in 1840, was ninety-seven years old when interviewed by the Freeman's Bureau. He recalled the way his master was known for spoiling his slaves by allowing them to date and wed.

> He was funny about us marryin', too. He would let us go a-courtin' on the other plantations near anytime we liked, if we were good. And if we found somebody we wanted to marry, and she was on a plantation that belonged to one of his kinfolks or to a friend, he would swap a slave so that the husband and wife could be together. Sometimes, when he couldn't do this, he would let a slave work all day on his plantation and live with his wife at night on her plantation. Some of the other owners was always talkin' about his spoilin' us.[9]

Not all owners were as gracious. Ida Belle Hunter, a mulatto man who had an African-American slave father, said he never met his mother or father. He was taken as a child to Texas and whipped every day by his slaveholding grandfather until he understood the ways of oppression. He also recalled the dating process for slaves on plantations that allowed courting among slaves.

> They didn't allow you to come to see a gal 'less she was eighteen and you was twenty-one. The cause of this was

> to raise good stock. The gals couldn't marry till they was eighteen, neither, but they could have chillen [children]. You had to have a pass to see your gal, even. Now you got your pass from your master. Iffen [if] you was under fifteen, you could go play and didn't need no pass, but all over fifteen just had to have a pass.[10]

Teenage slave boys and girls at courting age were under a lenient, but complicated, system of slavery that took from them both typical dating traditions and their virginity. Ida's story revealed that, while a girl could not marry until eighteen, she could have children before then. The age of dating and childbearing among slaves was different than those for Whites. An underage White girl would have been ashamed to have a child out-of-wedlock at a young age, and suitable marriage partners would have avoided her. Among slaves, it was common for women to have children out-of-wedlock.

The Human Need for Marriage and Family

Man-made laws will never innately remove the natural laws that God has placed in the souls of humanity. In the face of forced captivity and anti-marriage laws, African-American couples found companionship any way they could, and often married without the master's consent. There were those masters who prohibited their slaves from having the satisfaction of a spouse and family, while others saw the good in slaves having marriages for companionship. Slaves acknowledged their slave marriages; they also knew at anytime they could be separated, sold or forced to mate with others. All of these factors could break up slave marriages at any time the master desired.

Because slaves were not in control of their marriages, they were often bred with healthier slaves to produce a capable offspring for labor purposes. The ungodly requirements attached to the Slave Codes speaks clearly to the words of Jesus, "No one can serve two masters, for either he will hate the one and love the other, or he will be devoted to the one and despise the other. You cannot serve God and money" (Matt. 6:24. ESV). Slaveholders, in essence, made themselves gods and required slaves to serve and obey them at all cost.

In rare occurrences, a plantation owner allowed the marrying of their slaves based upon marriage ceremonies that the owner designed. Nonetheless, "these were quasi-marriages and were intended to complement the needs of the owners and make slaves more committed to living a slave's life."[11] Heather Williams also provided some insight on why some owners allowed slave marriages. She said, "Despite the likelihood of breaking up families, family formation helped owners to keep slavery in place. Owners debated among themselves the benefits of enslaved people forming families."[12]

Slaveholders were able to use to their advantage the needs of enslaved men and women for intimate companionship, both with their children and the opposite sex. Some compassionate slavers understood slaves needed to be parents, brothers and sisters, and they allowed them to develop these relationships without the full commitment of the usual family roles. Both slave and owners realized that slave marriages and families were unstable and totally within the master's control. However, for the slave, having a spouse and family fulfilled a need that could last a lifetime, even when living abroad. For slave owners, marriages and families produced a safeguard to their financial investments. Heather Williams continued, "Many of them reasoned that having families made it much less likely that a man or woman would run away, thus depriving the owner of valuable property."[13]

For the slave, love of family was all that they could control. Their submission to the control of slave masters was easier to tolerate when slaves had the love and support of a family structure. This philosophy within the slave system made illegitimate marriages worthwhile for slaves and owners. "Many owners encouraged marriage, devised the practice of 'jumping the broom' as a ritual that enslaved people could engage in, and sometimes gave small gifts for the wedding."[14] Often, when owners allowed an elaborate makeshift wedding for slaves, they used the event to better control every resistance of a slave to captivity. "Some owners honored the choices enslaved people made about whom their partners would be; other owners assigned partners, forcing people into relationships they would not have chosen for themselves."[15]

A slave's marriage, family and home life all depended on the personality of their owners. Some slaveholders were men of high to moderate cruelties, while other owners were kind and compassionate. Ex-slave Addie Vinson, at almost one hundred and eight years old in 1938, recalled her wedding day attire.

> What! Is I got to tell you 'bout dat (that) old Nigger I got married up wid (with)? I don't want to talk 'bout dat low

> down, no 'count devil. Anyhow, I married Ed Griffeth and, sho (sure) dat, I had a weddin'. My weddin' dress was jus' de purtiest thing; it was made out of parade cloth, and it had a full skirt wid ruffles from de knees to de hem. De waist fitted tight and it was cut lowneck wid three ruffles 'round de shoulder. Dem puff sleeves was full from de el-bow to de hand. All dem ruffles was aidged wid lace and, 'round my waist I wore a wide pink sash. De underskirt was trimmed wid lace, and dere was lace on de bottom of de drawers laigs. Dat was sho one purty outfit dat I wore to marry dat no 'count man in. I had bought dat dress from my young Mist'ess.[16]

The majority of slaves were on small, impoverished plantations, with owners that treated them with strictness according to the laws designed to control bondage. There is an inaccuracy that enslavement was only associated with the Southern states. A study of America's slavery timeline reveals that both Northern and Southern states had laws that permitted slaveholding. Slavery was reported in New York, which was known as the New Netherlands, as early as 1621. The first African-American slave in the colony of Delaware was named Anthony and was brought up from the West Indies in 1639. Delaware remained a slave state from 1639 until 1865. In 1641, Massachusetts was among the first North American colonies to recognize enslavement as a legal institution. Slavery was also mentioned in the state of Connecticut as early as the year 1639 and lasted until 1848. Pennsylvania, while a part of the New Netherlands, reported African slaves working there as early as 1639. Colonization as a state did not happen until 1681, and their slaves were given freedom in 1780, making them among the first states to abolish captivity.

The state of New Hampshire began slavery in 1645; however, by 1810, there was no slave counted in the state. Slavery in New Hampshire did not become officially abolished until the 13th amendment of the Constitution. New Jersey upheld bondage from 1662 until 1846 when the legislature of the state outlawed the institution, but through a loophole, allowed slave-holders to retain their slaves by renaming them "apprentices." In a majority of Northern states, slavery was abolished as a gradual process over many years. According to the last United States Census, slave schedules enumer-ated in 1860 reported 393,975 named persons holding 3,950,546 unnamed slaves, for an average of about ten slaves per holder. Slave Codes existed in both the Northern and Southern states of America.

Northern states were more lenient regarding marriages between slaves, often allowing lawful nuptials. It was clear, though, that there were many difficulties with the North's version of slavery. "Black slaves in New England were not allowed to marry in a civil and religious ceremony after the late seventeenth century. However, their marriages were hampered, since in many instances husbands and wives were owned by different masters and thus lived apart."[17] This positioned enslaved marriages in the predicament of trying to please two masters while satisfying each other. In contrast, Jesus said, "No one can serve two masters." Such separate ownership had a decidedly negative impact on slave families, causing lower than average rates of natural increase (children born to the couple). "New England slave families suffered because of the frequent refusal of masters, on economic grounds, to allow enslaved parents to keep their children."[18]

The Sin and Shame of America

Sadness and frustration, heartache and shame have reigned in the hearts of multi-generations of African-Americans when seeking an answer to the questions of how their forefathers could be so void of willpower and fighting prowess as to live under the atrocities of slavery. Why did they not fight to the death for freedom at every plantation?

Within the Slave Codes, that regulated the lives of slaves, are the fundamental principles that caused the social factors that continue to make the marriages and families of African-Americans an at-risk institution. Bondage laws in America established a corrupt system that claimed its merits on the erroneous teachings that it was the will of God to enslave the African-American race.

Scriptures warn us "All have sinned and come short of the glory of God" (Rom. 3: 23 ESV). Sinful men who were corrupt wrote the laws that regulated American slavery. They created laws designed for mental and physical maltreatment upon slaves to live among a nation of people who preferred just legislation for themselves and unjust regulations for others. The horrors imposed upon African-Americans by slavers are examples of the sinfulness that men will indulge in when they have total control over the life of another human. Judicial laws that protected the breakup up of families created many unusual hardships for African Americans slaves.

> A man once married his mama and didn't know it. He was sell from her when 'bout eight years old. When he grow to a young man, slavery then was over, he met this woman who he like and so they were married. They was married a month when one night they started to tell of their experiences and how many times they was sold. The husband told how he was sold from his mother who liked him dearly. He told how his ma faint when they took him away and how his master then use to brand his baby slaves at a year old. When he showed her the brand she faint 'cause she then realize that she had married her son.[19]

Sin, slavery and bondage are often referred to in the same context in scripture. Jesus answered them, "Truly, truly, I say to you, everyone who practices sin is a slave to sin." The conditions of slavery were created in the sinful hearts of slaveholders in America. There was no degree of corruption and immorality withheld from American slaves under these codes. The apostle Peter says, "but they themselves are slaves of corruption. For whatever overcomes a person, to that he is enslaved" (1Peter 2:19 ESV). According to this biblical teaching, slavery placed slavers, owners and masters in the position of being enslaved to the sin of slavery by how they treated their slaves.

Abolitionist Fredrick Douglass said, within the content of several of his speeches, that slavery is the sin and shame of America.

> Standing with God and the crushed and bleeding slave on this occasion, I will, in the name of humanity, which is outraged, in the name of liberty, which is fettered, in the name of the Constitution and the Bible, which are disregarded and trampled upon, dare to call in question and to denounce, with all the emphasis I can command, everything that serves to perpetuate slavery -- the great sin and shame of America![20]

The African-American family in America suffered a broken bloodline because of the sin of captivity, which was empowered within the judicially regulated Slave Codes, that can never be recovered.

Jumping the Broom

Figure 21. A Marriage Broom from the African-American Slave Tradition

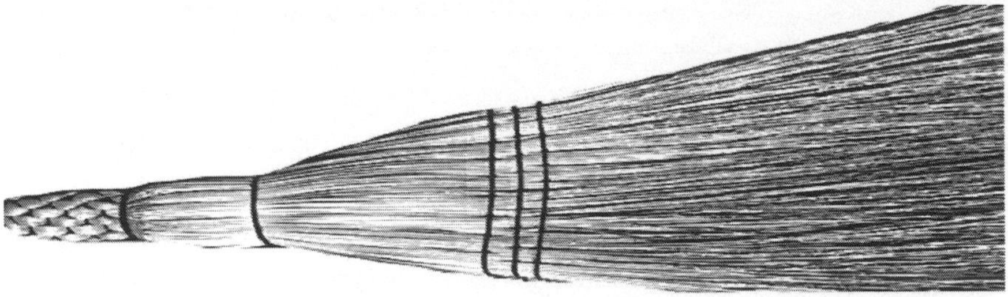

Initially, the Jumping the Broom wedding of slaves was created as a mock ritual by owners. It gave them a clear conscience in light of the fact that their slaves were forced to live a life of cohabitation. Some historians have reported the custom of jumping the broomstick was devised by slaves and approved by masters as an acceptable practice for validating slave marriages. The Broom ceremony became a celebrated event for slaves who honored and considered their marriages as sacred in their hearts. In the following interviews, we will see that marriage was not until death, but until they were parted or separated. Matrimony was viewed differently on each plantation depending on the requirements of owners. Some did not allow slave unions of any kind among their slaves. In these circumstances, jumping a broom made secret marriages easy for slaves. The procedure was usually quaint enough that it could be done with or without the consent of an owner. In spite of its simplicity, most of the slaves who were interviewed remembered the celebration of jumping the broom and the other gala aspects of the marriage ceremony. Annie L. Burton, who wrote *Memories of Childhood's Slavery Days*, said, "If a slave man and woman wished to marry, a party would be arranged some Saturday night among the slaves. The marriage ceremony consisted of the pair jumping over a stick. If no children were born within a year or so, the wife was sold."[21] The marriages of slaves were always for the benefit of the owners, and separation could happen at the master's will.

When recalling her life as a slave who nursed children in the home of Georgia's governor, Rachel laughed when she said, "I was a old maid when I married. 'De broom wuz de law. All we hadder do was step over de broom befo' witnesses and we wuz marry!"[22]

Susie Johnson, from Griffin Georgia, when asked about the negro marriage customs of slavery days, remembered the story of her parents wedding day as told to her by her mother. "She and Jim (Susie's daddy) when they got in love and wanted to marry, jest held each others hands and jumped over the broom and they was married."[23]

Various forms of the jumping the broom ceremony have become very popular in the twenty-first-century for African-Americans. Jumping over a broom is an attempt to honor the resilient commitment of slaves for marriage. This part of twenty-first century African-American weddings is an act of appreciation for slaves who established a high value on marriages and families in the face of being sold the next day. Jumping the broom today is in honor and acknowledgment of the atrocities slave ancestors were required to endure as they kept and maintained their family structures.

According to an article, written by David Walbert and Maren Wood, entitled *Marriage in Colonial North Carolina*, jumping the broom "was a ceremony, imported from Africa, in which two people would hold a broom at the base of a door and the couple would hold hands and jump over it. This signified that they had chosen each other as life partners."[24] Mary Reynolds, an ex-slave, described her wedding day. She said, "After a while, I take a notion to marry, and Massa and Missy marries us, same as all the niggers. They stands inside the house with a broom held crosswise of the door, and we stands outside. Missy puts a little wreath on my head they kept there, and we steps over the broom into the house. Now, that's all they was to the marryin.' After freedom I gets married and has it put in the book by the preacher."[25]

Slaves devised a ceremony that had rich meaning for them. For example, connected to the broom were many symbols that would represent the home life of a slave. In some cases, the groom would take the broomstick and sweep around the bride and himself as a representation of cleaning away all past negative baggage and energies from their past relationships. Because of the laws defining their conditions as slaves, many lived promiscuously, were abused sexually by their master or other slaves, or were made to breed before marriage. At this point in the ceremony, an announcement was made to give notice to all in attendance that the slave couple would protect their relationship from any outside interference. These negative energies were symbolically removed by the sweeping of the broom. The groom would then take the broomstick and give it to the bride who would lay it on the ground in front of the couple. By doing this, she served notice to all that she was assuming the domestic responsibilities of her new husband and home. "Sometimes, this rite of passage included a scriptural reading. Occasionally, owners saw to it that their slaves were united in a conventional religious ceremony."[26]

Figure 22 Honoring the Marriage Institution of Slave Ancestors in 2014

According to former slave Elmo Steele, his grandfather taught him that jumping the broom originated in Africa. Steele recalled this story about marriages in Africa.

> Dey had a queer way ob gittin' married. If two boys wuz in love wid de same girl an' dey couldn't decide who would git her, she would run an' de two boys would run after her, an' de one dat kotched her would marry her. De marriage

> ceremony was simple. Dey used branches from bushes for brooms, an' one ob dese brooms wuz laid across de floor, an' de boy an' gal run an' jumped over it an' dey wuz married.[27]

In some instances, a bride and groom were allowed to hold a celebration at a local church or in the master's home. As always, this depended on the character of the master. Many weddings were followed by a reception with plenty of food and cake. Ex-slave Wade Owens of Opelika, Alabama said, "Atter I got growed I married Leila Benford at Mr. Lockhart's house, an' us had a nice little frolic, wid cake, syrup pudding an' wine. It was a fine night wid me, 'caze all kissed de bride. Us had fourteen children, jes' eight living, Minnie, Wade, Robert, Walter, Viola, Joe, Jim and Johnnie, an' ten grand-chilun."[28]

Millie Evans, a slave born in 1849, reported how marriage was approved by her "good old master." She said:

> All Old Master's niggers was married by de White preacher, but he had a neighbor who would marry his niggers his self. He would say to de man: 'Do you want this woman?' and to de girl: 'Do you want this boy?' Den he would call de Old Mistress to fetch de broom, and Old Master would hold one end and Old Mistress de other and tell de boy and girl to jump this broom, and he would say: "Dat's your wife." Dey called marryin' like dat "jumpin' de broom.[29]

This was not much of a ceremony, and the vows were without constructive meaning to what marriage means; nevertheless, Millie took pride in having a White preacher officiate her wedding. Notice that the wedding ceremonies of slaves usually involved the participation of the owners on their plantations. It was understood that even when the masters joined in performing the wedding ceremonies of his slaves, that owner was in charge.

W.W Dixon recalled that he was born in 1854 in Winnsboro, South Carolina. When asked about the marriages of slaves, he described how class among slaves was often a determining factor for eligible candidates. He said:

> De lowest class was de common field niggers. A house nigger might swoop down and mate with a field hand's

> good lookin' daughter, now and then, for pure love of her, but you never see a house gal lower herself by marryin' and matin' with a common field-hand nigger. Dat offend de White folks, 'specially de young misses, who liked de business of match makin' and matin' of de young slaves.[30]

House slaves and field slaves were usually at odds with each other because of their job responsibilities. It was considered to be beneath a house slave to marry one who worked in the fields. Cohabitating couples made no commitment to each other as a spouse. They lived together as husband and wife without any confirmation of their relationship by their community or family.

John Smith, an ex-slave at the time of his interview, was living in Uniontown, Alabama. John responded to the interviewer's question about his marriage and children:

> "Now John tell me about your wife and children," I said. "How many children did you have?" "Gawd, I don't know mistess. Dey runnin' 'roun' de country like hawgs. Dey don't know me an' I don't know dem. I ain't never been mai'ed. Niggers didn't marry in dem days. I jes' tuk up wid one likely gal atter anoder. I ain't even mai'ed to de one I got now. I jes' ain't gwine tie myse'f down. Effen I's free, I's gwine to be free."[31]

John Smith's indifferent attitude toward his children and marriage is a response often used by dead-beat dads today. For John, this could be an attempt to cover-up the pain associated with having no control over relationships with his children and their mothers. Perhaps he actually had no feeling about the separation and loss of his family, because he was guided to do so by society. "A study of slave records by the Freedmen's Bureau of 2,888 slave marriages in Mississippi (1,225), Tennessee (1,123) and Louisiana (540), revealed that over 32 percent of marriages were dissolved by masters as a result of slaves being sold away from the family home."[32] These records were compiled after slavery when interviewing former slaves living in these three states. John was never married, but serves as an example of how slave families were in crisis.

The research team of Katherine Anderson, Don Browning and Brian

Boyer, when composing their documentary "Marriage-Just a Piece of Paper: Just a Piece of Paper," discovered the crisis of cohabitation continues from slavery. They reported, "When African-Americans do get married or cohabit, they have the highest rate of marital or cohabitation disruption. When they divorce or their unions break up, they have the lowest rate of remarriage or getting back into unions. The result of all this is one simple, tragic fact - African-Americans are the most unpartnered group of people in the nation."[33] African-Americans have the lowest rate of marriage among all racial groups. Their percentage is 36, compared to Asian American at 61.5 percent, White-Americans at 56 percent and Hispanics at 50.5 percent, all according to the 2010 US Federal Census Bureau.[34]

A Legal Marriage Between Slaves

Figure 23 Dred and Harriett Scott Legally Married 1837[35]

The legitimate marriage of slaves was rare in the first three hundred years of America history; however, one of the few instances of a matrimony between slaves created an avalanche of legal issues that forced a divide between the Northern and Southern states. Dred Scott and his wife Harriett Robinson (enslaved African-Americans living in a free state) were united in a civil (lawful) marriage. Scott was sold to Dr. John Emerson and met and legitimately married Harriett in a civil union.

> In 1836, Emerson moved with Scott from Illinois to Fort Snelling, which was located in the Wisconsin territory in what would become the state of Minnesota. The United States Congress prohibited slavery in the Wisconsin Territory (some of which, including the location of Fort Snelling, was a part of the Louisiana Purchase) under the Missouri Compromise. During his stay at Fort Snelling,

> Scott married Harriet Robinson in a civil ceremony by Harriet's owner, Major Lawrence Taliaferro, a justice of the peace who was also an Indian agent. The ceremony would have been unnecessary if Dred Scott were a slave, as slave marriages had no recognition in the law.[36]

Although their masters never gave the Scotts their freedom, both owners consented to a lawful marriage for the couple. Their union created some issues that led to the landmark decision in a lawsuit filed by Scott to acquire his freedom. "In 1857, the U.S. Supreme Court held, in Dred Scott v. Sanford, that the Constitution did not apply to African-Americans because they were not citizens when the Constitution was written."[37]

The decision determined that free African-Americans in free states were not American citizens and could not sue in federal court—neither could slaves in the Southern states be granted freedom by a court decision. This verdict also endangered the liberty of Northern African-Americans living in free states and free Blacks residing in the South, making them candidates to be enslaved. The outcome of the Dred Scott decision placed the United States in a position where the system of slavery could end only by Civil War.

As the stage was set for civil war, states began to take sides. They were equally divided from 1859 thru 1860 with no state having more than a two advantage until 1861. With the start of the Civil War, the free states outnumbered the slave states 19 to15. The Abolitionist Movement of the 1800s was stronger than ever in its efforts to remove the immoral treatments of slaves. The Nineteenth Century Era took the marketing of the abolitionism from newspaper articles, flyers and pamphlets to printing books that described the condition of enslaved families.

Perhaps the grace of God allowed the lawful marriage of slaves Dred and Harriett Scott to set the stage for the lawsuit that served as the critical factor in dividing Northern and Southern states and causing the war that finally emancipated all African-Americans. The reconstruction of the United States began after this war because "new laws were necessary for the purpose of extending civil liberties to the former slaves."[38]

The Thirteenth Amendment outlawed slavery by overruling the 1662 slave law defining African-Americans as slaves for life. "In 1865, the Thirteenth Amendment to the Constitution was enacted to make Slavery and other forms of Involuntary Servitude unlawful. Also, Congress received the power to pass laws that were necessary to enforce this new amendment."[39] It also set the precedence for the enactment of new laws that would provide all African-Americans with a second-class U.S. Citizenship for the next one hundred years. Although the mention of citizenship for slaves and free Blacks does not plainly get defined in the Fourteenth Amendment, it is implied. "The Fourteenth Amendment, ratified in 1868, states that every individual who is born or naturalized in the United States is a citizen and ensures that a state may not deprive a citizen or resident of his or her civil rights, including Due Process of Law and Equal Protection of the laws. Congress is also empowered to enact laws for the enforcement of these rights."[40]

> As a period of history, the "Jim Crow era" can be set off by two significant decisions made by the U.S. Supreme Court, each determining the constitutionality of racial segregation. On one end, *Homer Plessy v. John H. Ferguson* 163 U.S. 537 (1896) sanctioned racial segregation and discrimination with the doctrine of "separate but equal," arguing that the Fourteenth Amendment "could not have been intended to abolish distinctions based upon color, or to enforce social, as distinguished from political equality, or a commingling of the two races upon terms unsatisfactory to either." On the other end of a timeline, *Oliver Brown, et al. v. Board of Education of Topeka, et al.* 387 U.S. 483 (1954) outlawed racial segregation in public schools arguing that "separate educational facilities are inherently unequal." *Brown* opened the door to question and to challenge other forms of racial inequity.[41]

The battle for African-American families to have equality in this country has been a long struggle through various courts. Each Judicial victory made room for inclusion of African-Americans into the American way of life. These changes made life better for those who were able to overcome centuries of inequalities. African-Americans have lived in the shadow of a past filled with dysfunctions, and many have failed to pull themselves out of the racial disparities that keep their marriages and families in hardships. Marriages and families suffered because of unemployment and poverty, illiteracy and poor schools, slavery and their inability to make contracts.

In contrast, the marriage covenant in the hearts of a couple represents the way they battle through their issues, enduring whatever it takes to make a marriage work. The Apostle Peter reminds couples of the way the parents of faith, Abraham and Sarah, stayed committed to marriage through difficult times. "For this is how the holy women who hoped in God used to adorn themselves, by submitting to their own husbands, as Sarah obeyed Abraham, calling him lord. And you are her children if you do good and do not fear anything that is frightening. Likewise, husbands, live with your wives in an understanding way, showing honor to the woman as the weaker vessel, since they are heirs with you of the grace of life, so that your prayers may not be hindered" (1 Peter 3: 5-7 ESV). Abraham and Sarah went through many hardships in their marriage, spouse sharing, a child by Hagar, a blended family, allowing Sarah to be courted by another man, and much more.

African-Americans, in their efforts to have marital relationships, fought through the Slave Codes and Jim Crow laws to establish their cultural marriage covenants. The wedding vows are a commitment to stay faithful to marriage through all the difficulties in life. Marriage necessitates couples to draw closer in sickness and health, for richer and poorer, forsaking all others and keeping only unto each other, until death separates them. None of these principles can be maintained without a marriage covenant of the heart.

Chapter 10

Family Incarceration on Plantations

> Then the LORD said to Moses, "Go in to Pharaoh and say to him, 'Thus says the LORD, the God of the Hebrews, Let my people go, that they may serve me'" (Exodus 6:9 ESV).

> I shall possess within the veil,
> A life of joy and peace.

During slavery, a majority of slave owners considered themselves professing Christians, receiving backing from a Christian government that sanctioned the denial of the rights of a lawful marriage and family to their slaves. One justification for the ills of holding humans in bondage was the idea of doing evangelism among Africans. "The Europeans justified the taking of slaves by arguing that they were providing an opportunity for Africans to become Christians. By the 17th century, the removal of slaves from Africa became a holy cause that had the full support of the Christian Church."[1]

On the one hand, the evangelistic movement said it wanted to save souls, while on the other, it said slaves had no souls. "Over the first half of the nineteenth century, as conversion experiences and church-going became the expected thing for proper White citizens, most Christianized enslavers abandoned the claim that African-Americans had no souls to be saved."[2] George Washington Williams, an early African-American sociologist, said, "Slavery did not exist at sufferance. It was a crime against the weak, ignorant, and degraded children of Africa, systematically perpetrated by an organized Christian government, backed by an army that grasped the farthest bounds of civilization, and a navy that overshadowed the oceans."[3] The United States of America has from its beginning claimed a Christian identity, although its laws and principles were not always in line with the teachings of Jesus.

Frederick Douglass often pointed out the discrepancies between Christianity and the horrors of slavery. He called slaveholders "men stealers," a term used in 1 Tim. 1:10. The Bible connects men stealers with several other sinful lifestyles that are not of sound doctrine. Men stealers are also among a list of immoral lifestyles that are also mentioned in I Corinthians 6:9-10 (ESV) as sins that will keep a person from inheriting the kingdom of heaven. 1 Timothy tells us that the people involved in slave trading are men stealers, kidnappers and slave traders. The online *Your Dictionary* also defines men stealers as a slave-dealer, or someone who seizes other persons to hold those persons as a slave. It also includes someone who sells another human into slavery, or *more loosely:* a slaveholder.[4] These definitions put both the slave trader and slave owner in danger of losing their salvation.

Douglass said, when speaking of slaves, that they have a desire for a marriage and family, even though their lives are trapped under the system of captivity. "If any of these three million find for themselves companions, and prove themselves honest, upright, virtuous persons to each other, yet in these cases—few as I am bound to confess they are—the virtuous live in constant apprehension of being torn asunder by the merciless men-stealers that claim them as their property."[5]

Slaves viewed the slave system as a thief that took from them their rights to the most important relationships and possessions in life. Slave narratives tell us that one of their great fears was being stolen away from families by owners, patrollers and slave traders. For example, William Craft in his autobiography *Running A Thousand Miles for Freedom* said, "I have myself conversed with several slaves who told me that their parents were White and free; but that they were stolen away from them and sold when quite young. As they could not tell their address, and also as the parents did not know what had become of their lost and dear little ones, of course all traces of each other were gone."[6] Slaves considered the selling and buying of a slave as stealing by both the owner and the buyer.

> "My mother and uncle Robert and Joe," said Margaret Nickerson of Florida, "[they] was stole from Virginia and fetched here." Lewis Brown explained his own genealogy in this way: "My mother was stole. The speculators stole

> her and they brought her to Kemper County, Mississippi, and sold her." Over and over, enslaved people said that when they were sold, or otherwise forced to move, they had been "stolen." In so telling their personal histories, they accomplished two things. First, they used a newly common tongue to make their own personal histories part of a larger story. And second, they made it clear that this common story was a crime story. Buying and selling people was a crime. Buyers and sellers were criminals.[7]

The rules for slavery on and off plantations were the same, and were not much different from the regulations for incarcerated prisoners. The enslaved life on plantations kept slaves in ignorance of the principles necessary to acquire a successful lifestyle. African-American mothers and fathers found themselves confronted with a matter of life and death to keep their children illiterate.

Ninety-year-old ex-slave Victoria Adams said, "White folks never teach us to read nor write much. They learned us our A, B, C's, and teach us to read some in de testament. De reason they wouldn't teach us to read and write, was 'cause they was afraid de slaves would write their own pass and go over to a free county. One old nigger did learn enough to write his pass and got 'way wid it and went up North."[8] The cruelest plantation owners would enforce this rule to the maximum degree. Any family member who violated this rule created the possibility of losing their life. Former slave William Ballard said, "We didn't have a chance to learn to read and write, and master said if he caught any of his slaves trying to learn he would 'skin them alive.'"[9] Learning to read and write put the family at the risk of being sold away to set an example for the remaining slaves on the plantation.

The majority of slaves living on a plantation were field hands whose purpose was to plant and harvest a crop. They were daily confined to plantation fields and slave dwellings without the ability to take vacations or have leisure time. The food for slaves was usually sparse and unhealthy, and many testimonies written in the accounts given by former slaves report them living in hunger. Slaves ate whatever owners choose to feed them on plantations. This is very much like prison life. Robert Fall, an ex-slave remembered:

> "They didn't half feed us, either. They fed the animals better. They gives the mules roughage and such, to chaw

> on all night. But they didn't give us nothing to chaw on. Learned us to steal, that's what they done. Why, we would take anything we could lay our hands on, when we was hungry. Then they'd whip us for lying when we say we don't know nothing about it. But it was easier to stand when the stomach was full."[10]

On plantations, the slaves who cooked food for their masters did not have a part in determining the menu. Most times they ate only what they could produce from the earth in the evening hours. On a good day, they received food that was from the leftover parts of the master's meals. Most of their meat was from the discarded parts of the animals that their owners refused to eat. They used the waste parts from cows and pigs to make meals that, to them, became a delicacy.

Past and Present African-American Incarceration

Michelle Alexander determined in her book, *The New Jim Crow*, "There are more African-Americans under correctional control today — in prison or jail, on probation or parole — than were enslaved in 1850, a decade before the Civil War began."[11] She could have also said there are more African-Americans in jail today than those living on plantations each decade from 1619 to 1860. She continued, "One in eleven African-American adults were under correctional supervision at year end 2007, or approximately 2.4 million people. According to the 1850 Census, approximately 1.7 million adults (ages 15 and older) were slaves."[12] These numbers do not include children under age 15, but when they are considered, the number of incarcerated slaves goes up to 3,204,313 in 1850. Considering the total populations of enslaved African-Americans in 1850, the number is more than those imprisoned today. However, ten years earlier the numbers were nearly the same. In 1840, slaves totaled 2,487,355, compared to 2007 when there were 2.4 million incarcerated African-Americans.

Historical stats reveal that there are more African-Americans in today's prisons than were free African-Americans during the history of slavery. For example, the most substantial number of free African-Americans in the 1790-1860 US. Census enumerations were 488,070, far below the 2.4 million incarcerated African-Americans listed in 2007. The US Census from 1850 reported a total count of free African-Americans at 434,495 thousand for a percentage of 11.9% of the Negro population. This history contributed significantly to the overwhelming racial disparity in American prisons and jails in 2016. Statistics show that African-Americans are "13% of the US population and 40% of all the incarcerated in correctional institutions."[13] The reality that enslavement is synonymous with captivity and imprisonment leads us to understand why African-Americans have historically had high rates of incarceration.

The First American Police

The comparisons between prisons of today and slave plantations with overseers are in many ways identical. Every plantation had its system of rules and regulations that was dependent on the compassion or cruelty of the slave master. The enslavement of African-American families was a form of imprisonment, where slaves were confined to plantations and could not leave without a signed pass by their owners. The need for slaves to carry a pass came about, "After an aborted slave insurrections in 1649 slaves were required to carry a pass while traveling away from their plantations."[14] To resolve problems of runaway slaves, slaveholders employed men to patrol. These paid patrollers had the jobs of keeping slaves in fear so that they did not run away, and checking the intent of any slave found off a plantation. During early colonial times, they usually worked together in groups of five or six. As their authority became established and recognized, they traveled in twos.

Robert M. Bohm and Keith N. Haley, in their book *The Structure of American Law Enforcement: Introduction to Criminal Justice*, (textbook designed to teach at police academies) explained, "In the South, the earliest form of policing was the plantation slave patrols. Slave Patrollers have been designated 'the first distinctively American police system.'"[15] In the beginning, patrols policed both slaves and indentured servants, but with the increase of slavery and White indentured servanthood ceasing, it left only African-American slaves to be watched by the patrollers. "The slave patrols were created to enforce the infamous Slave Codes, the first of which was enacted by the South Carolina legislature in 1712. Eventually, all the Southern colonies enacted Slave Codes."[16] American slavery was the reason for the development of the first policemen in this country.

Figure 24 Running for Freedom[17]

Vol. III. No, VII JULY, 1837. Whole No. 31.
This picture of a poor fugitive is from one of the stereotype cuts manufactured n this city for the southern market, and used on handbills offering rewards for unaway slaves.
THE RUNAWAY.

Undoubtedly, owners saw patrols as security blankets in the event that they had runaway slaves. Many patrollers were necessary. "All White men aged six to sixty, were required to enlist and conduct armed patrols every night which consisted of searching slave residences, breaking up slave gatherings, and protecting communities by patrolling the roads."[18] These guards had the authority to whip, with fifteen lashes, any slave found without a pass. These whippings could take place even if no resistance occurred.

Patrollers were often brutal and dishonest, and whippings were a mere part of their actions. Ex-Slave Sally Carder recalled, "De patrollers would go about in de quarters at nights to see if any of de slaves was out or slipped off. As we sleep on de dirt floors on pallets, de patrollers would walk all over and on us and if we even grunt dey would whip us. De only trouble between de Whites and Blacks on our plantation was when de overseer tied my mother to whip her and my father untied her and de overseer shot and killed him."[19]

Ex-slaves also reported that the patrollers would sometimes take slaves, even those who had a signed pass from their owner, and kidnap them to sell to other owners. Many patrollers were so dishonest that they captured free African-Americans, as was the case for Solomon Northup in the book and movie *12 Years a Slave.* Free Blacks were consistently subject to the tricks of patrollers. The danger of being captured and enslaved required free African-Americans to carry a Certificate of Freedom in their possession at all times. Solomon Barwick of Kent, Delaware provided Negro Stephen the following papers to protect his freedom. It stated:

Figure 25. Certificate of Freedom Negro Stephen Transcribed[20]

Know all men by these present that I Solomon Barwick of Kent, County on Delaware do think it wrong and apprehensive to hold Negros in Bondage and do hereby mandate and set absolutely free Negro Stephen/ who I lately purchased of William Kelly and the widow wing So that from the date of his purchase he shall be free and at his liberty to act for himself in all causes whatever. And I do hereby Warrant and Defend the freedom of the said Negro against me my Heirs Prosecutors and Administrators- In witness whereof I have hereto set my hand and Seal this 8 day of August 1792——

Solomon Barwick Seal

Test
Tilmon Blades
James Barwick

Documents of freedom were essential to Delaware free blacks, because the state remained a slave state even while it was surrounded by mostly free

Northern states. Our nation's capital, Washington, DC, was also a difficult place for free Blacks, because of its authorization and support of slavery. Documents of Freedom were also required of free Blacks, even when they were born free. This was the case with Harriet Beall Beans in the following transposed figure.

Figure 26. Document of Freedom 1825 Harriet Beall Beans[21]

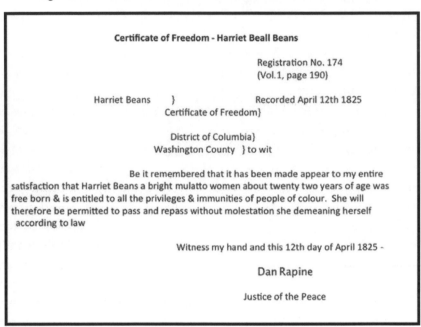

Certificate of Freedom - Harriet Beall Beans

Registration No. 174
(Vol.1, page 190)

Harriet Beans } Recorded April 12th 1825
Certificate of Freedom}

District of Columbia}
Washington County } to wit

Be it remembered that it has been made appear to my entire satisfaction that Harriet Beans a bright mulatto women about twenty two years of age was free born & is entitled to all the privileges & immunities of people of colour. She will therefore be permitted to pass and repass without molestation she demeaning herself according to law

Witness my hand and this 12th day of April 1825 -

Dan Rapine

Justice of the Peace

Although free Blacks were given Documents to prove their freedom, they were still required to live by a different set of rules than Whites. This is explained on the Certificates of Freedom website:

> Free blacks in Washington D.C., life was better than for African-Americans living further south. However, the District of Columbia's Municipal Code, like that of most southern cities placed curfews of the movements of all blacks, free and enslaved and required free blacks to carry on their person a "certificate of freedom." Without a certificate of freedom an individual could be jailed as runaway slave. A typical certificate of freedom not only indicates how the person became free, but may lists physical

> characteristics that could be used to establish identity. These include height, eye color, complexion, and hair color and texture.[22]

Any slave who could get a written Document of Freedom could pass as a free man or woman, which at the time made the patroller's job difficult to perform. It was always helpful if you knew who the owner was of each slave in your area. Therefore, given the advantages of keeping slaves confined, these patrollers, at times, were made up of local slave owners who took shifts to watch over each other's slaves. With this in mind, "Slave patrols had three primary functions: (1) to chase down, apprehend, and return to their owners, runaway slaves; (2) to provide a form of organized terror to deter slave revolts; and, (3) to maintain a form of discipline for slave-workers who were subject to summary justice, outside of the law, if they violated any plantation rules."[23]

Slaves who lived in big cities were also subject to patrols and found themselves regulated by a nightly curfew and city boundaries. The primary job of the patrols was to put enough fear into the hearts of slaves that they would not leave their plantation for any reason. Silas Jackson who was born a slave, in either 1846 or 1847, in Ashbie Gap, Virginia, recalled his experience with patrollers. He said, "There were a number of slaves on our plantation who ran away. Some were captured and sold to a Georgia trader; others were never captured. To intimidate the slaves, the overseers were connected with the patrollers, not only to watch our slaves but sometimes for the rewards for other slaves who had run from other plantations."[24]

Slave patrols also served as bounty hunters who looked for slaves who had a price on their head. The patrollers racially profiled every slave they caught off plantations. Overall, the patroller's principle incentive was to find Blacks when they left plantations as runways, bounty or not. This job description of a slave patroller was the beginning of racial profiling that continues to be a major fear and problem among African-Americans in 2017. "One of the most heated issues in law enforcement is the profiling of individuals based solely on the race, ethnicity, or national origin of the individual. Statistics show that African-Americans are several times more likely to be arrested and incarcerated than White-Americans."[25]

Racial profiling today is based on stereotypical assumptions by a law enforcement official that a particular race is more likely to be involved in law-breaking offenses because they are of that certain race. In the year

2000, the office of Attorney General in the Department of Justice reported, "Six percent of Whites and 42 percent of Blacks responded that the police because of their race had stopped them, and 72 percent of Black men between ages 18 and 34 believed they had been stopped because of their race."[26]

Eleven years later, African-Americans still find themselves routinely pulled over at a higher rate than White-Americans. One example can be found in the New York Police Department (NYPD). "Stop-and-frisk" data revealed that in 2011, a record 684,330 people were stopped, 87 percent of whom were black and Hispanic individuals—although they comprise approximately 25 percent and 28 percent of New York City's total population respectively."[27] The above statics also showed that 47 percent of White-Americans surveyed said racial profiling did not exist, compared to the 72 percent of African-American who stated that they experienced being a victim. Racial profiling is one reason for the vast difference in the abundance of African-Americans in penal institutions today.

A Comparison: Plantation and Detention Officers

Figure 27 Slave Overseer, Men, Women and Children in a Cotton Field[28]

Another significant factor of slave plantation confinement was the overseers responsible for managing slaves while they were on the plantation. When combined with patrollers, they were a double-layer of security guards. Together, overseers and slave patrol had secured the exterior and interior of plantations to protect the investments of slave owners. Equally significant is the fact that synonyms for the word "incarcerated" also can be used to describe the home life for slaves: enslaved, imprisoned, confined, caged, jailed, interned and detained. Each word, in various ways, describes what it was like to live on plantations as a slave in America. All aspects of family life were lived in captivity and under the watchful eyes of owners and overseers. Today, we would call overseers either detention officers or prison guards.

> These men were a varied lot. Some were the sons of planters who served their fathers as overseers, learning the art of plantation management before striking out on their own. Others, perhaps the largest number, were semi-professional managers hoping one day to set up their own agricultural operations. And still, others lived up to the worst reputation of their class: violent men, often drunkards, unable to hold steady jobs, who moved repeatedly from plantation to plantation.[29]

Like the overseers in slavery, detention guards today continue as armed guards with shotguns to keep the detainees from disobeying the rules or leaving. In many instances, slaves received the same treatment as prisoners, who were escorted into the fields and watched as they worked throughout the day.

Frederick Douglass said, "That plantation is a little nation of its own, having its own language, its own rules, regulations, and customs. The laws and institutions of the state, apparently touch it nowhere. The troubles arising here are not settled by the civil power of the state. The overseer is generally accuser, judge, jury, advocate, and executioner. The criminal is always dumb. The overseer attends to all sides of a case."[30]

On plantations, there were three classes of individuals: slaveholders, overseers, and slaves. Slaves were the only ones who held no rights when justice was needed.

The disciplinary methods were often so severe that a slave would be better off to confess to a crime for which he or she was not guilty than to claim his innocence and risk a more severe punishment. Douglass reported, "The slave is sometimes whipped into the confession of offenses which he never committed. The reader will see that the good old rule— 'a man is to be held innocent until proven to be guilty'—does not hold good on the slave plantation. Suspicion and torture are the approved methods of getting at the truth here."[31]

In similar fashion to prisoners, slaves could not take restroom breaks or wander from their work area for any reason without the permission of their overseers. The enslaved worked from sunup to sunset for six days a week on a schedule that was determined by each individual plantation. The *Dictionary of American History* said,

> Overseers were the middlemen of the antebellum South's plantation hierarchy. As such, they occupied an impossible position. The masters expected them to produce profitable crops while maintaining a contented workforce of slaves—slaves who had little reason to work hard to improve the efficiency of the plantation. It would have required a prodigy to balance these competing pressures to the complete satisfaction of both the master and the slaves. Few overseers were prodigies.[32]

Overseers were usually uneducated and socially disadvantaged men. Their status in life placed them in a position where they were required to work in one of the lowest occupations of employment. For a slave overseer on a plantation, it was expected of them to manage a people that society narrowly placed in lesser a status than they were. They worked long hard hours watching and controlling the slaves in any weather condition, whether it be sun, rain, sleet, or snow.

Both slaves and owners often regarded overseers as White trash who were unacceptable for friendships. The disdain for the poor Whites created much of the harsh treatment that overseers displayed upon their slaves. W. J. Cash pointed out, "Slavery rested on force: the lash, chains and shackles, hounds and pistols to chase runaways, and mutilations and brandings (reflected in runaway slave advertisements). Cash also suggested that slavery hurt the White slaveholding population. Cash said, 'It was brutalizing to White men— releasing sadism and cruelty in masters and breeding in the common Whites a savage hate for African-Americans in response to the 'White trash' epithets they endured."[33] Within these statements by Cash, we can see how the residuals of enslavement affect this present generation of Black and White-Americans. It is reflected in the open racism displayed on a daily basis, and in the inequitable number of Black men who are in prisons across this country.

Slave overseers were usually White men. On many plantations, there was an additional position called a "driver." Drivers were typically a slave who had been taught to function as a handler, overseeing the slaves' activities during every phase of plantation life. These drivers served as the eyes and ears for slaveholders as informants, and were often harsher than their White counterparts who did the job.

> Drivers were another story. They were slaves appointed by masters to positions of authority on the plantation. Where masters were resident, black drivers often replaced overseers. On larger plantations, especially in the Lower South, black drivers worked under the supervision of White overseers. The drivers' jobs were manifold, but they were expected above all to maintain discipline in the fields and order in the quarters.[34]

The Treatment of Prisoners and Slaves

William Wells Brown, an abolitionist who wrote *The American Slave-Trade (1848)*, commented on the imprisonment of slaves before they reached the plantation. He reminisced on his visit to the South when he shared, "Few persons who have visited the slave states have not, on their return, told of the gangs of slaves they had seen on their way to the southern market. This trade presents some of the most revolting and atrocious scenes that the mind can imagine. Slave-prisons, slave-auctions, handcuffs, whips, chains, bloodhounds, and other instruments of cruelty are part of the furniture, which belongs to the American slave trade. It is enough to make humanity bleed at every pore, to see these implements of torture."[35] Slave men, women, boys and girls received the treatment of prisoners as they traveled in chains and shackles to various plantations after being sold. We can witness this similarity today in how prisoners are transported to prisons and courts in the penal systems in America today.

Upon arriving at the plantation, the shackles came off. Each time a slave was sold, it started a new prison sentence. American slavery produced this lifestyle for slaves, regardless of age or gender. Life in slavery required the same cruelty for every member of a slave family. When there was not complete total submission to the demands of plantation rules and work, all slaves were tortured into submission by many forms of punishment. The selling of family members was among the cruelest of punishments.

One difference between a slave plantation and a penitentiary is the correctional component to reform criminals, as is found in a penal institution. In contrast, slave plantations kept slaves incarcerated to maintain a free labor supply. Slaves were not criminals, but received the treatment of felons who had committed a federal offense. In essence, it was a conviction as a federal offense to be African-American during the years of bondage. Slavery was an institution that incarcerated African-Americans into a life of inferiorities, inequalities and injustices. Millions of slaves, from 1619 to 1865, had lived in confinement because of the color of their skin.

Could this provide some insights as to the reason African-American men and women find themselves imprisoned more than any other race in America today? "The prison population grew by 700 percent from 1970 to 2005, a rate that is outpacing crime and population rates. The incarceration rates disproportionately impact men of color: 1 in every 15 African-American men and 1 in every 36 Hispanic men are incarcerated in comparison to 1 in every 106 White men."[36] Katherine Anderson, in her book *Marriage—Just A Piece of Paper,* cited William Galston, who was the former deputy assistant to President Clinton for domestic policy. His perspective offers insights on the effect of imprisonment within the African-American community:

> In the African-American community, there are some difficulties that have to be acknowledged frankly. Our country, for good and for ill—and we can have a lengthy discussion about this—has embarked on a high prison incarceration strategy as its main approach to crime control in the past twenty years. That has had the effect of stripping the African-American community of many young men from their marriages and families. These facts are well known and greatly complicates the task of restoring marriage as a norm rather than a rare exception in the African-American community.[37]

During slavery, African-American marriages and families received a life sentence, without parole, designed for a prison or halfway house setting.

In many instances, some slaves never left the acreages of their plantation. The thought of patrollers was a constant reminder of the many dangers for slaves who went beyond the familiar surroundings of the owner's estate without a pass.

Figure 28. William and Ellen Craft, Escaped Slaves Married in 1846 While Slaves[38]

Regardless of the high level of security on slave plantations, many slaves found ways to escape to freedom. People like William and Ellen Craft demonstrated the constant pursuit of liberty. This slave couple escaped captivity in the year 1848 and wrote their story about the difficulties and experiences of being runaway slaves. William Craft said, "I must now give the account of our escape; but, before doing so, it may be well to quote a few passages from the fundamental laws of slavery; in order to give some idea of the legal as well as the social tyranny from which we fled."[39] One law read:

> If any slave, who shall be out of the house or plantation where such slave shall live, or shall be usually employed, or without some White person in company with such slave, shall REFUSE TO SUBMIT to undergo the examination of ANY WHITE person, (let him be ever so drunk or crazy), it shall be lawful for such White person to pursue,

> apprehend, and moderately correct such slave; and if such slave shall assault and strike such White person, such slave may be LAWFULLY KILLED."— 2 Brevard's Digest, 231.[40]

According to this law, any White person could lawfully kill a slave if they found a slave without a signed pass, and an ensuing struggle occurred during the arrest. This notice pointed out that slaves were required to submit to any Whites, regardless of their mental faculties, drunk or crazy. No slave could physically resist or protect themselves or their loved ones without risking death. William Craft continued his explanations of the dangers to a slave that was a part of everyday life on a plantation. He explained, "But, should the bondman, of his own accord, fight to defend his wife, or should his terrified daughter instinctively raise her hand and strike the wretch who attempts to violate her chastity, he or she shall, saith the model republican law, suffer death."[41]

Protecting one's family is a noble thing to die for in the case of any present-day husband or father. However, it would have been a daily possibility, and even norm, for a male African-American slave's life. Nevertheless, some "enslaved migrants ran away all the time, hiding in the woods to escape violence. However, most of them eventually came back to the slave labor camp. Slave patrols caught them. Random Whites caught them. Other slaves betrayed them. Most of them did not know the way back to wherever they had come from. And in between stood thousands of armed White people who would not be their friends."[42]

Bondage was never a voluntary institution; its fear element existed even among the best-treated slaves on a plantation. "More slaves are whipped for oversleeping than for any other fault. Neither age nor sex finds any favor. The overseer stands at the quarter door, armed with stick and cow skin, ready to whip any who may be a few minutes behind time."[43] American Slavery certainly sounds like the prison settings. In all fairness, though, to modern-day detention officers and police, their priority is safety. They are to serve and protect our communities, along with those incarcerated.

The Impact of Prisons and Slavery

Could there be a link between prisons on slave plantations and the American penal systems of today? There has been a lot of debate over the idea that plantations were prisons for slaves. Stanley M. Elkins, in *Slavery:*

A Problem in American Institutional and Intellectual Life argued, "The behavior exhibited by slaves was similar to that of concentration camp prisoners. John W. Blassingame contended that 'the system was not as closed' as Elkins asserts. 'Slaves, he argues, developed their own culture within the slave society.' This culture was dedicated to achieving freedom."[44] The merit of both arguments between Blassingame and Elkins was to expose that slavery was a prison camp where the enslaved did all within their power to win their freedom. They maintained as much human dignity as possible, while suffering through unspeakable injustices to their humanity. The era of captivity was entrenched with immorality by the White society. In 1861, Linda Brent wrote about the attitudes of many Southern women regarding slaves: "Southern woman often marries a man knowing that he is the father of many little slaves. They do not trouble themselves about it. They regard such children as property, as marketable as the pigs on the plantation." [45]

According to Howard McGary in *Between Slavery and Freedom: Philosophy and American Slavery Blacks in the Diaspora,* Kenneth M. Stampp wrote: "Slaves showed great eagerness to get some— if they could not get all— of the advantages of freedom."[46] It's important to understand the accommodating behavior slaves displayed in the context of the lives they were forced to live. "If slaves yielded to authority most of the time, they did so because they usually saw no other practical choice. Slaveholders understood this and worked to construct a system that would make slaves stand in fear."[47]

Mika'il DeVeaux quoted the research of Donald Clemmer, a pioneer whose work focused on the psychological effects of prison life, in his article "The Trauma of the Incarceration Experience a Harvard Civil Rights-Civil Liberties Law Review." In this article, he reported, "Indeed, the prison experience is unlike any other. Sociologist Donald Clemmer noted in his classic book, 'The Prison Community.'"[48] Deveaux says there are at least eight long-term effects of serving a prison term. He discovered:

1. "The prison experience is neither normal nor natural, and constitutes one of the more degrading experiences a person might endure."[49]
2. "People in prison are likely to report that their adaptations to the constant scrutiny of guards and the lack of privacy are psychologically debilitating."[50]

3. "Some literature suggests that people in prison experience mental deterioration and apathy, endure personality changes, and become uncertain about their identities."[51]
4. "Several researchers found that people in prison may be diagnosed with posttraumatic stress disorders, as well as other psychiatric disorders, such as panic attacks, depression, and paranoia."[52]
5. "Subsequently, these prisoners find social adjustment and social integration difficult upon release."[53]
6. "Other researchers found that the incarceration experience promotes a sense of helplessness, greater dependence, and introversion and may impair one's decision-making ability." [54]
7. "This psychological suffering is compounded by the knowledge of violence, the witnessing of violence, or the experience of violence, all too common during incarceration."[55]
8. "Some assert that the psychological effects of incarceration, developed during confinement, are likely to endure for some time following release."[56]

The above tenets are the same traits for an individual and any family member who would have spent any time incarcerated in either a prison or on plantations.

Herman Bell, an African-American, wrote, while imprisoned in the Eastern Correctional Facility in Napanoch, NY, about his prison experience. In this article entitled "The Psychological Effects of Long-Term Imprisonment," he languished, "For a African-American prisoner, his or her choice is like the Sword of Damocles suspended over his/her head by a hair. The historic enslavement of African-Americans in America and their maltreatment by White slaveholders is well documented, though much of it still remains to be told."[57] This illustration of the Sword of Damocles places an individual in a position of living while facing impending doom. The context is to live life the best you can in a situation in which you know that at any moment your life might end.

Herman Bell compared his incarceration in 2005 to what African-Americans endured in the days following the Civil War. "When Lincoln freed the US. Slaves, vestiges of the slave system remained firmly in place, and African-Americans remained subordinate to White authority. Although intervening years and subsequent battles won African-American civil rights victories, some would argue that the more things would seem to change for African-Americans, the more they remain the same."[58] Bell continued by expressing the distrust and fear of the legal authorities and systems that once enforced slavery and Jim Crow, and that titled African-Americans as subhuman and inferior. He continued taking this history into account – arrested by White police, prosecuted by White prosecutors, sentenced by White judges, and confined in American jails and overseen by White guards and administrators – how much to concede to authority weighed against its demands is no small consideration indeed. This very construct evokes strong imagery of overseer and slave on the plantation, complete with its psychological underpinnings.[59]

Although Bell wrote about the effects of slavery as an imprisonment of African-Americans, we should not neglect the consequences of slavery on White-Americans. Because America deemed African-Americans chattel and slaves as sub-human from 1619 to 1865, Black lives did not matter. This way of thinking continued from 1865 until 1965 when Black lives in freedom were legally second-class citizens under Jim Crow Laws (a time in which Black lives did not matter like White lives). Now we are only fifty-two years after the end of the Jim Crow Laws, and the residuals of racism from our past history are still in the hearts of many in our country. For many Whites today, the concept of superiority over African-Americans is associated with the belief that African-Americans should be feared or subjected to abuse because of what they endured in the past.

God's Grace for Prisoners

The amazing grace of God can manifest itself in the most challenging situations of life, even those of a prison setting. Jesus called for believers to comfort those in prisons. "I was in prison and you came to me. Then the righteous will answer him, saying, Lord, when did we see you? And when did we see you sick or in prison and visit you? And the King will answer them; Truly, I say to you, as you did it to one of the least of these, my brothers, you did it to me" (Matt.25: 36, 39-40 ESV). We have already discovered that God has compassion on those who care for the less fortunate in life. African-American slaves can be found in this passage many times, but prisoners of slavery and the least of these, they vividly stand out.

In another passage, the writer of Hebrews reminds us that God is at work when the Lord sends His Christian servants to supply the needs of the incarcerated. "For you had compassion on those in prison, and you joyfully accepted the plundering of your property, since you knew that you yourselves had a better possession and an abiding one. Therefore, do not throw away your confidence, which has a great reward. For you have need of endurance, so that when you have done the will of God you may receive what is promised" (Heb. 10:34–37 ESV). The work of abolitionists was by His Amazing Grace as they fought for the freedom of slaves throughout history, while using the word of God to justify their cause. The abolitionist and antislavery movements had compassion on African-American slaves when they found them incarcerated on slave plantations.

According to John MacArthur in *Slave: The Hidden Truth About Your Identity In Christ*, "Some of the earliest English translations, influenced by the Latin version of the Bible, translated *doulos* as "servant" because it was a more natural rendering of *servus*. Added to this, the term *slave* in sixteenth-century England generally depicted someone in physical chains or in prison." [60] Christians are to be committed to the cause of the gospel in every situation, or they become slaves to sin. The majority of times that the Greek word *slave* is used in New Testament translations, it is interpreted as *servant*. John MacArthur continued:

> The reason for this is as simple as it is shocking: the Greek word for slave has been covered up by being mistranslated in almost every English version—going back to both the King James Version and the Geneva Bible that predated it. Though the word slave (doulos in Greek) appears 124 times in the original text, it is correctly translated only once in King James. Most of our modern translations do only slightly better. It almost seems like a conspiracy.[61]

The difference between a slave and a servant is that a master owns the slave and the servant owns himself or herself. "Instead of translating *doulos* as 'slave,' these translations consistently substitute the word servant in its place. Ironically, the Greek language has at least half a dozen words that can mean servant. The word *doulos* is not one of them. Whenever it is used, both in the New Testament and in secular Greek literature, it always and only means slave."[62] Slaves who received a conversion experience to Christianity and who were fortunate to know the principles found in the teachings of Christianity, found strength in Christ while enduring the struggles of the American slave system.

African-American incarceration in 2017 continues to be a problem in the American legal system. I hope that the content covered in this chapter will serve as a deterrent to crime, by bringing awareness to our legislators, courts and law enforcement officers of some concerns within the African-American community. The judicial system is not an equitable system, and there is much work needed to be done to revise our courts and penal institutions so that it accurately reflects the racial breakdown of the American society.

America's modern-day justice system continues to institute laws that work to incarcerate people of color as a method of control and capitalism. For example, the most devastating legislation to African-American communities is the failure to regulate non-discriminatory ways to enforced laws. Over the last forty years, the United States has encountered a flood of arrests placing people of color behind bars. The National Association for the Advancement of Colored People lists the following "Criminal Justice Fact Sheet" for African-Americans:

Racial Disparities in Incarceration

1. African-Americans now constitute nearly 1 million of the total 2.3 million incarcerated populations.
2. African-Americans get incarcerated at nearly six times the rate of Whites.
3. Together, African-American and Hispanics comprised 58% of all prisoners in 2008, even though African-Americans and Hispanics make up approximately one-quarter of the US population.
4. According to Unlocking America, if African-American and Hispanics received incarceration at the same rates of Whites, today's prison and jail populations would decline by approximately 50%.
5. One in six black men had been incarcerated as of 2001. If current trends continue, one in three black males born today can expect to spend time in prison during his lifetime.
6. One in 100 African-American women are in prison.
7. Nationwide, African-Americans represent 26% of juvenile arrests, 44% of youth who are detained, 46% of the youth who are judicially waived to criminal court, and 58% of the youth admitted to state prisons (Center on Juvenile and Criminal Justice).[63]

It is disturbing to think of the two possible reasons the above statics are in existence: 1. A legal system slanted by race that is more lenient in enforcing the law toward the majority race. 2. African-Americans are inherently more sinful than other people groups and deserve to be locked up in higher numbers. Your life experiences and the side of the fence you stand on often determines the way a person feels about racial issues and the mass incarceration of African-Americans. Scripture challenges Christians to "remember those who are in prison, as though in prison with them, and those who are mistreated since you also are in the body" (Hebrew 13:3 ESV). Today, Americans are experiencing the residuals of slavery as demonstrated in the high numbers of African-Americans that are incarcerated in prisons and jails. These figures are escalated by the lack of knowledge and sensitivity for how past relationships continue to affect all Americans. With these comparisons in mind, one can see how race relationships has an impact on policing in America.

Chapter 11

The African-American Search for Identity

> But by the grace of God I am what I am, and his grace toward me was not in vain. On the contrary, I worked harder than any of them, though it was not I, but the grace of God that is with me (1 Cor. 15:10. ESV).

When we've been there ten thousand years
Bright shining as the sun

Africans, throughout the slave trade, were ripped by force from their families, friends and homeland to cross the Atlantic Ocean to America. They were then put to work on building its infrastructure and crops. On the shores of this country, they found themselves stripped of their names and their physical and mental dignity, while still struggling to hold onto their culture. A significant component of the African culture was ancestor adoration, from which they found strength and support for the difficult tasks of life. They looked for the spirit of their ancestors to communicate with them to lead, guide and protect them until they reunited with them after parting this life.

Of course, the first Africans in this country knew and understood their African heritage. But as time went by, and now 400 years later, their children search for identity. As an example, Cinque was a free African captured and brought to America aboard the *Amistad*. This was a slave ship still transporting slaves after slave trade had ended in 1807. Once the boat docked in America, Cinque found himself in a legal fight to obtain his freedom. He was forced to go through a series of hearings in front of the Supreme Court. He sought the support and strength from his deceased ancestors for reassurance and help, as he assisted ex-president John Quincy Adams to win back the freedom of all the captured free Africans on the ship. Cinque said, "We will not be alone. I meant my ancestors; I will call into the past, far back to the beginning of time, and beg them to come help me, at the judgment. I will reach back and draw them to me, and they must come. For at this moment I am the only reason they have existed at all."[1] Quincy Adams then used the argument as his defense to demonstrate they were free men born in Africa. This argument for ancestral unification created a defense that caused them to win their case for freedom. In the words of Adams, "When a member of Mende tribe encounters a situation where there appears that there is no hope at all, he invokes his ancestors, and it's a tradition. See the Mende believes that if one can summon the spirit of their ancestors, then they have never left. And the wisdom and strength they fathered and inspired will come to his aid."[2] Since the first Africans came to the shores of America in bondage, they have been on a quest to find self-identity, equality and a sense of belonging.

Social psychologist Thomas Pettigrew put it this way, "The pursuit for self-identity is the search for answers to the all-important questions: Who am I? What am I like as a person? Also, how do I fit into the world? These are not easy questions for anyone to answer in our complex, swiftly-changing society. Yet they offer even greater difficulties for Negro Americans."[3] One psychological effect on the first generation of slaves in America, compared to those that were born into slavery, was having had the taste of freedom and then having to grieve its loss. The first generation of African slaves suffered the agony of being forced to decrease in recognized personhood from human to inhuman within their lifetime.

Slaves: No Image of God and no Soul

The survival of African-American marriages and families, under a government that reduced the African-American to the status of animals, was not an intentional American concept in slavery. Defining African-American marital status as quasi-cognation reveals the intent of the Slave Codes to annul any family relations or the marriages by slaves. Cognation refers to having relationships by blood or having a common ancestor. One goal of the slave laws was to eliminate any connection of the slave to his heritage, which is reflected by the slaves' inability to have heirs, make wills or name their family. The ability to trace lineage was an attribute of humanity and not chattel, and having a family name would also provide a link for slaves to locate their families that were sold. If a slave could have located their family, the fear was that they would be tempted to run away to join them. Also, knowing family descent enhances the ability to discover family roots to the base of all humanity, all of the way back to Adam and Eve.

Sociologist Orlando Patterson explained why the quasi-cognation marriages and families of slaves held little value to keep long-lasting family relationships. He said, "The refusal to formally recognize the social relations of slaves produced profound lasting emotional and social implications for separated slave families. In all slaveholding societies, slave couples could be and were forcibly separated. And the consensual wives of slaves were obliged to submit sexually to their masters."[4] These laws endangered every principle leading to the marital satisfaction of couples.

The sad reality of American slavery is the ability of one race to define another race as existing outside of humanity. This epitomizes man's inhumanity to their fellow man. To suggest that God made African-American people a lower species is to question the Word of God in both the Old and New Testaments. "And he has made from one blood all nations of men to dwell on all the face of the earth and has determined the times before appointed, and the bounds of their habitation" (Acts 17:26 ESV). "And the LORD God formed man *of* the dust of the ground, and breathed into his nostrils the breath of life; and man became a living soul" (Genesis 1:26 ESV). This tenet of slavery took from African-Americans the legal right to be considered humans created by God.

It is staggering to think that theologians of the day could interpret these passages in any other way than as written, and yet several different unfounded theological minds were able to justify African-American people as chattel. For example, Buckner H. Payne, also known as Ariel, was theologically responsible for some of the false Bible teachings on the subject of Negro inhumanity. He said, "As Adam was the federal head of all his posterity, as well as the real head, so was this beast, the Negro, the federal head of all beasts and cattle, etc., down to creeping things—to things that go upon the belly and eat dust all the days of their life."[5] His interpretation of God's creation of man provides a distorted understanding that was the predominate theology used to remove the African-American from God's creation account of humanity. If the slaves were not human, the creation account did not apply to them.

Arguments regarding the humanity and personal status of African-Americans continued throughout the history of slavery and the Civil

Rights era. At the end of slavery, Payne Ariel published a book entitled *The Negro: what (sic) is His Ethnological Status?* Ariel questioned the legitimacy of the Negro's humanity. He asked several questions to promote the inferiority of African-Americans. "What is his Ethnological Status? Is he the progeny of Ham? Is he a descendant of Adam and Eve? Has he a Soul? Or is he a Beast, in God's nomenclature? What is his Status as fixed by God in creation? What is his relation to the White race?"[6] This book, written in 1866, was intended to prove that African-Americans were savage beasts outside of the human race. The theology behind this teaching is without any intelligent argument.

The content of this book is comparable to all the books written during the era of slavery and Jim Crow on the subject of African-Americans' bestiality. Payne's questions were designed to comfort a hurting and defeated Confederacy. These teachings also helped set the course for the Negro's future status and continued treatment as second-class citizens. This idea became widespread as a popular public opinion, which opened the door for racial hatred and the cruel and harsh attacks on African-Americans during Jim Crow. The book represents the mental attitudes of a nation from a past era concerning the human status of African-American people. The residuals of these false and unfounded assumptions continue to pollute the minds of many White-Americans in the twenty-first century.

African-Americans endured centuries of identity, personality, and character assignations designed to humiliate and degrade their ability to develop as people of integrity. False teachings, like those in Payne's book, created a struggle for African-American people to prove their humanity while still discovering their place in a broken American society. Millard J. Erickson, in *Christian Theology*, wrote about this issue. "The quest for identity has always been part of the normal process of maturation for forming an independent outlook of personal values and goals."[7] Slavery required them to live without integrity or fairness and as if they did not have a human soul. Because African-American couples were denied these needs, marital stereotypes became associated with black marriages and families today.

These stereotypes developed into the identity traits assigned to African-Americans by the White community during slavery and Jim Crow to exaggerate their promiscuous sins. If you take a close look at the sins of the owners during slavery, it is easy to see that the negative stereotypes that were assigned to slaves really were reflected in the owners. Slaveholder's sexually assaulted black women. They stole their lives and their labor. Owners treated their slaves like beasts - they killed, brutalized, raped and whipped those under their control.

Counselors and psychologists recognize this transferal of shamefaced behavior as *projection*: "A sociological phenomenon where members of a people group accuse members of another group of feeling or acting in a manner that they are engaging in, often to divert attention from their behavior. It is particularly common among groups living with high levels of fear or resentment."[8] Slaves were accused of the actions of their owners, like a husband or wife guilty of adultery who says their spouse committed the same wrong to hide their infidelity. Another example is a child who does something wrong, but instead of confessing, points his finger at his playmate and accuses them, in this way hiding his shame. Although there were many negative tenets of slavery projected onto slaves, the word of God is clear that the responsible parties will have their judgments. "For you may be sure of this, that everyone who is sexually immoral or impure, or who is covetous (that is, an idolater), has no inheritance in the kingdom of Christ and God" (Eph. 5:5 ESV).

Consequently, slavery forced slaves into these sinful, immoral and promiscuous lifestyles, and all the blame of its actions are represented in the stereotypes attached to them and their offspring. In contrast, the White community was not labeled with the same negative stereotypes as African-Americans, even while they were the originators of much immorality. Although in many cases slaves were often their willing partners, most victims were forbidden to refuse all invitations to corrupt living. Subsequently, many today have failed to escape this heritage and have established the enforced sexual attitudes and characteristics associated with African-Americans in slavery.

What's in a Family Name?

In the quest for identity, the family sets the stage for telling us who we are: the kind of person I am and how I am to fit in life. "Identity problems are unusually acute during certain periods in a person's life. These periods, these identity crises, often occur in the preschool years, later in adolescence, and again in young adulthood. All three of these periods impose additional stress on Negroes. Negro parents confess to great anxiety and ambivalence over telling their preschool children what it means to be a Negro in American society."[9] We can devise from the findings of Dr. Pettigrew that identity and self-esteem problems are intimately associated with the lack of family solidarity. In the case of the African-American family, this stems from generations of treatment as inferior. Historically, African-Americans have had little positive with which to measure themselves on the quest to find self-importance. Slavery and the second-class citizenship status appointed them in America have provided the most challenging and demeaning standards upon which to devise a self-identity.

First-generation slaves endured having their African names stripped from them, and being given American names chosen by their owners. The loss of a family name can have a devastating effect on a person. African-Americans were required to change their names for many reasons throughout slavery. Attached to family names are the answers to the questions in the search for self-identification. For most people, the family name is a source of pride, respect and honor, and this name requires protecting at all cost. The surname indicates bloodline and creates the most durable bonds for identification; however, the name of a slave was of little importance, because their family and marriages meant nothing in the American society. Prov. 22:1 (ESV) says, "A good name is rather to be chosen than great riches, and loving favor rather than silver and gold." The use of family surnames by a slave family was never permissible in the presence of owners in the American slave system. "The people who created it so perversely designed it to destroy any possibility of maintaining the family ties necessary to tracing one's ancestry, through the deviously brilliant act of obliterating our family names, our surnames."[10]

Due to the circumstances, numerous slaves, after receiving freedom, changed their names from that given by their former masters. As an illustration, the famous abolitionist Frederick Douglass changed his name to Douglass, a title he gave himself after gaining his freedom. Douglass, a runaway slave, Freeman and an abolitionist, changed his last name at least three times during his lifetime. He went from Bailey to Johnson and finally Douglass.

As slaves were sold from one owner to another, they were often required to accept the last name of whoever held ownership papers on them. It was unusual for a slave to not change names each time after suffering their sale to a new owner. Switching the names of slaves who were sold away to other plantations kept them from being traceable by family members who might run away looking for their children, mothers, fathers, and spouses. Consequently, slaves, according to the legislation defining slavery, had no lineage. The loss of ones' heredity, or having no human right to legacy, is found within the American Slave Codes starting in 1662 and lasting throughout the history of slavery.

A few years ago, I began to trace my family history and found a common genealogical brick wall for all African-Americans families. Henry Gates determined in his book, *In Search of Our Roots*, that "All African-Americans hit a genealogical brick wall somewhere in slavery. Slavery was constructed to deconstruct the Negro, in every way imaginable, except as pure labor, as a measurable commodity."[11] Before 1870, the Census enumerators from earlier years only listed slaves by age and gender, creating a wall for African-Americans who attempt to trace their heritage.

Figure 29 1860 Slave Schedule Ellis County Texas[12]

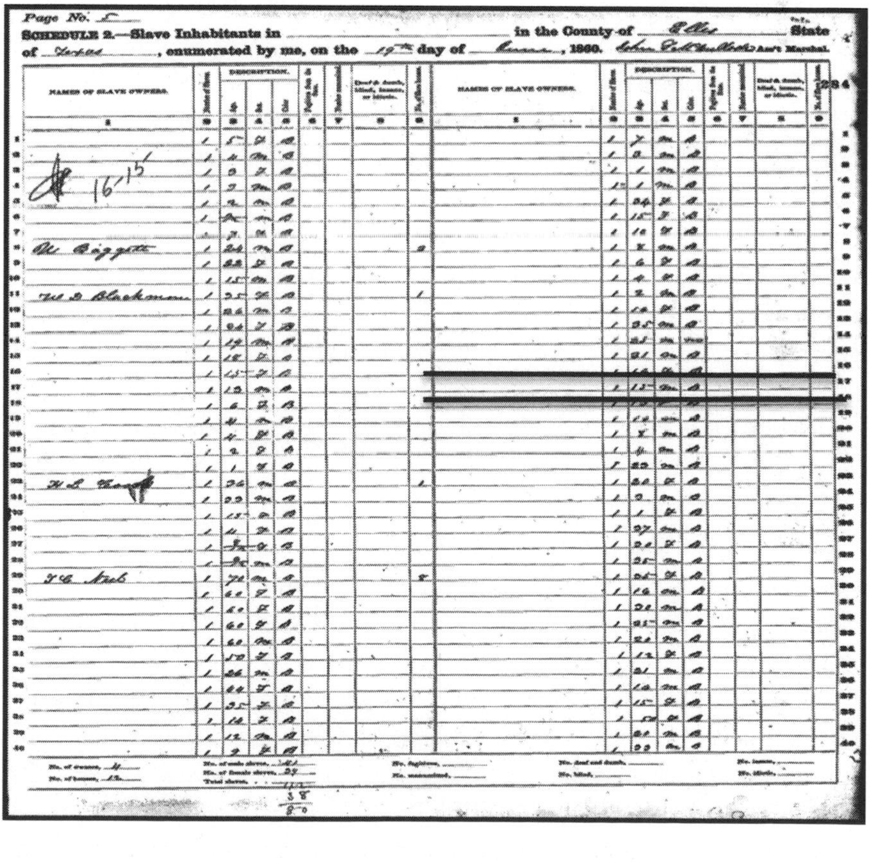
Page No. ___
SCHEDULE 2.—Slave Inhabitants in ___ in the County of ___ State of ___, enumerated by me, on the ___ day of ___, 1860. ___ Ass't Marshal.

> Slaves were enumerated separately during the 1860 Census, though, most schedules do not provide personal names. In most cases, individuals were not named but were simply numbered and can be distinguished only by age, sex, and color; the names of owners are recorded. However, some enumerators listed the given names of slaves, particularly those over one hundred years of age. These names are found in the "name of slave owners" column. Other questions asked include whether a fugitive from the state (meaning if the slave had fled and not returned); number manumitted (or freed); whether deaf and dumb, blind, insane, or idiotic; and number of slave houses.[13]

The 1870 brick wall, as referred to by ancestry research analysts, was the first time the United States Census included the households, names, birth year, and state of birth for the newly emancipated slaves. Frederick Douglass explained the real difficulty of slaves and birthdays. He said, "I never met with a slave who could tell me how old he was. Few slave-mothers know anything of the months of the year, nor of the days of the month. They keep no family records, with marriages, births, and deaths. They measure the ages of their children by springtime, winter time, harvest time, planting time, and the like; but these soon become indistinguishable and forgotten."[14] This Census also included, for the first time, financial assets, whether the person had the ability to read and write, what their gender was, and what occupation the former slaves held.

The previous chart is an example of the missing names for slaves on the 1860 US Census for Slaves. On this Slave Schedule from the 1860 Census in Ellis County in Texas, the outlined 15-year-old male slave could be Warren Turner. Warren Turner was first introduced in chapter one of this book as family risk factors were being explored. Like many slaves, Warren must have changed or assumed his surname upon receiving his freedom, because his name is different than his slave owner, who is listed as TC Neel. Possibly, Warren knew the name Turner as that of his previous owner in Georgia. He might have thought that assuming this surname allowed a connection to family that might be looking for him through the Freemans Bureau.

The Freemans Bureau was a government agency responsible for paving a way into society for former slaves after the Civil War. One of the agency's primary functions was helping sold and separated families get reunited.

For the first time in American history, "Former slaves had to undertake a task unknown to free-born Americans. They were required to adopt a surname. Although slaves often adopted family names for use among themselves, few masters wished to bestow upon their chattel the sense of dignity a surname implied."[15]

The assumption that Warren took the surname Turner for himself as a freedman is fairly safe, because no slaveholders had that name in Waxahachie, Ellis County Texas in 1860. "One former bondman insisted that adoption of a surname was a way to get 'clean' of slavery. In choosing a name, a small percentage adopted the family name of their master, either as a tie to an ancestral birthplace, or perhaps so that relatives might find them at war's end."[16]

Warren first appeared in records at the end of the Civil War in 1867 at age 20 when he filled out his Voter Registration information for African-American men who were former slaves. This was a US Government effort during the Reconstruction Movement, and it was beneficial in revealing Warren's past geographical location as Georgia. Also, it provided his time of residence. He had moved to Texas in Waxahachie, Ellis County 13 years earlier, which made him a 7-year-old child slave in 1854 migrating from Georgia.

Family research analysis experts instruct African-Americans who are looking for their ancestor families to search for the family name among the freedmen living in the same neighborhood. They found that most of the newly freed families stayed close to the area they were most familiar with after enslavement.[17] For this reason, I linked the other Turner households next-door as possibly his brothers, sister, and mother or grandmother. Another finding that helps piece together this family puzzle is all the Turner families in adjacent houses were also born in Georgia. The only exception was the youngest sibling who was born in Texas in 1854, the year they arrived in Texas from Georgia. The final keys for this link were the ages and genders of the slaves on the above Waxahachie, Ellis County slave schedule in 1860, and the name of the slaveholder, who is also from Georgia.

Another important consideration on the Slave Schedule is in knowing the slaveowner's name and residence. It is helpful to know when tracing the transitions of slaves as they moved around from one plantation to another. For example, "TC Neel the slave owner listed on the above slave schedule also moved from Hancock, Georgia to Texas in 1854 and to Waxahachie in

1855 with 80 slaves."[18] If Warren were the 15-year-old on the slave schedule, we could also assume the historical record of TC Neel's movement from Hancock, Georgia would also be Warren's. These documents, if correct, provide an ancestry trace that takes his family back to the year 1810. The year 1810 is the year that Ray Turner was born on the 1870 Census. She was living next door to Warren and was possibly his mother or grandmother.

The 1870 Census also listed a family with a mulatto father and his African-American wife, with her two mulatto children, living next door on the other side of Warren. They had the surname Neil. Possibly, they were related and slaves of TC Neel. One ancestery.com research user has identified the wife as Warren's sister. Perhaps the husband is a member of Neel's family, and the Census taker misspelled the surname, which was a common occurrence. When names were misspelled, it either indicated the slave was illiterate and could not correct the Census taker's mistake, or the broken English used by slaves was challenging to understand. In the case of Warren's African-American neighbors, everyone but one household listed themselves as illiterate. Another possibility was the pressure placed on ex-slaves by the United States government to register with surnames quickly, and the urgency to comply forced them to keep the former slaveholder's name. Maintaining the slaveholder's name was familiar for slaves who were the offspring of slaveholders, since surnames served as recognition of kinship and any possible inheritance. "The practice of naming simply varied from county to county and state to state and, indeed, from former slave to former slave."[19]

In contrast, a large majority of newly freedmen wanted to remove any connection to their former masters as they realized the significance of surnames. "The adoption of an owner's surname also implied a biological kinship that did not exist; should hundreds of liberated slaves on a large estate adopt the same name, that might suggest a family tie many neither recognized nor desired."[20] Also, when slaves stayed close to the plantations of their enslavement, some owners maintained a controlling influence over slaves. They often led them to adopt new names that the former owner selected. Elizabeth A. Regosin and Donald R. Shaffer, *In Voices of Emancipation: Understanding Slavery, the Civil War, and Reconstruction through the U.S. Pension Bureau Files* said, "Slaveholders generally did not assign slaves their own surnames, though they referred to slaves by their owner's surname as a means of signifying to whom they belonged."[21]

Legal records were also found revealing that Warren was connected to the family members of TC Neel following slavery. One example was the Bethel Church in Ellis, Texas, in which he was married after slavery, was a church that TC Neel assisted in founding. A final observation was after TC Neel's death in 1863, his ex-wife married William H. Getzendaner the first mayor of Waxahachie who signed the 1869 marriage license for Warren and Elvira Turner. Nevertheless, with all this genealogical research on the 1860 Slave Schedule, it is impossible to definitively say they are the same person.

Because of the difficulties in finding ancestry slave links, the search for identity among African-Americans today is problematic and often frustrating. Numerous slave families after the Civil War dropped the slave name of their owner and renamed themselves. The search for identity is evident in both the Pathological and Resilience sociological views. The missing link of a traceable family name within Black America has created mental anguish and is a tenet of the pathologies associated with slavery. While in contrast, the ability to rename oneself is adaptive or resilient among sociologist when found in African-Americans following slavery.

Without addressing the physical and mental wounds of racial trauma, which remained throughout their lifetimes, they were unable to heal from the mistreatments in their hearts. This silence served to develop a psychological block that perhaps only therapeutic methods could have cured; nevertheless, they used what was at their disposal.

Cultural Trauma

A link to cultural trauma exists between contemporary African-Americans and former slaves, and can be seen in the struggle to find an identity as a people group. Psychologists have identified the conflicts of slavery and all the distress involved in losing heritage by African-Americans as a Cultural Trauma. A team of sociologists from the University of California explained, "Cultural trauma occurs when members of a collectivity feel they have been subjected to a horrendous event that leaves indelible marks on their group consciousness, marking their memories forever and changing their future identity in fundamental and irrevocable ways."[22] Although most African-Americans have never heard of the theory associated with Cultural Trauma, they understand that the cruelties associated with discrimination in American history have altered their lives. Most would agree that the Cultural Trauma they presently experience was also existing over generations, beginning with slavery. One example can be illustrated in the way African-Americans have undergone numerous name changes regarding their racial identity: Nigger, Negro, Colored, Afro-American, Black-American, and African-American. When looking at all ethnicities, no other nationality has held so many different race related identifications over the course of American history. Every African-American born in the 1950s that is alive today has experienced each of the above changes to the cultural identity of African-Americans.

The decades of the 60s, 70s and 80s saw anthropologists and sociologists struggle to create a suitable description to identify the descendants of Africans into the American social system. African-Americans, until the 60s, endured offensive names like Negro, Colored, or Nigger. Today these terms are inappropriate to use. Slaves and Whites alike commonly used the word nigger during slavery, as it took on the meaning of degradation. Nevertheless, the oldest and most offensive term used to identify African-Americans is a nigger, a name that for hundreds of years has refused to fade away. The term nigger was given to the Africans by the American slave system to defile, slander, demean, and hate African-American people, and it continues as a term used by many African-Americans among themselves. The cultural resiliency in the African-American Community took the negatives out of the word and used it to express endearment among close African-American friends and families. The term nigger uttered in a pathological nature is a putdown by African-Americans and carries the original meaning. For this reason, today it is a volatile term when used by other ethnicities.

Nevertheless, the etymology, or "The history of the word nigger is often traced to the Latin word Niger, meaning Black. This word became the noun, Negro (Black person) in English, and simply the color Black in Spanish and Portuguese."[23] When reflecting on the origin of the term nigger, the negative connotation associated with the word is lost. If not for centuries of racial hatred in the hearts and minds of people, this would be a reasonable word. When the word is used in this book, it was not changed to keep the context of the day and time it was spoken. In contrast, the author, when referring to Black people, chose to use the preferred names selected by African descendants for themselves such as Black-Americans or African-Americans.

So, what name should be used? Black-American or African-American? Both are given names for the same people group. Black-American is a term that came into existence during the Civil Rights movements of the 60s and remained the preferred name until the 80s when African-American became popular. Today, the term African-American remains the most acceptable name for identifying a person of African descent.

These name changes for African-Americans, starting in the 60s with Black-Americans, were positive culturally to the identity of this people group and represented their advancement for recognition as a race. African-Americans have historically looked for the societal acceptance of the majority culture for their development and inclusion as a race of people. The attempt to find self-significance found some achievements by expressing creativity, pursuing spiritual understanding, and pursuing a quest for historical knowledge. Perhaps the need for self-significance or importance is at the heart of the 2017 movement that Black Lives Matter and are important too. This is also an attempt by modern-day African-American youths to express their need for acceptance by the majority culture one hundred and fifty years after slavery. Behind each of the historical struggles for civil rights in this country has been the need to acquire self-significance. This quest to find self-worth in America has been best fulfilled in their creative abilities in athletics, acting, dancing, singing, education, service to God, and knowledge of African-American history.[24] Each of these professions represents careers that African-Americans have found their most significant success after gaining freedom.

Also, the African-American search for self-significance and identity is an effort to reverse the stereotypes of being a lazy, uninterested people who have not contributed to the success of America in the sciences, arts, and comforts of the American way of life. Thomas Pettigrew reported that influential European writers of the late eighteenth and early nineteenth centuries first made these putdowns against all Americans.[25] As the English expressed superiority over the early inhabitants of the American colonies, the first American slaveholder conveyed these negative and inferior concepts to slaves. These stereotypes have made it very difficult for African-American people to fill a respectable place in American society. Although they were insults intended for all Americans, over the course of time, the majority culture has shaken off these negative innuendos. The putdowns have remained applicable only for African-Americans throughout history.

The battle continues to overcome centuries of putdowns and to bring normalcy to the African-American family structures among slave descendants. When tracing the history of African-American marriages and families in the United States, laws that governed each century during slavery revealed this identity crisis was intentional on the part of slaveholding states. This investigation also linked an identity crisis to the present high rates of social factors experienced by present-day African-American married couples and those of marriages in slavery. Mostly, the high failure rates among African-American marriages and families in the twenty-first century have remained practically unexplored by social scientists until this study. Most studies on the subject of slavery and its impact on African-Americans do not examine its consequence on families and marriages of today. Consequently, the Resilience and Pathology views are the two primary sociological studies included in this book, and both have limited their results to the era of slavery and the first half of the twentieth century. Sociologists who express the Resilience Theory contend that African-Americans received no negative affected influence from bondage. This is not true for every family, and their lack of researching and exploring the impact of slavery on the African-American family has left the African-American community in the dark. It is essential to remember the historical struggles endured by the ancestors of any people group if they endeavor to repair the present. Scripture also recommends knowing the negatives of our ancestors are of great benefit to explain our present suffering. "The Lord...visits the iniquity of the fathers on the children and the children's children, to the third and fourth generation" (Exodus 34:6-7 ESV).

The following chart will assist in reviewing the family crisis from 1790 through 1860 of the US Census enumerations. This diagram represents the percentages of the enumerated African-American individuals and families who were free and who were slaves, those who could marry and those who could not legally marry because of slavery. In an era when African-American marriages and families are at an all-time low in family stability, and high in social risk factors, marriage specialists are determined to discover why African-American families are overwhelmed with absentee and fatherless homes, a majority single mother households, extremely high out-of-wedlock births, and cohabitating couples. When examining the US Census statistics from 1790–1860, no family statistics were computed for slaves. Therefore, I am calculating the possibility of stable and unstable African-American individuals, marriages and families during this period. Having a status of slave or free was the determining factor for a family that was stable or in crisis. Whereas, free African-Americans during this time will be treated as possible stable marriages and families since they were without the crisis of slavery and could maintain family relationships independent of outside forces.

Figure 30. US Census African-American Marriage Statistics 1790-2010[26]

MARITAL CONDITIONS OF BLACK AMERICANS 15 AND OLDER 1790- 2010

The 1790 – 1860 US Census listed slaves under the owner's name and household, along with age, gender and race. The marriages of slaves were not legal; their marriages were considered cohabitation. Free Blacks were listed on the US Census in the same manner as White Americans. They, however, were not listed as Black but as *other persons* along with the ages of all male and female household members.

US CENSUS RESULTS 1790- 1860

	Free Blacks Legally Married Open To Marriage Choices Equitable Family Structures			Slave Marriages Prohibited Forced Cohabitating Families Inequitable Family Structure			
Year	Free Blacks	Percentage	Increase	Slave	Percentage	Increase	Total Blacks
1790	59,557	7.9%		697,624	92.1%	N/A	757,181
				Slave Trade ended 1808 breeding results			
1800	108,435	10.8%	82.2%	893,602	89.2%	28.1%	1,002,037
1810	186,446	13.5%	71.9%	1,191,362	86.5%	33.3%	1,337,808
1820	233,634	13.2%	25.3%	1,538,022	86.8%	29.1%	1,771,656
1830	319,599	13.7%	36.8%	2,009,043	86.3%	30.6%	2,328,642
1840	386,293	13.4%	20.9%	2,487,355	86.6%	23.8%	2,873,648
1850	434,495	11.9%	12.5%	3,204,313	88.1%	28.8%	3,638,808
1860	488,070	11.0%	12.3%	3,953,760	89.0%	23.4%	4,441,830

1870- 2010 US Census Results Percentages By Male and Female Ages 15 Up

1870 No marriage or family data was listed in the 1870 US Census. After 5 yrs. of freedom the Black population increased an average rate of a ten-year growth during slavery, 4,441,830 to 4,880,009 million people, an 8.9% increase.

1880 Blacks family structure acknowledged, they also quadrupled their average ten-year population growth over 100 yrs. with an increase of 1,700,784 (25.8%), totaling 6,580,793 million Black Americans.

	MARRIED	SINGLE	DIVORCED	WIDOWED
	After 100 years 1890 was the first US Census with data for marital status			
1890	55.5% M/54.6% F	39.8% M/30.0% F	0.2% M/0.5% F	4.3% M/14.7% F
1900	54.0% M/53.7% F	39.2% M/29.9% F	0.4% M/0.8% F	5.7% M/15.4% F
1910	57.2% M/57.2% F	35.4% M/26.9% F	0.7% M/1.1% F	6.2% M/14.8% F
	From 1920- 1950 the stats for divorces/widow were combined			
1920	60.4% M/59.0% F	32.6% M/24.1% F	N/A	5.9% M/14.8% F
1930	59.9% M/58.8% F	33.1% M/23.2% F	N/A	5.5% M/15.8% F
1940	60.0% M/58.5% F	33.5% M/23.9% F	N/A	6.2% M/15.7% F
	Male and Female stats were combined for singles, divorces, and widows			
1950	63.5% M/F	23.9% M/F	N/A	12.6% M/F
1960	60.9% M/59.8% F	29.6% M/F	2.4% M/F	4.6% M/F
1970	56.9% M/54.1% F	24.3% M/F	3.6% M/F	5.2% M/F
1980	44.8% M/44.6% F	30.5% M/F	8.9% M/F	8.4% M/F
1990	45.1% M/40.2% F	35.1% M/F	8.5% M/F	10.6% M/F
	Marriage stats are separated/combined for male and female			
2000	36.0% M/F	40.6% M/F	7.0% M/F	11.2% M/F
2010	39.0% M/33.0% F	48.8% M/45.2%F	9.1% M/12.4% F	2.7% M/9.1% F

US Census Bureau: Population and Housing, 1790-2010. https://www.census.gov/prod/www/decennial.html

When considering the difficulties of slave and free Negro families, the 1860 statistics provide some insight into why the pathological view came into existence. The Census enumeration from this year reveals the small percentages of African-American families that enjoyed a healthy family life. In effect, there were "3,953,760 million slaves living as someone's property with no control over their families and 488,070 free African-Americans. Free and slave African-Americans totaled 4, 441,830"[27] living in this country five years before the emancipation proclamation. These statistics also revealed that 11% of the African-American population was free to have a reasonable family life outside of slavery, and 89% were enslaved without legal family relationships. Consequently, an understanding of the system of chattel slavery specifies data for an evaluation of the social risk factors that were involved in enslaved family structures. This era of American history made being African-American a social issue, which made them susceptible to social risk factors, whether free or slave.

Equally important would be a 2014 comparison of 38,605,000 African-American adults with all the rights to assume family life as they chose, but having the same risk factors as their enslaved ancestors. With this in mind, statistics reveal an increased population of African-Americans after slavery experiencing a historical low of 33% married couples despite having the freedom to marry. With 72% of children born out-of-wedlock and only 31% of African-American children living in two-parent households, conditions are not much different from the days of slavery. Simply put, little has changed to improve the instability of the African-American family since slavery.

Many family historians argue that, for one hundred years after oppression (1890-1990), marital conditions among African Americas were unaffected by two and a half centuries of forced family crisis. The US Census findings revealed the rates for African-American marriages were the same for Black and White marital unions from 1890 to1990. These statistics suggest that enslavement had no negative impact on the matrimonial conditions of African-Americans.

Although slaves gained emancipation in 1860, family statistics were not a part of the Census until 1880, some twenty years after captivity. This actually reveals twenty years of undetermined family functioning among ex-slaves. Captivity was a battle both mentally and physically for African-Americans, and the Lord explains the warfare that must be waged if we are to have a plentiful or abundant life. "The thief comes only to steal and kill and destroy. I came that they may have life and have it abundantly" (John 10:10 ESV). American bondage took the possibility of finding the quality of life that was promised to Disciples of Christ who escape the captivity of Satan.

In my opinion, it's unrealistic that slaves could escape two hundred and fifty years of mental exploitations, of being taught they needed masters to provide for them as an inferior race, without wrestling with serious and numerous consequences even decades later. In bondage, their masters named them and disciplined them all like children. African-Americans controlled no aspect of their family relationships. They were bred like animals to produce children they could not raise as they decided. Couples were not able to protect each other from the sexual advances of any predator, owner, overseer or other bondmen without severe discipline or losing their life.

Under these circumstances, the mental oppression of slavery required them to act as if everything was normal in the midst of great pain. Their ability to keep their anger and frustrations tempered and unnoticed was a key to survival. However, what the statistics from the first 100 years of freedom, from 1890 to 1990, cannot reveal is the need for African-Americans to demonstrate their abilities for independent survival. They possessed a driving ambition to receive acceptance in every aspect of the American society. Freedom created an overwhelming enthusiasm about their new possibilities in life. No words could accurately express the excitement that accompanied hearing, "We Are Free." Their jubilation, no doubt, was the same as the psalmists, "This is the day that the Lord has made; let us rejoice and be glad in it" (Ps. 118:24 ESV).

Former slaves and their descendants, for 100 years after captivity, were in an extreme state of euphoria over having their freedom. They were the first to be free in the history of their African-American ancestors. Now, like never before, they could celebrate and make a commitment to a legitimate marriage. Above all, they could rejoice at becoming lawful husbands, wives and parents and control their own lives as independent adults and families. This excitement would last for generations as they told their children of the joy they received when getting their freedom, along with the thrill of knowing that the sufferings of being enslaved would no longer exist. They could now reveal openly the many brutalities used to condition them to accept their status in life, and the ideologies that falsely informed them of their inferiorities as chattel. Finally, they were excited to see that God heard and answered their prayers for freedom. This newfound freedom prompted the need to demonstrate their abilities to make their marriages and family relationships successful during the first 100 years after captivity.

However, racism and abuses inherent in the American society did not end with captivity. From 1865 through 1965, African-Americans were legally second-class citizens. In freedom, the strength of their families served as a safety net from the pathologies of continued bondage. After slavery, the pains suffered by African-American marriages and families remained suppressed to acquire total acceptance into an American society governed by racist laws. Quickly after the end of slavery, Jim Crow laws became redefined versions of discriminatory rules that regulated only African-Americans. From 1865 to1877, the United States government started the Reconstruction period as an effort to launch free African-Americans into society. This effort stopped as states established their own laws called the Black Codes. These Black Codes separated fathers, mothers, and children by making them criminals and placing them in prisons to serve years of hard labor for trivial charges. The use of these petty charges filled prison camps, which for the most, part leased workers to large industries and paid municipalities for supplementing the income of local and state governments after the Civil War.

Although African-Americans were victimized by institutionalized racism during the reconstruction period, they continued to celebrate freedom, needing to prove how capable they were with managing their own personal lives and families. The African-American family remained resilient as they faced life's inequitable hardships under the Black Codes. They found the ability to maintain life amidst new oppressions of unjust legislation by holding on to the support of God, spouses and families. Nevertheless, the pain and sufferings from captivity were smoldering as they lived in the shadow of oppression they suffered during slavery. Finally, as mentioned before, the US Census statistics for almost one hundred years (1890 to 1970) reported that 50 – 60% of African-Americans were married. The 1960s ushered in the social revolutions which brought liberating influences on the American society and played a significant role in the decline of marriage rates within African-American families. In 1980, the rates of marriage started to decline for African-American couples, hovering from low to mid 40% percent.

Figure 31. The Proportion of Married Adults Has Decreased 2011[28]

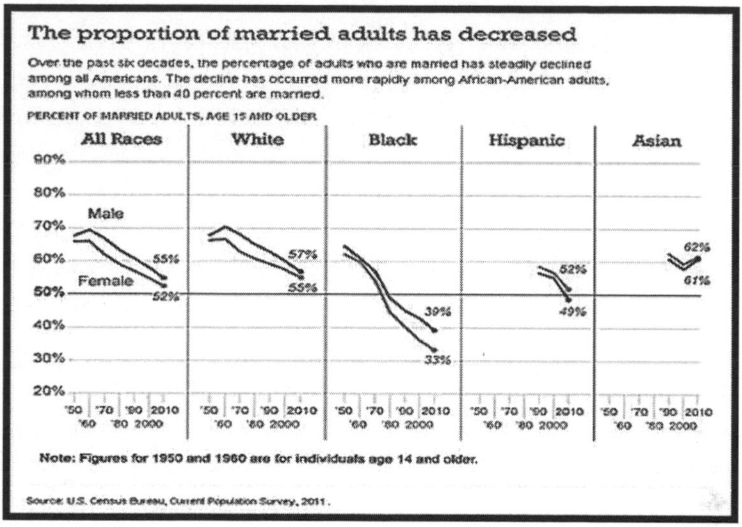

The above chart reveals that marriage rates for African-Americans experienced nearly a 30% drop compared to other ethnicities, during this 1960-2010 period. In 2014, 45.7 million African-Americans were living in the United States, residing in 9.9 million households, with 50% of those homes led by a married couple. The 2010 US Census reveals that when interracial marriages are included, half of African-Americans are married. But when factoring in homogenous marriages only, they drop significantly.

Knowing the Past to Understand the Present

"Remember the days of old, consider the years of all generations. Ask your father, and he will inform you, your elders, and they will tell you" (Deuteronomy 32:7 ESV). All people, regardless of ethnicity, want to know their ancestors. This is an effort to identify with the life of their forefathers and compare the impact of their lives to the present generation. One example of why this is important is how crucial it is knowing family history when attending the doctor for an initial appointment. Each patient is required to complete a family history form. This necessitates each person knowing and remembering past family health histories, which can often be emotional and draining. However, it is necessary information for the physician to obtain when diagnosing the possibilities of an illness. Having knowledge of one's family medical background can be the key to life or death as physicians attempt to treat patients with possible diseases.

My exploration of family health issues from 1940 back to the 1870 brick wall revealed a common thread for the causes of death among generations of my ancestors. I realized that, for more than a century, my ancestors suffered from similar or the same causes of death. It is essential to know the historical health records of ancestors from the past. This knowledge can help manage a person's own health. My heart is distressed when I think of the number of close relatives that died from the same causes as our ancestors. They might have been alive today had they known the family medical history. The same is true with family relational dynamics. Knowledge of past family relationships is essential to avoid similar failures in marriages and families.

Slave marriage and families required reproduction of children under unacceptable and sometimes unreasonable circumstances. For example, owners would sometimes select an unwanted partner over a spouse to father a child. Only in rare situations did owners prohibit the bearing of children, because they became adults who made the slavers more money. Slaves tolerated their family crises to fulfill their need to belong to a family structure. Intimate ties between husbands, wives, children and extended family created slave commitments that made unbearable situations a little easier, especially in comparison to how single men and women fared. Slave marriages and families found psychological security in the situations when owners allowed them to have an influence on maintaining their own family.

In contrast, owners used the innate needs of slaves to keep their marriages and families together as a source of sustaining guardianship and control. Good behavior was a requirement and rewarded; this allowed some slave marriages and families to have a sense of stability and longevity. Owners promised not to sell or separate families if they followed the rules; violations of regulations often led to the selling of family members to enforce the consequences of disobeying plantation laws.

When separated, slaves bitterly resisted the breakup by crying out with promises of obedience and holding on to sold family members until forced from their embrace. After the sale of family members, some slaves were never the same mentally or physically—some suffered from emotional trauma the remainder of their life. Others attempted suicide, ran away, or developed a no-fear stubborn attitude in the face of punishments.

Developing a tenacious or volatile opinion did not change the situation, because slaves knew their efforts to resist would be met with severe opposition, penalties and possibly death. Nevertheless, family ties were foundations of strength for enslaved men, women and children. Being sold and separated from the family created a void that might never have been restored. There is no doubt that each of the traumas created around family issues created risk factors within the families of slaves.

When connecting the social risk factors between this generation of African-Americans and the past histories of slavery, reconstruction, and the civil rights area, it is essential to consider the words of astronomer, writer, and scientist Carl Sagan: "You have to know the past to understand the present."[29] Knowledge of the past is essential to uncovering the present dysfunctions that trouble African-American marriages and families. God's vehicle for transmitting and teaching values and norms from one generation to the next is in the family structure as stated in Deuteronomy 32:7.

Figure 32. Government Regulated Institutionalized Racism

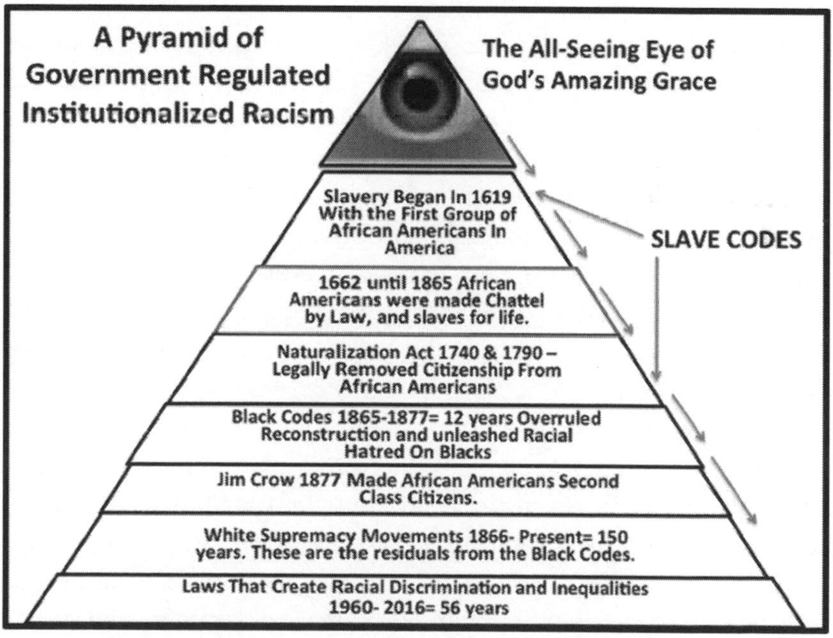

A Pyramid of Government Regulated Institutionalized Racism gives an account of the intentional laws that were created to cause an identity crisis among centuries of

> African-Americans. These laws removed the human rights of every African-American to achieve and have equality as a standard of life. They were created to influence a social identity crisis for African-American families.

For example, the majority of states developed Slave Codes that defined Negros as chattel. This started in 1662 and continued all the way through until states began dividing over slavery. The Colonial "Naturalization Act of 1740"[30] did not address the citizenship of Negros, and by not mentioning them, the silence left in the void perpetuated their status as slaves. Fifty years later, the "Naturalization Act of 1790"[31] was deliberate in legally defining all African-Americans, both free and slaves, as non-citizens. The "Black Codes"[32] of 1865 unleashed the hatred and pain of White supremacy groups on African-American families after the Civil War. These governmental legislations left African-Americans without legal protection and provided no consequences for killings, rapes, and acts of terror. The "Jim Crow" laws, which lasted until 1964, took the place of the Black Codes and allowed the same atrocities.

In light of the compelling evidence, it is impossible, unrealistic and unreasonable to expect slaves and their descendants to function as if slavery never happened. Likewise, it is impossible to assume slavers and their descendants could move on as if slavery had no influence on their lives. As a result, without any therapeutic initiatives designed to bring healing and rehabilitation to all Americans, the social risk factors created in slavery continues to manifest in both Black and White people groups. These social risk factors are associated with unemployment, the lack of education, inadequate housing, homogenous friendships, and segregated Sunday worship services throughout America. Each of these have been examined in previous chapters.

When all is considered, the key to eliminating the risk factors associated with today's dysfunctional family structures is in knowing the root of the problem and the marital hazards of past generations. In principle, African-American marriages must face the future in the same manner as their slave ancestry, invoking the same resiliency to repair the inherited ills of the past. They must realize they are the descendants of a determined and resilient people who went through centuries of family structure annihilation and survived. This generation of African-Americans must learn to discard the inherited risk factors to provide a clean slate for the next generation. This has been referred to as breaking the ruse of inheritance, or in other words, putting a stop to the tricks and wiles of Satan. Society reveals how the negatives incurred by parents are likely handed to their children in divorces, out-of-wedlock births, poor education and low-income housing, just to name a few.

Sociologist Ralph Richard Banks' book, *Is Marriage for White People? How the African-American Marriage Decline Affects Everyone,* is an attempt to provide legitimate answers to the reasons for the breakdown of African-American marriages. Banks led his readers through the social factors that presently affect the unions of African-American men and women. He suggested that Whites are more suited for marital relationships than Blacks, by placing the social issues associated with the Black male as the primary reason that African-American nuptials are in decline. Banks found that the African-American female has few suitable spouses among African-American men; therefore, she marries out of her race. Although this might be true, his theory fails to consider the impact of institutional racism on why there are few suitable men. Maybe the consideration of the historical influence of American Jim Crow laws, along with the separation of families during slavery, can help provide some answers for the decline of marriages among African-Americans.

These social issues help us understand why a study of the social risk factors that affect marriages and families depends significantly upon the facts of historians, sociologists, psychologists, and anthropologists. The many dysfunctional similarities for the African-American family structures studied by modern social scientists have no remedy in view. The social scientist cannot rectify the damage experienced by past and present generations without understanding the sovereignty of God's hand in history.

What is the damage that the social scientist must consider when using God and theology as a method for healing the atrocities of the past? The overarching problem is an inherent family structure of unusual characteristics from centuries of government regulated non-marital family development among African-Americans. Over three centuries of cohabitation, makeshift marriages, single-parent households, absentee fathers, and illegitimate births has trickled down to this present generation.

Each of the risk factors in the above list is a source of sexual and moral failure. Two hundred and fifty years of cohabitation as a form of marriage and family structure by African-Americans, whether forced or by consent, is a despicable act in the presence of God. When sin has infiltrated the lives of a people group, the outcome will be social issues that developed because of violating God's word. The breakdown of the family structures among African-Americans requires a biblical lens for a solution. Correcting the present with the word of God can rectify the past. Scripture reminds couples of their duties for intimacy to their spouse to maintain a satisfying marriage:

> It is good for a man not to have sexual relations with a woman. But because of the temptation to sexual immorality, each man should have his own wife and each woman her own husband. The husband should give to his wife her conjugal rights, and likewise the wife to her husband. For the wife does not have authority over her own body, but the husband does. Likewise, the husband does not have authority over his own body, but the wife does. Do not deprive one another, except perhaps by agreement for a limited time, that you may devote yourselves to prayer; but then come together again, so that Satan may not tempt you because of your lack of self-control (1Cor. 7:1-5 ESV).

Fictive Kinships

"He executes justice for the fatherless and the widow, and loves the sojourner, giving him food and clothing" (Deuteronomy 10:18 ESV). The essence of fictive kinships finds its origin in a need to belong in a family relationship. This was consoling for slaves who suffered the fate of becoming separated from their biological families. The nature of buying and selling child slaves of all ages created a need for pretend mothers, fathers, aunts and uncles to adopt orphan children as their own. In many cases, an adult mother or father who had been separated from their own biological children also needed to adopt children into their family unit for emotional healing.

Faye Zollicoffer Belgrave and Kevin Wendell Allison, in *African-American Psychology: From Africa to America,* established that "Fictive kin are those members of the family who are not biologically related nor related through marriage but who feel and function as family. Friends who are fictive kin are seen socially and emotionally as kin."[33] They are also "those individuals who are not biologically related or related through marriage but are treated as though they are." [34]

The adoption of family members who were not blood became common among slaves. Belgrave also said, "Slavery had a long lasting adverse impact on the African-American families due to the lack of legal recognition of unions between male and female slaves and the fact that children could be sold from their parents. Despite the fact that slavery had adverse effects on the African-American family, it supported a flexible and extended family and kinship system that continues today."[35]

The existence of fictive kin families continues to be a very active part of the African-American family culture. Most African-Americans have never heard of the term fictive kin and don't realize the historical link to slavery. They are unaware of where the tradition comes from when they give family titles, usually reserved for close relatives, to unrelated people. For example, today, when close friends call each other brothers and sisters and introduce themselves to strangers like they are biological siblings, they are acting as fictive kin. This also happens when an older woman or man take on the parental relationship with a younger person and are referred to as their momma or daddy. This kind of fictive kinship bonding takes place throughout all the family relationships based on the age and closeness of the people involved.

The slave community found Fictive Kin relationships as a way to keep the joy and pleasure in family structures that were deeply troubled. These connections also allowed them to fulfill moral obligations as they provided for the helpless and hopeless among both their young and old on the plantations. Gutman provided some insight into the resiliency of African-American slaves to develop and institute Fictive Kin relationships:

> Unrelated adults to one another thereby enlarged slave communities with conceptions of obligation that had flowed initially from kin obligations rooted in blood and marriage. The obligations to a brother or a niece were transformed into the obligations toward a fellow slave or a fellow slave's child, and behavior first determined by familial and kin obligation became enlarged social obligation. Just as the fictive aunts and uncles may have bound children to quasi-kin, so, too, the ties between a child and

its fictive adult kin may have bound children's parents to their fictive aunts and uncles.[36]

Due to the nature of fictive kin relationships among slaves, family structures endured situations that would have been contentious in communities outside of slavery. Couples learned to live with the pains of extramarital relationships and children born outside of marriage. Andrew Cherlin explains how "slavery forced African-Americans to have children outside of marriage, and African culture was tolerant of this practice because having children was so important to the lineage. Slavery forced slaves to depend on other kin because slave owners could separate parents and children, and African culture emphasized links to a network of kin in one's lineage."[37]

Given these points, the fictive kin titles of mom, dad, brother, sister, aunt, uncle, grandma and grandpa were relationship terms only used within the slave community for people who were not blood relatives. Slaves used a criterion of closeness between friendships and age to determine how to include these fictive family members. For example, an older man or woman considered a fictive mother or father to a young adult or child if their intimacy were to develop into a parental relationship. As a measure of safety, these terms were not used in the presence of unscrupulous owners and untrusted Whites, because family relationships could not be openly acknowledged by slaves. To be a slave required a person to relinquish all rights and authority to the most intimate biological relationships, including those of, husband, wives, parent, and children. Slaveholders took away their power to function in each of these family roles as they desired, regardless of the emotional and mental traumas suffered by slaves.

In spite of these difficulties, the institutions of marriage and family never lost its inspiration or significance for slaves, which required them to overlook the flaws in their family structures. Cherlin highlighted the enduring qualities within of slaves to have marriages and family relationships. "Whatever the mix of influences, African-American families were set on a track in which marriage mattered but childbearing outside of marriage was tolerated, and ties to one's parents or siblings were relatively more important than among Whites."[38]

In like manner, Edward Baptist, in *The Half Has Never Been Told*, quoted Charles Ball, a fugitive slave who wrote his own autobiography to enlighten his readers on why marriage was morally important for enslaved men. Baptist also highlighted Ball's need as a slave man to have children, even if they were fictive kin. "Being a husband or father mattered because enslaved men who wanted to live in a way defined by moral choice rather than fear had to turn to the long view (look in the future), to thinking of the people who would one day be left behind them. Even those who did not marry could establish new ties of blood or pseudo-blood."[39]

Ball, a slave, husband and father, sold, then separated, and finally as an escaped run away, explained a series of events he initiated to regain family relationships through fictive kinships. Baptist emphasized how, "Ball had left his family behind in Maryland."[40] Under the severest circumstances, and his need for family relationships as a fugitive, "In South Carolina, he became a contributing member of Nero's household and critiqued Lydia's husband for not being much of a caretaker."[41] He also became a member of Nero and Lydia's fictive kin family. Later, "he adopted a trade-orphaned little boy, the same age [as] my own little son, whom I had left in Maryland; and there was nothing that I possessed in the world, that I would not have divided with him, even to my last crust."[42]

This testimony by Ball expressed a need for belonging that every slave desired and felt as they lived in constant fear of losing their identity as a family member. Ball said, "What mattered was to matter— to count, to be essential in the life of another person. No need was greater than that of an orphan child for an adult—except, perhaps Charles Ball."[43] The following image is on the cover of Charles Ball's autobiography, which also could serve as a testament for every slave sold and separated from their biological family. This drawing depicts a slave that has been humbled and stripped of all worldly possessions as he pleads for recognition as a member of the human race.

Josiah Wedgwood is credited with coining the phrase at the bottom of the photo, "Am I not a man and a brother?"[45] The question is asked of all "*Am I not a fellow human being made in the image of God* (man) *and did Jesus Christ not die for the African just as He did for the European and people of all ethnicities?*"[46] This picture and question were leading influences in the movement to abolish slavery in Great Britain during nineteenth-century anti-slavery campaigns. The Bible says, "Let us then with confidence draw near to the throne of grace, that we may receive mercy and find grace to help in time of need" (Hebrews 4:16 ESV). God's grace on the road to freedom for African-Americans would be a long hard struggle, found in the efforts of the anti-slavery movements. In the final analysis, stories like those of Charles Ball's would touch the hearts of sympathetic observers, who would then make it their life's work to make a difference and free the slaves.

Figure 33. A Call for Freedom and Brotherhood for Slaves [44]

Likewise, as it pertains to God's grace, fictive kinships among slaves in America are an example of grace extended to the brokenhearted in their loss of family members. It allowed slaves to join together into family units with fictive relatives in an attempt to repair the pain of missing their own loved ones. Both the anti-slavery movements and fictive kinships are examples of God's grace extended in love in the midst of slavery.

A Biblical Understanding of Grace in Slavery

When reflecting on how grace works from a biblical perspective, both the Resiliency and Pathological views are on target theologically, "knowing that all things work together for the good to them that love the Lord and are called according to His purpose" (Rom 8:28 ESV). God's grace is evident in the risk factors existing in all the dysfunctions of life, because of the unmerited favor of God. Biblically speaking, God is working through the good and bad events of life to bring mankind into a closer relationship with Him. A majority of the victims of slavery found themselves living among people who professed a relationship with Christ, but the principles of Christianity was not evident in their actions. Many Christian owners mistreated their slaves as poorly as unbelievers did. Nevertheless, in spite of the abuse suffered by slaves at the hand of Christians, the gospel found its way into the lives of generations of the enslaved.

Slave descendants can affirm the good news, because God's Amazing Grace serves as a witness to the movement of God through three centuries of abolitionists who fought to obtain the human rights that African-Americans deserved. Furthermore, an understanding of soteriology would lead us to realize that it was all through God's Amazing Grace. Salvation for slaves and their descendants would provide spiritual and physical freedom from slavery, as well as the rights to marry and have a legitimate family. "The word 'salvation' is the translation of the Greek word 'soteria' which is derived from the word *soter* meaning 'savior.' The word' salvation' communicates the thought of deliverance, safety, preservation, soundness, restoration, and healing."[47] In other words, as Jesus said, "He has sent me to proclaim liberty to the captives and recovering of sight to the blind, to set at liberty those who are oppressed" (Luke 4:18 ESV).

Looking back at African-American history in its true context requires a hard analysis to find God's blessings in the persistent struggle to achieve equality in the American culture. A great measure of God's grace is that Africans found themselves removed from a land of traditional African religions to a land where salvation in Christ Jesus is free to everyone. Although African-Americans at first were denied the gospel in this country, God's word found a way into the lives of slaves by the power of the Holy Spirit. "And we impart this in words not taught by human wisdom but taught by the Spirit, interpreting spiritual truths to those who are spiritual" (1 Corinthians 2:13 ESV). Hearing the gospel is powerful in every situation of life, even when the message was for someone else to receive. African-Americans must appreciate the revelation that God's Grace was present in the power of the Comforter and Holy Spirit through four centuries of institutionalized slavery, Jim Crow laws, and family crisis.

Another positive thing for African-Americans during slavery was the way "Slave kinship patterns reflected the survivals of African cultural patterns. Traditionally, African society was organized by lineages, large groups of kin who traced their ancestry through the father's or mother's line; the members of a lineage cooperated and shared resources with each other."[48] Slaves looked for any associations that allowed for connection to their homeland, because it served as a confident stroke to their self-identity and worth as a person.

The single source of identity that has remained consistent for African-Americans is their ability to stay a spiritually healthy people. Marvin Andrew McMickle, "The Black Church Crisis," *An Encyclopedia of African-American Christian Heritage* stated:

> During the decades of slavery in America, slave associations were a constant source of concern to slave owners. For many members of White society, Black religious meetings symbolized the ultimate threat to White existence. Nevertheless, African slaves established and relied heavily on their churches. Religion offered a means of catharsis... Africans retained their faith in God and found refuge in their churches. However, White society was not always willing to accept the involvement of slaves in Christianity. As one slave recounted "the White folks would come in when the colored people would have prayer meeting, and whip every one of them. Most of them thought that when colored people were praying it was against them."[49]

In spite of all the hardships slaves endured, their unwavering trust in God's love, mercy, and grace to save them in the midst of their trials is evident by their consistent faith. A former Virginia female slave expressed it eloquently as she looked upon emancipation as something approaching a miracle. "Isn't I a free woman now! De Lord can make Heaven out of Hell any time, I do believe."[50] Her expression of joy and faith was the same in churches among Africans-Americans throughout the south after hearing of freedom. "In addressing his Nashville congregation, a black preacher interpreted the reason for emancipation was because of his people having kept the faith, even when it appeared as though there was no hope and that the Lord had forsaken them."[51] This faith is what God requires from every believer. "For by grace you have been saved through faith. And this is not your own doing; it is the gift of God" (Eph. 2:1-8. ESV).

Throughout the ages until this present generation, every ethnological people group aspires to know the divine blessing or absence of godly protection in the history of their people. As previously noted, the African-American search for identity through exploring the lives of our ancestors is on track with scriptural teachings. The Bible chronicles God using Moses to teach the importance of knowing the history of family. Therefore, in the book of Genesis, God inspired Moses to tell the story of the historical beginning of the human race: "This is the book of the generations of Adam. When God created man, he made him in the likeness of God. Male and female he created them, and he blessed them and named them Man [and Woman, Adam and Eve] when they were created."[52] Anyone who acknowledges the Bible as truth must realize they are the descendants of Adam and Eve, and therefore make a psychological connection to them as ancestors. Having the ability to trace their ancestral line was a great advantage for Hebrews (the people of God) to know their genealogical history. This knowledge revealed the blessings of God in the lives of their forefathers, and showed that He was capable of working in their personal situations as He had done for past generations. Scripture teaches that educational training in both Old and New Testaments for the Israeli and Jewish descendants of Abraham was so that they learned the stories of their family history. The term "generation" is to signify a continuous succession of race or a continuous offspring. According to John Calvin and John King's *Commentary on the First Book of Moses Called Genesis*, a genealogical list is designed "to inform us… there was always a number, although small, who worshipped God; and this number was wonderfully preserved by celestial guardianship, lest the name of God should be entirely obliterated, and the seed of the Church should fail."[53]

God chose the Israeli people for revealing His sovereignty to the entire world. Their bondage for 400 years in Egypt serves as an example for African-Americans, who endured enslavement for 250 years, that God's Grace is sufficient for everyone. African-Americans must also learn to appreciate that their time in American slavery is an example to the world of God's delivering power. The words of Jesus would lead Israel, African-Americans, and everyone else to realize that God is at work in every situation of their lives. He is working in both enemies and friends.

> "You have heard that it was said, 'You shall love your neighbor and hate your enemy.' But I say to you, Love your enemies and pray for those who persecute you, so that you may be sons of your Father who is in heaven. For he makes his sun rise on the evil and on the good, and sends rain on the just and on the unjust. For if you love those who love you, what reward do you have?" (Matt. 5:43-46a. ESV).

The essence of this Scripture cannot be lived unless Jesus is in a person's heart. It is the key to overcoming the mistreatments of others. Often, African-Americans remember the sufferings of slavery because little is known about the victories and lessons of endurance that God provided through the power of love. Winston Churchill said, "Those who fail to learn from history are doomed to repeat it."[54] God gave Israel the blessing of remembering the victories and sufferings of past generations; although we find them consistently repeating the failures of their forefathers, we also see them repeatedly return to God's loving kindness. African-Americans must also be held to the same standard. They need to acknowledge their history, see God's hand in deliverance from slavery, and return to Him from sin without reservation. God established an annual Feast of Unleavened Bread to serve as a reminder of their deliverance from Egyptian slavery (Exodus13: 3-10 ESV). Likewise, in America, the month of February is Black Heritage Month and recognized as a national holiday. Lawmakers have made a time for remembering the events of the 1960s Civil Rights Movements, since it was during these movements that African-Americans eventually won full citizenship.

In spite of the divisiveness surrounding the subject, any effort to bring healing to the cultural trauma created by slavery in African-Americans will require intentionality on many different fronts. A few suggestions: 1) members of the social science communities must be intentional and provide a historical knowledge base to reconcile hurting African-American couples to the resiliency of their ancestors. 2) All avoidance techniques must end and a national dialogue opened. The failure to talk about, confront and embrace the distressed past will only serve to perpetuate centuries of abused family structures by canceling a knowledge base for research. 3) Churches in America today must stand as a unified body against the racial prejudice in the pew and in society. For centuries, the Church has permitted its members to embrace prejudice. The Church across America must unite and recognize the historical errors of the past within American Christianity that promoted slavery and Jim Crow. When pastors and churches of different ethnicities become intentional to befriend and worship with others from diverse ethnic backgrounds, healing can overcome past traumas.

In light of these suggestions for healing the African-American community from the outside, African-Americans must also do their part. One dilemma that African-American marriages and families face today is their inability to reverse the tragedy of the past and correct the present. African-American unions suffer from the highest rates of divorce and family separation; therefore, they must be determined to stay together at all cost. Statistically, more children are born to unwed parents among African-Americans. To offset these risk factors, life changes are needed. One such change is to abstain from sexual relationships outside of marriage. Also, more African-American children live in single-parent households than any other American ethnic group, so single parents must use their lives as an object lesson to teach what's missing in the home. Raising children in a dual parent household is God's design for the family. When one parent is missing, children get only half of their parental blessing. Single parents must be willing to instill in the lives of their children the importance of getting married before having children. They must also teach the blessings and staying married, as well as the failures of divorce. As a people group, African-Americans have come a long way; however, there is still a long way to go before the damage done to their family structures will be corrected.

The Bible offers encouragement for husbands, fathers, wives, mothers, and children of both African-American and Anglo-American descent. It is essential to consider that the sovereign God was at work before slavery existed in America. Jesus spoke of the psychological effects of sin and suffering in bondage when He said, "The Spirit of the Lord is upon me because he has anointed me to proclaim good news to the poor. He has sent me to proclaim liberty to the captive and the recovering of sight to the blind, to set at liberty those who are oppressed, to proclaim the year of the Lord's favor" (Luke 4: 18-19 ESV). God, in his sovereignty through Jesus, revealed the outcome for those who are in need of spiritual and physical deliverance from oppression. Slavery, captivity and bondage all represent the positions of those who are under the control of sin. In Scripture, slavery and sin are synonymous, and their power can only be broken through the power of Jesus' blood.

The New Testament epistles teach the concept of slavery as a requirement for living the Christian life. According to Scripture, men of God referred to themselves as slaves of God, and they taught others in the church to imitate the behavior of a good slave in Christ. James' and Paul's letters to the churches start with a reminder of their enslavement to the gospel and the Lord Jesus Christ. The need for every Christian to acknowledge Jesus as the Lord of one's life and to accept Him as personal savior is a requirement for believers. When Jesus is Lord, each of the terms that apply to the relationship between slave and owner is in effect. Jesus is master, owner, and ruler of all who would give their lives to Him as a Christian.

Whenever there is a lord over the people, those who serve him are slaves. "The word slave (doulos in Greek) appears 124 times in the original text, it is correctly translated only once in King James. Most of our modern translations do only slightly better. It almost seems like a conspiracy. Instead of translating doulos as "slave," these translations consistently substitute the word servant in its place."[55] Jesus gave slaves a new outlook on how to live their lives in captivity and oppression. One key was to have peace of mind as they complied with the rules of the slave system.

In Christianity, the brutalities of American slavery are not looked upon favorably. One reason is because of the principle to "love one's neighbor" found within the Christian faith. We must investigate how good slaves take on the same qualities of good Christians; they exemplify a spirit of humility, submission, obedience, truthfulness, forgiveness, and commitment. Also, Christians and slaves alike need to be loyal, selfless and compassionate towards their masters. The fruit of the Spirit is the making of devout Christians and slaves. "But the fruit of the Spirit is love, joy, peace, patience, kindness, goodness, faithfulness, gentleness, self-control; against such things, there is no law" (Gal. 5:22-23. ESV).

Equally important is how Paul referred to his chains and shackles as evidence that he was a slave of the Lord. "Praying at all times in the Spirit, with all prayer and supplication. To that end keep alert with all perseverance, making supplication for all the saints, and also for me, that words may be given to me in opening my mouth boldly to proclaim the mystery of the gospel, for which I am an ambassador in chains, that I may declare it boldly, as I ought to speak" (Eph. 6:18 ESV). All Americans must strive to educate both themselves and others about the dark history of slavery, if there is to be an understanding of the goodness of God in every life. The Christian principles found in humbling oneself as a slave to Jesus will educate and motivate racial unity among the descendants of all who still suffer from ethnic injustices. Every Christian believer should have the knowledge that God wants us to live in peace and brotherly love with all men.

> Live in harmony with one another. Do not be haughty, but associate with the lowly. Never be wise in your own sight. Repay no one evil for evil, but give thought to do what is honorable in the sight of all. If possible, so far as it depends on you, live peaceably with all. Beloved, never avenge yourselves, but leave it to the wrath of God, for it is written, "Vengeance is mine, I will repay, says the Lord." To the contrary, "if your enemy is hungry, feed him; if he is thirsty, give him something to drink; for by so doing you will heap burning coals on his head." Do not be overcome by evil, but rather overcome evil with good (Rom.12: 16-21 ESV).

The Christian principles found in Rom.12:16-21 must be a treasured source of knowledge and a valued condition of the heart. The Bible says in Hosea 4:6: "My people perish (are destroyed) for lack of knowledge." Black and White-Americans have been miseducated, and they need to be reeducated in regard to the impact slavery had on all Americans. Americans must rethink the advantages and disadvantages that exist in the residuals of the slave institution, which we know today has had an impact on both ethnicities. Alexis De Tocqueville (*American Democracy)* evaluated the effects of slavery on both slave and owner. He said, "Slavery, as we shall afterwards show, dishonors labor; it introduces idleness into society, and with idleness, ignorance and pride, luxury and distress. It enervates the powers of the mind, and benumbs the activity of man."[56]

This statement by De Tocqueville shared a unique perspective about White slave owners that could possibly help us, in the 21st century, to understand the mental gap that exists between the races, specifically over the suffering of slave ancestors. In light of this eighteenth-century statement, I find it difficult to understand why some Christians remain biased and unaware of the historical racial differences that perpetuate race problems. Beyond that, it should help Christians acknowledge how racial issues that had their root in slavery still exist in present-day Black America.

Whenever public attention turns its focus to racial problems in our society, those who find it concerning express their naivety to the root cause. America must be educated on the sin of racism, or perish for lack of knowledge. Racial unity is essential before revival will come to America. Perhaps the illustration given to us by Jesus of becoming as a little child will help end our problems with race relationships. "One of the most complex relationships was the one that existed between White children and their African-American caretakers. This picture, of slave nurse Louisa and her charge, H. E. Hayward, suggests the inherent tension of these relationships."[57]

Figure 34 The Closeness of a Child and Nanny[58]

The ability to see others as God sees them is the key to overcoming the racial divide in America. "White children were often in the unnatural position of standing to inherit the people who raised them, and enslaved nannies were in the similarly unnatural position of caring for the children who would grow up to be their masters."[59] Nevertheless, the nanny, in spite of her status in life, would provide nourishment for a White baby's health, and the child would love the nanny until taught differently. Jesus put it this way, "And calling to him a child, he put him in the midst of them and said, 'Truly, I say to you, unless you turn and become like children, you will never enter the kingdom of heaven. Whoever humbles himself like this child is the greatest in the kingdom of heaven'" (Matt. 18:3-4 ESV).

The above scripture explains why having a humble heart is a great gift in the sight of our Lord, and attached to it is the promise of entrance into heaven. Jesus uses the humble spirit of an infant, like the one in the picture, to warn against adult aggression and pride in life. It was essential to the American slave system for every slave to keep a childlike demeanor in the presence of any White person, regardless of age. "White Southerners had convinced themselves that black people were a childlike and irresponsible race wholly incapable of surviving as a free people if they were emancipated and compelled to compete with White-Americans. Most White people believed the black race would decline and disappear if slaves were freed."[60]

The stage of infancy puts one in the position of needing someone to care for them. For every slave to keep his or her sanity, while remaining totally dependent on another adult to provide for every need, required an enormous amount of self-control, and was an acquired mannerism. For the same reason, "Elkins concluded that the psychological impact of slavery was to reduce most male slaves to behavioral patterns associated with the childlike 'Sambo' character. The Sambo personality, he insisted, was not a black characteristic; instead, it was the reaction of most humans caught in a similar situation."[61]

The system of American slavery took the Christian principles of being childlike, obedient and humble to create a lifestyle for slaves requiring them to stay inferior to their masters. Jesus, in contrast, illustrated this example to mean that all mankind is expected to be submissive and dependent on God by developing a lifestyle of humility. The healing of African-American families and marriages from racial oppression can only be accomplished when slavery is viewed through the word of God, and institutionalized racism is acknowledged and ended. Finally, when slaves took on the personal characteristics required by Christianity and slavery, this placed them in favor with God. What man meant for evil, God meant for good. Joseph said these words to his brothers after they sold him into slavery, "As for you,

you meant evil against me, but God meant it for good, to bring it about that many people should be kept alive, as they are today" (Genesis 50: 20 ESV). America would not be the wonderful country it is today without the hard work and free labor of African-American slaves.

Chapter 12

When Love Conquers

> Love is patient and kind; love does not envy or boast; it is not arrogant or rude. It does not insist on its own way; it is not irritable or resentful; it does not rejoice at wrongdoing, but rejoices with the truth. Love bears all things, believes all things, hopes all things, endures all things (I Cor. 13: 4-7 ESV).

We've no less days to sing God's praise
Than when we've first begun.

Praise the Lord! It's true that the same grace that was with African-American slaves two and a half centuries, as they struggled through a life of family crisis, would finally serve to free them to pursue healthy marriages and families. Every African-American that desired marriage could finally apply for a legal license to marry, and have marriages that legally represented its eternal spiritual meaning. A Council of Trent summary from *Catechism of the Catholic Church* tells us, "The sacrament of Matrimony signifies the union of Christ and the Church. It gives spouses the grace to love each other with the love with which Christ has loved his Church; the grace of the sacrament thus perfects the human love of the spouses, strengthens their indissoluble unity, and sanctifies them on the way to eternal life."[1] African-American slaves waited 246 years before given the legal right to consummate their wedding vows. Before a wedding takes place, there is an engagement period where the couple prepares for the marriage ceremony. The couple and their needs normally determine the time of engagement. There have been marriage engagements that have lasted for several years, whereas others lasted only a few days or months. The longest engagement described is the wedding between Christ and His bride, the Church, which will take place in the last days of time. The battle of Armageddon is the setting for the wedding of Christ and the Church. "Hallelujah! For the Lord our God the Almighty reigns. Let us rejoice and exult and give him the glory, for the marriage of the Lamb has come, and his Bride has made herself ready; it was granted her to clothe herself with fine linen, bright and pure" (Rev. 19: 6b-8a ESV).

God's Amazing Grace in the US Civil War

The Civil War was the setting in which centuries of illegitimate families and marriages for slaves would end, and God's most prized institution of marriage and family would become legitimate for slaves. God caused the institution of slavery to be stopped by a Civil War, after being so immersed in a season where marriages and families were routinely and intentionally separated.

Slavery's end actually started years before with the prophetic visions by two of the most feared and hated men by many in American History. Nate Turner and John Brown loved freedom so much that each said only by bloodshed would this country free its slaves. Today we are confronted with the question of whether God really did speak to these men, and if their message of God's Amazing Grace of love extended to the American slave.

John Brown was a man who was willing to risk everything to rid America of the institution of slavery. He referred to slavery as the guilt of America. "I, John Brown, am quite certain that the crimes of this guilty land will never be purged away, but with blood, I had, as I now think, vainly flattered myself that without very much bloodshed it might be done."[2] Brown gave his final prophecy in a speech minutes before being put to death. He wrote, "Now if it is deemed necessary that I should forfeit my life for the furtherance of the ends of justice, and mingle my blood further with the blood of my children and with the blood of millions in this slave country whose rights are disregarded by wicked, cruel and unjust enactments, I submit. So let it be done."[3]

The death of Nat Turner revealed an extensive look at his prophecy. According to his final words in the *Confessions of Nat Turner* during his trial, he gave this testimony from his jail cell before his death sentence. "And about this time I had a vision--and I saw White spirits and black spirits engaged in battle, and the sun was darkened--the thunder rolled in the Heavens, and blood flowed in streams--and I heard a voice saying, 'Such is your luck, such you are called to see, and let it come rough or smooth, you must surely bare it.'"[4] We have said much about the spiritual qualities of God's grace found in the lives of both slave and master. One characteristic of grace that is more profound than either forgiveness or mercy is the power of love. "This is my commandment, that you love one another as I have loved you. Greater love has no one than this, that someone lay down his life for his friends. You are my friends if you do what I command you" (John 15:13-14 ESV).

God's loving-kindness to people in bondage was first found in the deliverance of Israel from Egyptian slavery when the army of Egypt drowned in the Red Sea. This same grace is again witnessed as it is extended to the African-American slave with the defeat of the Confederate army. In the American Civil War, there was no sea in which the Army of the oppressor could drown. Instead, God soaked the fields of the South with blood by turning the hearts of brothers and friends against each other over the evil system of slavery. Wars fought at God's direction are waged to overcome corrupt regimes. "Then I saw an angel standing in the sun, and with a loud voice he called to all the birds that fly directly overhead, 'Come, gather for the great supper of God, to eat the flesh of kings, the flesh of captains, the flesh of mighty men, the flesh of horses and their riders, and the flesh of all men, both free and slave, both small and great.' And I saw the beast and the kings of the earth with their armies gathered to make war against him who was sitting on the horse and against his army" (Rev. 19: 17-19 ESV).

The American Civil War Facts reported 620,000 men were killed on battlefields, 476,000 wounded and another 400,000 captured or missing for an estimate of 1.5 million Civil War casualties.[5] This war cost the most in lives and casualties of any war in American history. The Union Army had more significant number of victims with 642,427 of the 2,672,241 total enlisted men. The Union casualities included approximately 40,000 thousand Colored soldiers of the 178,975 who enlisted. These men were prohibited from legally carrying guns before they joined the Union Army.[6]

On the side of the Confederate Army, there were 750,000 to 1,227,890 total enlisted men, of which 483,026 were killed in the conflict.[7] These lives were lost as a partial effort to keep those enslaved who were historically considered legal chattel. The loss of the war by the Confederate Army remains a sore spot for many Southerners today, but they are also provided a way of restoration in the Scripture. "But love your enemies, and do good, and lend, expecting nothing in return, and your reward will be great, and you will be sons of the Most High, for he is kind to the ungrateful and the evil" (Luke 6: 35 ESV). Desperate actions were needed before God's Amazing Grace could be extended to free millions of enslaved African-American men, women and children from the horrors of slavery.

The signing of the Emancipation Proclamation in 1863 gave freedom to nearly 4 million slave men, women and children. President Abraham Lincoln described the difficulty of freeing American slaves.

> Hartford, Connecticut, on Mar. 5, 1860, If slavery is not wrong, nothing is wrong. Lincoln acknowledged the difficulty of ending slavery in a day, a week, or a year. Slavery, he said, was like a gruesome metastatic wen (cancer) growing on a man's neck. "He dares not cut it out. He bleeds to death if he does, directly." Slavery, he said, was also like a rattlesnake that crawled into "a bed where the children are sleeping. Would I do right to strike him there? I might hurt the children." Or the awakened serpent "might bite the children." But leave it coiled in the bed, let the wen (cancer) grow, and the result was also death. Permit expansion, and, as the past seventy years had shown, you deepen American slavery's severity, entrench more securely its "immense pecuniary interest."[8]

At the time of his presidential election, Lincoln had no intentions of freeing the slaves. Only after pressure was placed on his administration to keep the United States intact by the Southern states did he fulfill his threat to free the slaves. In Abraham Lincoln's inaugural address, he expressed his desire to maintain slavery: "I have no purpose, directly or indirectly to interfere with the institution of slavery in the United States where it exists. I believe I have no lawful right to do so, and I have no inclination to do so."[9]

Legal Marriages and Families Among the Freedmen

The separation of families during slavery is perhaps the most devastating consequence of the breakdown the family structure, and has had the longest lasting negative influences on the African-American family. The newly-freed American slaves would have the right to develop their family structures without the fear of suffering separation for the first time after the Civil War. However, these freedmen couples experienced much damage after slavery through White supremacy movements that started in 1865, the year following the end of slavery. The actions like those committed by "the Ku Klux Klan (founded in 1865) and the Knights of the White Camellia (1867) were secret groups, while members of the White League (1874) and the Red Shirts (1875) were publically known."[10]

These hate movements put African-Americans in difficulties that forced them to remain committed to marriage and family, while still living in desperation and fear to protect each other. The goal of White supremacy groups was to keep Black-Americans from experiencing success in life. During reconstruction, two-parent households proved beneficial to overcome the poverty created by leaders of these racist movements. These leaders were known at times to be lawmakers in every sphere of local and state legislative branches ascending as high as governors. They made laws that violated the commandment of the Savior when He responded to the question of what the greatest law was. After giving an answer as to what the first great law was, Jesus then said, "The second is this: 'You shall love your neighbor as yourself.' There is no other commandment higher than these" (Mark 12:34 ESV). Love would keep these new couples and families together. African-American marriages shared their highest rates of success during this era, even amidst the trials from hate movements.

Couples enjoyed love, safety, and security in numbers by living near family members and friends. This allowed them some security from the possible activities of these hate groups. Living alone without the protection of neighbors and family could be life-threating. White supremacy movements forced African-American families to live in appalling conditions of extreme poverty. If a Black reached any measure of success, it put them on the hit list of these race-driven hate groups. The Democratic Party served as the political arm for these groups, and used its leadership to legislate laws to torment Blacks and to keep them from moving out of poverty. "All four groups used violence to intimidate blacks and Republican voters. Their efforts succeeded, and with the end of Reconstruction in 1877, White supremacy became the reality of the South."[11]

While slave laws legislated that Blacks would remain uneducated, the hate groups utilized their own strategy to keep Blacks uneducated. Their strategy was new segregation laws. These laws made learning to read or write an additional hardship. The new laws successfully perpetrated a philosophy within the American culture that African-Americans were inferior, couldn't learn, and therefore, didn't deserve to have equal education.

There was also a lack of judicial courts designed to protect African-American marriages from the invasion of a corrupt society filled with racist extremist groups. This caused lots of difficulty for African-American couples and their families as they assimilated into the American society. This time was mentally and physically challenging, for the next one hundred years, as they attempted to overcome the hindrances of Jim Crow. After the war was a time in which pain from the devastation caused many divisions between the North and South, Black and White. Americans have come a long way since those days, but we must continue to apply the biblical principle that informs us how, "Hatred stirs up strife, but love covers all offenses" (Proverbs 10:12 ESV). Dr. Martin Luther King in his book *A Gift of Love: Sermons from Strength to Love* explained it this way, "Why we should love our enemies is that love is the only force capable of transforming an enemy into a friend. We never get rid of an enemy by meeting hate with hate; we get rid of an enemy by getting rid of enmity. By its very nature, hate destroys and tears down; by its very nature, love creates and builds up. Love transforms with redemptive power."[12]

The privilege of belonging was rewarding for African-American couples after having no control over their lives. The family served as the primary source of love and security as they depended on each other for the basic physical and emotional needs in life. Their struggle for normalcy within a majority culture was a consistent reminder that they were not welcome in an America that was showing little love to its new second-class citizens. This fight continued well into the mid-1960s when Jim Crow laws became abolished.

James T. Patterson quotes the Moynihan Report when recognizing the condition of African-American marriages: "That cultural damage from slavery and segregation, savage though it had been, had not greatly afflicted all Black people: roughly half of African-Americans, displaying considerable ambition and talent, had risen into the middle classes. Those who married were especially likely to do well: the income of married African-American people was nearly as high as it was for married White people of the same age. This was a group of African-Americans 'for whom the legacy of slavery has been overcome.'"[13] Bowen System of Family Theory would explain those who overcame slavery as having a Differentiation of Self, or the ability to change by defeating the influences of families that negatively affect their members.

This report revealed that all African-Americans have not entirely overcome the legacy of slavery. However, love in marriage improves the likelihood of overcoming past traumas. Educational attainment and the ability to earn a real income are essential needs in a postmodern society for a satisfying marriage. The research team of Lorraine Blackman, Obie Clayton, Norval Glenn, Linda Malone-Colon, and Alex Roberts suggest that for "African-Americans, satisfying, healthy marriages promote physical health and psychological well-being, just as they do among Americans of European descent."[14] In contrast, M. Corra, S.K. Carter, J.S. Carter, D. discover, "African-Americans tend to be less happy with their marriages and exhibit higher levels of conflict than do Whites."[15] A.J. Cherlin in Marriage and Marital Dissolution Among African-Americans say, when compared with Whites, Asians, and Hispanics, "African-Americans are more likely to have children outside of marriage and are less likely to marry at all, and if they do marry, are more likely to end their unions in divorce."[16]

As the country moved toward Civil War, the states began to take sides, with the North and South dividing almost equally. Although slavery was also in the North, all the Blacks in Northern states were allowed their freedom. However, the number of African-Americans in the South far exceeded those in the North. E. Franklin Frazier, in his comprehensive book *The Negro Family In The United States,* provided the following Census data on the early Negro population. When the first US Census was tabulated in 1790, the total Negro population in America was 757,181. The breakdown of slave and free was: enslaved Negros totaled 697,624 compared to 59,557 free. Seventy years later, the 1860 Census reported the number of free Negros had risen to 488,070, while the enslaved had risen to 3,943,760. "When freedom came, tens of thousands of former slave men and women—some seeking to marry for the first time and others attempting to solemnize long-standing relationships—sought help from Union Army clergy, provost marshals, Northern missionaries, and the Freedmen's Bureau."[17] The emancipation proclamation created a helpless situation spiritually.

> With its hundreds of thousands of men, women, and children just broken forth from slavery, was, so far as these were concerned, lying under an almost absolute physical

> and moral interdict. There was no one to baptize their children, to perform the marriage, or to bury the dead. A ministry had to be created at once--and created out of the material at hand. The courage of the leaders of our church is to be commended in that, in the face of the great crying need, so apparent to all, they dared to lay hands on men, not fearing the criticism of those who openly proclaimed in Charleston in 1865 that the A. M. E. Church had "neither the men nor the money" to carry on work in the South.[18]

A Marriage License Legislated for the Freedman

> The Freedmen's Bureau—established in the War Department by an act of Congress on March 3, 1865—was responsible for "the supervision and management of all matters relating to the refugees and freedmen and lands abandoned or seized during the Civil War." With duties resembling those of a modern-day social services agency, the bureau provided freed people with food and clothing, medical attention, employment, support for education, help with military claims, and a host of other socially related services—including assisting ex-slave couples in formalizing marriages they had entered into during slavery.[19]

Former slaves could now experience Holy Matrimony as husbands and wives based on biblical principles and state legislation. For the first in American history, the majority of African-American men could assume the leadership role in their households. "Likewise, husbands, live with your wives in an understanding way, showing honor to the woman as the weaker vessel, since they are heirs with you of the grace of life, so that your prayers may not be hindered" (1Peter 3:7 ESV). Now they could experience the totality of the marriage institution as a lifestyle based on the word of God. Husbands could live with their wives in love and understanding as the man in her life and not a slave. He could give her the honor she deserved as his spouse and the mother of his children. Having a family life initiated the blessings and promises of God that allowed them to become heirs of the grace of life. This is to be interpreted that God would give them homes they could call their own, children who would bear their names and all the benefits of a Christian family. However, most importantly, their prayers would not be hindered, as they could call on God.

> The Freedman's Bureau 1865 Rules For Marriage, from June to September 1865, both Florida and Georgia were under the jurisdiction of the Freedmen's Bureau in South Carolina. In late summer 1865, the assistant commissioner for South Carolina issued an elaborate set of "marriage rules" for all three states. The matrimony rules outlined the duties of former slave couples and who was eligible to marry and remarry, who could grant permits and solemnize marriages, the responsibilities of husbands to former wives, and the rights of female spouses and children. Each state passed legislation-legalizing freedmen marriages that contained the same provisions as the spousal rules issued by the assistant commissioner for South Carolina.[20]

In states where the union army remained after the Civil War to protect the freedman, local governments were forced to submit to the new regulations for the marriages of former slaves. States that committed to follow the new legislation were the first to develop rules for the Freedman's inclusion into society. Benjamin Mason and Sarah White would have been among the first former slaves to receive an official marriage license.

> On April 19, 1866, former slaves Benjamin Berry Manson and Sarah Ann Benton White received an official marriage certificate from the Freedmen's Bureau, officially known as the Bureau of Refugees, Freedmen, and Abandoned Lands.
>
> The Wilson County, Tennessee, couple had lived as slave man and wife since October 28, 1843, and for the first time in more than two decades their marriage had finally received legal recognition. For the Mansons—who had lived intermittently on separate farms—the marriage certificate issued by the Freedmen's Bureau was more than a document "legally" sealing the sacred bonds of holy matrimony. Listing the names and ages of 9 of their

> 16 children, it was for them a symbol of freedom and the long-held hope that they and their children would one day live free as a family in the same household.[21]

Below is a copy of John and Emily Pointer's marriage license. This first license was very detailed listing the names of all their children born in slavery. This was an effort to solidify the whole family as legitimate and belonging to each other. This was exciting to every Freedman who now possessed papers saying they belonged to their wives, husbands and children, and not their masters. This made them feel like they were human beings that held a place in life. They now had papers legally making them members of each other. Paul said that oneness in marriage comes from God, "nevertheless, in the Lord woman is not independent of man nor man of woman; for as woman was made from man, so man is now born of woman. And all things are from God" (1Cor. 11:11-12 ESV).

Figure 35 Marriage License Freedmen's Bureau 1866[22]

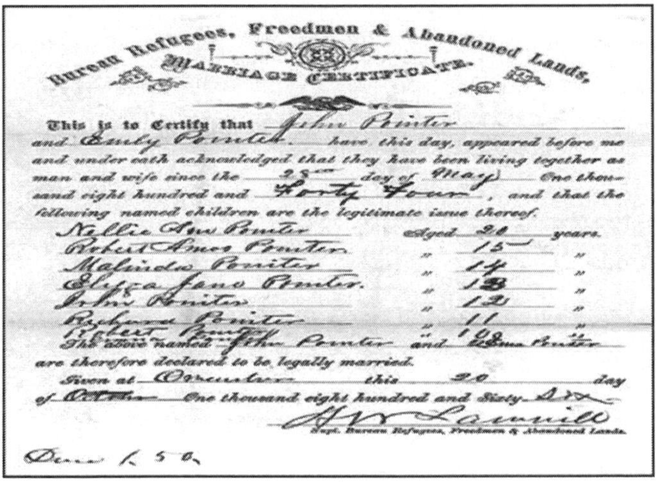

Bureau Refugees, Freedmen & Abandoned Lands,
Marriage Certificate.

This is to Certify that John Pointer
and Emily Pointer have this day, appeared before me and under oath acknowledged that they have been living together as man and wife since the 25th day of May One thousand eight hundred and Forty Four, and that the following named children are the legitimate issue thereof.

Nellie Ann Pointer aged 21 years.
Robert Amos Pointer " 15 "
Malinda Pointer " 14 "
Eliza Jane Pointer " 13 "
John Pointer " 12 "
Richard Pointer " 11 "
Robert Pointer " 10 "

The above named John Pointer and Emily Pointer are therefore declared to be legally married.

Given at [illegible] this 20 day of [illegible] One thousand eight hundred and Sixty Six

H. W. Lawrill
Supt. Bureau Refugees, Freedmen & Abandoned Lands.

[illegible] 1. 5 [illegible]

The Freedmen's Bureau was also responsible for the management of abandoned lands after the Civil War. General William T. Sherman issued order #15 on Monday, March 3, 1865, to help former slaves and their families become landowners as a method to assimilate them into the American society. This order became known as the 40 acres and a Mule order, which was supported by Congress and signed by President Lincoln. This rule would allow the Freedmen's families to establish a livelihood by working the land as landowners. The law was short-lived after Lincoln's death. Jackson abolished the Freedmen's Bureau and took back land from 40,000 Freedmen. This left African-American families without government provisions and protection.

Marriage According Legislation or Dormancy Law

Texas was the last state to free its slaves after the end of the Civil War. For two more years, Texas defied the laws of emancipation and kept its slaves in bondage. They finally liberated them in 1865. Freedom for the slaves brought the need for legislation that would determine African-American family structure. During slavery, marriages of slaves had no lifetime commitments, which created a legal and moral problem that would now need to be solved. Many slaves had more than one sexual partner and family, depending on how many times their slaver required them to cohabitate. This would mean that children could also exist in each of these quasi-marriages. At times, there were problems with slaves who returned to former plantations to find their spouse married to someone else.

The Texas Judicial System also defied the rights of slaves to be married for two extra years, ruling in 1867 that the status of slave marriages had not changed.

> The court in Timmins vs. Lacy stated Contubernal was the matrimony of slaves; a permitted cohabitation not partaking of lawful marriage, which they could not contract. The progress of society in civilization, more correct notions on the subject of moral obligation, and, above all, the benign influence of the Christian religion, have softened many of the of the rigors attendant on slavery among the ancients. But the rights of the slave, in respect to marriage, remains and the acquisition of property by way of inheritance remains on the same ground. These authorities show very conclusively that the permitted cohabitation existing formerly among our slave population did not partake of lawful marriage. If we could say legal rights of husbands and wife, parent and child, spring from these connections, it must be held that corresponding disabilities flow from them, many of which are of a severely penal character,

> affecting almost this entire portion of our population. Timmins vs. Lacy, 30 Tex. 115, 136 (Tex. 1867)[23]

However, Texas took another four years after the emancipation to give African-Americans the rights of marriage. After two more years of court proceedings, the Supreme Court of Texas finally handed down a decision allowing the marriages of African-American men and women. In "Timmons, 30 Tex, at 1 15.1869,"[24] the validity of slave marriages was finally resolved by the Texas legislature with the adoption of the following Constitution, "TEX. CONST. art. 12, § 27 (Vernon 1869)."[25] This statute validated the marital relations of former slave couples where the couples continued to cohabit at the time the Constitution passed. It also applied retroactively to authorize slave marriages where one of the spouses died before the passage of the curative legislation.

America, following the Civil War, was unloving and extremely unfriendly to former slave men and women. The war left tremendous casualties in both the Northern and Southern states. Anger and hostilities filled the air on both sides that viewed the freemen as the reason for their pain, financial instability, and lost families. The freedmen and women started a new life with all the benefits of freedom in the midst of a violent society. At the top of the list for most adults was the privilege of going to the local authorities and getting a marriage license to legalize their family:

> Every opportunity was maliciously seized to taunt the colored people with their complexion. A gentleman of the highest worth stated that several years ago he applied to the proper officer for a license to be married. The license was accordingly made out and handed to him. It was expressed in the following insulting style: "T---- H----, F.M., is licensed to marry H---- L----, F.C.W." The initials F.M. stood for free mulatto and F.C.W. for the free colored woman! The gentleman took his knife and cut out the initials, and was then threatened with a prosecution for forging his license.[26]

The right to get a marriage license brought honor and legitimacy to the marriages of the slaves, whether first married as a slave or those newly married after slavery. Those who married by slave laws and traditions could now turn their illegal marriages into a legitimate marriage, and do the same for their family. In the opinion of Judge Matthews, when deciding the case of Girod vs. Lewis in the state of Louisiana, the law profoundly gave validity to slave marriages that were never before considered legitimate. The ruling stated, "Emancipation gives to the slave his civil rights, and a contract of marriage, legal and valid by the consent of the master, and moral assent of the slave, from the moment of freedom. Although dormant during slavery, contubernial produced all the effects which result from such contract among free persons."[27]

The Freedman's Bureau of the United States Government, working with each state, established legislation to provide legal marriages for the freedmen and women. "After the Civil War ended, the newly formed Freedman's Bureau, which oversaw the relief efforts for emancipated slaves, issued marriage rules. The bureau told African-Americans, who could not marry under slavery that now they must marry: 'No parties ... will be allowed to live together as husband and wife until their marriage has been legally solemnized.' Several Southern states passed laws making a living together without legal marriage a misdemeanor punishable by a fine."[28] Some states gave these men and women their rights of marriage at the time of the signing of the Emancipation Proclamation; these laws were implemented by the Legislation of the Law. The marriages of freedmen and women, in states that were forced to give former slaves the right to marry through lawsuits, were established by Dormancy Law court proceedings. "Given the opportunity, newly freed slaves legitimated relations which previously had no standing in law, joining together to celebrate weddings and to register their marriages in official records often of their own making."[29] There were no specific laws in Texas governing ex-slave marital relations when Commissioner Howard issued his orders on the subject. When Texas became a republic in 1836, slaves were prohibited from marrying, even with the consent of their owners, and free Blacks could not live in the state.

> The bureau's assistant commissioner for Texas issued a circular in March 1866 containing marriage rules and encouraged the Texas legislature to recognize the marriages of former slave couples who lived in accordance with the state's common law marriage practices. The question concerning marriages of "persons of color" was eventually addressed by the Texas constitution of 1869, and an act

of the state legislature on August 15, 1870, legalized the marriages of persons "formerly held in bondage" and declared their children legitimate. By this time, however, Freedmen's Bureau activities in Texas, except matters relating to freedmen of education, had been withdrawn from the state. There is no evidence in Texas Bureau records that the field offices registered or issued marriage licenses and certificates. The legal legitimatization of long-standing relationships gave Black people a freer hand in performing everyday duties, as husbands and wives, parents, and sons and daughters.[30]

Freedom to Marry at All Cost

"An excellent wife who can find? She is far more precious than jewels. The heart of her husband trusts in her, and he will have no lack of gain. She does him good, and not harm, all the days of her life" (Prov. 31:10-12 ESV). African-American marriages and families remained in a state of crisis following slavery. Those who decided to leave their former masters were destitute, and because of their lack of education, were without the ability to provide for themselves outside of their slave jobs. Many roamed the country looking for spouses and families they loved and had been separated from. Others that were fortunate enough to be with their families had to work jobs at poverty wages. Fractured families that were suffering and impoverished they did all they could to bring normalcy to their lives.

Dr. Herbert Gutman, defending his theory that slave families were resilient and adaptive in their circumstances, observed the struggle for a couple to have legal marriages. He discovered over "20,000 African-American couples in seventeen North Carolina counties paid a fee of 25 cents to have their marriages legally registered"[31] at the end of the Civil War. "The court stated: Persons married in North Carolina while slaves, who continued to cohabit after the abolition of slavery, were ipso facto legally married (Act 1866, Chap. 40), and no acknowledgment before an officer was essential."[32] These individuals were married without any further actions on the part of the couple or the government. They allowed their quasi-slave marital relationship to remain intact without receiving any written acknowledgment of legitimacy. According to the law, they were a legitimately married couple. "The marriage was complete before the prescribed acknowledgment made before the clerk, even if such acknowledgment were not made at all."[33] This was also the case among older couples whose children were grown. They had already gained an established reputation as a married couple in their community. When couples are moved by love, they will do the right thing and make their relationships legal. A moral sense of love reminds lovers, it is the best for the one they love to be in a legitimate marriage. In "six counties of Virginia 2, 817 former slave couples had their marriages renewed."[34] Every Southern state legislature was confronted with the issue of resolving the marriage relationships of its freedmen and women. Virginia, like North Carolina, left things in the hands of the couples and their desire to formalize their marriage with a legal contract:

> The curative act passed by the Virginia legislature recognized marriages entered into by agreement of the parties, even absent a formal ceremony to solemnize the same. The agreement to marry could be either express or implied by the "acts, conduct, and conversation of the parties." When determining the existence of a slave marriage by implication, Virginia courts considered such factors as duration of cohabitation, reputation as a married couple by members of the community and extended family, public acknowl edgment by a couple of relationship to each other, and the conception and rearing of children during the union. An express indication of a slave couple's intent to marry was generally demonstrated by their participation in a "jumping the broom" ceremony or some other informal public solemnization of their union by a preacher or the plantation's master.[35]

Most couples wanted to legitimize their marriages, children, and families upon gaining their freedom. The marriage contract became the first legal agreement that the freedmen had the privilege to make as they attempted to exist as persons in America.

> Slave couples living in Kentucky who joined together in putative antebellum marriages were not permitted to legally marry until February 14, 1866, when the state passed legislation specifically addressing this issue. Section 2 of the Act

> of 1866 provided that such relationships would be deemed lawful marriages if the slave couple had "heretofore lived and cohabited, and do now live together as husband and wife ..." The Act imposed an affirmative duty upon the slave couple to appear before the county clerk, pay a nominal fee, and declare "that they have been, and desire to continue, living together as husband and wife ..." Upon the issuance of the certificate of the declaration, the slave couple would have proof that their marriage was a legally recognized union, and that their children were legitimate.[36]

Marriage records are a precious resource for genealogists as they tie together two direct ancestors. In most cases, they are the key to identifying and potentially unlocking family trees. When bearing in mind the biblical perspective of marriage, the license or certificate is not a requirement. Marriage is the making of a covenant between God, man, and woman for life. Not all marriages are made in covenant. Only those that are entered into with God in the midst are biblical marriages. Many of these unions were for legal purposes alone, which made them marriage contracts.

In 1868, former slaves found some freedom in their ability to make marriage contracts but still, they were plagued with the effects of their past bondage. "Henry was suddenly a man. Mary was a woman, a slave girl no more. Here they stood, bride and groom, before John Wesley Starr, the coarse old preacher who a blink of an eye before had spent his Sundays teaching White people that slavery was the manifestation of a human order ordained by God, and preaching to Black people that theirs was a glorified place among the chickens and the pigs."[37]

This pastor could legally marry two people who were, a short time ago, legally chattel. They had only moments before been slaves, inhuman and without the ability to consent to their marriage. This couple gave their approval and was proud to be their own master. Jumping the broom was not a necessary part of their wedding - now they made a true marriage commitment without a broom. They were married with the understanding that they could love each other until death, and not distance, parted them. Only the power of God's love could have delivered the African-American slave from the grip of the most powerful nation in the world. Certainly Lord, Certainly Lord, It's by God's Amazing Grace that Four Centuries of African-American Marriages and Families are now Reconciled.

The lives of slaves and African-Americans today have bridged the gap between slavery and freedom. We are able to see how love is the greatest of all virtues, and found in its power is the ability to heal all relationships. In the past, God used the love of abolitionists and heroes during the Civil Rights movement to bring freedom and a measure of equality to African-Americans. In the present and future, African-Americans marriages and families must realize that all the trials of our troubled past work for our good in Christ Jesus. "And we know that for those who love God all things work together for good, for those who are called according to his purpose" (Rom. 8:28 ESV). God's love and His Amazing Grace has brought us this far, and will lead us on as exemplified on this final chart.

Figure 36 The Pyramid of God's Amazing Grace to African-Americans

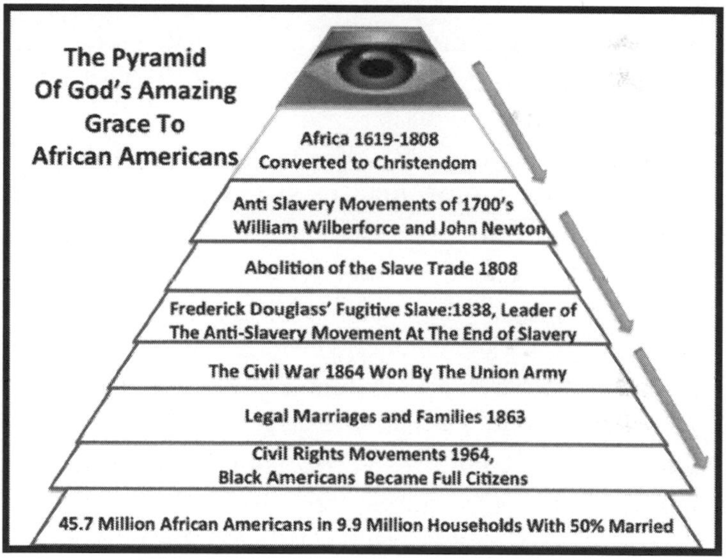

13 Principles from Slavery to Achieve Marital Satisfaction

1. African American marriages and families have the most excellent example of keeping God in their lives through test and trails. Slaves understood that marital happiness was not as important as keeping the family together.
2. Couples today should find in their testimonies of marriage and family a faith that teaches them how to survive by trusting in God's word when all hope is lost.

3. The difficulties involved in maintaining families and marital relationships in the face of promiscuous lifestyles should teach couples how to love one another.
4. Slaves considered their marriages as ethical institutions, which made their marital relationships right with God, although not legal by law. African-Americans today should strive for sexual purity as singles and in marriage, because it can provide spiritual insights and build character.
5. Understanding the history of marriage and family in the African-American context, couples and family members should develop a code of moral honor and respect for each other found in God's word.
6. African-Americans have historically trusted in God through a personal relationship with Him, and kept their family and marriages bathed in prayer. Families today must emulate the same spiritual lifestyle to find the peace that overcomes their failures and develop a good marriage.
7. Marriage and families are designed to draw couples closer to God. As spouses give accountability to each other, it helps them to live right – plus, it keeps the relationship in good standing with each other.
8. Living holy with our spouse provides us a sense of God's presence in our marriages and families. Marriage is designed to make each other aware of God's presence and favor.
9. African-American marriages and families must develop an immediate past that represents spiritual endurance and commitments upon which to build a future.
10. Learning to appreciate the struggles and difficulties of slaves will develop interpersonal strength. It encourages us to eliminate the shame of having been a captive people, and it allows us an opportunity to build character.
11. Broken marriages and family relationships teach the critical Christian principle of forgiveness. African-Americans cannot move forward in American society without being committed to forgiving.
12. Slavery, like marriage, teaches families to put others before themselves. In doing so, members develop the servant's mind that was also in Christ.

13. Marriage teaches couples to serve our spouse, family and others as a ministry to God. Christian slaves were committed to fulfilling Scripture in their service in the most difficult of circumstances. This made their status in life better as they lived life unto God. They were forced to remember that, in Christ, families are Christian servants to one another.

We are called to follow the example of Jesus, who was a suffering servant. In the end, we will find He is more for us than the all the world against us. The Apostle Paul reminds us of God's everlasting love to His suffering people:

> What then shall we say to these things? If God is for us, who can be against us? He who did not spare his own Son but gave him up for us all, how will he not also with him graciously give us all things? Who shall bring any charge against God's elect? It is God who justifies. Who is to condemn? Christ Jesus is the one who died—more than that, who was raised—who is at the right hand of God, who indeed is interceding for us. Who shall separate us from the love of Christ? Shall tribulation, or distress, or persecution, or famine, or nakedness, or danger, or sword? As it is written, "For your sake we are being killed all the day long; we are regarded as sheep to be slaughtered." No, in all these things we are more than conquerors through him who loved us (Rom. 8: 31-37. ESV).

God has given us the most excellent example of His work within the lives of our African American ancestors. He has revealed to this modern generation what love can accomplish through God's Amazing Grace to Reconcile Four Centuries of African American Marriages and families. When we love God and serve Him, we can rectify the ills of our past history and create an inheritance of healthy families.

Endnotes

Introduction

1 William Wells Brown, (2011-03-24). *Clotel; or, the President's Daughter.* 1853 p. 70. Kindle Edition.
2 William Wells Brown. P.2.
3 Angela J. Hattery, Earl Smith, (2007-04-19). *African-American Families* (Kindle Locations 533-534). SAGE Publications. Kindle Edition.

Chapter 1 What's Wrong With My People

1 The Spirituals Project at the University of Denver. "African Tradition, Proverbs, and Sankofa." 2004, Retrieved 19 February 2017. https://www.berea.edu/cgwc/the-power-of-sankofa/
2 Texas, County Marriage Records, 1837-1977, the database with images, *Family Search* (https://familysearch.org/ark:/61903/1:1:QV14-2Q88: accessed 29 September 2015), Warren Turner and Elvira Davis, 06 Feb 1869, Marriage; citing Ellis, Texas, United States, Citing county clerk offices, Texas; FHL microfilm 1,034,617.
3 "Texas Births and Christenings, 1840-1981," database, *FamilySearch* (https://familysearch.org/ark:/61903/1:1:VR3M-Y12: 8 December 2014), Willie Ann Turner, 15 Jan 1883; citing Ennis, Ellis, Texas, reference; FHL microfilm 1651033 IT 1-4.

Chapter 2 The Apple Doesn't Fall Far from The Tree

1 *Handbook of Cultural Psychology.* Guilford Publications. (2007-06-25) p. 289 Kindle Edition.
2 Douglass K. Blount and Joseph D. Wooddell, *The Baptist Faith and Message 2000: Critical Issues in America's Largest Protestant Denomination*(Lanham, MD: Rowman & Littlefield Publishers Inc., 2007), 4317, Kindle Edition.

3 Act XII, *Laws of Virginia,* December 1662 (Hening, *Statutes at Large,* 2: 170). Laws Pertaining Slavery http://www.bowdoin.edu/~prael/projects/gsonnen/page3.html
4 Darlene Clark Hine, Stanley C. Har; William C. Hine (2013-08-28). *The African-American Odyssey, Combined Volume* (Page G-6). Pearson Education. Kindle Edition
5 Full in wider, Robert, *"Affirmative Action,"* *The Stanford Encyclopedia of Philosophy* (Winter 2014 Edition), Edward N. Zalta (ed.). Accessed, November 20, 2015. http://plato.stanford.edu/archives/win2014/entries/affirmative-action.
6 National Association for the Advancement of Colored People ("NAACP") website www.naacp.org Retrieved May 13, 2017.http://www.naacp.org/criminal-justice-fact-sheet/
7 Robert J. Priest, Alvaro L. Nieves, (2006-12-07*). This Side of Heaven: Race, Ethnicity, and Christian Faith* (p. 26). Oxford University Press. Kindle Edition.
8 *The Physical and Psychological Effects of Slavery on the Slave Body,* 2014 Accessed November 8, 2015. http://prezi.com/x7nhxy6_o8ti/?utm_campaign=share&utm_medium=copy&rc=ex0share
9 American Psychiatric Association (2013). *Diagnostic and Statistical Manual of Mental Disorders* (5th ed.). Arlington, VA: American Psychiatric Publishing. pp. 271–280.
10 Dr. Joy DeGruy. *Post Traumatic Slave Syndrome: America's Legacy of Enduring Injury and Healing,* Joy DeGruy Leary. Uptone Press (2005). P. 121.
11 Dr. Joy DeGruy. *Post Traumatic Slave Syndrome: America's Legacy of Enduring Injury and Healing,* Joy DeGruy Leary. Uptone Press (2005). Retrieved December 17, 2015,http://www.quazoo.com/q/Post Traumatic_Slave_Syndrome.
12 Charles Ball, (2012-12-18). *Fifty Years in Chains Or, the Life of an American Slave* (pp. 12-13). Kindle Edition.
13 John Simkin, (2014-01-11). *Slavery in the United States* (Kindle Locations 13052-13054). Spartacus Educational Publishers. Kindle Edition.
14 McGoldrick, Monica (2005-08-18). *Ethnicity and Family Therapy, Third Edition* (p. 83). Guilford Press. Kindle Edition.
15 Michael P. Nichols, Richard C. Schwartz, *Family Therapy: Concepts & Methods.* Psyche page, retrieved Dec. 24, 2015. 2012. P.1. http://www.psychpage.com/learning/library/counseling/bowen.html
16 HYPERLINK "https://www.google.com/search?tbo=p&tbm=bks&q=inauthor:%22Michael+P.+Nichols%22."
17 Warren Beck and Myles Clowers, *Understanding American History Through Fiction* (New York: McGraw-Hill, 1975), 1: ix. In James W. Loewen, (2008-04-08). *Lies My Teacher Told Me: Everything Your American History Textbook Got Wrong* (p. 135). The New Press. Kindle Edition

18 Warren Beck and Myles Clowers, *Understanding American History Through Fiction* (New York: McGraw-Hill, 1975), 1: ix. In James W. Loewen, (2008-04-08). *Lies My Teacher Told Me: Everything Your American History Textbook Got Wrong* (p. 135). The New Press. Kindle Edition.

19 Carolyn Baker, *U.S. History Uncensored: What Your High School Textbook Didn't Tell You.* 2006. http://www.thepeoplesvoice.org/TPV3/Books.php/2010/09/12/u-s-history-uncensored-what-your-high-sc

20 Angela Hattery and Earl Smith (2007-04-19). *African-American Families* (Kindle Locations 1019-1024). SAGE Publications. Kindle Edition.

21 (Frankenburg 1993; Hartigan 2000; Keating 1995; Rodriguez 1999). In Robert J Priest, Nieves, Alvaro L. (2006-12-07). *This Side of Heaven: Race, Ethnicity, and Christian Faith* (p. 29). Oxford University Press. Kindle Edition.

22 Roberta M. Gilbert, (2011-10-18). *The Eight Concepts of Bowen Theory* (p. 70). Leading Systems Press. Kindle Edition.

23 Isaac Allen, Aughey, John Hill; Baring, Evelyn; Bibb, Henry Walton; Fowler, William Warde; Thompson, Charles (2016-03-09). *Slave Narrative Six Pack 6 - Slavery in the Bible, Henry Bibb, Portuguese Slavery, Slavery and Secession, The Slave Preacher and Roman Slavery* (Illustrated) (Kindle Locations 1999-2013. Kindle Edition.

24 Edward E. Baptist, (2014-09-09). *The Half Has Never Been Told: Slavery and the Making of American Capitalism* (Kindle Locations 4441-4444). Basic Books. Kindle Edition

25 Ibid.,

26 Patricia Dixon, (2013-06-17). *African-American Relationships, Marriages, and Families: An Introduction* (Kindle Locations 125-142). Taylor and Francis. Kindle Edition.

27 R. Staples, The myth of the Black matriarchy. In R. Staples (Ed.), *The Black family: Essays and studies*. Belmont, Wadsworth, California 1971. PP.149-159.

28 U.S. Department of Labor, Office of Policy Planning and Research. (1965/1981). The Negro family: The case formational action. Westport, Connecticut: Green-wood Press. pp. 29-32.

29 Moynihan Report." International Encyclopedia of the Social Sciences. 2008. *Encyclopedia.com*. Retrieved April 4, 2016. http://www.encyclopedia.com/doc/1G2-3045301638.html

30 Tristan L. Tolman, *The Effects of Slavery and Emancipation on African-American Families and Family History Research*. Crossroads Journal (March 2011): P. 6. Accessed July 15, 2016.

31 Dixon, Patricia (2013-06-17). *African-American Relationships, Marriages, and Families: An Introduction* (Kindle Locations 125-142). Taylor and Francis. Kindle Edition.

32 Ibid.,

33 Orlando Patterson, *Rituals of Blood: Consequences of Slavery in Two American Centuries* (New York: Basic Civitas, 1998), 25.
34 Herbert Gutman, *The Black Family In Slavery & Freedom 1750-1925*. Pantheon Books, New York. 1976. P3.
35 Dixon, Patricia (2013-06-17). *African-American Relationships, Marriages, and Families: An Introduction* (Kindle Locations 143-147). Taylor and Francis. Kindle Edition.
36 Faye Z. (Zollicoffer) Belgrave; Kevin W. (Wendell) Allison. *African-American Psychology: From Africa to America* (Kindle Locations P.61.). Kindle Edition.

Chapter 3 God's Amazing Grace: A Response to The African Dilemma

1 Philip D. Curtin, *The Atlantic Slave Trade* (Madison: University of Wisconsin Press, 1969), p. 266. In Sowell, Thomas (2008-08-01). *Ethnic America: A History* (p.185-186). Basic Books. Kindle Edition.
2 Stan Griffin, *Amazing Grace--More Than A Hymn. Workers For Jesus*. P.1. Retrieved May 18, 2016. Hymn. http://www.workersforjesus.com/amaz.htm
3 Wintley Phillips, *Amazing Grace*, Carnegie Hall-YouTube. New York, New York. 2012. Video. Retrieved November 2, 2015. https://vimeo.com/56399119
4 History of Calabar, NKA NKORI YE NSONGONDA EFIK, EFUT YE ABAKPA. 2015. P.1. Retrieved November 2, 2015. http://www.arikwings.com/discover-cross-river/.
5 Ibid.,
6 Randy J. Sparks. *The Two Princes of Calabar: An Eighteenth-Century Atlantic Odyssey* (Kindle Locations 338-341). Kindle Edition.
7 Wesley, John (2014-07-25). *Thoughts Upon Slavery* (Short & Rare Works Series) (Kindle Locations 482-488). Hargreaves Publishing. Kindle Edition.
8 Site © Wesley's Chapel & Leysian Mission 2007, 49 City Road, London EC1Y 1AU Registered Charity No: 1137321. Retrieved 8/27/2016. http://www.wesleyschapel.org.uk/jwesley.htm
9 public domain picture of John Wesley - Image details [[File: John Wesley 1.jpg|thumb|John Wesley 1]] This image is available from the United States Library of Congress's Prints and Photographs division under the digital ID cpn.3m00154. https://en.wikipedia.org/wiki/File:John_Wesley_1.jpg
10 Public domain picture of John Newton. Work this author published before January 1, 1923 are in the **public domain** worldwide because the author died at least 100 years ago. Translations or editions published or editions later may be copyrighted based on how long they have been published in certain countries and areas. Unidentified painter 18th-century portrait painting of men, with Unspecified, Unidentified or Unknown artist and location. - http://www.nndb.com/people/494/000103185/.

11 Jonathan Aitken, (2007-06-07). John Newton (Foreword by Philip Yancey): *From Disgrace to Amazing Grace*. Crossway. P. 12. Kindle Edition.

12 Ibid.,

13 Harriet Beecher-Stowe, *Uncle Tom's Cabin* (p. 566). Fair Price Classics. Kindle Edition. In Jonathan Aitken, John Newton (Foreword by Philip Yancey): From Disgrace to Amazing Grace (p. 235). Crossway. Kindle Edition.

14 James Michael Brodie, *Equal The Lives and Ideas of Black American Innovators*. Bill Adler Books, Inc. William Morrow and Co. Inc. New York. 1993 P1.

15 Jonathan Aitken, (2007-06-07). John Newton (Foreword by Philip Yancey): *From Disgrace to Amazing Grace* (p. 233).

16 Mark Roads, *Amazing Grace: Some Early Tunes, New Britain*. Anthology of American Hymn Tunes, Bethel University, St. Paul, MN. P.1. Retrieved May 18, 2016. http://www.markrhoads.com/amazingsite/index.htm

17 James Michael Brodie, *Equal The Lives and Ideas of Black American Innovators*. P.1.

18 Robert J. Priest, Alvaro L. Nieves. (2006-12-07). *This Side of Heaven: Race, Ethnicity, and Christian Faith* (p. 26). Oxford University Press. Kindle Edition.

19 Monica McGoldrick, (2005-08-18). *Ethnicity and Family Therapy*, Third Edition (p. 17). Guilford Press. Kindle Edition.

20 Erika Margaret Reiko, *But I Can't Possibly Be Racist, My Mother is Asian. The Secret History of America*, Essays in American Studies from UC Berkeley. 2015. P.1. https://medium.com/the-secret-history-of-america/but-i-can-t-possibly-be-racist-my-mother-is-asian-ac7e0f9ee821#.zdif672km. In Brockhaus' Small conversational lexicon. Encyclopaedic dictionary. Fourth Completely Revised Edition, Leipzig 1886; First volume. German website. Quelle: Brockhaus' Kleines Conversations-Lexikon. *EncyclopädischesHandwörterbuch*. Vierte *Vollständig*umgearbeitete Auflage, Leipzig 1886; Erster Band. http://www.enzyklopaedie.ch/dokumente/handlungstraeger.html#AnkerOben

21 Ibid.,

22 Johann Friedrich Blumenbach, Karl Friedrich Heinrich Marx, Pierre Flourens, Rudolph Wagner, and John Hunter, *On the Natural Varieties of Mankind: De generis humani varietate native*, 1795, ed. and trans. Thomas Bendyshe, published for the Anthropological Society of London by Longman, Green, Longman, Roberts & Green (London: Bergman Publishers, 1865), 148.

23 Steven Jay Gould, "The Geometer of Race," *Discover Magazine*, November 1994, 1.

24 Monica McGoldrick, *Ethnicity and Family Therapy*, 3rd ed. (New York: Guilford Press, 2005), 16. Kindle Edition

25 J. A. Rogers, Sex and Race, Volume 1: *Negro-Caucasian Mixing in All Ages and All Lands -- The Old World* (p. 24). Helga Rogers. 2014. Kindle Edition.

26 Suman Fernando, *Mental Health, Race and Culture* (Kindle Locations 581-583). Palgrave Macmillan. 2010. Kindle Edition.

27 SLAVERY RACE AND THE AMERICAN LEGAL SYSTEM 1700-1872 93 (Paul Fink lm an, ed. 1988) [hereinafter SLAVERY RACE] (Reprint of Sketch of the Laws relating to Slavery in the several states of the United States of America, George M. P. 23.1827.

28 Martha W. McCartney, Lorena S. Walsh, *A Study of the Africans and African-Americans on Jamestown Island and at Green Spring, 1619-1803 The Evolution of Slavery as an Institution, Colonial Williamsburg Foundation.* Williamsburg, Virginia. 2003. P.118. 8/25/2016 https://www.nps.gov/jame/learn/historyculture/upload/African%20Americans%20on%20Jamestown%20Island.pdf

29 Jessie Carney Smith Black First: 2,000 years of extraordinary achievement, 1994 Visible Ink Press, Detroit, MI. ISBN 0-8103-9490-1 8/25/2016.

30 Jessie Smith, *First Black*. P. 1.

31 Martha W. McCartney, Lorena S. Walsh, *A Study of the Africans and African-Americans on Jamestown Island and at Green Spring, 1619-1803The Evolution of Slavery as an Institution, Colonial Williamsburg Foundation*. Williamsburg, Virginia. 2003. P.94 https://www.nps.gov/jame/learn/historyculture/upload/African%20Americans%20on%20Jamestown%20Island.pdf

32 John Hope Franklin, *From Slavery to Freedom* (Page 53). McGraw-Hill Higher Education -A. Kindle Edition.

33 Ibid.,

34 Jennifer Hallam, *The Slave Experience: Family.* PBS Slavery and The Making of America, A production of Thirteen/WNET, New York. @2004 Educational Broadcasting Corporation. P 2. http://www.pbs.org/wnet/slavery/experience/family/history.html

35 Ibid.,

36 Christopher L. Webber, *American to the Backbone: The Life of James W. C. Pennington, the Fugitive Slave Who Became One of the First Black Abolitionists* (Kindle Locations 1003-1006). Pegasus Books. Kindle Edition.

37 David Walbert, L. Maren Wood, *Marriage in colonial North Carolina.* P1.

38 Ibid.,

39 Theodore D. Weld, *American Slavery As It Is: Testimony of a Thousand Witnesses*, The American Anti-Slavery Society. New York. 1839. P. 51.

40 Norman Yetman, *When I Was a Slave: Memoirs from the Slave Narrative Collection.* Dover Thrift Editions Dover Publications. Mineola, New York. Kindle Edition. 2012. P.77.

41 Ralph L. Beals, Harry Hoijer, and Alan R. Beals, *An Introduction to Anthropology, 5th ed.* (New York: Macmillan, 1977), 97, quoted by Charles Kraft, *Anthropology for Christian Witness* (New York: Orbis Books, 1997), 2987. Kindle Edition.

42 Robert Staples, *Exploring Black Sexuality* (Kindle Locations 713-716). Rowman & Littlefield Publishers. 2006. Kindle Edition

43 Benjamin Griffith Brawley, *A Social History of the American Negro Being a History of the Negro Problem in the United States. Including A History and Study of the Republic of Liberia* (p. 42). 2012 Kindle Edition.

44 Anna Belle Pfau, *Three Stories of Black Women American History*, The New Agenda, 2011 P.1. Retrieved 8/25/2016. In Public domain, Albrecht Durer-The Negress Katherina - WGA07097.jpg. Wikimedia Commons, the free media repository. Retrieved 8/25/2016 http://thenewagenda.net/2011/02/10/three-stories-of-black-women-from-american-history/

45 Brendan Wolfe, "Free Blacks in Colonial Virginia." *Encyclopedia Virginia*. Virginia Foundation for the Humanities, 24 Jan. 2014. Web. 2 Nov. 2015.

46 Act XII, *Laws of Virginia*, December 1662 (Hening, *Statutes at Large*, 2: 170). Laws Pertaining Slavery http://www.bowdoin.edu/~prael/projects/gsonnen/page3.html

47 William Goodell, *The American Slave Code In Theory And Practice: Its Distinctive Features Shown By Its Statutes, Judicial Decisions, & Illustrative Facts* 90 (1853). P. 105-108.

48 Act XII, *Laws of Virginia*, December 1662 (Hening, *Statutes at Large*, 2: 170). Laws Pertaining Slavery http://www.bowdoin.edu/~prael/projects/gsonnen/page3.html

49 Ross Kimmel, "The Origins of the Law of Slavery in British North America," 17 Cardozo Law Review 1711-1792 (1996). In Ross Kimmel, Blacks Before The Law In Colonial Maryland. Retrieved March 30, 2016, http://msa.maryland.gov/msa/speccol/sc5300/sc5348/html/footnotes3.html#fn5

50 General Assembly, *An act concerning Servants and Slaves, XX, 1705*, P. 454. William Waller Hening, ed., *The Statutes at Large; Being a Collection of All the Laws of Virginia from the First Session of the Legislature, in the Year 1619*, (Philadelphia: R. & W. & G. Bartow, 1823), 3:447–463. In *Encyclopedia Virginia*. Retrieved April 16, 2016, from http://www.EncyclopediaVirginia.org/Indentured_Servants_in_Colonial_Virginia.

51 Ibid.,

52 Elizabeth Hyde Botume, *First Days among the Contrabands* (Boston,1893), p. 160-161.

53 Frances Smith Foster. *'Til Death or Distance Do Us Part: Love and Marriage in African America* (Kindle Locations 1777-1782). Kindle Edition.

54 Elizabeth Hyde Botume, p.160-161.

55 Suman Fernando, (2010-01-29). *Mental Health, Race and Culture* (Kindle Locations 1458-1462). Palgrave Macmillan. Kindle Edition. (Anon., 1851) (Thomas and Sillen, 1972, p. 16) (Plummer, 1970).

56 Sue, Derald Wing; Sue, David (2012-07-10). *Counseling the Culturally Diverse: Theory and Practice* (Wiley Desktop Editions) (Kindle Locations 10924-10926). Wiley. Kindle Edition.

57 Ross Kimmel, *Blacks Before the Law In Colonial Maryland.* Retrieved March 30, 2016, http://msa.maryland.gov/msa/speccol/sc5300/sc5348/html/footnotes3.html#fn5

58 Ibid.,

59 Ibid.,

60 William Hand Browne. *BLACKS BEFORE THE LAW IN COLONIAL MARYLAND, FREEDOM OR BONDAGE -- THE LEGISLATIVE RECORD.* Archives of Maryland, (in progress; Baltimore, 1883 to date), XIII, pp. 546-549.

61 Joshua Rothman, *Notorious in the Neighborhood: Sex and Families Across the Color Line in Virginia, 1787–1861*, published 2003 and Thomas E. Buckley (The Great Catastrophe of My Life: Divorce in the Old Dominion, published 2002).

62 David L. Walbert, L. MAREN WOOD, *Marriage in colonial North Carolina.* Learn North Carolina, The University of North Carolina at Chapel Hill, Chapel Hill, NC .2008 P. 299. http://www.learnnc.org/lp/editions/nchist-colonial/4079

63 George Washington Williams (2012-05-17). *History of the Negro Race in America From 1619 to 1880. Vol 1 Negroes as Slaves, as Soldiers, and as Citizens* (Kindle Locations 5590-5591). Kindle Edition

64 Benjamin Griffith Brawley (2012-05-17). *A Social History of the American Negro Being a History of the Negro Problem in the United States. Including A History and Study of the Republic of Liberia* (p. 323). Kindle Edition.

65 B. A. Botkin, ed., *Lay My Burden Down: A Folk History of Slavery* (Chicago: University of Chicago Press, 1945), 54, http://www.questia.com/read/91249698/lay-my-burden-down-a-folk-history-of-slavery.

66 George Washington Williams, (2012-05-17). *History of the Negro Race in America From 1619 to 1880. Vol 1 Negroes as Slaves, as Soldiers, and as Citizens* (Kindle Locations 5590-5591). Kindle Edition

67 William Craft; Craft, Ellen; Du Bois, W. E. B.; Keckley, Elizabeth; Henson, Josiah; Truth, Sojourner; Gilbert, Olive; Still, William (2015-08-06). *Slave Narrative Six Pack 2 - Running a Thousand Miles for Freedom, The Souls of Black Folk, Behind the Scenes, Life of Josiah Henson, Narrative of Sojourner Truth and William Garrison* (Illustrated) (Kindle Locations 193-197). Kindle Edition.

68 Mary V. Thompson, *Slavery and Marriage.* Mount Vernon Estate and Gardens, Digital Encyclopedia, accessed November 13, 2015. http://www.mountvernon.org/research-collections/digital-encyclopedia/article/slavery-and-marriage/

69 Ibid.,

70 Ibid.,

71 Ibid.,

72 Ibid.,

73 Thomas Jefferson Public Domain, Thomas Jefferson. Wikimedia Commons, the free media repository. https://commons.wikimedia.org/wiki/File:Mather_Brown_-_Thomas_Jefferson_-_Google_Art_Project.jpg

74 History.com, Sally Hemings. A+E Networks. Accessed November 25, 2015. 2010 http://www.history.com/topics/sally-hemings.

75 *Notes*, ed. Peden, 138. The 1832 edition is available online. See Jefferson, *Notes on the State of Virginia* (Boston: Lilly and Wait, 1832), 144.

76 Jefferson to Edward Coles, August 25, 1814, in *PTJ: RS*, 7:604. Transcription. http://founders.archives.gov/documents/Jefferson/03-07-02-0439

77 Ibid.,

78 Read more at http://www.phillymag.com/news/2014/04/11/10-facts-thomas-jefferson-slavery-at-jeffersons-monticello-national-constitution-center/#huc5iaVTSiSXBhqI.99

79 James Oliver Horton, (2011-05-10). *Slavery and Public History: The Tough Stuff of American Memory* (p. 136). New Press, The. Kindle Edition. *In Lucia Stanton, Slavery at Monticello* (Charlottesville, VA: Thomas Jefferson Memorial Foundation, 1996), 13. Horton, James Oliver (2011-05-10). *Slavery and Public History: The Tough Stuff of American Memory* (p. 239). New Press, The. Kindle Edition.

80 William Wells Brown (2011-03-24*). Clotel; or, the President's Daughter.* London: Partridge & Oakey, 1853. (p.2-4). Kindle Edition.

81 James Oliver Horton, (2011-05-10). *Slavery and Public History: The Tough Stuff of American Memory* (p. 136). New Press, The. Kindle Edition. In Lucia Stanton, Slavery at Monticello (Charlottesville, VA: Thomas Jefferson Memorial Foundation, 1996), 13. Horton, James Oliver (2011-05-10). *Slavery and Public History: The Tough Stuff of American Memory* (p. 239). New Press, The. Kindle Edition.

82 Ibid.,

83 Anthony Iaccarino, Encyclopædia Britannica Online, s. v. "The Founding Fathers and Slavery," accessed November 13, 2015, http://www.britannica.com/topic/The-Founding-Fathers-and-Slavery-1269536.

84 Thomas Jefferson, *The Writings of Thomas Jefferson: Being His Autobiography, Correspondence, Reports, Messages, Addresses, and Other Writings, Official and Private* (Washington, D.C.: Taylor & Maury, 1853-1854). Accessed November 25, 2015,/ http://www.Blackpast.org/primary/declaration-independence-and-debate-over-slavery#sthash.q1bdX2on.dpufhttp.

85 *The Holy Bible: English Standard Version* (Wheaton: Standard Bible Society, 2001), Ec 7:29.

Chapter 4 Slave Marriages, Conversion, and the Church

1 Frederick Douglass, *The Narrative of the Life of Frederick Douglass* [with Biographical Introduction]). Neeland Media LLC. Kindle Edition. (pp. 105-106).

2 Matthew Henry, *Matthew Henry's Commentary on the Whole Bible: Complete and Unabridged in One Volume* (Peabody: Hendrickson, 1994), 2318.

3 Edward E. Baptist, *The Half Has Never Been Told: Slavery and the Making of American Capitalism*. 2014. (Kindle Locations 4376-4378). Kindle Edition.

4 Marcus W. Jernegan, "Slavery and Conversion in the American Colonies," *The American Historical Review* 21.3 (1916): 504–527. In Documents relating to the Colonial History of New York, III. P.36. See also Calendar of State Papers, Colonial, I574-I660, pp. 492-493.

5 John C. Hurd, *Law of Freedom and Bondage*, I. 160-161. P.508

6 William Goodell. P. 219.

7 Fredrick Douglass, *My Bondage and My Freedom*. P. 26.

8 Helen T. Catterall (ed.), *Judicial Cases Concerning American Slavery and the Negro* (Washington, D.C., 1926), pp. 57.

9 Edward E. Baptist, (Kindle Locations 4320-4325).Kindle Edition.

10 Ibid.,

11 B. A. Botkin, ed., *Lay My Burden Down: A Folk History of Slavery* (Chicago: University of Chicago Press, 1945), 26, http://www.questia.com/read/91249670/lay-my-burden-down-a-folk-history-of-slavery.

12 Neil Brown, June 26, 1821, Neill Brown Papers, Duke. Baptist, Edward E. (2014-09-09). *The Half Has Never Been Told: Slavery and the Making of American Capitalism* (Kindle Location 9953). Basic Books. Kindle Edition.

13 Sparks, *On Jordan's Stormy Banks*, 66– 71, 116– 117, 125– 139; David T. Bailey, "A Divided Prism: Two Sources of Black Testimony on Slavery," JSH 46 (1980): 392; Randolph Scully, "' I Come Here Before You Did and I Shall Not Go Away': Race, Gender, and Evangelical Community on the Eve of the Nat Turner Rebellion," JER 27, no. 4 (2007): 661– 684; Janet Duitsman Cornelius, Slave Missions and the Black Church in the Antebellum South (Columbia, SC, 1999); Isaac Johnson, Slavery Days in Old Kentucky (Ogdensburg, NY, 1901), 25– 26; Solomon Northup, Twelve Years a Slave (Auburn, NY, 1853), 94. Baptist, Edward E. (2014-09-09). The Half Has Never Been Told: Slavery and the Making of American Capitalism (Kindle Locations 9947-9952). Basic Books. Kindle Edition.

14 Ibid.,

15 Faye Z. (Zollicoffer) Belgrave; Kevin W. (Wendell) Allison. *African-American Psychology: From Africa to America* (Kindle Locations 2851-2854). Kindle Edition.

16 Edward E. Baptist, (Kindle Locations 4432-4433). 2014. Kindle Edition.

17 Ibid.,

18 Ibid.,4434-4438.

19 Negro Spiritual, *Certainly Lord*, African-American Heritage Hymnal (2001), p.1055 http://www.hymnary.org/hymn/AAHH2001/678.

20 Richard J. Chacon; Michael Charles Scoggins. *The Great Awakening and Southern Backcountry Revolutionaries.* Springer, (2014). Pp. 36–37.

21 Baptist, Edward E. (2014-09-09). *The Half Has Never Been Told: Slavery and the Making of American Capitalism* (Kindle Locations 4306-4310). Basic Books. Kindle Edition.

22 Ephesians 6: 5, Colossians 3: 22; James Smylie, Review of a Letter, from the Presbytery of Chillicothe, to the Presbytery of Mississippi, on the Subject of Slavery (Woodville, MS, 1836), 3. Retrieved September 13, 2017. https://archive.org/details/reviewofletterfr00smyl. And Edward E. Baptist, (2014-09-09). InThe Half Has Never Been Told: Slavery and the Making of American Capitalism (Kindle Locations 9987-9988). Basic Books. Kindle Edition.

23 William Goodell. *The American Slave Code Letter From The Honorable William Jay Letter To The Author.* New York, 25th, January 1853.

24 Jonathan Edwards, *The Injustice and Impolicy of The Slave Trade and of the Slavery of Africans.* New Haven Anti-Slavery Society. Whitmore & Buckingham, New Haven, Ct. 1833. P.11.

25 Jonathan Edwards, *The Injustice and Impolicy.* P.31.

26 Jonathan Edwards, *The Injustice and Impolicy.* P.32.

27 Marcus W. Jernegan, "Slavery and Conversion in the American Colonies," *The American Historical Review* 21.3 (1916): 504–527. In Documents relating to the Colonial History of New York, III. P.36. See also Calendar of State Papers, Colonial, I574-I660, pp. 492-493.

28 James Roberts, *The Narrative of James Roberts, a Soldier Under Gen. Washington in the Revolutionary War, and Under Gen. Jackson at the Battle of New Orleans, in the War of 1812: "a Battle Which Cost Me a Limb, Some Blood, and Almost My Life": James Roberts 1753.* Documenting The American South, Academic Affairs Library, UNC-CH University of North Carolina at Chapel Hill, 2001. P. iv. Retrieved 05, 07, 2016, http://docsouth.unc.edu/neh/roberts/roberts.html.

29 Baptist, Edward E. (2014-09-09). *The Half Has Never Been Told: Slavery and the Making of American Capitalism* (Kindle Locations 2367-2369). Basic Books. Kindle Edition.

30 Baptist, Edward E. *The Half Has Never Been Told*, Kindle Location 3970.

31 James Roberts, *The Narrative of James Roberts. P. iv.*

32 Ibid.,

33 Ibid.,

34 Faye Z. Belgrave; Kevin W. Allison. *African-American Psychology: From Africa to America* (Kindle Locations 2677-2680). Kindle Edition.
35 Rick Paskin, *African-American Funeral Service Rituals.* Funeralwise, Wilmette, Ill. (2007). P.1. Retrieved 5/9/16. https://www.funeralwise.com/customs/african_american/
36 Rick Paskin, *African-American Funeral Service Rituals.*
37 Rick Paskin, *African-American Funeral Service Rituals.*
38 B. A. Botkin, ed., *Lay My Burden Down: A Folk History of Slavery* (Chicago: University of Chicago Press, 1945), 26, http://www.questia.com/read/91249670/lay-my-burden-down-a-folk-history-of-slavery.
39 William Goodell, P.106.
40 John Simkin, (2014-01-11*). Slavery in the United States* (Kindle Locations 5345-5348). Spartacus Educational Publishers. Kindle Edition.
41 Theodore D. Weld, *American Slavery As It Is: Testimony of a Thousand Witnesses*, The American Anti-Slavery Society. New York. 1839. P. 48.
42 Ibid.,
43 George Washington Williams, (2012-05-17). *History of the Negro Race in America From 1619 to 1880. Vol 1 Negroes as Slaves, as Soldiers, and as Citizens* (Kindle Locations 4270-4272). Kindle Edition.
44 Norman R. Yerman, (2012-03-15). *Voices from Slavery: 100 Authentic Slave Narratives* (African-American) (p. 26). Dover Publications. Kindle Edition.
45 Thornton Stringfellow, P. 28.
46 Phillip Schaff, *History of the Christian Church*, (Oak Harbor, WA: Logos Research Systems, Inc.) 1997. This material has been carefully compared, corrected and emended (according to the 1910 edition of Charles Scribner's Sons) by The Electronic Bible Society, Dallas, TX, 1998. P. 1.
47 William Wells Brown, (2011-03-24). *Clotel; or, the President's Daughter.* London: Partridge & Oakey, 1853. (p.100). Kindle Edition.
48 Carter Godwin Woodson, *The History of the Negro Church 2012*. (Kindle Locations 1339-1349).
49 Ibid.,
50 Ibid.,
51 William Goodell, *Slavery and Anti-Slavery, a History of the Great Struggle in Both Hemispheres*, 2010. Kindle. p.3707-3721.
52 Ibid.,
53 Ibid.,
54 Ibid.,
55 Ibid.,
56 Ibid.,
57 Ibid.,
58 Frederick Douglass, "Baptists, Congregationalists, the Free Church, and Slavery: An Address Delivered in Belfast, Ireland, on December 23, 1845."

Belfast News Letter, December 26, 1845, and *Belfast Northern Whig*, December 25, 1845. Blassingame, John (et al., eds.). *The Frederick Douglass Papers*: Series One--Speeches, Debates, and Interviews. New Haven: Yale University Press, 1979. Vol. I.

59 Rev. James M. Simms, *The First Colored Baptist Church in North America Constituted at Savannah, Georgia, January 20, A.D. 1788*. Philadelphia J. B. Lippincott Company1888. Philadelphia, PA. P.18.

60 Ibid., P.18.

61 Ibid., P.55-56.

62 Eighmy, *Churches in Cultural Captivity*, 10– 16; Nancy Tatom Ammerman, Baptist Battles: Social Change and Religious Conflict in the Southern Baptist Convention (New Brunswick: Rutgers University Press, 1990), 31– 32. In Newman, Mark (2011-04-08). Getting Right With God: Southern Baptists and Desegregation, 1945-1995 (Religion & American Culture) (p. 213). University of Alabama Press. Kindle Edition.

63 Southern Baptist Convention, Resolution Concerning Lynching And Race Relations Oklahoma City, Oklahoma – 1939. Executive Committee of the Southern Baptist Convention. Nashville, Tennessee. http://www.sbc.net/resolutions/879/resolution-concerning-lynching-and-race-relations. In Mark Kelly, U.S. House apologizes for slavery, 'Jim Crow' laws, Baptist Press, Southern Baptist Convention. Nashville, Tenn. 2008. Retrieved 8/29/2016. http://www.bpnews.net/28564/us-house-apologizes-for-slavery-jim-crow-laws.

64 Southern Baptist Convention, Resolution Concerning Lynching And Race Relations Oklahoma City, Oklahoma – 1939. Executive Committee of the Southern Baptist Convention. Nashville, Tennessee. http://www.sbc.net/resolutions/879/resolution-concerning-lynching-and-race-relationsMark Kelly, U.S. House apologizes for slavery. Retrieved 8/29/2016

65 Southern Baptist Convention, Resolution, On Racial Reconciliation On The 150th Anniversary of The Southern Baptist Convention, Atlanta, Georgia - 1995. Executive Committee of the Southern Baptist Convention. Nashville, Tennessee. In Mark Kelly, U.S. House apologizes for slavery. Retrieved 8/29/2016

66 Mark Kelly, "U.S. House apologizes for slavery." Retrieved 8/29/2016

67 United States. Work Projects Administration (2011-03-23). *Slave Narratives: A Folk History of Slavery in the United States From Interviews with Former Slaves Georgia Narratives, Part 2* (Kindle Locations 1464-1470). Kindle Edition

68 E. A Randolph, Picture, *The Life of Rev. John Jasper, Pastor of Sixth Mt. Zion Baptist Church, Richmond, Va., from His Birth to the Present Time, with His Theory on the Rotation of the Sun*. Richmond, VA. R. T. Hill & CO Publisher.1884. P.10-11. Public domain, John Jasper 1911.jpg Created: 31 December 1910. E. A Randolph, Picture, The Life of Rev. John Jasper, Pastor of

Sixth Mt. Zion Baptist Church, Richmond, Va., from His Birth to the Present Time, with His Theory on the Rotation of the Sun. Richmond, VA. R. T. Hill & CO Publisher.1884. P.10-11. https://commons.wikimedia.org/w/index.php?search=John+Jasper+&title=Special:Search&profile=default&fulltext=1&searchToken=dzwfw80bz7kk68x65ar5qkdgi#/media/File:John_Jasper_1911.jpg.

69 Ibid.,

70 *The Life of Rev. John Jasper.* P. 11.

71 Ibid., 12.

72 Ibid., 33.

73 Albert J. Raboteau, (1980-02-07). Slave Religion: The "Invisible Institution" in the Antebellum South (p. 98). Oxford University Press. Kindle Edition.

74 McCartney, Martha. P.

75 Carter Godwin Woodson, (2012-02-28). *The History of the Negro Church* (Kindle Locations 757-762). Kindle Edition.

76 Wolfe, Brendan. "Free Blacks in Colonial Virginia." *Encyclopedia Virginia.* Virginia Foundation for the Humanities, 24 Jan. 2014. Web. 2 Nov. 2015.

77 Virginia Slaves and Indentured Servants. Retrieved April 13, 2016. http://web.csulb.edu/~jlawler/Course%20DW/VirginiaSlaveLaws.htm

78 SLAVERY AND THE MAKING OF AMERICA is a production of Thirteen/WNET New York. © 2004 Educational Broadcasting Corporation. Retrieved April 13, 2016, http://www.pbs.org/wnet/slavery/timeline/1662.html

79 George M. Stroud, A Sketch of the Laws relating to Slavery.1827.

80 FREEDOM OR BONDAGE -- THE LEGISLATIVE RECORD, Archives Md., II, p. 272., Excerpt From Goodell, William, 1829-1894. "The American slave code in theory and practice: its distinctive features are shown by its statutes, judicial decisions and illustrative facts.

81 Albert J. Raboteau. (1980-02-07). Slave Religion: The "Invisible Institution" in the Antebellum South (p. 99). Oxford University Press. Kindle Edition.

82 Ibid., 99.

83 Judith Weisenfeld, "Religion in African-American History." American History: Oxford Research Encyclopedias. 2015-03-02. Oxford University Press. Date of access 25 May. 2016, <http://americanhistory.oxfordre.com/view/10.1093/acrefore/9780199329175.001.0001/acrefore-9780199329175-e-24

84 Judith Weisenfeld. *Religion in African-American History.*

85 Albert J. Raboteau. (1980-02-07). *Slave Religion: The "Invisible Institution" in the Antebellum South* (p. 100). Oxford University Press. Kindle Edition. Quoted by Edgard Legate Pennington, Thomas Bray's Associates and Their Work Among the Negroes (Worcester, Mass.: The American Antiquarian Society, 1939), pp. 38– 39.

86 Albert J. Raboteau, *Slave Religion: The "Invisible Institution.* P. 39-39.

87 Ibid.,

88 Ibid.,

89 George Washington Williams, *History of the Negro Race in America.* Kindle P. 4272.

90 Carter G. Woodson, The History of the Negro Church 2012 (Kindle Locations 149-152). Kindle Edition.

91 Ulrich Bonnell Phillips, (2012-05-17). American Negro Slavery A Survey of the Supply, Employment and Control of Negro Labor as Determined by the Plantation Regime (Kindle Locations 7385-7387). Kindle Edition.

92 Henry Chase, "Proud, free and Black: Petersburg - visiting the Virginia location of the largest number of 19th century free slaves, *American Visions,*" Jun-Jul 1994, accessed 27 Dec 2008.

93 Stroud's Sketch, p. 94. "Jay's Inquiry," In Goodell, William, The American Slave Code P1829.

94 William Goodell, 1829. P. 139. Mississippi Rev. Code, 390. Stroud's Sketch, p. 94. Jay's Inquiry,

95 Carter G. Woodson, Carter, *The History of the Negro Church.* Kindle, P. 1563-1565.

96 United States. Work Projects Administration (2011-03-23). *Slave Narratives: A Folk History of Slavery in the United States From Interviews with Former Slaves Georgia Narratives, Part 2* (Kindle Locations 2708-2713). Kindle Edition.

97 Robert Joseph Taylor, Linda M. Chatters, and Jeff Levin, *Religion in the Lives of African-Americans.* Sage Publication Inc., Thousand Oaks, Calif. 2004. P.33.

98 Faye Z. (Zollicoffer) Belgrave; Kevin W. (Wendell) Allison. *African-American Psychology: From Africa to America* (Kindle Locations 2851-2854). Kindle Edition.

Chapter 5. Slave Codes: Their Impact on Marriages and Families

1 Beecher-Stowe, Harriet. *Uncle Tom's Cabin* (p. 567). Fair Price Classics. Kindle Edition

2 Samuel Bruce Chilbolton III, (2013-08-16). *Slavery According to the Bible* (Kindle Locations 108-109). Kindle Edition.

3 George M. Stroud, *A Sketch of the Laws Relating to Slavery In Several States of The United States. Kimbmer and Sharpless,* Philadelphia, 1827. Preface i.

4 Ibid.,

5 Ibid.,

6 Ibid., 26.

7 Ibid., 30.

8 Ibid., 35.

9 Ibid., 44.

10 Ibid., 45.
11 Ibid.,50.
12 Ibid.,51.
13 Ibid.,57.
14 Ibid.,57.
15 Ibid.,59.
16 Ibid.,61.
17 Ibid., 25.
18 James C. Thompson, *Women And Slavery In The Ancient Rome: Women In The Ancient World.* July 10, P. 1. http://www.womenintheancientworld.com/women%20and%20slavery%20in%20ancient%20rome.htm
19 Schaff, Philip, *Christianity and Slavery,* History of the Christian Church. Volume1. (Oak Harbor, WA: Logos Research Systems, Inc.) 1997. This material has been carefully compared, corrected and emended (according to the 1910 edition of Charles Scribner's Sons) by The Electronic Bible Society, Dallas, TX, 1998. P. 1.
20 Katherine Anderson; Don Browning; Brian Boyer. *Marriage-Just a Piece of Paper: Just a Piece of Paper* (Kindle Locations 2705-2707). Kindle Edition.
21 William Goodell, 105-108.
22 Katherine Anderson; Don Browning; Brian Boyer.(Kindle Locations 2444-2445).
23 PBS Slavery and The Making of America, A production of Thirteen/WNET, New York. @2004 Educational Broadcasting Corporation. http://www.pbs.org/wnet/slavery/timeline/1712.html.
24 Reginald Washington, *Sealing the Sacred Bonds of Holy Matrimony Freedmen's Bureau Marriage Records.* Prologue Magazine, Freedmen's Bureau Marriage Records, Spring 2005, Vol. 37, No. 1. *https://www.archives.gov/publications/prologue/2005/spring/freedman-marriage-recs.html*
25 The Narrative of Lunsford Lane, Formerly of Raleigh, N.C. (Boston,1842). P.11.
26 Angela (Angie) J Hattery. Earl Smith, (2007-04-19). *African-American Families* (Kindle Locations 731-733). SAGE Publications. Kindle Edition.
27 Thomas Morris, D. *Southern Slavery and The Law* 1619-1860 76-77,83, 96, 437-438 (1996).
28 W. Bradford Wilcox. *Why Marriage Matters, Third Edition: Thirty Conclusions from the Social Sciences* (Kindle Locations 88-92). Kindle Edition
29 Opinion of Daniel Dulany, Esq. Attorney General of Maryland, 1 Maryland Reports, 561, in Stroud, George M., *A Sketch of the Laws Relating to Slavery In Several States of The United States. Kimbmer and Sharpless*, Philadelphia, 1827. p. 26. 88-89.
30 William Goodell, Picture at Massachusetts Historical Society: Image Resource. Your resource was viewed at this page: MHS Collections Online:

William Goodell with this URL:http://www.masshist.org/database/viewer.php?item_id=1135&img_step=1&mode=large#p.age1. Frederick Gutekunst [Public domain], via Wikimedia Commons. https://commons.wikimedia.org/wiki/File%3AWilliam_Goodell.jpg

31 Stroud, George M., *A Sketch of the Laws Relating to Slavery In Several States of The United States. Kimbmer and Sharpless*, Philadelphia, 1827. p. 61.

32 William Goodell, *The American Slave Code In Theory And Practice: Its Distinctive Features Shown By Its Statutes, Judicial Decisions, & Illustrative Facts* 90 (1853). P. 105-108.

33 Edward E. Baptist, (2014-09-09). *The Half Has Never Been Told: Slavery and the Making of American Capitalism* (Kindle Locations 1030-1032). Basic Books. Kindle Edition.

34 Stroud, George M., *A Sketch of the Laws*. P. 61.

35 William Goodell, *The American Slave Code In Theory And Practice: Its Distinctive Features Shown By Its Statutes, Judicial Decisions, & Illustrative Facts 90* (1853). P. 108.

36 Contubernium. *A Law Dictionary, Adapted to the Constitution and Laws of the United States*. By John Bouvier.. 1856. 30 Sep. 2015 http://legal-dictionary.thefreedictionary.com/Contubernium

37 United States. Work Projects Administration (2011-03-24). Slave Narratives: a Folk History of Slavery in the United States From Interviews with Former Slaves Georgia Narratives, Part 4 (Kindle Location 1834). Kindle Edition.

38 *West's Encyclopedia of American Law, edition 2*. S.v. "Natural Law." Retrieved October 8, 2015, from http://legal-dictionary.thefreedictionary.com/Natural+Law.

39 *West's Encyclopedia of American Law, edition 2*. S.v. "Natural Law." Retrieved October 8, 2015, from, http://legal-dictionary.thefreedictionary.com/Natural+Law

40 William Goodell, 105-108.

41 *West's Encyclopedia of American Law, edition 2*. S.v. "Civil Rights." Retrieved October 17, 2015 from http://legal-dictionary.thefreedictionary.com/Civil+Rights.

42 *A Law Dictionary, Adapted to the Constitution and Laws of the United States. By John Bouvier*. S.v. "Bill of Rights." Retrieved October 17, 2015, from http://legal-dictionary.thefreedictionary.com/Bill+of+Rights.

43 W. Bradford Wilcox. *Why Marriage Matters, Third Edition: Thirty Conclusions from the Social Sciences* (Kindle Locations 88-92). Kindle Edition.

44 Ibid.,

45 Velma Bell, United States. *Work Projects Administration (2011-03-23). Slave Narratives: A Folk History of Slavery in the United States From Interviews with Former Slaves Georgia Narratives, Part 2* (Kindle Location 1243). Kindle Edition.

46 William Goodell, 108
47 Ibid., 108.
48 William Goodell, P. 105-108.
49 Ibid.,108
50 Charters and Laws of Mass., p. 748. Williams, George Washington (2012-05-17). *History of the Negro Race in America From 1619 to 1880. Vol 1 Negroes as Slaves, as Soldiers, and as Citizens* (Kindle Location 4933). Kindle Edition.
51 Ibid.,
52 William Goodell, 105-108.
53 David Walbert, L. Maren Wood. *Marriage in colonial North Carolina*. P. 299.
54 Martha W. McCartney, Lorena S. Walsh, *A Study of the Africans and African-Americans on Jamestown Island and at Green Spring, 1619-1803 The Evolution of Slavery as an Institution, Colonial Williamsburg Foundation*. Williamsburg, Virginia. 2003. P.118.https://www.nps.gov/jame/learn/historyculture/upload/African%20Americans%20on%20Jamestown%20Island.pdf
55 Ira Berlin. *Many Thousands Gone: The First Two Centuries of Slavery in North America* (Kindle Locations 2104-2106). Kindle Edition.

Chapter 6. The Marriage Covenant of Slaves

1 John Simkin, (2014-01-11). *Slavery in the United States* (Kindle Locations 284-286). Spartacus Educational Publishers. Kindle Edition.
2 George M. Stroud, *A Sketch of the Laws Relating to Slavery In Several States of The United States. Kimbmer and Sharpless*, Philadelphia, 1827. p. 45.
3 Ibid.,57.
4 Ibid.,59.
5 Ibid., P. 61.
6 The "Opinion of Daniel Dulany, Esq." Attorney General of Maryland, 1 Maryland Reports, 561, 563. In William Goodell, The American Slave Code In Theory And Practice: Its Distinctive Features Shown By Its Statutes, Judicial Decisions, & Illustrative Facts 90 (1853). P. 105-108.
7 William Goodell, 105-108.
8 Katherine Anderson; Don Browning; Brian Boyer. *Marriage-Just a Piece of Paper: Just a Piece of Paper* (Kindle Location 3597). Kindle Edition.
9 Alan E. Kazdin, Encyclopedia of Psychology: 8Volume Set, American Psychological Association, Sexual Abuse. http://www.apa.org/topics/sexual-abuse/.
10 Patterson, James T. (2010-04-13). *Freedom Is Not Enough: The Moynihan Report and America's Struggle over Black Family Life--from LBJ to Obama* (Kindle Locations 668-671). Basic Books Kindle Edition. P.21.

11 James T. Patterson, (2010-04-13). *Freedom Is Not Enough: The Moynihan Report and America's Struggle over Black Family Life--from LBJ to Obama* (Kindle Locations 668-671). Basic Books Kindle Edition. In the Negro American Family, W.E.B. Dubois. Atlanta University Press, Atlanta, Georgia. 1908. P.41.

12 John Hope Franklin, (2010-01-20). *From Slavery to Freedom* (Page 150). McGraw-Hill Higher Education -A. Kindle Edition

13 Staples, Robert (2006-04-27). *Exploring Black Sexuality* (Kindle Locations 2397-2400). Rowman & Littlefield Publishers.

14 W.E.B. Dubois, *In the Negro American Family.* Atlanta University Press, Atlanta, Georgia. 1908. P. 42.

15 William Goodell, 107.

16 Biography.com Editors, *Josiah Henson Biography,* /Retrieved 8/25/216. http://www.biography.com/people/josiah-henson-541392. Picture/Retrieved 8/25/216. https://commons.wikimedia.org/wiki/Category:Josiah_Henson#/media/File:Josiah_Henson.jpg

17 Josiah Henson, (2015-03-08). *The Life of Josiah Henson: Formerly a Slave, Illustrated* (Kindle Locations 30-39). Kindle Edition.

18 Josiah Henson, (2015-03-08). *The Life of Josiah Henson.* P. 30-39.

19 John W. Blassingame, *The Slave Community: Plantation Life in the Antebellum South,* Oxford University Press. Oxford, New York, 1979. P 173.

20 Robert Staples, (2006-04-27). *Exploring Black Sexuality* (Kindle Locations 710-712). Rowman & Littlefield Publishers. Kindle Edition.

21 *The New King James Version* (Nashville: Thomas Nelson, 1982), 1 Th 4:3–7.

22 Charles Swindoll, Insight for Living, *Counseling Insights: A Biblical Perspective on Caring for People* (Plano, TX: Insight for Living, 2007), 202.

23 William Goodell, 105-108.

24 Freda McKissic Bush and Joe S. McIlhaney, Jr., *Hooked: New Science on How Casual Sex is Affecting Our Children* (Chicago: Moody Publishers, 2008), 39. Kindle Edition.

25 Hummer and Hamilton, *Fragile Families,* 115.

26 Bush and McIlhaney, *Hooked,* 105.

27 Patterson, *Rituals of Blood,* 73.

28 Amato, Booth, Johnson, and Rogers, *Alone Together,* 2788-2800. Kindle Edition.

29 Michael Layman and Gina Kolata, *Sex in America,* 97–98, quoted in Freda McKissic Bush and Joe S. McIlhaney Jr., *Hooked: New Science on How Casual Sex is Affecting Our Children* (Chicago, IL: Moody Publishers, 2008), 96. Kindle Edition.

30 Anderson, Browning, and Boyer, *Marriage Just a Piece of Paper,* 274-277.

31 Ibid.,

32 Michael J. Rosenfeld and Kim Byung-Soo, "The Independence of Young Adults and the Rise of Interracial and Same-Sex Unions," Department of Sociology Stanford University: Stanford CA. 2005. In Rosenfeld and Byung-Soo 2005, 541 1. Accessed March 10, 2014. http://www.stanford.edu/~mrosenfe/Rosenfeld+Kim%202005%20final.pdf. quoted in Riedmann and Lamanna, *Marriages, Families, and Relationships*, 10. Kindle Edition.

33 Patterson, *Rituals of Blood*, 73.

34 Larry L. Bumpass, "The Declining Significance of Marriage: Changing Family Life in the United States." Paper presented at the Potsdam International Conference, "Changing Families and Childhood," December 14–17, 1994. Larry L. Bumpass and James A. Sweet, "National Estimates of Cohabitation," Demography 26 (1989): 615–625. D. T Lichter, Z. Qian, L.M. Mellott, "Marriage or dissolution? Union transitions among poor cohabiting women," Demography (May 2006): 43(2):223–40. Larry Bumpass, Hsien-Hen Lu, "Trends in Cohabitation and Implications for Children's Family Contexts in the United States," Population Studies, Vol. 54, No. 1 (Mar. 2000), 29–41. Bush, Freda McKissic; McIlhaney Jr., Joe S. (2008-08-01). Hooked: New Science on How Casual Sex is Affecting Our Children. Moody Publishers. Kindle Edition.

35 Lee A. Lillard, Michael J. Brien, and Linda J. Waite, "Pre-Marital Cohabitation and Subsequent Marital Dissolution: Is It Self-Selection?" Demography 32 (1995): 437–458. Elizabeth Thomson and Ugo Collela, "Cohabitation and Marital Stability: Quality or Commitment?" Journal of Marriage and the Family 54 (1992): 259–268. Bush, Freda McKissic; McIlhaney Jr., Joe S. (2008-08-01). Hooked: New Science on How Casual Sex is Affecting Our Children. Moody Publishers. Kindle Edition.

36 Larry L. Bumpass, R. Kelly Raley, and James A. Sweet, "The Changing Character of Stepfamilies: Implications of Cohabitation and Nonmarital Childbearing," Demography 32: 425–436. Bush, Freda McKissic; McIlhaney Jr., Joe S. (2008-08-01). Hooked: New Science on How Casual Sex is Affecting Our Children. Moody Publishers. Kindle Edition.

37 Marriage, Bush, Freda McKissic; McIlhaney Jr., Joe S. (2008-08-01). *Hooked: New Science on How Casual Sex is Affecting Our Children.* Moody Publishers. Kindle Edition.

38 C. T. Kenney, S. S. McLanahan, "Why are cohabiting relationships more violent than marriages?" Demography (Feb. 2006): 43(1):127–40. Bush, Freda McKissic; McIlhaney Jr., Joe S. (2008-08-01). Hooked: New Science on How Casual Sex is Affecting Our Children. Moody Publishers. Kindle Edition. Bush and McIlhaney Jr., *Hooked*, 97. Kindle Edition.

39 L. Dickson, *The future of marriage and family in Black America.* Journal of Black Studies, *23 (4). 1993, 472-49.* In S. South, S.J. Racial and ethnic differences in the desire to marry. Journal of Marriage & the Family, *55(2),*

1993. 357-370. In S. Kelly, (2001). The effects of negative racial stereotypes and Afrocentricity on Black couple relationships. *Journal of Family Psychology, 15(1), 110-123.*

40 W. E Harris Jr, Kelly D. Bradley, *The Impact of Stereotypes on Black Male College Student's Perception of Marriage.* University of Kentucky: Lexington, Ky. 2001.4, Accessed April 7, 2014, http://www.uky.edu/~kdbrad2/Stereotypes%20and%20Marriage.pdf.

41 Deloras Williams. *Sisters in the Wilderness: The Challenge of Womanist Talk*, Maryknoll, NY: Orbis, 1993.1473. Kindle Edition.

42 Bell Hooks, *Ain't I a Woman?* (Boston: South End Press, 1981). 52. In Williams, Delores S. (2013-10-25). Sisters in the Wilderness: The Challenge of Womanist God-Talk (Kindle Location 4848). Orbis Books. Kindle Edition.

43 Ibid.,

44 Lee H. Butler Jr., *A Loving Home: Spirituality, Sexuality, and Healing Black Life*. Minneapolis: Fortress Press. 2007. 1411-1412. Kindle Edition.

Chapter 7. Marriage Is for Humans Only

1 George M. Stroud, A Sketch of the Laws Relating to Slavery In Several States of The United States. Kimbmer and Sharpless, Philadelphia, 1827. p. 51.

2 William Goodell, *The American Slave Code In Theory And Practice: Its Distinctive Features Shown By Its Statutes, Judicial Decisions, & Illustrative Facts* 90 (1853). P. 105-108.

3 Ibid., P. 105-108

4 Ibid.,

5 Ibid.,

6 Manning Marable, *How Capitalism Underdeveloped Black America: Problems in Race, Political Economy, and Society* (Cambridge, MA: South End Press, 2000), 72.

7 Ibid.,

8 Yetman, Norman R. (2012-03-15). *Voices from Slavery: 100 Authentic Slave Narratives* (African-American) (p. 92). Dover Publications. Kindle Edition.

9 The United States. Work Projects Administration (2011-03-24). *Slave Narratives: a Folk History of Slavery in the United States From Interviews with Former Slaves Georgia Narratives, Part 4 (*Kindle Locations 2148-2151*).* Kindle Edition.

10 The United States. Work Projects Administration (2011-05-02). *Slave Narratives: A Folk History of Slavery in the United States From Interviews with Former Slaves: Volume I, Alabama Narratives* (Kindle Locations 1332-1334). Kindle Edition.

11 Pamela D. Bridgewater, UN/RE/DIS COVERING SLAVE BREEDING IN THIRTEENTH AMENDMENT JURISPRUDENCE, 7 Wash. & Lee Race & Ethnic Anc. L. J. 11 (2001). Available at: http://scholarlycommons.law.wlu.edu/crsj/vol7/iss1/4. P18.

12 Pamela D. Bridgewater, P. 15.

13 Stroud's "Sketch of the Slave Laws," p.6l.

14 Pamela D. Bridgewater, P18.

15 Pamela D. Bridgewater, P.14.

16 Roberts James. *The Narrative of James Roberts, a Soldier Under Gen. Washington in the Revolutionary War, and Under Gen. Jackson at the Battle of New Orleans, in the War of 1812: "a Battle Which Cost Me a Limb, Some Blood, and Almost My Life": James Roberts 1753.* Documenting The American South, Academic Affairs Library, UNC-CH University of North Carolina at Chapel Hill, 2001. P. 26. Retrieved 05, 07, 2016, http://docsouth.unc.edu/neh/roberts/roberts.html.

17 Andreas J. Kostenberger, David Jones, (2010-05-05). *God, Marriage, and Family (Second Edition): Rebuilding the Biblical Foundation* (p. 84). Crossway. Kindle Edition.

18 Ibid.,

19 Charles C. Ryrie, "Depravity, Total," ibid., 312. See also Edwin H. Palmer, The Five Points of Calvinism (Grand Rapids: Guardian, 1972), 9–13. Found in Enns, Paul (2008-02-01). The Moody Handbook of Theology (Kindle Locations 10842-10843). Moody Publishers. Kindle Edition.

20 Charles C. Ryrie, *Survey of Bible Doctrine* (Chicago: Moody, 1972), 111. In Enns, Paul (2008-02-01). The Moody Handbook of Theology (Kindle Locations 6683-6684). Moody Publishers. Kindle Edition.

21 Paul Enns, (2008-02-01). *The Moody Handbook of Theology* (Kindle Locations 10716-10718). Moody Publishers. Kindle Edition.

22 Goodell, William (2010-10-31). *Slavery and Anti-Slavery, a History of the Great Struggle in Both Hemispheres, With a View of the Slavery Question in the United States* (Kindle Locations 7329-7344). Kindle Edition.

23 Pamela Bridgewater, P. 15.

24 Murray Bowen, *Multigenerational Transmission Process.* The Bowen Center For The Study of The Family. 1975. Pg.1. https://thebowencenter.org/theory/eight-concepts/

25 *The New King James Version* (Nashville: Thomas Nelson, 1982), Ex 20:5–6.

26 Emasculate." *Merriam-Webster.com.* Merriam-Webster, n.d. Web. 23 Nov. 2015. http://www.merriam-webster.com/dictionary/emasculate.

27 Ibid.,

28 Ibid.,

29 Charles Ball, *Slavery in the United States: a narrative of the life and adventures of Charles Ball, a Black man.* New York, J. S. Taylor. 1837. P.36.

30 Emasculate." *Merriam-Webster.com*. Merriam-Webster, n.d. Web. 23 Nov. 2015. http://www.merriam-webster.com/dictionary/emasculate.
31 *When I Was a Slave: Memoirs from the Slave Narrative Collection* (Dover Thrift Editions) (pp. 125-126). Dover Publications. 2012. Kindle Edition.
32 Robert Staples, (2006-04-27). *Exploring Black Sexuality* (Kindle Locations 2412-2415). Rowman & Littlefield Publishers. Kindle Edition.
33 Robert Staples, (2006-04-27). *Exploring Black Sexuality* (Kindle Locations 2404-2407). Rowman & Littlefield Publishers. Kindle Edition.
34 Wayne Grudem, (2006-08-31). *Recovering Biblical Manhood & Womanhood: A Response to Evangelical Feminism* (Kindle Locations 9657-9659). Good News Publishers. Kindle Edition.
35 Fredrick Douglass, *My Bondage and My Freedom*. P. 26.
36 W.E.B. Dubois, *The Negro American Family*. Atlanta University Press, Atlanta, Georgia. 1908. P. 49.
37 Ibid., 56.
38 Napp Nazworth, "Scholar Feminists Have Made Men Afraid To Embrace Their Manhood," *Christian Post* (2013): 1, accessed January 12, 2014, http://www.christianpost.com/news/scholar-liberals-feminists-have-made-men-afraid-to-embrace-their-manhood-92043/.
39 Jacques Étienne Victor Arago [Public domain], via Wikimedia Commons. 1839. https://commons.wikimedia.org/wiki/File%3AEscrava_Anastacia.jpg
40 William Goodell, 105-108.
41 Douglass K. Blount and Joseph D. Wooddell, *The Baptist Faith and Message 2000: Critical Issues in America's Largest Protestant Denomination*(Lanham, MD: Rowman & Littlefield Publishers Inc., 2007), 4317, Kindle Edition.
42 Sonya C. Tonnesen, *The Hit It And Quit It: Response To Black Girls victimization in School*. Intersectionality Race, Racism and the Law. P. 6. Retrieved November 7, 2016. http://racism.org/index.php?option=com_content&view=article&id=1664:blackgirlsvictimization&catid=72&Itemid=215&showall=&limitstart=5
43 Ibid.,
44 Ibid.,
45 Ibid.,
46 Faye Z. (Zollicoffer) Belgrave; Kevin W. (Wendell) Allison. *African-American Psychology: From Africa to America* (Kindle Locations 988-990). Kindle Edition.
47 Robert Mallard, *Plantation Life Before the Emancipation*. WHITTET & SHEPPERSON, RICHMOND, VA.1892. Academic Affairs Library, University of North Carolina at Chapel Hill, Digital Version 1998. P. 200-201. http://docsouth.unc.edu accessed October 12, 2017.
48 Ibid., P.9.

49 Black women often breastfed the white children they looked after from slavery times and long after abolition. #wetnurse www.pinterest.com 385 × 522 HYPERLINK "https://www.google.com/searchbyimage?image_url=https%3A%2F%2Fs-media-cache-ak0.pinimg.com%2F564x%2F59%2F90%2Fe6%2F5990e68fef649ef41907bed54f70cade.jpg&sbisrc=imghover&bih=741&biw=1043"

50 Andrew J. Cherlin, (2010-12-08). *The Marriage-Go-Round: The State of Marriage and the Family in America Today* (Vintage) (Kindle Locations 814-827). Knopf Doubleday Publishing Group. Kindle Edition.

51 (2012-03-01). *When I Was a Slave: Memoirs from the Slave Narrative Collection* (Dover Thrift Editions) (p. 20). Dover Publications. Kindle Edition.

52 Faye Z. Belgrave; Kevin W. (Wendell) Allison. *African-American Psychology: From Africa to America* (Kindle Locations 988-990). Kindle Edition.

53 John Hope Franklin, (2010-01-20). *From Slavery to Freedom* (Page 151). McGraw-Hill Higher Education -A. Kindle Edition.

54 PBS Slavery And The Making of America, A production of Thirteen/WNET, New York. @2004 Educational Broadcasting Corporation. http://www.pbs.org/wnet/slavery/timeline/1712.html.

55 Robert Staples, (2006-04-27). *Exploring Black Sexuality* (Kindle Locations 654-657). Rowman & Littlefield Publishers. Kindle Edition.

56 Kathryn Cullen-DuPont, "State of Missouri v. Celia, a Slave: 1855." Great American Trials. 2002. *Encyclopedia.com.* (October 13, 2015). http://www.encyclopedia.com/doc/1G2-3498200071.html

57 United States *Work Projects Administration (2011-03-24). Slave Narratives: a Folk History of Slavery in the United States From Interviews with Former Slaves Georgia Narratives, Part 4 (Kindle Locations 3357-3360). Kindle Edition.*

58 Dan McKanan, *Identifying the Image of God.* New York: Oxford University Press. 2002. P.129. InKilner, John F. (2015-01-08). Dignity and Destiny: Humanity in the Image of God (p. 11). Wm. B. Eerdmans Publishing Co. Kindle Edition.

59 The quotation is from Weld's January 2, 1833 letter to William Lloyd Garrison (in Barnes and Dumond, 1965: 97-98; cf. discussion in D. Davis, 2008: 252-53). Channing (1836: 25; cf. 9-10, 76-77) considered slaves' creation in "God's image" to be "the great argument against seizing and using a man as property"; cf. discussion in H. S. Smith, 1972: 137. IN Kilner, John F. (2015-01-08). Dignity and Destiny: Humanity in the Image of God (p. 51). Wm. B. Eerdmans Publishing Co. Kindle Edition.

60 Brady E. Hamilton; Joyce A. Martin; Michelle J.K. Osterman; Sally C. Curtin; and T.J. Mathews, M.S, *Births: Final Data for 2014.*Center For Disease Control National Vital Statistics Reports Volume 64, Number 12 December 23, 2015 Division of Vital Statistics. P. 7. Retrieved June 4, 2016. http://www.cdc.gov/nchs/data/nvsr/nvsr64/nvsr64_12.pdf

61 Paul Kalra, *From Slave To Untouchable: Lincoln's Solution* (p. 68).
62 John Hope Franklin, (2010-01-20). *From Slavery to Freedom* (Page 58). McGraw-Hill Higher Education -A. Kindle Edition.
63 Ibid.,
64 Catherine Clinton, (2004-02-02). *Harriet Tubman: The Road to Freedom* (Kindle Locations 803-808). Little, Brown and Company. Kindle Edition. In Five Hundred Thousand Strokes for Freedom: A Series of Anti-Slavery Tracts by the Friends of the Negro, Leeds Antislavery Series, no. 68 (London: W. & F. Cash, 1900).
65 MedlinePlus, U.S. National Library of Medicine. U.S. Department of Health and Human Services National Institutes of Health. Bethesda, MD. 2017. Retrieved May, 15, 2017, https://medlineplus.gov/connect/overview.html
66 Ira Berlin. *Many Thousands Gone: The First Two Centuries of Slavery in North America* (Kindle Locations 2101-2104). Kindle Edition.
67 Harriet Ann Jacobs, *Incidents in the Life of a Slave Girl Written by Herself* (p. 7). 2012. Kindle Edition.
68 Paul Kalra, *From Slave To Untouchable: Lincoln's Solution* (p. 68). Antenna Publishing Co. Kindle Edition.
69 Ibid.,
70 Jason Kander, *The Code Noir in Colonial Louisiana*, P.1.
71 Roger Baudier, *The Catholic Church in Louisiana* (New Orleans, 1939); Robin, Voyages dans Louisiane, III. In Paul Kalra, *From Slave To Untouchable: Lincoln's Solution* (p. 68).
72 *Slave Code for the District of Columbia: Slaves and the Courts, 1740-1860*. The Library of Congress, 2002, District of Columbia, P. 1. https://www.loc.gov/collections/slaves-and-the-courts-from-1740-to-1860/about-this-collection/
73 Ibid.,
74 Katherine Anderson; Don Browning; Brian Boyer. *Marriage-Just a Piece of Paper: Just a Piece of Paper* (Kindle Locations 782-784). Kindle Edition.
75 Paul Taylor, "The American Family Today," Parenting In America. *Pew Research Center* (2015): P.1, accessed July 4, 2017, 2016, http://www.pewsocialtrends.org/2015/12/17/1-the-american-family-today/
76 W. Bradford Wilcox. *Why Marriage Matters, Third Edition: Thirty Conclusions from the Social Sciences* (Kindle Locations 88-92). Kindle Edition.

Chapter 8 Marriage the First Institution: God's Grace Designed for Mankind

1 Douglass K. Blount and Joseph D. Wooddell, *Comparison of 1925, 1963, and 2000 Baptist Faith and Message Blount,* Douglas K.; Wooddell, Joseph D. (2007-06-07). In *The Baptist Faith and Message 2000*: *Critical Issues in*

America's Largest Protestant Denomination (Lanham, MD: Rowman & Littlefield Publishers Inc., 2007), 4317, Kindle Edition.

2 Ibid.,

3 Karen Seccombe, Rebecca L. Warner, *Marriages and Families Relationships In Social Context*. Wadsworth, Thomson Learning Center, Belmont, CA. 2004. P. 231- 233.

4 Douglass K. Blount and Joseph D. Wooddell. 4317-4318, Kindle Edition.

5 Karen Seccombe, Rebecca L. Warner, *Marriages and Families Relationships In Social Context*. Wadsworth, Thomson Learning Center, Belmont, CA. 2004. P. 231- 233.

6 A. Isaksson, *Marriage, and Ministry in the New Temple*, as cited in William F. Luck, *Divorce and Remarriage: Recovering the Biblical View* (San Francisco: Harper & Row, 1987), p. 17.

7 Ibid. p.17.

8 A. Isaksson, *Marriage and Ministry in the New Temple*, as cited in William F. Luck, *Divorce and Remarriage: Recovering the Biblical View* (San Francisco: Harper & Row, 1987), p. 17.

9 Ibid.,

10 Ibid.,

11 Douglass K. Blount and Joseph D. Wooddell, *The Baptist Faith and Message 2000: Critical Issues in America's Largest Protestant Denomination* (Lanham, MD: Rowman & Littlefield Publishers Inc., 2007), 4317, Kindle Edition.

12 Andreas J. Kostenberger, Jones, David (2010-05-05). *God, Marriage, and Family (Second Edition): Rebuilding the Biblical Foundation* (p. 22). Crossway. Kindle Edition.

13 Orlando Patterson, (1985-03-15). *Slavery and Social Death* (Kindle Locations 4429-4432). Harvard University Press. Kindle Edition.

14 Wayne Grudem, (2006-08-31). *Recovering Biblical Manhood & Womanhood: A Response to Evangelical Feminism* (Kindle Locations 2258-2259). Good News Publishers. Kindle Edition.

15 Howard J. Markman, Scott M. Stanley, and Susan L. Blumberg *Fighting for Your Marriage: A Deluxe Revised Edition of the Classic Best-seller for Enhancing Marriage and Preventing Divorce* (San Francisco: Jossey-Bass, 2010), 33. Kindle Edition.

16 David Olson Ph.D., Amy Olson-Sigg, and Peter J. Larson Ph.D., *The Couple Checkup: Find Your Relationship Strengths* (Nashville, TN: Thomas Nelson, 2006), 20. Kindle Edition.

17 Wayne Grudem, (2006-08-31). *Recovering Biblical Manhood & Womanhood: A Response to Evangelical Feminism* (Kindle Locations 8712-8714). Good News Publishers. Kindle Edition.

18 Andrew J. Cherlin, (2010-12-08). *The Marriage-Go-Round: The State of Marriage and the Family in America Today* (Vintage) (Kindle Locations 814-827). Knopf Doubleday Publishing Group. Kindle Edition.

19 Terry Turner, "Gods Amazing Grace: Reconciling Four Centuries of African-American Marriages and Families" Chart Marital Conditions of African-Americans 1790-2010. P. 14. 2017.

20 N. Sudarkasa, (1980). *African and Afro-American family structure. The Black Scholar, November–December, 37–60. And N. Sudarkasa,* (1997). African-American families and family values. In H. P. McAdoo (Ed.), Black families (3rd ed., pp. 9–40). In Patricia Dixon, (2013-06-17). *African-American Relationships, Marriages, and Families: An Introduction* (p. 3). Taylor and Francis. Kindle Edition.

21 Robert A. Hummer and Erin R. Hamilton, "Race and Ethnicity in Fragile Families," *The Future of Children* 20, no. 2 (2010): 133.

22 Ibid. 133.

23 W. Bradford Wilcox, Ph.D., Paul Taylor, and Chuck Donovan, "When Marriage Disappears: The Retreat from Marriage in Middle America." National Marriage Project at the University of Virginia and the Institute for American Values, December 2010, pp. 13ñ60, at http://stateofourunions.org/2010/SOOU2010.pdf (February 1, 2011). P. 5.

24 Stephanie Coontz, PP. 145-146.

25 Katherine Anderson; Don Browning; Brian Boyer. *Marriage-Just a Piece of Paper: Just a Piece of Paper* (Kindle Location 2705). Kindle Edition.

26 United States. Work Projects Administration (2011-03-23). *Slave Narratives: A Folk History of Slavery in the United States From Interviews with Former Slaves Georgia Narratives, Part 2* (Kindle Location 2684). Kindle Edition.

27 Stephanie Coontz, (2006-02-28). *Marriage, a History: How Love Conquered Marriage* (pp. 145-146). Penguin Publishing Group. Kindle Edition.

28 Stephanie Coontz, PP. 145-146.

29 Katherine Anderson; Don Browning; Brian Boyer. *Marriage-Just a Piece of Paper: Just a Piece of Paper* (Kindle Locations 4054-4056). Kindle Edition.

30 Williams, George Washington (2012-05-17). *History of the Negro Race in America From 1619 to 1880. Vol 1 Negroes as Slaves, as Soldiers, and as Citizens* (Kindle Locations 4231-4234). Kindle Edition.

31 Bureau of Vital Statistics, Texas Department of Health, Austin, TX

32 Ibid.,

33 Ibid.,

34 Ibid.,

35 *The Holy Bible: English Standard Version* (Wheaton: Standard Bible Society, 2001), Ro 13:1–3.

36 United States. Work Projects Administration (2011-03-24). *Slave Narratives: a Folk History of Slavery in the United States From Interviews with Former*

Slaves South Carolina Narratives, Part 1 (Kindle Locations 871-872). Kindle Edition.

37 Dana Fillmore, "New Study Shows Marriage in Danger at 10 Years" StrongMarriageNow.com, https://www.strongmarriagenow.com/new-study-shows-marriage-in-danger-at-10-years/

38 Douglass, Frederick Douglass, *Life and times of Frederick Douglass: His Early Life as a Slave, His Escape from Bondage, and His Complete History.* Written by himself. London, Collier Books, 1962, p. 205.In Webber, Christopher L. American to the Backbone: The Life of James W. C. Pennington, the Fugitive Slave Who Became One of the First Black Abolitionists (Kindle Locations 10168-10170). Pegasus Books. Kindle Edition.

39 Frederick Douglass, (2012-05-16). *My Bondage and My Freedom* (p. 178). Kindle Edition.

40 Public Domain, Fredrick and Anna Douglass Photograph first published in Rosetta Douglass Sprague, "My Mother As I Recall Her", 1900 - http://memory.loc.gov/mss/mfd/02/02007/0002.jpg Photograph of Anna Murray Douglass (1813–1882), the first wife of Frederick Douglass File: Anna Murray-Douglass.jpg Created: circa 1860. https://en.wikipedia.org/wiki/Anna_Murray-Douglass#/media/File:Anna_Murray-Douglass.jpgFrederickDouglass-https://docsouth.unc.edu/neh/douglass/douglass.html This work was published before January 1, 1923, and is in the public domain worldwide because the author died at least 100 years ago. https://en.wikisource.org/wiki/Narrative of the Life of Frederick Douglass, An American Slave

41 Kate Lawson, Larson, Kate Clifford (2009-02-19). *Bound for the Promised Land: Harriet Tubman: Portrait of an American Hero* (Many Cultures, One World) (Kindle Locations 152-153). Random House Publishing Group. Kindle Edition.

42 Catherine Clinton, Harriet Tubman: *The Road to Freedom.* Little, Brown and Company. Kindle Edition. 2004. Kindle Locations 488-490.

43 Catherine Clinton, *Harriet Tubman*. Kindle Locations 492-494.

44 Ibid.,

45 Kate Clifford Larson, (2009-02-19). *Bound for the Promised Land: Harriet Tubman: Portrait of an American Hero* (Many Cultures, One World) (Kindle Locations 1535-1537). Random House Publishing Group. Kindle Edition.

46 "The Origins of the Law of Slavery in British North America," Retrieved March 30, 2016.

47 John Hope Franklin, (2010-01-20). *From Slavery to Freedom* (Page 54). McGraw-Hill Higher Education -A. Kindle Edition.

48 John H. Russell, *The Free Negro in Virginia* (Baltimore, 1913), p. 40-41. In E. Franklin Frazier, *The Free Negro Family: A Study of Family Origins Before the Civil War,* (Nashville: Fisk University Press, 1932): 2.

49 Ibid.P.2.

50 Jeffrey R. Brackett, *The Negro in Maryland* (Baltimore, 1889), p. 175-176.

Chapter 9. The Marriage Covenant of Slaves

1 Williams, George Washington (2012-05-17). *History of the Negro Race in America From 1619 to 1880. Vol 1 Negroes as Slaves, as Soldiers, and as Citizens* (Kindle Locations 4251-4260). Kindle Edition.

2 Carter G. Woodson, *The Journal of Negro History, Volume 1, January 1916*. Gutenberg EBooks, 2004. (Kindle Locations 5911-5914).

3 American Anti-Slavery Society (2012-05-12). The Anti-Slavery Examiner, Part 3 of 4 (Kindle Locations 446-450). Kindle Edition.

4 John Simkin, (2014-01-11). *Slavery in the United States* (Kindle Locations 1367-1368). Spartacus Educational Publishers. Kindle Edition

5 Stephanie Coontz, (2006-02-28). *Marriage, a History: How Love Conquered Marriage* (p. 20). Penguin Publishing Group. Kindle Edition.

6 Stephanie Coontz, P.20.

7 B. F. French, *Historical Collections of Louisiana: Embracing Translations of Many Rare and Valuable Documents Relating to the Natural, Civil, and Political History of that State* (New York: D. Appleton, 1851). In Dr. Quintard Taylor, Jr., Scott and Dorothy Bullitt, *Primary Documents Louisiana's Code Noir,* University of Washington, Settle Washington. Retrieved October 24, 2015, http://www.blackpast.org/primary/louisianas-code-noir-1724

8 Letter of A. R. Wright, Louisville, Georgia, to Howell Cobb at Cherry Hill in the same county, in Phillips, Documentary History of American Industrial Society: Plantation and Frontier (Cleveland, 1910-11), II, 45

9 Norman Yetman, *When I Was a Slave: Memoirs from the Slave Narrative Collection.* Dover Thrift Editions. Dover Publications. Mineola, New York. Kindle Edition. 2012. P.56.

10 *When I Was a Slave: Memoirs from the Slave Narrative Collection* (Dover Thrift Editions) Dover Publications. 2012. Kindle Edition. P. 79.

11 Terry Turner, *Comparing Christian Marital Satisfaction Among Multiple Ethnic Couples*, Dissertation Project. Dallas Theological Seminary: Dallas. Abstract. P. 18.

12 Heather Andrea Williams, "How Slavery Affected African-American Families,"*Freedom's Story,* Teacher Serve. National Humanities Center, accessed July 22, 2013, 1, http://nationalhumanitiescenter.org/tserve/freedom/1609-1865/essays/aafamilies.htm.

13 Ibid.,

14 Ibid.,

15 Ibid.,

16 United States. Work Projects Administration (2011-03-24). Slave Narratives: a Folk History of Slavery in the United States From Interviews with Former Slaves Georgia Narratives, Part 4 (Kindle Locations 1249-1254). . Kindle Edition.

17 Franklin, John Hope, *From Slavery to Freedom*. McGraw-Hill Higher Education -A. 2010. Kindle Edition. P. 58

18 Ibid.,

19 B. A. Botkin, ed., *Lay My Burden Down: A Folk History of Slavery* (Chicago: University of Chicago Press, 1945), 55, http://www.questia.com/read/91249699/lay-my-burden-down-a-folk-history-of-slavery.

20 Frederick Douglass, "What to the Slave Is the Fourth of July?" An Address Delivered in Rochester, New York, on July 5, 1852.

21 Annie L. Burton, *Memories of Childhood's Slavery Days*. 1909. P.2. *In* Simkin, John (2014-01-11). Slavery in the United States (Kindle Location 652). Spartacus Educational Publishers. Kindle Edition.

22 United States. Work Projects Administration (2011-03-24). Slave Narratives: a Folk History of Slavery in the United States From Interviews with Former Slaves Georgia Narratives, Part 4 (Kindle Locations 2460-2461). Kindle Edition.

23 The United States. *Slave Narratives: Former Slaves Georgia Narratives, Part 2* (Kindle Locations 3562-3564). Kindle Edition.

24 David L. Walbert, L. Maren Wood, *Marriage in colonial North Carolina*. P. 299.

25 *When I Was a Slave: Memoirs from the Slave Narrative Collection* (Dover Thrift Editions) 2012. (p. 109). Dover Publications. Kindle Edition.

26 Martha W. McCartney, P.118.

27 James Mellon, (2014-12-23). *Bullwhip Days: The Slaves Remember: An Oral History* (Kindle Locations 4049-4052). Grove/Atlantic, Inc. Kindle Edition.

28 United States. Work Projects Administration (2011-05-02). Slave Narratives: A Folk History of Slavery in the United States From Interviews with Former Slaves: Volume I, Alabama Narratives (Kindle Locations 3621-3623). . Kindle Edition.

29 *When I Was a Slave: Memoirs from the Slave Narrative Collection* (Dover Thrift Editions) 2012. (p. 35). Dover Publications. Kindle Edition.

30 (2012-03-01). *When I Was a Slave: Memoirs from the Slave Narrative Collection* (Dover Thrift Editions) (p. 138). Dover Publications. Kindle Edition.

31 United States. Work Projects Administration.mSlave Narratives: A Folk History of Slavery in the United States From Interviews with Former Slaves: Volume I, Alabama Narratives (Kindle Locations 4088-4090). 201. Kindle Edition.

32 John Simkin, (2014-01-11). *Slavery in the United States* (Kindle Locations 5353-5355). Spartacus Educational Publishers. Kindle Edition.

33 Katherine Anderson; Don Browning; Brian Boyer. *Marriage-Just a Piece of Paper: Just a Piece of Paper* (Kindle Locations 787-789). Kindle Edition.

34 Sarah Torre, *Fact of The Week: Fewer Americans Are Marrying: "The Portion of Married Adults has Decreased,* US Bureau of Census (Washington DC: The Heritage Foundation. 2011), 1, accessed January 19, 2012, http://blog.heritage.org/2011/12/15/family-fact-of-the-week-fewer-americans-are-marrying/," 1.

35 Dred Scott. Harriet, wife of Dred Scott, Digital ID: (digital file from original print) ppmsca 38385 https://www.loc.gov/resource/ppmsca.38385/ (digital file from original print) LC-USZ62-5092 (b&w film copy neg. of Dred Scott) LC-USZ62-5067 (b&w film copy neg. of Harriet Scott). Repository: Library of Congress Prints and Photographs Division Washington, D.C. 20540 USA http://images.mohistory.org/image/09C4C4A6-B4E0-1960-AE52-E9E24AB9C36E/original.jpg Gallery: http://collections.mohistory.org/resource/148594

36 Paul Finkelman, (2007). "Scott v. Sandford: The Court's Most Dreadful Case and How it Changed History" (PDF). *Chicago-Kent Law Review*82 (3): 3–48. And in "Missouri's Dred Scott Case, 1846-1857". *Missouri Digital Heritage: African-American HIstory Initiative.* Retrieved 15 July 2015.

37 *A Law Dictionary, Adapted to the Constitution and Laws of the United States. By John Bouvier.*

38 Ibid.,

39 Ibid.,

40 Ibid.,

41 Jim Crow." International Encyclopedia of the Social Sciences. *Encyclopedia.com.* (May 16, 2017). http://www.encyclopedia.com/social-sciences/applied-and-social-sciences-magazines/jim-crow

Chapter 10. Family Incarceration on Plantations

1 John Simkin, (2014-01-11). *Slavery in the United States* (Kindle Locations 27-29). Spartacus Educational Publishers. Kindle Edition.

2 Edward E. Baptist, (2014-09-09). *The Half Has Never Been Told: Slavery and the Making of American Capitalism* (Kindle Locations 4376-4378). Basic Books. Kindle Edition.

3 George Washington Williams (2012-05-17). *History of the Negro Race in America From 1619 to 1880. Vol 1 Negroes as Slaves, as Soldiers, and as Citizens* (Kindle Locations 6055-6057). Kindle Edition.

4 men-stealer." Your Dictionary, n.d. Web. 27 April 2017. <http://www.yourdictionary.com/men-stealer Read more at http://www.yourdictionary.com/men-stealer#Pe0qFBlo5Mgc707i.99

5 Fredrick Douglass, *My Bondage and My Freedom*. P. 178.

6 William Craft; Ellen Craft; W.E.B. Du Bois; Elizabeth Keckley; Josiah Henson; Sojourner Truth; Olive Gilbert; William Still; (2015-08-06). *Slave Narrative Six Pack 2 - Running a Thousand Miles for Freedom, The Souls of Black Folk, Behind the Scenes, Life of Josiah Henson, Narrative of Sojourner Truth and William Garrison* (Illustrated) (Kindle Locations 225-227). Kindle Edition.

7 Edward E. Baptist, (2014-09-09). *The Half Has Never Been Told: Slavery and the Making of American Capitalism* (Kindle Locations 4039-4044). Basic Books. Kindle Edition.

8 The United States. Work Projects Administration (2011-03-24). Slave Narratives: a Folk History of Slavery in the United States From Interviews with Former Slaves South Carolina Narratives, Part 1 (Kindle Locations 262-265). Kindle Edition.

9 The United States. Work Projects Administration (2011-03-24). Slave Narratives: a Folk History of Slavery in the United States From Interviews with Former Slaves South Carolina Narratives, Part 1 (Kindle Locations 262-265). Kindle Edition.

10 United States. Work Projects Administration. Slave Narratives: a Folk History of Slavery in the United States From Interviews with Former Slaves Tennessee Narratives (Kindle Location 150). Kindle Edition.

11 Michelle Alexander, *The New Jim Crow, The New Press*. Kindle Edition. 2012. P. 179.

12 Michelle Alexander, *The New Jim Crow* P. 288.

13 Peter Wagner, Bernadette Rabuy, *Mass Incarceration: The Whole Pie. Prison Policy Initiative.* 2016. P. 1. Accessed August 22, 2016. Northampton, MA. http://www.prisonpolicy.org/reports/pie2016.html

14 Sally E. Hadden, *Slave Patrols: Law and Violence in Virginia and The Carolinas.* Cambridge, MA. Harvard University Press. 2001. P.11.

15 Robert M. Bohm, Keith N. Haley, *The Structure of American Law Enforcement.* Introduction to Criminal Justice, Updated 4th Edition, McGraw-Hill Global Education Holdings, LLC. New York, NY. 2016. P.144.

16 Robert M. Bohm, Keith N. Haley, *The Structure of American Law. P.144.*

17 "The Underground Railroad from Slavery to Freedom" By Wilbur Henry Siebert, Albert Bushnell Hart Edition: 2. Published by Macmillan, 1898, pg. 26. Runaway_slave.jpg (400 × 580 pixels, file size: 98 KB, MIME type: image/jpeg). This media file is in the **public domain** in the United States. This applies to U.S. works where the copyright has expired, often because its first publication occurred prior to January 1, 1923. https://commons.wikimedia.org/wiki/File:Runaway_slave.jpg

18 Sally E. Hadden, *Slave Patrols: Law and Violence in Virginia.* P. 73.

19 United States. Work Projects Administration (2011-03-24). Slave Narratives: a Folk History of Slavery in the United States From Interviews with Former Slaves Oklahoma Narratives (Kindle Locations 428-431). Kindle Edition.

20 Solomon Barwick, Slavery Papers 3555.55 Manumission of Negro Stephen Image 22. Kent County, Delaware. 1792. Accessed 6/28/2017. https://archives.delaware.gov/slavery-papers/, solomon_1792-355555barwick, solomon_1792-1.jpg

21 John G. Sharp, *Manumission and Emancipation Record 1821 -1862* District of Columbia, Volume 1 page 190. Accessed 6/28/2017. The original transcription was made from a digital image of Manumission and Emancipation Record 1821 -1862 District of Columbia, Volume 1 page 190.The spelling, punctuation and the use of ampersands are those of the original document. My thanks to Mr. Robert Johnson Archives Specialist, National Archives and Records Administration, Washington DC for generously allowing me to copy this document. John G. Sharp, July 29, 2008. http://www.genealogytrails.com/washdc/slavery/cofbeans.html.

22 Certificates of Freedom, Washington D.C. Genealogy Trails. 2006-2017. Retrieved 08/20/2017. http://www.genealogytrails.com/washdc/slavery/certoffreedomindex.html

23 Dr. Gary Potter, *History of Policing In The United States,* Eastern Kentucky University, Richmond, KY. 2013. P. 1. Retrieved 5/19/2017. http://plsonline.eku.edu/insidelook/history-policing-united-states-part-1

24 Norman Yetman, R. (2012-03-15). *Voices from Slavery: 100 Authentic Slave Narratives* (African-American) (p. 178). Dover Publications. Kindle Edition.

25 *West's Encyclopedia of American Law, edition 2*. S.v. "Racial Profiling." Retrieved May 14, 2017, from http://legal-dictionary.thefreedictionary.com/Racial+Profiling

26 Janet Reno, *A Resource Guide on Racial Profiling Data Collection Systems, "Nature and Extent of Perceptions of Racial Profiling."* U.S. Department of Justice, Washington, DC. 2000. P. 4. Retrieved 5/14/2017. https://www.ncjrs.gov/pdffiles1/bja/184768.pdf

27 Jorge Rivas, "NYPD 2011 Data Reveals Highest Number of Stop-and-Frisks Ever," Colorlines.com, Retrieved 5/14/2017, https://www.colorlines.com/articles/nypd-2011-data-reveals-highest-number-stop-and-frisks-ever

28 Cotton planter and pickers 1908.jpg. Photo from the United States Library of Congress and in the public domain. https://thecroydoncitizen.com/history/far-come-slavery-civil-rights-contemporary-racism/ (August 21, 2016). http://www.encyclopedia.com/doc/1G2-3401803120.html

29 Overseer and Driver." Dictionary of American History. 2003. P. 1.

30 Fredrick Douglass, *My Bondage and My Freedom*. P. 31.

31 Ibid., P.122.

32 Overseer and Driver." Dictionary of American History. 2003. *Encyclopedia.com*. (August 21, 2016).

33 Bonekemper III, Edward H. (2015-10-05). *The Myth of the Lost Cause: Why the South Fought the Civil War and Why the North Won* (Kindle Locations 487-490). Regnery Publishing. Kindle Edition.
34 Overseer and Driver." Dictionary of American History. P.1.
35 John Simkin, (2014-01-11). *Slavery in the United States* (Kindle Locations 567-571). Spartacus Educational Publishers. Kindle Edition.
36 Sophia Kerby, Race And Ethnicity, *The Top 10 Most Startling Facts About People of Color and Criminal Justice in the United States,* Center For American Progress. 2012. P. 1. Retrieved 5/14/2017. https://www.americanprogress.org/issues/race/news/2012/03/13/11351/the-top-10-most-startling-facts-about-people-of-color-and-criminal-justice-in-the-united-states/
37 Katherine Anderson, Don Browning, and Brian Boyer, *Marriage-Just a Piece of Paper: Just a Piece of Paper,* Religion, Marriage, and Family Series (Grand Rapids: Eerdmans, 2002), 3767-3770. Kindle Edition.
38 William and Ellen Craft fugitive slaves, The Liberator newspaper (1831-1865) files (http://www.theliberatorfiles.com/liberator-photo-gallery/) abolitionisthttps://en.wikipedia.org/wiki/Ellen_and_William_Craft#/media/File:Ellen_and_William_Craft.png. William and Ellen Craft fugitive slaves, The Liberator newspaper (1831-1865) files (http://www.theliberatorfiles.com/liberator-photo-gallery/) This media file is in the **public domain** in the United States. This applies to U.S. works where the copyright has expired, often because its first publication occurred prior to January 1, 1923. See this page for further explanation. abolitionisthttps://en.wikipedia.org/wiki/Ellen_and_William_Craft#/media/File:Ellen_and_William_Craft.png
39 William Craft, Ellen Craft; Du Bois, W. E. B.; Keckley, Elizabeth; Henson, Josiah; Truth, Sojourner; Gilbert, Olive; Still, William (2015-08-06). *Slave Narrative Six Pack 2 - Running a Thousand Miles for Freedom, The Souls of Black Folk, Behind the Scenes, Life of Josiah Henson, Narrative of Sojourner Truth and William Garrison* (Illustrated) (Kindle Location 316). Kindle Edition.
40 William Craft; Ellen Craft, Kindle Locations. 326-329.
41 Ibid., 332-334.
42 Edward E. Baptist, (2014-09-09). *The Half Has Never Been Told: Slavery and the Making of American Capitalism* (Kindle Locations 3718-3721). Basic Books. Kindle Edition.
43 Frederick Douglass, (2012-05-16). *My Bondage and My Freedom* (p. 48). Kindle Edition.
44 Howard McGary Jr., Lawson, Bill E. (1993-02-22). *Between Slavery and Freedom: Philosophy and American Slavery (Blacks in the Diaspora)* (pp. 2-3). Indiana University Press. Kindle Edition.
45 Linda Brent, *Incidents in the Life of a Slave Girl* (Boston: By the author, 1861), p. 57. Howard McGary Jr., Lawson, Bill E. Between Slavery and Freedom. P. 9.

46 Howard McGary Jr., Lawson, Bill E. P. 2-3.

47 Ibid.,

48 DONALD CLEMMER, THE PRISON COMMUNITY (1940). In Mika'il DeVeaux, *The Trauma of the Incarceration Experience.* Harvard Civil Rights-Civil Liberties Law Review Vol. 48. P. 259. http://harvardcrcl.org/wp-content/uploads/2013/04/DeVeaux_257-277.pdf

49 Samuel G. Kling, The Prison Community, 54 HARV. L. REV. 722, 722 (1941). In Mika'il DeVeaux, *The Trauma of the Incarceration Experience.* Harvard Civil Rights-Civil Liberties Law Review Vol. 48. P. 259. http://harvardcrcl.org/wp-content/uploads/2013/04/DeVeaux_257-277.pdf

50 FACING THE LIMITS OF THE LAW, supra note 7; see also Terry A. Kupers, Prison and the Decimation of Pro-Social Life Skills, in THE TRAUMA OF PSYCHOLOGICAL TORTURE 127, 129 (E. Almerindo Ojeda ed., 2008). In Mika'il DeVeaux, *The Trauma of the Incarceration Experience.* Harvard Civil Rights-Civil Liberties Law Review Vol. 48. P. 259. http://harvardcrcl.org/wp-content/uploads/2013/04/DeVeaux_257-277.pdf

51 Lorna A. Rhodes, *Pathological Effects of the Supermaximum Prison*, 95 AM. J. PUB. HEALTH 1692, 1692 (2005). In Mika'il DeVeaux, *The Trauma of the Incarceration Experience.* Harvard Civil Rights-Civil Liberties Law Review Vol. 48. P. 259. http://harvardcrcl.org/wp-content/uploads/2013/04/DeVeaux_257-277.pdf

52 Clara Geaney, Grounds, supra note 7, at 169, *That's Life: An Examination of the Direct Consequences of Life-Sentence Imprisonment for Adult Males Within the Irish Prison System 29* (2008) (unpublished M.A. thesis, Dublin Institute of Technology). In Mika'il DeVeaux, *The Trauma of the Incarceration Experience.* Harvard Civil Rights-Civil Liberties Law Review Vol. 48. P. 259. http://harvardcrcl.org/wp-content/uploads/2013/04/DeVeaux_257-277.pdf

53 See Grounds & Jamieson, supra note 7, at 347. In Mika'il DeVeaux, *The Trauma of the Incarceration Experience.* Harvard Civil Rights-Civil Liberties Law Review Vol. 48. P. 259. http://harvardcrcl.org/wp-content/uploads/2013/04/DeVeaux_257-277.pdf

54 Richard A. Schill & David K. Marcus, Incarceration and Learned Helplessness, 42. INT'L J. OFFENDER THERAPY & COMP. CRIMINOLOGY 224 (1998). In Mika'il DeVeaux, *The Trauma of the Incarceration Experience.* Harvard Civil Rights-Civil Liberties Law Review Vol. 48. P. 259. http://harvardcrcl.org/wp-content/uploads/2013/04/DeVeaux_257-277.pdf

55 Joycelyn M. Pollock, *Prisons: Today And Tomorrow* (2d ed. 2006); Shelley Johnson Listwan et al., How To Prevent Prisoner Reentry Programs From Failing: Insights From Evidence-Based Corrections, 70 FED. PROBATION 19, 23 (2006); William J. Morgan, Jr., Major Causes of Institutional Violence, AM. JAILS, Nov.–Dec. 2009, at 62 (2009); Steven Patrick, Differences in Inmate-Inmate and Inmate-Staff Altercations: Examples from a Medium

Security Prison, 35 SOC. SCI. J. 253, 253 (1998); Rebecca Trammell, A Qualitative Approach to Understanding the Connection between Race, Gender and Prison Violence 1 (2006) (unpublished conference paper, American Sociological Association Conference), available at HTTP://citation.allacademic.com/meta/p_mla_apa_research_citation/1/0/3/2/4/pages103246/p103246-1.php.

56 See, e.g., CLEMMER, supra note 11, at 315; HANEY, supra note 7, at 13; Kling, supra note 12, at 723.

57 Herman Bell, *The Psychological Effects of Long-Term Imprisonments,* Eastern Correctional Facility. Napanoch, NY. 2005. P. 1. Retrieved 8/25, 2016. https://4strugglemag.org/2005/11/11/the-psychological-effects-of-long-term-imprisonment/

58 Ibid.,

59 Ibid.,

60 Murray J. Harris, *Slave of Christ* (Downers Grove, IL: InterVarsity Press, 1999), 184. In John MacArthur, (2010-12-28). *Slave: The Hidden Truth About Your Identity in Christ* (p. 18). Thomas Nelson. Kindle Edition.

61 Ibid.,

62 Ibid.,

63 National Association for the Advancement of Colored People ("NAACP") website www.naacp.org Retrieved May 13, 2017.http://www.naacp.org/criminal-justice-fact-sheet/

Chapter 11. The African-American Search For Identity

1 Steven Spielberg (Director), David Franzoni (writer), *Amistad.* Dreamworks Video, Washington, D.C. 1997.

2 Steven Spielberg (Director), David Franzoni (writer), *Amistad.*

3 Thomas F. Pettigrew, *A Profile of the Negro American* (Princeton, NJ: D. Van Nostrand, 1964), p. 6,

4 Patterson, Orlando (1985-03-15). *Slavery and Social Death* (Kindle Locations 316-318). Harvard University Press. Kindle Edition.

5 Payne, Buckner H. 'Ariel' (2011-03-24). *The Negro: what is His Ethnological Status?* 2nd Ed. 1867. (Kindle Locations 832-834).

6 Payne, Buckner H. 'Ariel'. P. 7-9. Kindle Edition.

7 Millard J. Erickson, (2013-08-15). *Christian Theology* (p. 428). Baker Publishing Group. Kindle Edition.

8 CGST, Projection. Urban Dictionary, 2016 https://www.urbandictionary.com/define.php?term=Projection Retrieved 6/9/17.

9 Thomas F. Pettigrew, *A Profile of the Negro American* (Princeton, NJ: D. Van Nostrand, 1964), p. 7.

10 Henry Louis Gates Jr, *In Search of Our Roots: How l9 Extraordinary African-Americans Reclaimed Their Past* (Kindle Locations 131-133). (2008-12-27) Crown/Archetype. Kindle Edition.

11 Henry L. Gates Jr, (2008-12-27). *In Search of Our Roots: How l9 Extraordinary African-Americans Reclaimed Their Past* (Kindle Locations 6188-6189). Crown/Archetype. Kindle Edition.

12 Ancestry.com. *1860 U.S. Federal Census - Slave Schedules* [database on-line]. Provo, UT, USA: Ancestry.com Operations Inc, 2010. Original data: United States of America, Bureau of the Census. *Eighth Census of the United States, 1860.* Washington, D.C.: National Archives and Records Administration, 1860. M653, 1,438 rolls.Ancestry.com. *1860 U.S. Federal Census - Slave Schedules* [database on-line]. Provo, UT, USA: Ancestry.com Operations Inc, 2010.

13 Ibid.,

14 Frederick Douglass, *My Bondage and My Freedom* (pp. 19-20). Kindle Edition.

15 Douglas R. Egerton (2014-01-21). *The Wars of Reconstruction: The Brief, Violent History of America's Most Progressive Era* (Kindle Locations 1464-1467). BLOOMSBURY PUBLISHING. Kindle Edition.

16 Ibid.,

17 Crista Cow, African-American Family History Research: Breaking the 1870 Wall. Ancestery.com/video https://youtu.be/-hgUIDXEHz4. https://youtu.be/-hgUIDXEHz4NzYw--?p=african+american+family+history+research%3A+breaking+the+1870+wall+Acestery.com&fr=yhs-rotz-001&hspart=rotz&hsimp=yhs-001

18 Charlotte Carpenter Johnson, *Foot Prints Through Time.* Rootsweb, An Ancestry.com Community. 2011. P.1. Retrieved 7/15/2016. http://wc.rootsweb.ancestry.com/cgibin/igm.cgi?op=GET&db=charcarpjohn&id=I194

19 Henry L. Gates Jr, (2008-12-27). *In Search of Our Roots: How l9 Extraordinary African-Americans Reclaimed Their Past* (Kindle Locations 6202-6203). Crown/Archetype. Kindle Edition.

20 Douglas R. Egerton, (2014-01-21). *The Wars of Reconstruction: The Brief, Violent History of America's Most Progressive Era* (Kindle Locations 1473-1476). BLOOMSBURY PUBLISHING. Kindle Edition.

21 Elizabeth A. Regosin; Donald R. Shaffer (2008-05-24). *Voices of Emancipation: Understanding Slavery, the Civil War, and Reconstruction through the U.S. Pension Bureau Files* (p. 25). NYU Press. Kindle Edition.

22 Jeffery C. Alexander, *Cultural Trauma and Collective Identity.* University of California Press, Berkeley California, 2004. P.1.

23 Phil Middleton, David Pilgrim, Dr. David Pilgrim. *Nigger (The Word) A Brief History*, African-American Registry, Dept. of Sociology Ferris State University, 2001. Retrieved October 31, 2015.https://aaregistry.org/story/nigger-the-word-a-brief-history/

24 Robert M. Entman, Andrew Rojecki (2010-02-15). *The Black Image in the White Mind: Media and Race in America* (Studies in Communication, Media, and Public Opinion). University of Chicago Press. Kindle Edition.
25 Thomas F. Pettigrew, *A Profile of the Negro American* (Princeton, NJ: D. Van Nostrand, 1964), p. xi.
26 US Census Bureau: Population and Housing, 1790-2010. https://www.Census.gov/prod/www/decennial.html.
27 Bureau of the Census, Negro Population in the United States, 1790-1915 (Washington, 19I8), p. 53.
28 Sarah Torre, *Fact of The Week: Fewer Americans Are Marrying: "The Portion of Married Adults has Decreased,* US Bureau of Census (Washington DC: The Heritage Foundation. 2011), 1, accessed January 19, 2012, http://blog.heritage.org/2011/12/15/family-fact-of-the-week-fewer-americans-are-marrying/," 1.
29 Carl Sagan, Smart Quotes. http://statusmind.com/smart-quotes-336/
30 M.S. Giusepppi, *Naturalizations of Foreign Protestants in the American and West Indian Colonies (Pursuant to Statute 13 George II, c.7)* (Baltimore: Genealogical Publishing Co., 1979)
31 Shiho Imai, *Naturalization Act of 1790.* (2013, March 19). *Densho Encyclopedia.* Retrieved 07:46, May 11, 2017, from http://encyclopedia.densho.org/Naturalization_Act_of_1790/
32 *West's Encyclopedia of American Law, edition 2.* S.v. "Black codes." Retrieved May 11, 2017, from http://legal-dictionary.thefreedictionary.com/Black+codes
33 Faye Z. (Zollicoffer) Belgrave; Kevin W. Allison. 979-982. Kindle Edition.
34 Faye Z. (Zollicoffer) Belgrave; Kevin W. Allison. 688-689. Kindle Edition.
35 Faye Z. (Zollicoffer) Belgrave; Kevin W. (Wendell) Allison. African-American *Psychology: From Africa to America* (Kindle Locations 1261-1263). Kindle Edition.
36 Herbert Gutman, *The Black Family*, p. 220. (2013-01-11). American Families: A Multicultural Reader (Kindle Location 2964). Taylor and Francis. Kindle Edition.
37 Andrew J. Cherlin, (2010-12-08). *The Marriage-Go-Round: The State of Marriage and the Family in America Today* (Vintage) (Kindle Locations 814-827). Knopf Doubleday Publishing Group. Kindle Edition.
38 Andrew J. Cherlin, *The Marriage-Go-Round.* Location 814-827 Kindle Edition.
39 Baptist, Edward E. (2014-09-09). *The Half Has Never Been Told: Slavery and the Making of American Capitalism* (Kindle Locations 5993-5999). Basic Books. Kindle Edition
40 Ibid.
41 Edward E. Baptist, *The Half Has Never Been Told.* Kindle Locations 5993-5999
42 Ibid.
43 Ibid.

44 Bernard F. Reily, *Am I Not A Man And A Brother*, Published in American political prints, 1766-1876 / Boston: G.K. Hall, 1991, entry 183716.http://www.loc.gov/pictures/resource/cph.3a44497/

45 Ibid.

46 Ibid.

47 Lewis Sperry Chafer, *Systematic Theology Abridged Edition*, Vol.2, John Walvoord, editor, Donald K. Campbell, Roy Zuck, Consulting editors, Abridged Edition, Victor Books, Wheaton IL, 1988, p. 21.

48 Andrew J. Cherlin, (2010-12-08). *The Marriage-Go-Round: The State of Marriage and the Family in America Today* (Vintage) (Kindle Locations 814-827). Knopf Doubleday Publishing Group. Kindle Edition.

49 Marvin Andrew McMickle, "The Black Church Crisis," An Encyclopedia of African-American Christian Heritage. Judson Press, Copyright 2002. ISBN 0-817014-02-0.

50 Leon F. Litwack, (2010-12-15). *Been in the Storm So Long: The Aftermath of Slavery* (p. 218). Knopf Doubleday Publishing Group. Kindle Edition.

51 Ibid.,

52 *The Holy Bible: English Standard Version* (Wheaton: Standard Bible Society, 2001), Ge 5:1–2.

53 John Calvin and John King, *Commentary on the First Book of Moses Called Genesis*, vol. 1 (Bellingham, WA: Logos Bible Software, 2010), 227.

54 Winston Churchill, House of Commons, 12 May 1935, Stresa Conference, My book p. 490. Retrieved 08/05/2016. https://www.nationalchurchillmuseum.org/blog/churchill-quote-history/. And in George Santayana, *The Life of Reason*, 1905.

55 John MacArthur, (2010-12-28). *Slave: The Hidden Truth About Your Identity in Christ* (pp. 15-16). Thomas Nelson. Kindle Edition.

56 Alexis De Tocqueville, (2007-06-13). *Democracy in America, Volume I and II* (Optimized for Kindle) (Kindle Locations 1150-1152). Kindle Edition.

57 H. E. Hayward and slave nurse Louisa Image Credit: Digital image ©1998 Missouri Historical Society, St. Louis. Retrieved 8/27/2016. H. E. Hayward and slave nurse Louisa. Image Credit: Digital image ©1998 Missouri Historical Society, St. Louis Retrieved 8/27/2016 http://www.pbs.org/wgbh/aia/part4/4h3140.html

58 Ibid.,

59 Ibid.,

60 Darlene Calrk Hine, Stanley C Har; William C. Hine (2013-08-28). *The African-American Odyssey,* Combined Volume (Page 230). Pearson Education. Kindle Edition.

61 Randolph B. Campbell, (1991-08-01). *An Empire for Slavery: The Peculiar Institution in Texas, 1821--1865* (Kindle Locations 178-180). LSU Press. Kindle Edition.

Chapter 12. Love Conquers All

1 A Council of Trent summary from Catechism of the Catholic Church. P 463. In Kurt Bruner, Jim Ware. The Purpose of Passion: Dante's Epic Vision of Romantic Love (Kindle Locations 2332-2333). Tyndale House Publishers. Kindle Edition.

2 Samuel Vanderlip Leech (2011-03-30). *The Raid of John Brown at Harper's Ferry as I Saw It* (p. 36). Kindle Edition.

3 Ibid. P. 24.

4 Nat Turner, (2013-10-02). *The Confessions of Nat Turner, the Leader of the Late Insurrection of Southampton, Va* - Annotated (Kindle Locations 242-244). Oshun Publishing. Kindle Edition.

5 American Civil War, Chart showing Total Civil War Killed, Wounded, Missing and Captured. Courtesy CivilWar.Org. http://www.thomaslegion.net/americancivilwarcasualtiesfatalitiesbattlestatisticstotalskilledwoundedcasualtyfatalityfacts.html

6 American Civil War, Chart showing Total Civil War Killed, Wounded, Missing and Captured. Courtesy CivilWar.Org. http://www.thomaslegion.net/americancivilwarcasualtiesfatalitiesbattlestatisticstotalskilledwoundedcasualtyfatalityfacts.html

7 Ibid,

8 Abraham Lincoln, *Collected Works of Abraham Lincoln.* Volume 4. "Speech at Hartford, Conn., Mar. 5, 1860," LINCOLN, P. 5– 6. In Edward Baptist, E. (2014-09-09). In *The Half Has Never Been Told: Slavery and the Making of American Capitalism* (Kindle Locations 10784-10785). Basic Books. Kindle Edition.

9 Abraham Lincoln, *Inaugural Addresses of the Presidents of the United States.* Washington, D.C., U.S. G.P.O., 1989; Bartleby.com, 2001. www.bartleby.com/124/.

10 Douglass Blackmon, *Slavery by Another Name: White Supremacy and Terrorism*, PBS. 2012. Retrieved June 12, 2017. http://www.pbs.org/tpt/slavery-by-another-name/themes/white-supremacy/.

11 Ibid.,

12 Martin Luther King Jr, *A Gift of Love: Sermons from Strength to Love and Other Preachings* (King Legacy) (pp. 50-51). Beacon Press. Kindle Edition.

13 James T. Patterson, *Freedom Is Not Enough: The Moynihan Report and America's Struggle over Black Family Life--from LBJ to Obama* (Philadelphia, PA: Basic Books, 2010), 3564-3569. Kindle Edition.

14 Lorraine Blackman, Obie Clayton, Norval Glenn, Linda Malone-Colon, and Alex Roberts, *The Consequences of Marriage for African-Americans: A*

Comprehensive Literature Survey(New York: Institute for American Values, 2005), 5.

15 M. Corra, S.K. Carter, J.S. Carter, and D. Knox, "Trends in Marital Happiness by Gender and Race: 1973-2006,"Journal of Family Issues 30 (2009): 1379-1404.

16 Andrew J. Cherlin, *"Marriage and Marital Dissolution among Black Americans,"Journal of Comparative Family Studies*29, no.1, 1998. P. 1. Accessed December 16, 2013, https://www.jstor.org/stable/pdf/41603552.pdf?seq=1#page_scan_tab_contents

17 Reginald Washington, *Sealing the Sacred Bonds of Holy Matrimony Freedmen's Bureau Marriage Records.* Prologue Magazine, Freedmen's Bureau Marriage Records, Spring 2005, Vol. 37, No. 1.

18 T. G. Steward, *Fifty Years in the Gospel Ministry* [Philadelphia, 1922 P. 33).

19 Ibid., 1.

20 Ibid., 1.

21 Reginald Washington, *Sealing the Sacred Bonds of Holy Matrimony Freedmen's Bureau Marriage Records.* Prologue Magazine, Freedmen's Bureau Marriage Records, Spring 2005, Vol. 37, No. 1.

22 Reginald Washington, *Sealing the Sacred Bonds of Holy Matrimony.* The marriage certificate of John and Emily Pointer lists their children and their ages. (Records of the Bureau of Refugees, Freedmen, and Abandoned Lands, RG 105) image https://www.archives.gov/publications/prologue/2005/spring/freedman-marriage-recs.html

23 Darlene C. Goring, *The History of Slave Marriage in the United States*, 39 J. Marshall L. Review, (2006). 299.

24 Ibid.,

25 Ibid., 322.

26 American Anti-Slavery Society (2011-03-24). The Anti-Slavery Examiner, Part 2 of 4 (Kindle Locations 5757-5764). Kindle Edition.

27 The opinion of Judge Matthews, a case of Girod vs. Lewis, May Term, 1819; 6 Martin's "Louisiana Reports," p. 659. Wheeler's "Law of Slavery," p. 199.

28 Andrew J. Cherlin, (2010-12-08). *The Marriage-Go-Round: The State of Marriage and the Family in America Today* (Vintage) (Kindle Locations 929-932). Knopf Doubleday Publishing Group. Kindle Edition.

29 Reginald Washington, *Sealing the Sacred Bonds of Holy Matrimony* . No. 1.

30 Ira Berlin. *Many Thousands Gone: The First Two Centuries of Slavery in North America* (Kindle Locations 3160-3162). Kindle Edition.

31 William Loren Katz, *Breaking The Chains African-American Slave Resistance.* Atheneum Macmillan Publishing Company, New York, NY. 1990. P. 34.

32 William Loren Katz, *Breaking The Chains.* P.34.

33 Darlene C. Goring, *The History of Slave Marriage in the United States*, P. 332.

34 William Loren Katz, *Breaking The Chains African*, P. 34.

35 Darlene C. Goring, *The History of Slave Marriage in the United States*, P. 324.

36 The Laws of Kentucky, Chapter 556, An Act in relation to the marriage of negroes and mulattoes, Act of February 14, 1866, page 37. The Act also legitimized children born of said relationships. See Stewart v. Munchandler, 65 Ky. 278, 281 Dowd v. Hurley, 78 Ky. 260, 262 (1880).

37 Douglass Blackmon, A. (2008-12-27). *Slavery by Another Name: The Re-Enslavement of Black Americans from the Civil War to World War II* (p. 13). Knopf Doubleday Publishing Group. Kindle Edition.